Pearson
BTEC National
Applied Psychology

Student Book

Elizabeth Barkham

Dr Adam Gledhill

Susan Harty

Pamela Hughes

Georgina Shaw

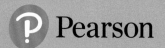

Published by Pearson Education Limited, 80 Strand, London, WC2R 0RL.

www.pearsonschoolsandfecolleges.co.uk

Copies of official specifications for all Pearson qualifications may be found on the website: qualifications.pearson.com

Text © Pearson Education Limited [2019]

Typeset by PDQ Media

Original illustrations © Pearson Education Limited 2019

Picture research by Integra

Cover design © Pearson Education Ltd

The rights of Elizabeth Barkham, Dr Adam Gledhill, Susan Harty, Pamela Hughes and Georgina Shaw to be identified as authors of this work have been asserted by them in accordance with the Copyright, Designs and Patents Act 1988.

First published 2019

22 21 20 19

10 9 8 7 6 5 4 3 2 1

British Library Cataloguing in Publication Data

A catalogue record for this book is available from the British Library

ISBN 978 1 292 27755 4

Acknowledgements

The publisher acknowledges the use of the following material.

Text

The publisher acknowledges the use of the following material.

P 130, Jessica Faulkner, P 148, SAGE: Persuasion: Theory and Research, Daniel J. O'Keefe,©SAGE Publications,1990; **P 148, Elsevier:** Bandura, A. (1994). Self-efficacy. In V. S. Ramachaudran (Ed.), Encyclopaedia of human behaviour (Vol. 4, pp. 71-81). New York: Academic Press. (Reprinted in H. Friedman [Ed.], Encyclopaedia of mental health. San Diego: Academic Press, 1998); **P 166, AddictionHelper:** Addiction Statistics© AddictionHelper; **P 225 Simple Psychology:** Kohlberg's Stages of Moral Development, Saul McLeod,©Simple Psychology; **P 290, World Health Organization, 2014:** World Health Organization, 2014; **P 301, Devon Heritage Centre:** Adapted from Devon County Mental Hospital© Devon Heritage Centre. Used with Permission; **P 310, Mental Health Foundation:** Black, Asian and minority ethnic (BAME) communities,©Mental Health Foundation.

Photographs

The publisher acknowledges the use of the following material.

123RF: Dolgachov 131c, Maksym Mzhavanadze 295l, Stockbroker 331c; **Alamy Stock Photo:** ART Collection 45tl, The History Collection 45tr, geogphotos 54br, Marmaduke St. John 73c, Ilene MacDonald 81c, Science History Images 104cr AB Forces News Collection 180cr, Tribune Content Agency LLC 220t, Israel images 242tl, Cultura RM 275cl, Mike Goldwater 296tr, Bax Walker 299b, Eddie Gerald 306tl, Galló Gusztáv 319b, Axel Bueckert 329tr, Colin Underhill 341r ; **Jessica Faulkner:** 130tr; **Getty Images:** Thomas D. McAvoy 244cl, Bettmann 270bl; **Pearson Education :** BTEC Sport and Exercise Science student book,© Pearson Education 2016 340,342,343,344,360, Edexcel AS/A level Psychology Student Book,©Pearson Education,2015 32; **Safia Suatt :** 233tr; **Shutterstock:** 215tl, GrAl 1c, James Steidl 5br, Fer Gregory 24b, postolit 34bl, Africa Studio 34br, Levent Konuk 60b, Wavebreakmedia 94tl,128c, 351tl, vgstudio 94tr, NAN728 101tl, Antonio Guillem 108tr, Julian Rovagnati 146t, Gcpics 163t, Welcomia 171tl, William Perugini 173b, AJR_photo 190tr, Prath 197c, Cristi C 212tr, Mettus 218t, Ken Regan/Orion/Kobal 230cr, Myvisuals 234tl, Alena Ozerova 235c, Rawpixel 255c, Jacob Lund 263c, Apollofoto 286tr, Lightspring 28c, Jane September 308bl, Irina Mitin 314bl, shipfactory 330tl, India Picture 338tr, Bobex-73 362c, mimagephotography 364tr, Jim Pruitt 365tl.

Cover image: Front: a-poselenov / iStock / Getty Images

All other images © Pearson Education

Websites

Pearson Education Limited is not responsible for the content of any external internet sites. It is essential for tutors to preview each website before using it in class so as to ensure that the URL is still accurate, relevant and appropriate. We suggest that tutors bookmark useful websites and consider enabling students to access them through the school/college intranet.

Notes from the publisher

1.

In order to ensure that this resource offers high-quality support for the associated Pearson qualification, it has been through a review process by the awarding body. This process confirms that this resource fully covers the teaching and learning content of the specification or part of a specification at which it is aimed. It also confirms that it demonstrates an appropriate balance between the development of subject skills, knowledge and understanding, in addition to preparation for assessment.

Endorsement does not cover any guidance on assessment activities or processes (e.g. practice questions or advice on how to answer assessment questions), included in the resource nor does it prescribe any particular approach to the teaching or delivery of a related course.

While the publishers have made every attempt to ensure that advice on the qualification and its assessment is accurate, the official specification and associated assessment guidance materials are the only authoritative source of information and should always be referred to for definitive guidance.

Pearson examiners have not contributed to any sections in this resource relevant to examination papers for which they have responsibility.

Examiners will not use endorsed resources as a source of material for any assessment set by Pearson.

Endorsement of a resource does not mean that the resource is required to achieve this Pearson qualification, nor does it mean that it is the only suitable material available to support the qualification, and any resource lists produced by the awarding body shall include this and other appropriate resources.

2.

Pearson has robust editorial processes, including answer and fact checks, to ensure the accuracy of the content in this publication, and every effort is made to ensure this publication is free of errors. We are, however, only human, and occasionally errors do occur. Pearson is not liable for any misunderstandings that arise as a result of errors in this publication, but it is our priority to ensure that the content is accurate. If you spot an error, please do contact us at resourcescorrections@pearson.com so we can make sure it is corrected.

Contents

Introduction to your Applied Psychology Student Book

Welcome to your BTEC National Applied Psychology course. Your BTEC National Applied Psychology qualification will give you the opportunity to gain specific knowledge, understanding and skills that are relevant to your chosen subject or area of work. This new BTEC is a great foundation for you to build the skills you need for employment or further study.

A BTEC National qualification is widely recognised within the industry and in higher education as the signature vocational qualification. Choosing to study for a BTEC National Applied Psychology qualification is a great decision to make for lots of reasons. The qualification will help you to gain knowledge and experience that will help you to prepare for university or employment in a range of different sectors; including health care, social care, sports psychology and within the criminal justice system. Whatever career path you are interested in, this course will help you build and develop the skills you need to make a success of higher education, employment or both.

About the authors

Elizabeth Barkham

Elizabeth is a Consultant Forensic Psychologist working in clinical practice. She has spent many years working in prisons and secure units. She has been an examiner for Edexcel for almost 15 years, working as a Team Leader for various psychology qualifications and as part of the review process of exam development. She has previously contributed to the development of psychology textbooks and is published in the area of Forensic Psychology. Elizabeth is keen to promote psychological knowledge as a basis for future careers in psychology.

Dr Adam Gledhill

Adam has over 15 years' teaching and leadership experience within further and higher education settings. For Pearson, Adam has been involved in the development of other qualifications, as an International Standards Verifier, as an Assessment Associate; and as an author for many textbooks. Adam is a British Association of Sport and Exercise Sciences (BASES) Accredited Sport and Exercise Scientist with significant experience providing sport psychology support to a range of athletes and teams. He is currently an Associate Editor for the British Journal of Sports Medicine with a specific focus on psychology of sports injury and is the current Deputy Chair of the BASES Division of Psychology.

Susan Harty

Susan has been teaching psychology at different levels for over 20 years and indeed only took up teaching in order to maintain her knowledge of psychology. She has taught undergraduates on introduction to psychology courses, GCSE level, BTEC students and A level students. She is an experienced examiner in psychology and has contributed to several books on the subject.

Pamela Hughes

Pamela has over 20 years' of experience in secondary education across a number of social science disciplines. As a head of curriculum area, she currently oversees multiple subjects at Key Stages 4 and 5. She also works as a trainer, principal examiner and moderator across different qualifications. Pamela is a classroom practitioner who strives to develop the academic skills of her learners in addition to ensuring they aspire to fulfil their potential within higher education, employment or apprenticeship pathways.

Georgina Shaw

Georgina is a psychologist and has over 20 years' experience as a lecturer in Further and Higher Education, in a range of subjects including Psychology, Law, and Health and Social Care. She has been a contributing author to many BTEC textbooks and teaching materials. She is also a Senior Verifier and Chief Examiner for other qualifications. Georgina now runs her own business consultancy company, but still retains close links to her work in motivating young people to engage and succeed in their education and employment.

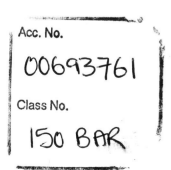

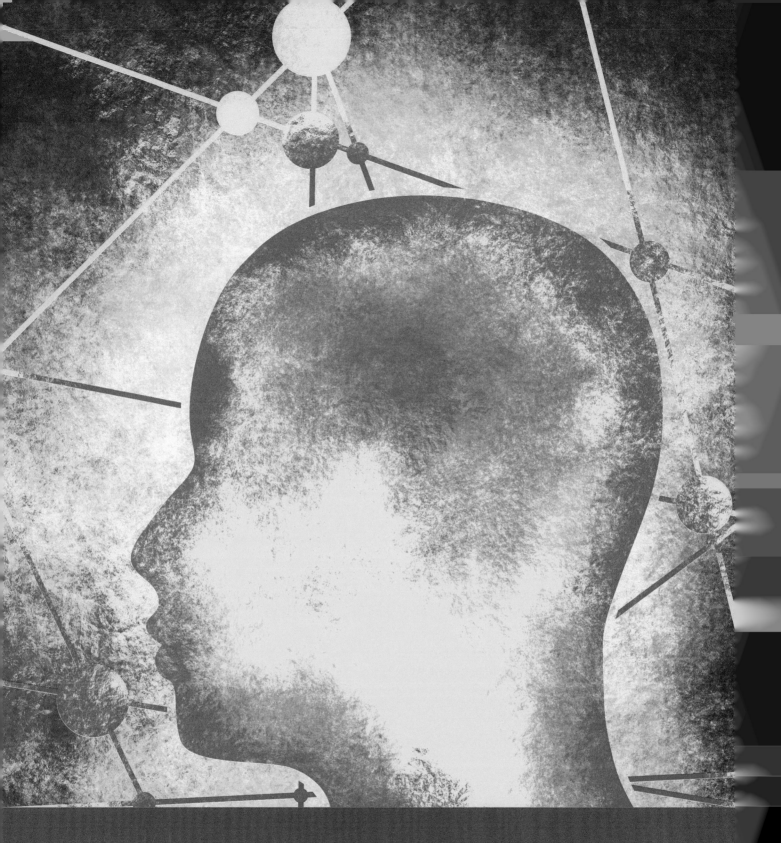

Psychological Approaches and Applications

1

Getting to know your unit

This unit gives you a basic understanding of what psychology is, how it works and what it is used for. It introduces you to some different psychological approaches to understanding human minds and behaviour. It starts with an exploration of four different approaches to understanding psychology and then examines some key theories relevant to each approach, together with some research that has been done to test those theories. The theories are then put into practice to explain and change aspects of human behaviour.

How you will be assessed

This unit will be assessed by an externally set and marked exam. This is a 90-minute exam with three sections totalling 72 marks.

The paper will consist of a variety of question types, including: extended open-response questions relating to psychological approaches to understanding and explaining human behaviour, and scenario-based questions relating to vocational contexts.

If you are hoping to gain a Merit or Distinction, you should also make sure that you practise a range of exam answers under timed conditions (some are provided for you in this book and there are sample assessment materials available online). Use mark schemes where possible to help you to see the level at which you are working and how you can improve.

You will be tested on three different assessment outcomes (AOs), each of which asks you to demonstrate specific skills (see Table 1.1).

▶ **Table 1.1:** Assessment outcomes (AOs) and command words

AO	Description	Command words and marks
1	Demonstrate psychological knowledge, be able to recall key assumptions, concepts and research.	Describe, Give, Give a reason why, Identify, Name, State. Marks: range from 1 to 4 marks.
2	Demonstrate understanding by explaining the link between psychological assumptions, concepts and research to behaviour in society.	Describe, Explain, Interpret, Justify. Marks: range from 1 to 4 marks.
3	Apply and evaluate psychological assumptions, concepts and research to explain contemporary issues of relevance to society.	Analyse, Assess, Compare, Discuss, Evaluate, Explain. Marks: range from 1 to 9 marks.

Psychologists are employed usefully in many areas of life. Think about some of these areas and come up with a list of applications for psychology. If you are struggling to find information, a good source is the British Psychological Society (BPS) website where you can search for BPS careers to get an overview.

A Psychological approaches and assumptions

Approaches and assumptions

Psychology aims to understand and explain minds and behaviour, but it does this in different ways. Each way of looking at minds and behaviour is called an approach (also known as **perspective**). You will begin by looking at four approaches, each of which assumes that behaviour is influenced by a particular aspect of a person's psychology.

Cognitive assumptions

The **cognitive** approach looks at how the mind deals with information. This includes the cognitive processes of language, thought, attention, memory and **perception**. It assumes that behaviour is influenced by how you process information from the world around you.

Assumption 1

The mind is an information processor with features that are similar to a computer (also known as the computer **analogy** – see Figure 1.1). Computers have **data** input, for example through the keyboard. This data is processed and stored and can be brought back as a form of output, for example printing a document. Similarly, your mind takes in data from your senses (sight, touch, taste, sound, smell, and so on), processes the information (for example converts to words and stores it as memory), and this then affects how you behave (output).

> **Key terms**
>
> **Perspective** – a specific way of seeing and explaining things.
>
> **Cognitive** – working through thoughts to process information.
>
> **Perception** – becoming cognitively aware through the processing of sensory information.
>
> **Analogy** – a comparison between one thing and another for the purpose of explanation.
>
> **Data** – information gathered during the course of research applied to a specific question.

> **Theory into practice**
>
> Dan is sitting in a classroom when a loud siren goes off (input). He thinks about what this means, drawing on his knowledge of alarms, and decides if it is a threat or just a drill (the processing stage). Dan decides it is not a drill so gets up quickly and leaves the classroom (output).
>
> Which cognitive processes does Dan use?

Link

Go to page 12 to learn about some of the cognitive biases that affect information processing.

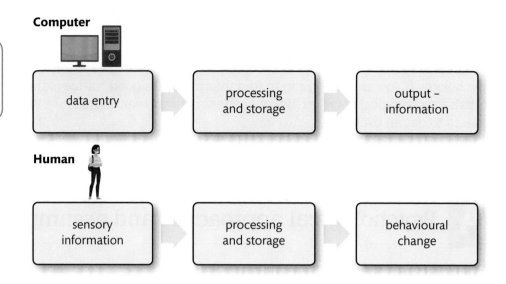

▶ **Figure 1.1:** The computer analogy

Assumption 2

Taking this assumption further, you can see how all your behaviour is therefore a product of how you process information. The way you think about something will determine how you feel about it, which will then affect how you behave towards it.

Theory into practice

Lily thinks her tutor does not like her. This makes her feel bad and angry. So, when the tutor asks her a question, Lily thinks she is picking on her and finds it hard to answer. When the tutor tries to help her answer, Lily feels worse and finds it even harder. Eventually she refuses to try at all.

Explain why Lily's refusal to try to answer the question is a direct result of her beliefs about her tutor.

Evaluation of the cognitive approach

Evaluation is a skill you will be asked to demonstrate in the exam; it involves judging the worth of something.

The cognitive approach has worth as it is useful to understand how our information processing affects our behaviour. This means it has useful applications to many areas of life, as almost everything you do involves cognitive processing. For example, it is used in therapy for mental health disorders in the form of cognitive behavioural therapy.

Furthermore, it has worth because it uses a scientific method in order to test its ideas. There is value and trust in science because ideas are supported by evidence.

However, unlike some areas of science, it is not possible actually to see a physical thing at work when you process information. For example, when you describe how memory works you are basing this on assumptions that fit the data from the experiments, and not what you can actually see happening when you remember something.

Social assumptions

This approach assumes that behaviour occurs in a social context. Therefore, your behaviour is influenced by what is going on within the situation in which you find yourself. Humans are often described as social animals. Part of the success of the human species is due to people having the ability to cooperate in groups to form **societies**. As such, people are sensitive to information from, and about, other people.

Assumption 1

This approach assumes that behaviour is affected by the real or imagined presence of other people. There is a tendency to do what seems right in order to fit in with other people in the situation.

> **Theory into practice**
>
> When Nish studies alone he usually plays music and often sings along, but when studying near other people, he does not sing even though the music is still playing. His behaviour changes because of the social context.
>
> When would he be likely to sing with others present?

Assumption 2

Behaviour is affected by the **norms** and **culture** in which it is situated. From birth, you are **socialised** to learn the rules of behaviour for your culture and your society. These help you to exist in a group: the world would be chaotic if everyone just did what they wanted without regard for the rules, customs or traditions of the groups.

Some of these rules are formal and have become laws in society as a whole, for example you do not take other people's property without their permission. Other rules are informal and often apply to smaller groups or cultures. These are social or cultural norms, which are the unwritten rules of behaviour that affect how people act. Different cultures and societies have different norms, therefore behaviour changes according to the culture and society in which it is displayed.

> **Key terms**
>
> **Societies** – large groups of people living together with shared laws, values and traditions.
>
> **Norms** – informal guidelines about what is considered correct in specific situations.
>
> **Culture** – the ideas, customs and social behaviour of a particular society.
>
> **Socialised** – the process of learning to behave in ways acceptable to society.

> **Case study**
>
> People dress according to cultural and social norms. In most Western societies it is not the norm for males to wear skirts unless you are Scottish (and usually only on special occasions as the kilt is a traditional costume or custom for the Scottish people). Remember, it is only relatively recently that females started wearing trousers or even showing their legs; the custom was to wear floor-length dresses or skirts. People chose their clothes to fit the customs.
>
> 1 Can you think of other items of clothing that are specific to a particular situation or setting?
>
> 2 Why would it be less socially acceptable to wear a kilt if you are not Scottish and are not at a formal occasion?
>
> 3 How might other people react to someone wearing unusual clothing?

Evaluation of the social approach

This approach has given many useful insights about how people actually behave in society. This is of value because if you understand how the context affects behaviour, then the context can be changed in order to support a preferred behaviour.

Although the approach uses the **scientific** method to test its ideas, the studies tend to be done in less controlled contexts than a laboratory. This means that the data is sometimes inconclusive allowing challenges about whether the theories are valid and useful.

Furthermore, many of the studies that test the theories from this approach are regarded as unethical because of the way they manipulate people's beliefs and behaviour.

Learning assumptions

This approach forms the **nurture** part of the **nature** vs. nurture debate, which examines whether you are born with behavioural characteristics (nature) or whether you learn them (nurture).

Assumption 1

All behaviour results from direct environmental experience. All animals (including humans) are **conditioned** by their environment to behave in specific ways. So, if you experience something bad in a specific environmental situation, you will learn that the situation is to be avoided in the future.

Theory into practice

Dogs quickly learn to associate particular noises they hear in their environment with food. The noise of a tin opener or the rattle of biscuits in a box causes them to go to the place where the noise is being produced because they know from experience that the noise comes before feeding time.

Can you think of any other examples of how animals learn from experience?

Assumption 2

You also learn behaviour from observing and imitating other people. Humans (and some animals) do not always need direct experience in order to learn behaviour; they learn from observing what happens to others when they do something. Babies show an early preference for watching people in the environment rather than objects. Even with young children, much of their attention is directed to other people's actions. This is called **social learning** where you watch what someone does to see what happens to them, and then in the future you **imitate** what they did.

Theory into practice

Jamal sees his older brother being praised by his mother and getting a nice dessert after he ate all of his broccoli. Jamal was then offered broccoli and was happy to eat it. On another occasion, Jamal's brother rejected tomatoes but his mother ignored it.

What would happen if Jamal saw his brother getting punished for eating vegetables?

Evaluation of the learning approach

This approach takes a very scientific approach to the development of theories, focusing only on what can be directly observed. This approach has theoretical value because it is supported by evidence.

The approach has contributed many useful techniques which have benefits for society such as setting up systems of rewards in classrooms to help young children develop good behaviour in class.

However, this approach ignores the role of nature in its theories which means that it lacks the ability to explain many aspects of human behaviour.

> **Research**
>
> Investigate the nature vs. nurture debate in psychology. Find out what type of behaviour is said to be primarily nature and what is primarily nurture.
>
> Do you think any behaviour is only one or the other?

Biological assumptions

This approach takes the nature side of the nature vs. nurture debate and assumes that most of our behaviour is innate, meaning that it occurs without learning.

Assumption 1

Much of your behaviour is influenced by physical aspects of yourself including your **central nervous system (CNS), genes** and **neurochemistry**. You inherit your genes and they shape the structure and chemistry of your CNS (which is made up of the brain and the spinal cord). The brain controls our behaviour so behaviour is directly influenced by how the brain is structured.

> **Theory into practice**
>
> The MAOA gene (also known as the warrior gene) is associated with impulsive aggression. People who have this gene are more likely to act aggressively when threatened than people who do not have it.
>
> What do you think the gene changes about a person that would make them more aggressive?

Assumption 2

Your genetic makeup (and therefore your physiological makeup) is a product of evolution. Evolution is a slow process of genetic change in response to environmental pressures. Genes that program the brain to make some behaviour or trait more likely will be passed onto the next generation if that behaviour made the person more successful (that is, they are able to live longer, attract more mates and produce more offspring). The genetic difference created an **adaptive advantage** for that person with it. They then survived better than those without this genetic difference so their genes are more likely to be passed on. As genes change slowly over generations, modern humans still have genes suited to the environment that were successful in prehistoric times. This is called **genome lag**.

> **Key terms**
>
> **Central nervous system (CNS)** – the brain and the spinal cord.
>
> **Genes** – units of inheritance that provide the basic plan for physical makeup.
>
> **Neurochemistry** – the balance of chemicals in the brain.
>
> **Adaptive advantage** – any characteristic or behaviour that help the organism possessing it survive in the environment they live in.
>
> **Genome** – all the hereditary information contained in the genes of an organism.
>
> **Genome lag** – the idea that evolution works slowly, so genes that developed in the past are still present even though the environment is very different.
>
> **Adrenaline** – hormone that is released during stress that helps to prepare the body for action.

> **Link**
>
> Go to page 36 to learn more about genome lag.

Humans respond to threat through the activation of the 'fight or flight' mechanism. This makes the body ready for action, to run away from danger or to face up to it and fight. In both cases it involves the release of **adrenaline** which is an automatic response to threat. This would have conveyed an advantage to your prehistoric ancestors, where the dangers they faced were physical and immediate. The human who acted immediately to respond to a threat would have been more successful than one who took longer to reason it out, so that human would live longer, have more sex and therefore pass on the genes for fight or flight.

1 How are the threats you face in modern society different from those in your prehistoric past?

2 Why might this be a problem for modern humans?

3 Why do you still have the 'fight or flight' mechanism when it no longer conveys a clear, adaptive advantage?

Evaluation of the biological approach

This approach is very scientific as it examines physical data such as the structure of brains, the chemicals present and your genetic makeup and investigates how changes in these can be used to explain changes in behaviour.

It provides many useful applications based on an understanding of how your brain works, for example using drugs to change the chemistry of the brain to treat mental health disorders. These drugs have benefited many people.

However, this approach minimises the influence of free will in human behaviour and makes it seem as if everything you do is caused by biological changes beyond your control. This suggests that behaviour, whether good or bad, is not chosen by the person displaying the behaviour but is beyond their control. In most cases this is simply not true.

PAUSE POINT Outline the four different approaches to psychology that you are required to know.

Hint Use a simple spider diagram with psychology in the middle and each approach named and briefly outlined in each corner.

Extend Think of some examples of behaviour that clearly illustrates each approach. Try not to use the ones from the student book.

B | Key concepts

Each approach will have many concepts or theories that explain different kinds of behaviour. These concepts and theories are tested through research studies which gather and analyse data that can then be used to determine if the theory is valid or not.

Cognitive approach

The cognitive approach views the information processing system as a fundamental influence on behaviour. Perception, memory, attention, thought and language all interact to give you your experience of the world and to produce your reaction to it. In this section you will learn about some concepts involved in this with a focus on reconstructive memory and cognitive biases, including the idea of priming. You will learn how these concepts can be applied to explain experience and behaviour, and you will learn about three key research studies that illustrate or investigate information processing.

Reconstructive memory

Human **memory** is complex, and psychologists are yet to understand fully all the processes involved. Bartlett, working in the early twentieth century, proposed that memory is dynamic. When you **recall** information, you do not passively retrieve data from a store and replay it in your mind as you would a video clip. Instead, when you recall information you reconstruct it from different sources and create a version of the original event. This means that memory is flexible; it is influenced by what you already know and by what you learn later. Your memory for an event is therefore a combination of all the relevant knowledge you have about it and other similar events.

Bartlett used the idea of **schema** as an explanation for the way memory is organised and why it is dynamic. He proposed that memory is organised as a set of interconnected schema which develop throughout your life and are personal to you. These schema become activated when something in an event triggers them and they are then used to make sense of the event. Your memory for the event is altered by the schema you have, especially as time passes.

For example, most people will have a schema for a bank robber (see Figure 1.2), usually developed through watching films and TV. The characteristics associated with being a bank robber are linked together to make a schema. If you are ever a witness to a bank robbery and are asked to describe the person then your memory for them is likely to be affected by what you already know.

> **Key terms**
>
> **Memory** – the process of encoding storing and recalling previously learned information.
>
> **Recall** – bring a memory back into one's mind; remember.
>
> **Schema** – hypothetical cognitive framework that organises and stores information.

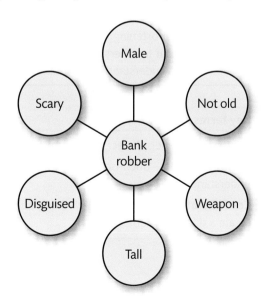

▶ **Figure 1.2:** Simple schema for a bank robber

Link

Go to the Loftus and Palmer key study on page 16 and explain how schema affected the recall of the **participants** in this study.

Research

One way in which schema have been shown to affect how you recall information is through leading questions. This is a question that contains information about the expected answer. For example, if someone witnesses a bank robbery and you ask them if they saw the knife you could be biasing them to remember a knife when they may not have seen one at all.

Discussion

Stefan and Katarina are both witnesses to a crime. When the police interview them separately two days later, they observe that although there is quite a lot of agreement in their statements there are also some significant differences, especially about the physical characteristics of the criminal who they both saw for only a few minutes.

Why do they have different memories for the same event?

Link

Go to Bartlett's key study on page 13 to help you understand this. It will give you a clear example of the concepts described here.

Research has shown some other ways that schema affect recall from memory. You will learn about three ways.

▶ **Rationalisation** – when something does not make sense to you, you work on it until it does; this can involve changing the memory to fit with your existing schema. So, if confronted with something unfamiliar, your memory for it will become distorted as you use your prior knowledge to make sense of it.

▶ **Confabulation** – you fill in gaps in your recall from past experiences so two or more memories could merge to make one new one. This involves transforming the information in some way. This is especially true if the two memories are similar.

▶ **Shortening** – your memory for an event typically becomes shorter than the actual event, indicating that a lot of information is being left out.

Discussion

Think of a film you have recently watched and summarise what happens. The film probably lasted for about two hours but your summary is unlikely to exceed a few minutes. This is shortening. Is there any confabulation in your recall? There might be if the film is similar to others you have watched. Have you rationalised parts of the film you did not understand, for example applying a motive to a character's actions?

Key terms

Participants – people recruited to take part in research.

Rationalisation – unconsciously changing recall of a memory so it is more understandable to you.

Confabulation – unconsciously mixing up of memories from different sources to create a different memory.

Cognitive scripts

These are collections of **schemata** which link together to produce a series of expectations relevant to the situation you are in. These scripts guide you on what to expect and how to behave in specific situations. They develop over time and with repeated experience of social situations

Cognitive priming

This happens when exposure to one stimulus influences how you respond to subsequent stimuli. It is a bit like planting an idea in someone's mind. The experience of seeing and hearing one thing leads you to see and hear another more quickly. This is called **positive priming** as it speeds up how you respond to things after you have been primed. Theorists suggest this is because you use schema to store information in your memory. Schema are linked to each other depending on similarity of the concepts involved. So, when an experience activates a concept in a schema, this then primes linked concepts so that they are more accessible to your consciousness than those that are not linked. **Negative priming** occurs when exposure to the **prime** slows the response to the subsequent things.

There are several different types of **priming**, the ones you need to know are:

▶ **Repetition** – this is a form of direct priming in which experience of something primes you so that response to the situation is quicker in the future. For example, if you are asked to say the word 'poke' several times and then are asked what the white part of an egg is called, you will probably say 'yolk' because you have been primed to do so.

▶ **Semantic** – the prime and the target belong to similar categories and share features so thinking of a specific item within the category can prime you to process information relevant to other members of the category more quickly. For example, if you are primed to think of dogs you will be able to identify a picture of a wolf more quickly than you would a leopard because wolves and leopards belong to different categories.

▶ **Associative** – priming happens when the prime and the target are regularly associated but do not have to be from the same conceptual category. For example, fish and chips: fish acts as a prime for chips.

> ### Key terms
>
> **Schemata** – plural of schema.
>
> **Positive priming** – stimulus that makes response to a prime faster.
>
> **Negative priming** – stimulus that makes response to a prime slower.
>
> **Priming/Prime** – stimulus that subconsciously affects how you respond to something.
>
> **Semantic** – the meaning of something.

> ### Theory into practice
>
> Try this out on some friends. Prime them with either numbers or letters first, and then ask them what the middle item in this list is. You could get them to recite the alphabet first or count up to 20.
>
>
>
> What kind of priming do you think is likely to have happened here?

Cognitive biases

You process masses of information all the time. This puts a high demand on your processing capacity. The brain works out some short cuts that enable fast processing without the need to attend consciously to every detail before making a decision. These shortcuts are called cognitive **heuristics**. Mostly this is highly efficient but sometimes they lead to biases in the way you process information, which therefore causes bias in how you think and feel about your experiences.

▶ The **fundamental attribution error** (FAE) happens when you over-emphasise the role of intention as a cause of behaviour of other people, and under-emphasise its role in your own behaviour. When something happens to someone else it is their fault, but when it happens to you it is due to random factors beyond your control.

Theory into practice

Arran is walking through college with an armful of books. Another student he knows called Ellie rushes past and bumps into him nearly knocking the books out of his grasp. Arran scowls at her and thinks she is rude and selfish. Arran turns around to go to his next class and immediately bumps into someone else.

Where will Arran attribute blame for the second episode?

Key terms

Heuristic – a mental shortcut, like an algorithm in a computer.

Fundamental attribution error – the tendency to underestimate the effect of your own motives or behaviour in a situation but overestimate the motives or behaviour of others in the event.

Confirmation bias – the focus is directed towards information that is consistent with your opinions and/or knowledge.

Hostile attribution bias – the tendency to think that the ordinary behaviour of other people is actually threatening towards you.

▶ **Confirmation bias** leads you to pay attention to information that supports your views and to ignore information that does not.

Theory into practice

Later in the day Arran is at lunch in the cafeteria with his friend Nish when Ellie comes in and starts to have an argument with another student in the queue. The other student is angry and Ellie walks away. A tutor comes in and asks Nish and Arran what they saw. Arran emphasised that Ellie started it whereas Nish focused on how angry the other student was.

Why do Nish and Arran have different accounts of the same event?

▶ The **hostile attribution bias** (HAB) causes you to attribute negative intentions to someone else's behaviour leading you to feel victimised by them, and perhaps retaliating against them. For example, in a social situation someone vulnerable to HAB would interpret someone simply looking at them as disrespectful and/or threatening and, as a result, might respond with aggression.

Theory into practice

Nish shares a class with the angry student. During a class discussion the other student argues against Nish's view. Nish gets angry and shouts at the student accusing her of deliberately trying to show him up. He storms out of the class. Later, when questioned about his actions Nish said that he knew she was 'out to get him' so got in first.

Why might Nish have thought this?

All of these biases operate without your conscious awareness and provide you with quick and easy judgements about your environment and especially about other people. This enables you to make fast judgements about potential problems and react quickly.

⏸ PAUSE POINT

Before you go on to learn about the key studies that test these ideas, it is a good idea to check your knowledge on what you have done so far. Summarise each of the cognitive concepts described in this section.

Hint   Turn your summaries into bullet points using as few words as possible but which will allow you to reconstruct the description effectively.

Extend   Think of some different examples to illustrate each one. For example, consider how the police and the criminal justice system might benefit from knowing about cognitive biases. You can use this as an evaluation point for these concepts and theories as they have useful application to the real world.

Cognitive approach key studies

A study is an investigation which tests the claims of a theory or concept. It gathers data which is then applied to the theory. All studies have an aim (linked to the theory being tested), a procedure (a way of gathering data), some results (analysis of the data) and conclusions. Results and conclusions are referred to as findings.

Bartlett (1932) 'War of the Ghosts'

Bartlett felt that the study of memory should incorporate social context and meanings. He proposed that memory must be understood as a creative process, putting him in opposition to the view at the time that memory is a singular process for keeping information until needed. He developed new ways of testing memory including this famous study.

Aim: To investigate the role of existing personal semantic knowledge in the formation of memory.

Procedure: This research does not follow the normal rules of experimental research so is difficult to describe exactly. British participants were told a story from North American culture (the 'War of the Ghosts'). They then had to tell the story to someone else, who then told it to someone else and so on, until it had been retold several times. This is called **serial reproduction**.

In another version of the study, people were told the story by the researcher and were asked to recall it after a long time (up to two years).

In both versions, Bartlett recorded the recall of the story and looked for the ways the story changed. Bartlett also asked participants to read the story two times at their own pace, and then to recall it later. This could be weeks, months or even years after the initial reading. This is **repeated reproduction**.

Link

Go to Unit 2 to learn about the way research is conducted.

Key terms

Serial reproduction – a technique used in memory research where one person gives information to the next, who then gives it to another person, and so on. Similar to Chinese whispers.

Repeated reproduction – the same person repeatedly recalling information.

Link

Go to Unit 2 to read about the ethical guidelines for doing research involving people.

Key terms

Levelling – leaving out parts of original information resulting in shortening of the memory.

Sharpening – focusing on small details in the original memory so they become more important.

Longitudinal research – research that tests the same people over a long period of time comparing their responses between time periods.

Ecological validity – how much the study's procedure and/or conclusions genuinely reflect real life events and behaviour.

Population validity – how much the characteristics of the participants reflect the characteristics in the general population.

Findings: Participants distorted the story as they recalled it. The story became shorter, it lost a lot of detail (**levelling**) and the order in which the events happened tended to change in order to fit with the cultural expectations of the participant (**sharpening**). They found that the things that happened in the story that were least familiar to British culture were transformed so that they became more understandable (rationalisation).

Conclusions: This study shows that memory is an active process; it is reconstructed at the point of recall rather than just retrieved from storage. It shows the effect that pre-existing schema have in creating the memory through the way that the recall is distorted to fit with cultural expectations.

Research

Try a replication of Bartlett's serial reproduction study. You will need to recruit at least four participants. You will need a quiet room and the 'War of the Ghosts' study (you can find this online). Get your first participant to come into the room. Read out the story to them. Then invite your second participant in and ask participant one to tell them the story as accurately as possible while you record what they say. Thank the first participant and let them go, and invite participant three into the room. Ask participant two to tell them the story, record what they say, thank participant two and invite participant four. Repeat the process until all participants have told the story; the final participant should tell the story to you.

Next, analyse the data. Look for examples of sharpening, rationalisation and/or confabulation.

Use the ethical guidelines whenever you are doing research with people, even informally like this.

▶ Evaluation of the study

Strengths	Limitations
One of the studies had a **longitudinal research** design. This gives a clear picture of what happens to your memory over a long period of time so increases the **ecological validity** of the research as it represents how memory is used in real life.	This study lacked control; it did not follow the appropriate scientific format in reporting what was done and what was found, so it is hard to judge how reliable the data is. Another researcher looking at the same data might interpret it differently.
The conclusions from this study have useful application. For example, understanding how memory changes over time means that you need to treat eyewitness memory for long-ago events with caution.	The study had limited **population validity** as it only tested 20 English people for their recall of a North American folk tale.

Harris, Bargh and Brownell (2009) Priming effects of television food advertising on eating behaviour

Some psychologists investigate the influences that may contribute to unhealthy behaviour and provide scientific evidence to show these influences. These can then be used to form behavioural interventions designed to improve the health of the population. One major area for research is childhood obesity, so cognitive psychologists investigate how people think about food and what influences that thinking. For example, they investigate whether priming affects eating behaviour.

Aim: To investigate the impact of TV advertising for junk food on eating behaviour.

Procedure: Two laboratory experiments were conducted on people of different ages.

Experiment 1: The participants were 118 children aged between 7 and 11 years old. The **sample** consisted of both genders and a range of bodyweights and ethnicities. They were recruited as volunteers by their parents in response to letters sent out from their schools. They were tested at school after lessons.

The participants were **randomly allocated** to one of two groups (conditions) but each participant was tested alone. All children watched the same 14-minute cartoon which had two short advert breaks in which four adverts were shown, but one group was exposed to adverts for junk food promoting fun and happiness, and the other was exposed to adverts for non-food products.

Both groups were provided with cheesy cracker snacks and water during their time watching the cartoon.

Experiment 2: 98 adult participants (university students) of both genders and varied ethnicity, were randomly allocated to three groups (conditions). They were told that the study was to investigate the effect of TV on mood. All watched the same 16-minute TV programme alone with four minutes of adverts which included either four junk-food adverts, four nutritious food adverts, or no food adverts.

None of the groups were provided with snacks during their viewing but were later asked to taste a range of healthy and unhealthy snacks and rate them for how much they liked them.

Researchers in both experiments measured the amount of food consumed by the participants in each group, how long they spent eating and their liking for the product.

Findings: Groups exposed to adverts for food consumed more snacks than groups not exposed to food adverts.

In the first experiment, the children in the junk-food group ate 45 per cent more than the other children.

The adults consumed more snacks (both healthy and unhealthy) when exposed to food adverts.

There was no link between consumption and actual hunger.

They concluded that food advertising primes the viewer to eat more by triggering automatic eating habits whether they are hungry or not. The content of an advert can prime eating behaviour.

> **Key terms**
>
> **Sample** – people selected to participate in a specific research study.
>
> **Random allocation** – putting participants from the sample into the conditions of the experiment using a random technique. This could be putting all names in a hat and drawing out one at a time until one group is populated, then doing the same for the next group if there are more than two conditions.

▶ Evaluation of the study

Strengths	Limitations
The study is likely to have produced reliable data because of the controls in the procedure. For example, the random allocation of participants to conditions controls for researcher bias of putting the 'most likely to eat more' participants in the junk-food condition. We can be sure that the effect was due to the exposure to the adverts and not due to the characteristics of the participants.	The study may lack ecological validity as the children and adults watched TV alone and were in an unusual location for watching TV (at school); viewing is usually a social activity. This may have affected how much they were influenced by the adverts and caused them to eat more. In normal conditions they might not have behaved in the same way.
The study has important application as it demonstrates how people, and especially children, are affected by how food is advertised. As there is a real concern about increasing childhood obesity, it would therefore suggest that food adverts should not be shown during children's TV or before children's films in order not to encourage snacking.	The study could not pinpoint the exact cause of the increased snacking other than to state that it was the advert itself. The content of the advert (for healthy food or junk food) did not seem to matter. This therefore limits the usefulness of these results, especially as similar tests of priming do not always show the same results.

Research

Investigate the types of adverts shown on children's TV. Choose a day and a channel to watch for about an hour at a time when you might expect children to be watching and note down the type of adverts that occur. Analyse the data to see if there are any types of adverts that might influence the behaviour of the children.

Loftus and Palmer (1974) Reconstruction of automobile destruction

Elizabeth Loftus has spent many years studying how memory can be distorted and changed as a result of misinformation. She has applied her expertise to many court cases, helping judges and juries understand issues with witness memory. One of her best-known studies is a test of the effect of misinformation in the form of leading questions.

Aim: To test whether the way a question is worded will affect recall of the circumstances of a car crash.

Procedure: This was a laboratory experiment where 45 student participants were divided into five groups (**conditions**). Each student watched short films of several car crashes. They were then asked to recall what they had seen and were given a **questionnaire** with a critical question: 'how fast were the cars going when they … each other?'. Each group was given a different verb describing the crash: contacted; hit; bumped; collided or smashed. So, in one of the five conditions the critical question was 'how fast were the cars going when they hit each other?'. The participants had to report their estimate of the speed in miles per hour and their answers were compared across the various conditions.

Key terms

Conditions – in an experiment, a condition is the way the tested variable is applied to the participants.

Questionnaire – self-report method where the participants give written answers to pre-determined questions.

Findings: Table showing mean estimates of speeds of cars in each condition.

Verb	Speed (MPH)
Smashed	40.8
Collided	39.3
Hit	38.1
Bumped	34
Contacted	31.8

Conclusions: As the intensity of the verb increased, so too did the measure of speed. This may be because the verb activated a schema which affected the recall of the car's speed. For example, 'smash' indicates high speed so the participant remembered the car as travelling faster.

▶ Evaluation of the study

Strengths	Limitations
Employed a lot of **controls** to ensure that the data was reliable. For example, exactly the same film clip was shown in all the conditions suggesting that any change in recall was due to the wording of the question and not changes in the actual crash.	May lack population validity as all the participants were students of a similar age. It may be that students of this age are more likely to pick up cues in the question because they are unlikely to have lots of experience of judging speed.
Has very useful **application** as it shows that the way questions are asked can distort the recall of an event. Police must be careful about using leading questions because they might cause the witness to recall events inaccurately perhaps leading to miscarriages of justice where the wrong person is convicted of a crime.	Might lack ecological validity as it asked the participants to judge the speed of cars on a video clip. This is different from the real world as they are in a controlled situation. In the real world there would be more noise and panic and so their recall might be more accurate in that situation where they were more emotionally aroused.

Key terms

Controls – in research, it is essential to hold as many **variables** constant as possible so as only the variable being tested changes between the conditions.

Application – the way the findings of a study are used in society.

Variables – anything that can change.

Conformity – changing your mind or behaviour to that of the group.

Normative social influence – changing your mind or behaviour to that of the group in order to fit in with them and not stand out as different.

Informational social influence – changing your mind or behaviour to that of the group in order to do the right thing in a situation where you are uncertain.

Social approach

Social influence is a major factor that affects how you behave. Humans are social animals, living and working in groups. Your survival depends on successful interaction with each other. Some would argue that humans have evolved to be social because this gave them an advantage over other species. This means that social information, such as other people, has a big impact on your behaviour.

For example, the groups you belong to fundamentally affect how you behave towards others. This can lead to aggression and to cooperation between groups. Membership of different social groups can also affect the individuals in those groups in terms of how they think, feel and behave. There is an overlap with cognitive psychology here in terms of how social situations affect information processing. In this section you will learn about conformity, social categorisation and stereotyping.

Key concepts

Conformity

You belong to many different social groups, for example your group of friends, your family, your culture or your interests. When you are with the group, and sometimes as a result of belonging to a group, this will change how you think and how you behave. **Conformity** is a type of social influence involving a change in belief or behaviour in order to fit in with a group.

Jade is on her way to a football match with her friends. As they near the stadium her friends start shouting football chants insulting the other team and their fans. Jade knows people who support the other team including people in her own family, but she joins in the chants.

1 Explain why this is an example of normative social influence.

2 Does Jade truly believe that the supporters of the other team are inferior?

Deutsch and Gerard (1955) proposed that groups influence people in one of two ways:

▶ **Normative social influence**: this involves a change in the behaviour or attitude of an individual in order to fit in with the behaviour of the group. You change your behaviour to avoid standing out as different from other people around you. This is unlikely to lead to long-lasting change in attitudes or behaviour as the person could do something completely different when in a different group. It is sometimes referred to as the 'desire to be liked'.

▶ **Informational social influence**: this involves a change in the behaviour or attitude of an individual to be more like the behaviour or attitude of the group they are with. It occurs when the individual believes the group knows more than them. This is more likely to lead to long-lasting changes in attitude and behaviour. It is sometimes referred to as the 'desire to be right'.

Types of conformity

The depth of the conformity varies depending on how much and how long lasting the change is towards the group's behaviour and attitudes, and whether the change is only in public but not in private.

- **Compliance** is the least enduring and most superficial level. It is likely to be of short duration and only persists while the person is with the group. Although publicly they may agree with the group, privately they don't so there is no real change of attitude, only behaviour.
- **Identification** happens when the person lines up with the group's attitudes and behaviour in order to be a member of the group. They agree publicly with the group's values and are more likely to agree privately too. This can happen in terms of group work: when you are working as a team, you adopt the team values, but these are not necessarily permanent.
- **Internalisation** is the deepest level of conformity, where the change in attitude and behaviour is both public, private and permanent. It is most likely to result from informational social influence.

Case study

Declan does not know much about rugby and has no strong feelings about it. When he starts college, he has a group of new friends who are all keen rugby supporters. Declan says that he likes rugby too.

1 What level of conformity does Declan show here?

As Declan gets to know his friends better, he begins to discuss rugby with them and learns more about the game, until he is able to talk confidently about rugby issues when in the group.

2 What level of conformity does Declan show here?

Eventually Declan really gets into rugby and discusses it with his parents, even asking for a replica team strip for his birthday.

3 What level of conformity does Declan show here?

Factors that affect whether you conform or not

Psychologists have researched what makes people more or less likely to conform to group pressure. They suggest it involves:

- the **status** of the group, especially when informational social influence is applied. A high-status group is expected to know more than most people so you might be more likely to conform to their opinions because they are experts, especially if you have little or no knowledge on the topic.
- the size of the group. Generally, there is an increase in conformity when the group consists of three or more people, although it does not necessarily follow that very large groups will cause more conformity. Research shows that three people in a group saying the same thing are likely to affect the behaviour of an individual.
- **unanimity** in the group. When every member of the group says and does the same thing then conformity is more likely to happen.
- task difficulty. When groups are undertaking a difficult or **ambiguous** task, conformity increases.

Key terms

Status – perceived power of the person or group of people.

Unanimity – total agreement between members of the group.

Ambiguity/Ambiguous – situation where there is no clear and obvious way to act.

Social categorisation

People constantly try to categorise themselves and each other as this or that type of person. These **categories** are types of schema that tell you something about the person without you having to know them and which create expectations about the other person and how they will behave. Social categorisation is the process of classifying people into groups based on specific characteristics, for example age, nationality, profession, gender, and so on.

You use these categories to make **assumptions** about the people who belong to them; you might assume that a sporty person is more likely to be young. These assumptions influence how you interact with them. For example, people that you categorise as belonging to social groups other than your own (out-group members) might, in some cases, trigger a more hostile response than those you categorise as belonging to your own group (in-group members). In-group and out-group behaviour has been proposed as a basis for many types of prejudice such as that leading to racism.

> **Discussion**
>
> Imagine your boyfriend or girlfriend invites you home to meet their parents for the first time. How would your expectations change if your boyfriend or girlfriend first tells you they are both surgeons compared to shop-workers?
>
> Do you think this might affect how you interact with them?

> **Key terms**
>
> **Category** – grouping of things that are similar.
>
> **Assumption** – a decision about something based on minimal knowledge.
>
> **Stereotype** – a common, but simplistic, view of a person or thing.

Categorising people leads to you making superficial judgements about them based on background knowledge of the social categories they belong to. This leads to stereotyping, which affects how you think and feel about them and ultimately how you behave towards them.

A **stereotype** is a schema containing your knowledge about a particular category. For example, surgeons are brainy, they like classical music, they use long words, and they dress smartly. Everyone develops stereotypes; they operate unconsciously and are automatically triggered in situations where they become relevant. You use them often and they can lead to bias in the way you treat other people.

> **Discussion**
>
> Think about nurses. What kind of qualities do you think they have? Describe a typical nurse. Of course, by now you will realise that there is no such thing as a typical nurse, nevertheless, if you are honest, you will be able to come up with a set of qualities that are associated with your schema for nurses.

Social approach key studies

Asch (1951) Experimental investigation of conformity to the majority

Asch was an influential social psychologist; much of his work was done in the mid-twentieth century in the USA. He said that 'most social acts have to be understood in their setting and lose meaning if isolated'. His research is therefore focused on the social setting in which behaviour occurs and his most famous research is his investigation into conformity.

Aim: To investigate whether participants would conform to the obviously wrong judgement of a majority.

Procedure: Asch used a sample of 123 male university students. Each participant took part on their own, but were led to believe they were part of a bigger group of eight participants. The other seven were confederates (people that look like other participants but have been given a specific role to play).

The task given to the participants was to judge which line matched the standard line.

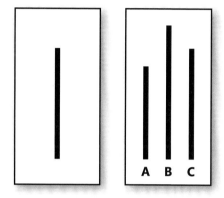

▶ **Figure 1.3:** Each person in the room had to state aloud which comparison line (A, B or C) was most like the standard line

By manipulating the appointment time for the true participant to arrive he made it so that they had to sit in a certain place, so were second from last to give their judgement. Each participant took part in 18 trials where they were asked to match the line to the standard. The correct answer was always obvious, and pre-testing on a control group showed that the vast majority of people were able to do this task quickly, easily and accurately. There were 12 critical trials where the confederates were instructed to all give the same wrong response; the data gathered on these trials was used to measure conformity.

Findings: 25 per cent of the participants never conformed; 75 per cent did (at least once). Overall, the total level of conformity on the critical trials was 36.8 per cent. Participants were interviewed after the study and asked about their decisions. The dissenters (those that did not conform) said that they felt uncomfortable going against the group but had enough confidence to do so. Those that yielded (agreed with the group) lacked this confidence even though many suspected that people in the group were deliberately giving the wrong answers so went along with the group so as not to stand out against them.

Conclusions: Normative social influence affected many participants as they did not want to stand out as a dissenter. Even the ones who did dissent felt socially uncomfortable in doing so. Some dissenters also showed informational social influence as they conformed because of the desire to be right.

▶ Evaluation of the study

Strengths	Limitations
There were many controls used in this study. For example, the same confederates were used throughout and they always gave the same answers to the different participants, so you can be sure that any change in the response of the participant was due to the social pressure rather than what the confederates said.	Although the sample was large, the study only used one type of participant (male undergraduate students at a university in the USA), so it is likely that they only represent that sub-set of the population and would not generalise to other segments. Furthermore, at that time in American history, conforming to the majority view was a strong social norm, which might not influence similar studies carried out in other times and places.
The data gathered was objective and not open to interpretation because it consisted of whether they acted independently of the group by disagreeing with them or not. This means that there was no chance of researcher bias in their interpretation of the results. Even though the actual level of conformity was 36.8% (which does not seem high), comparing this to the control where almost everyone always got the answer right, it does show a big shift to the group opinion.	The study had low ecological validity, the line length judgement task given to the participants was artificial and had no meaning for them, so they might be more likely just to agree with the group than if they were in a position where what they said mattered.

Research

Look at other studies of conformity and see if they agree with Asch's findings, for example studies in the UK by Perrin and Spencer (1980; 1981). Why did Perrin and Spencer get different results to Asch?

Chatard, Guimond & Selimbegovic (2007) 'How good are you in math?' The effect of gender stereotypes on students' recollection of their school marks

You have expectations about how to behave and how others should behave based on the group norms which are widespread within your culture. These norms become internalised as schema. A stereotype is a social schema about a group or category of people. One of the most basic categories is gender. Gender stereotypes affect how you think about yourself and other people, sometimes distorting what you perceive and remember so it fits the stereotype. One common gender stereotype is that males are better at maths whereas females are better at creative subjects.

Aim: To see if commonly held gender stereotypes about maths and arts ability affect students' recall of their actual grades in those subjects.

Procedure: They recruited 64 French high-school students all of a similar ability and from the same school (29 females and 35 males aged on average 14.2 years). During the last school year, the students had all undergone standardised testing for which they received a maths and an arts score.

The participants were randomly allocated to either the high or low **gender salient** condition. This means that the stereotype was made more obvious. Gender salience was manipulated by getting them to think about stereotypes before they thought about their own ability. They did this by administering a questionnaire asking them to rate their agreement (on a **Likert scale**) with statements about male and female maths and arts ability. For example, "Women are gifted at mathematics" or "Men are gifted at arts". Following this, they then had to rate their own ability at maths and arts, for example "I am gifted at mathematics".

▶ Example of a Likert scale

Totally disagree	Mostly disagree	Disagree somewhat	Neither agree or disagree	Agree somewhat	Mostly agree	Totally agree
1	2	3	4	5	6	7

In the high-salience condition, they were given the stereotype statements to complete first followed by the self-statements. The researchers believed that this would prime them to think stereotypically. In the low-salience condition the participants completed the self-statements first.

They then had to report their scores for both maths and arts on their last national standardised test.

Findings: The data was analysed to measure the amount of bias in the students' recall of their standardised test scores. They did this by comparing their recall of their standardised test score with their actual score (see Table 1.2).

In the low-salience conditions where participants were not primed for gender stereotypes there was some recall bias for both genders across both maths and arts in that both recalled their scores as higher than they were, but in the high-salience condition there was a significant difference between girls and boys in arts where girls overestimated much more than boys, and in maths girls underestimated whereas boys overestimated.

> **Key terms**
>
> **Gender salience** – salience means to make relevant, so gender salience is to make gender relevant, for example by reminding people of the stereotype it makes it more important.
>
> **Likert scale** – **quantitative** method of measuring attitudes by assigning numbers to levels of agreement.

▶ **Table 1.2:** Table to show recall bias based on difference score (recall of grade and official marks)

	Arts		Maths	
Gender	Low salience	High salience	Low salience	High salience
Female	0.39	0.83	0.38	-0.60
Male	0.72	0.14	0.12	0.57

A minus number indicates underestimation whereas a positive one indicates overestimation.

Conclusions: The researchers concluded that both genders were affected by stereotypes, but girls were negatively affected by stereotypes about maths and recalled a significantly worse score than they actually achieved.

▶ Evaluation of the study

Strengths	Limitations
The findings of this study are consistent with results from similar studies and therefore increase the validity of the conclusions. These have practical implications for education as it shows how easy it is for a stereotypical view to affect how you rate your own ability. Also, tutors must be aware of how stereotypes can affect performance and remind female students that maths is for girls too.	The study has limited **generalisability** because of the age group used; it may be that older students who have more confidence in their ability are less likely to respond to stereotypes in the same way and so might be more or less influenced by exposure to stereotypical ideas.
The study had a representative sample size and employed good controls, for example the participants' actual grades obtained independently of the research were used to determine whether they had over or underestimated their abilities. This is objective and therefore a reliable way of measuring the outcome.	**Demand characteristics** might have affected the data. Students will have been aware of the experiment and this could have changed their behaviour to be more or less likely to support the hypothesis, for example the girls might have wanted to be more helpful than the boys and this is why there was a gender difference.

> **Key terms**
>
> **Quantitative** – numerical data.
>
> **Generalisability** – the extent to which the findings from a study can be applied to other groups in the wider population.
>
> **Demand characteristics** – participants change their behaviour to fit with the aims of the experiment.

Haney et al (1973) A study of prisoners and guards in a simulated prison

The US Navy wanted to understand more about the way prisoners and guards interacted and funded Haney et al to run this study. Following Asch's research on conformity, they were interested in finding out about how the situation, and especially the social roles in a situation, affects behaviour.

Aim: To investigate the effect of social roles on behaviour in a prison setting.

▶ Are people influenced by the social role they find themselves in?

Procedure: A mock prison was set up in the basement of Stanford University. 24 participants were selected from a pool of volunteers who answered an advert in the local paper asking for participation in a study on prison life. Those selected to participate were checked to make sure that they were mentally healthy and had no prior criminal record. They were made aware of what the study entailed and were randomly allocated to being either a guard or a prisoner (12 guards and 12 prisoners). Guards received some training and were given uniforms including a night stick and sunglasses.

Prisoners were unexpectedly arrested at home by real police officers and processed like real criminals before being transported to the 'prison'. They were stripped, showered and given particular clothes to wear. The prisoners were given a number by which they were known throughout the study.

Guards had to enforce the rules (without physical violence) and the study was to last 14 days. All participants were to be paid $15 a day. The researchers took the role of superintendent and wardens. The situation was watched by the researchers 24/7: they took notes, some data was videotaped, conversations were recorded and regular questionnaires about mood were given out.

Findings: Very quickly the guards' interaction with the prisoners was reduced to giving orders. They soon started to humiliate the prisoners, for example by doing pointless counts on the prisoners making them line up and state their numbers. They also made them carry out degrading acts.

The prisoners became submissive and several showed signs of real mental distress with one prisoner having a breakdown and being 'released' after only 36 hours.

When the prisoners referred to themselves (for example in discussions with a priest) they used the number they were given, and talked about parole rather than withdrawal from the study. The study was cancelled after six days when a researcher visiting for the first time was appalled by the situation and objected on ethical grounds to what was happening.

Conclusions: The situation caused normal young men to become either abusive or submissive according to the role they were assigned. One third of the guards showed genuinely sadistic behavior, which showed that the roles had the power to change people.

Link

What do you think of the ethics of this study? Should this study have been allowed? Go to Unit 2 where you will learn about the ethical guidelines that should be applied to research. Once you have learned about these you can gain further evaluation of this study by discussing why it was or was not ethical.

▶ Evaluation of the study

Strengths	Limitations
This study controlled for the difference in personalities between the guards and the prisoners. All participants were screened before and the guards and prisoners were randomly allocated to groups so as there could be no effect of participant variables affecting the outcome. This ensured that it was the role allocated, and their expectations associate with that role, which influenced their behaviour.	There have been no successful replications of this study. In one similar British study by Reicher and Haslam (2006) conducted with the BBC and televised, there were very different results as the guards failed to adopt their role allowing the prisoners to have more power. This calls into question the study's conclusions about the power of the situation to shape behaviour.
The study had high ecological validity because the set-up had many similar aspects to real prison. The prisoners were arrested at home, for example, and taken to the cells by real police officers making it seem more real to them and reinforcing the role they were given. The study has therefore been used to explain real-world examples of prison abuse.	The researchers became too involved in the action. They lost their objectivity and the experiment got out of control. They therefore allowed things to happen that ethically should not have happened and had to be reminded about their duty of care by an outside observer. This means that the data gathered was not objective and was probably biased towards the aim of the study.

PAUSE POINT

You have now learned about six key studies. Before you move into the learning approach, it would be a good idea to consolidate your learning of these.

Hint

Try picking out the key features and findings of each study and write each one onto a sticky note. This will help you summarise the aims, procedures, findings and conclusions effectively, as you have only a small space to write on.

Extend

Once you have completed the sticky notes summarising all six, mix them up and then reassemble them. This will help you to firmly revise the content of each one; you may also start to see similarities in the methods which might help you apply the evaluations more easily.

Learning approach

The learning approach makes the assumption that all behaviour is almost entirely a product of nurture. It is learned as a result of our experience within our environment. Early theorists were called behaviourists. They focused on learning through direct experience (you have to do something yourself in order to learn from it). This is sometimes known as stimulus-response (SR) learning, but the introduction of social learning theory in the late 1960s softened these views to include your ability to learn through indirect experience too.

Key concepts

Classical conditioning

Pavlov discovered classical **conditioning** by accident when investigating the role of saliva in digestion. He unexpectedly found that the dogs began to salivate before food was presented to them and theorised that they had learned to associate the noises caused by producing and delivering the food with the food itself.

Initially the noise would not cause any response in the dog as it was a **neutral stimulus**, whereas food always caused the response of salivation. This is because the natural response to the smell of food is to salivate, this prepares their body to start digesting food in their mouths, and the food smell causes a **reflex** response. This is called an **unconditioned stimulus (UCS)**. The salivation is the **unconditioned response (UCR)** to the food, because they have not had to learn this. Eventually, even without the food, the dogs salivate to the noise. This response has been learned so the sound of the bell becomes the **conditioned stimulus (CS)** and the salivation is a **conditioned response (CR)**.

Pavlov demonstrated this in a very famous study, as seen in Figure 1.4.

1	UCS (food)	= UCR (salivation)
2	NS (bell)	= no response
3	NS (bell) + UCS (food)	= UCR (salivation)
4	CS (bell alone)	= CR (salivation)

▶ **Figure 1.4:** Pavlov's dogs

Key terms

Conditioning phase – the period during conditioning where the neutral stimulus is presented alongside the unconditioned stimulus in order to acquire its power.

Neutral stimulus (NS) – an object or event that initially has no power to cause behaviour.

Reflex – an innate (inborn) physical response to specific stimuli.

Unconditioned stimulus (UCS) – an object or event that naturally has the power to produce a reflex response.

Unconditioned response (UCR) – a naturally occurring reaction to a specific stimulus.

Conditioned stimulus (CS) – an object or event that has acquired the power to cause a specific response through association.

Conditioned response (CR) – a learned response to a specific stimulus.

Theory into practice

When Rajesh was small, he was visiting a farm park to see the animals when he was given some aniseed sweets that had a very distinctive smell. He was standing next to the goats and one of them put his head through the fence and took the bag of sweets from Rajesh's hand, nipping his fingers at the same time. Rajesh even as an adult cannot tolerate the smell of aniseed.

Explain why he reacts this way.

Link

Go to page 34 if you are struggling with this and look at the 'Little Albert' study conducted by Watson and Rayner (1920).

Operant conditioning

The theory of operant conditioning was developed by Skinner who thought that classical conditioning was too simple to explain all aspects of learning. He believed that learning was a more active process than suggested by classical conditioning, and that the best way to understand learning was to look for the causes of action. Specifically, he proposed that people learn as a direct result of experiencing the consequences of your actions. You are constantly acting (or operating) on your environment and the effect this has on you determines whether or not you are likely to repeat a behaviour or not.

Consequences can be nice, neutral or nasty. Neutral consequences do not affect learning but nice consequences will increase the chances that the behaviour will be repeated; these are known as **reinforcers**. There are two types of reinforcement: **positive reinforcement** and **negative reinforcement**. A nasty consequence will prevent you from repeating a behaviour again, by giving something unpleasant as a consequence of your action (**punishment**).

Research

Operant conditioning is used in many situations, but especially in training animals. Using a reward system, devise a way to encourage a puppy to pee only in the garden.

Classical and operant conditioning together make up the behaviourist approach to explaining behaviour. This is sometimes referred to as stimulus response learning. It ignores what happens inside the mind between the experience of the stimulus and the behavioural response.

Social learning theory

A further development in learning theories was proposed by Bandura. Although he agreed that conditioning was certainly part of the process of learning, he believed that there was more to it than that. Social learning theory works on the basis that most behaviours are learned through the observation and **imitation** of other people's actions. Although this is still learning from the environment and is consistent with the nurture view of the behaviourists, it adds cognitive processing to learning. It provides an explanation of what goes on in the mind between the stimulus and the behavioural response.

This theory says that you pay more **attention** to certain people in your environment and they become **models** for you. Models tend to be those who are important to you, similar in some way and often of higher status. You observe what they do and what happens to them when they do it. Sometimes you **retain** this information and use it in the future to perform similar actions but only if you know that you can **replicate** it successfully. You do this in order to **identify** with the model and because you and/or they are reinforced for doing so.

The behavioural processes involved in this are observation, modelling, imitation, and reinforcement. Reinforcement can be both direct, which is when you are reinforced for the imitation of the model, or indirect where the model is reinforced. This is called **vicarious reinforcement**.

The cognitive processes involved in this are attention, retention, replication and **motivation**. You choose who is to be your model and what to watch, you store information about their actions as memory, you decide whether you can actually physically do what they do, and you copy them when you are motivated to do so. This cognitive component to the theory means that you do not automatically just copy everything you see other people doing, and it explains why you do not need **direct reinforcement** from the environment in order to change your behaviour.

Research

Advertising campaigns often involve celebrities using a product and looking happy about doing so. Certain celebrities might be models for certain groups of people and these campaigns successfully target these groups. If their behaviour is simple enough to retain and to replicate, the person watching the advert might be motivated to buy the product in order to imitate the model and identify with them.

Imagine you are asked to produce an advertising campaign for a new sports drink targeting teenage girls. You want to include a celebrity. Who would you choose? What would you want the celebrity to do in the advert?

Watch some adverts involving celebrity endorsements and see if you can apply social learning theory to explain why, and how, advertisers use them.

Learning approach key studies

Bandura (1961) Transmission of aggression through imitation of aggressive models

Albert Bandura was interested in explaining aggression in young people. He felt that the traditional conditioning explanation was not sufficient to be able to do this so he proposed adding a cognitive and social element to learning. Learning in humans mostly occurs in a social context. You learn from observing and imitating other people, but this also involves cognition – how you process the information you observe is an important element which determines whether or not you repeat the behaviour you see. Bandura tested young children to see if he could make them more or less aggressive by exposing them to an aggressive model of either the same sex as them, or a different sex.

Aim: To demonstrate that if children witness a real-life aggressive model, they would imitate the aggressive behaviour if given the opportunity.

Procedure: 72 children, 36 males and 36 females, between the ages of 3–5 years, recruited from Stanford University Crèche took part. The participants were divided into eight experimental conditions (of six children each) and a control group (24 children). All of the children were matched for physical and verbal aggression before the experiment, based on the ratings of the experimenter and nursery teacher. This meant that equally aggressive children were distributed into each of the conditions to make sure that all the aggressive ones did not end up in the same condition.

The experimental conditions were whether the children watched aggressive or non-aggressive models of the same or different gender to the child (see Figure 1.5 for the allocation to each condition).

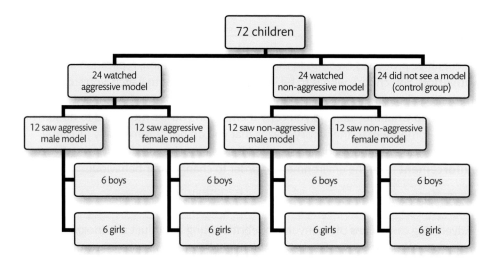

▶ **Figure 1.5:** The allocation of the children to each condition of the experiment

The children were tested individually. They were taken into a corner of a room and shown how to design a picture. The adult model was taken to an opposite corner and to their 'play area' which contained a table, chair, mallet, tinker toy (construction set) and a bobo doll (large inflatable doll with weights in the bottom that automatically stands up when knocked over).

In the aggressive condition, the model played with the tinker toy for a minute and then began to act aggressively towards the bobo doll. In the non-aggressive condition, the model continued to play with the toy. Ten minutes later the child was taken to another room and given toys to play with, which the experimenter then took away to cause frustration. The child was then taken to an experimental room containing aggressive and non-aggressive toys (including the bobo doll). The child was left to play there for 20 minutes while their behaviour was observed through a one-way mirror. The observer counted acts of imitated aggression (a direct copy of what the adult did) and non-imitated aggression (aggression not modelled by the adult).

Findings: Children exposed to the aggressive model showed significantly more acts of aggression (including all aggressive acts, not just those displayed by the model) than the children exposed to the non-aggressive model and those in the control group.

More than 50 per cent of the total acts of aggression (both verbal and physical) was done by the 24 children in the aggressive model condition.

Aggression was more pronounced in boys than girls, particularly when they had been observing a model of the same sex.

Male children showed more aggression in every condition.

Conclusions: If a child is exposed to an aggressive model, they are likely to imitate the aggressive acts they see, especially if the model is in some way similar to them.

Furthermore, just seeing a model behaving aggressively is likely to increase the amount of aggression shown even when the aggression being demonstrated by the witness is not the same as the aggression demonstrated by the model.

Research

Bandura followed this study up with others that tested the effect of the aggressive model being rewarded or punished for their aggression. He found that this also had an effect on whether the children copied the behaviour they saw.

Use your knowledge of vicarious reinforcement to explain what might happen in this study.

Bandura also did further research involving cartoons rather than live models. He found that social learning still happened.

Do an internet search to find out more.

▶ Evaluation of the study

Strengths	Limitations
Can be usefully applied to benefit society because it demonstrates that it is possible to learn from watching other people. This information can be used to reduce anti-social behaviour and to promote pro-social behaviour, for example by controlling what appears in children's TV programmes and by imposing a watershed for TV violence.	There are claims that the children may have been acting in a way they thought was expected of them. By placing them in a room with the bobo, after witnessing an adult hitting one, they could have been acting in accordance with expectation but not how they would respond in a more ecologically valid environment.
Controlled conditions were used and so you can be relatively sure that the differences observed were due to the actions of the model the children were exposed to.	The conclusions are limited to 3–5-year-old children. Children above this age may not respond in the same way when exposed to aggressive role models. They could be affected by other developmental milestones, such as moral development.

Case study

The Sesame Street effect has been attributed in part to social learning. The programme aims to promote kindness and smartness in its child viewers. It models this behaviour through its characters and through the behaviour of the children and adults that appear in the programme.

1 Find out a little more about this effect and use it as evidence to support the concept of social learning.

2 Look at the links between violence on TV and violence in society, especially where young people are watching the violence.

Skinner (1932) On the rate of formation of a conditioned reflex

Skinner believed it was useful to study the acquisition of behaviour through controlled observations and by manipulating the consequences of that behaviour through reinforcement and punishment. He put animals (mostly rats and pigeons) in controlled environments and developed techniques to control the consequences of the animal's behaviour. In this way he built up the theory of operant conditioning. In this section you will learn about Skinner's basic methodology and findings rather than a particular study.

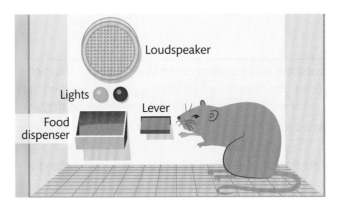

▶ **Figure 1.6:** A Skinner box

Aim: To test whether the behaviour of an animal is more likely to be repeated if followed by pleasant consequences (reinforced).

Procedure: Skinner designed apparatus that came to be known as a 'Skinner box' (see Figure 1.6). The box contained a food dispenser which allowed a food pellet to be issued into a food tray. There was also a lever. Before learning took place, the rats were placed into the boxes for short periods of time to adapt to the apparatus and also to get accustomed to the noise when a food pellet was issued to the food tray (operated by the experimenter). The food they received was rationed to keep rats below their natural weight in order to maintain high levels of hunger, making food a very pleasant reward. During this period the lever was detached so it could not trigger the dispenser.

The following day the lever was moved so that it could be pressed downwards to release a food pellet. The rats were then placed back into the box and the number of times the rat pressed the lever was measured in intervals. Initially, the rat was not interested in the lever, but during exploration of the box the rat would accidentally press it and food was immediately available to it. Food is positive reinforcement for a hungry rat. The rat would continue to explore and might by chance hit the lever again until this was reinforced. The rat soon came to associate lever pressing with the reward of food and would quickly go to the lever and repeatedly press it to gain food.

When testing negative reinforcement, the rats were subjected to an unpleasant electric current through an electrified cage floor. Again, the rat would engage in natural exploratory behaviour and would, by chance, press the lever. When the lever was pushed down it turned off the current which stopped the rats' discomfort. After a few trials the rat was able to go quickly to the lever and press it repeatedly.

Findings: When the rats were first placed in the Skinner box, they would engage in what Skinner termed 'investigatory behaviour' which involved moving around the box. Skinner found that rats placed in the box for an hour took on average 9 minutes and 45 seconds to press the lever for the first time, but at the end of one hour they were pressing it on average every 16 seconds.

Conclusion: Positive reinforcement strengthens a behaviour through providing a reward. Negative reinforcement also strengthens behaviour through the removal of something unpleasant.

> **Research**
>
> You can watch online video clips of some of Skinner's research. For example, there is a demonstration of a pigeon changing its behaviour from turning to pecking when the sign in the Skinner box changed to each command. These clips often include Skinner himself explaining what he found.
>
> Think about how Skinner might have used reinforcement in order to create this behaviour in the pigeon.

▶ Evaluation of the study

Strengths	Limitations
Used controlled, standardised procedures in which all rats were exposed to the same experimental conditions. This consistency increases the reliability of the research.	Some would argue that the findings of this research are not generalisable and so it is not possible to establish how humans learn by using animal studies. Humans have the capacity to think about what they do and to make reasoned decisions. This suggests that human behaviour cannot always be explained using simple stimulus–response processes.
The findings have huge benefits for society. For example, understanding the role of reward in reinforcing positive behaviour has been adapted to develop reward programmes used to manage behaviour in prisons and mental health institutions.	The research could be seen as unethical as the rats were deliberately underfed in order to keep them hungry which would be unpleasant for them. Skinner used small sample sizes, however, (in his original study he only used four rats), reducing the ethical implications.

> **Case study**
>
> During the Second World War, Skinner worked with the US Navy to develop pigeon-guided missiles. This was called Project Pigeon. Pigeons were trained to peck a viewfinder when the target in it deviated off course. The pigeon had three viewfinders with the target initially in the central one. As long as the target was central the pigeon did nothing and the missile did not change course. When the pigeon pecked to one or other side of the central target, the missile changed course because the pecking of the viewfinder was connected to the missile's steering process.
>
> This is a genuine case, although it was never actually used during the war as electronic guidance was developed at the same time and was more reliable.
>
> 1 Explain, using concepts from operant conditioning, how the pigeons could be trained in this way.
>
> 2 Can you think of any other ways that animals could be trained to carry out important behaviour (e.g. think about hearing dogs)?

Watson and Rayner (1920) Conditioned emotional reaction – 'Little Albert'

Background: Watson and Rayner investigated whether classical conditioning could be demonstrated in humans. They chose a baby for the study to rule out the effects of prior learning. The baby, called 'Albert' to protect his identity, was the son of an employee of the university where they worked.

Aim: To demonstrate that the principles of classical conditioning can be used to explain how humans acquire phobic behaviours. Also to show that a fear response can be created within a young child to a stimulus which does not naturally produce this response.

Procedure: As this was a study of one child it is regarded as a case study, although the basic procedure used a laboratory experiment. It consisted of three distinctive steps or trials.

▶ When Little Albert was nine months old, he was given a variety of different stimuli and his response was recorded. These included a white rat and other furry animals as well as the loud noise caused by a steel bar being struck by a hammer behind him. Albert showed only a fear response to the loud noise, making this an unconditioned stimulus (UCS) as no learning was required to produce the response of fear. This established a baseline.

▶ Two months later, he was again given the white rat to play with, but when Albert reached for the rat the steel bar was struck behind him causing the loud and unexpected noise. This process was repeated five times the next week and twice more 17 days later. This was the conditioning phase.

▶ A short time after that, Albert was shown the rat on its own and his response was recorded and compared to the previous times, especially the baseline.

Findings: After the first trial Albert showed some distress but this was not necessarily directed towards the rat. During the second trial he seemed suspicious of the rat. By the third trial Albert avoided the rat. He leaned away from it and cried when a rat was put next to him. He showed a learned fear response.

The researchers saw Albert again seven weeks later and showed him objects that resembled the white rat, including the fur collar of his mother's coat and a Santa beard. Albert cried and showed fear in response to these.

▶ Does classical conditioning work on humans?

Conclusion: It is possible to produce a fear response to a previously unfeared object in a human using the process of classical conditioning and it is possible for this fear to **generalise** to other objects that have similarity to the conditioned stimulus. They had given Albert a **phobia** for white furry objects.

Key terms

Generalisation – in the case of conditioning it means applying the learned response to other similar stimuli (it means something different when you are discussing the representativeness of a sample in a study).

Phobia – mental health disorder characterised by extreme irrational fear of an object or situation which affects daily life as the sufferer actively avoids the object.

▶ Evaluation of the study

Strengths	Limitations
Useful application in helping understanding of the development of phobias, which helped towards the development of effective treatments for phobic behaviour.	Low ecological validity; the method used created an unnatural situation which may not reflect learning in everyday life. Therefore, this study does not offer a full explanation for the development and maintenance of phobias.
Used scientific principles, therefore it has high internal validity. Due to the controlled nature of the experiment you can say with a high degree of certainty that Albert's fear was created due to an association made between the rat and the loud noise rather than anything else.	As this was a case study, you cannot generalise to others, and therefore the findings may be limited to Albert. Albert might have been very easy to condition compared to other people so you cannot make an assumption (based on this case alone) that all phobias develop through a negative experience.

Research

Research what flooding and systematic desensitisation are. A simple internet search will give you the information you need and you may even be able to access videos of actual therapy. Think about how they both rely on the principles of classical conditioning. This will help you apply classical conditioning to other situations, something you may be asked to do in the exam. This will be particularly beneficial if you go on to study Unit 3.

⏸ PAUSE POINT

Once you have studied Unit 2, particularly the ethical issues that are important when conducting research, you could develop a further limitation of this study based on its ethics. You should consider informed consent, protection from harm and anything else you think relevant. Remember that when researching children, it is not the child that consents, but the parent or guardian. So, it was not Albert who had to give his consent, but his mother.

Hint

In this case, Watson argued later that it was always his intention to decondition Little Albert after the study, but Albert's mother removed him from the university before they could do this. If they had been able to desensitise him would that have made the study acceptable?

Extend

Whenever ethical guidelines are broken and participants are disadvantaged in some way, there must be some justification. If the results are ground breaking, there may be the potential to help many other people. For each study you have learned about so far you can analyse the costs to the participants against the benefits for society. This makes good evaluation of studies and the theories and concepts they have tested.

Biological approach

In contrast to the behaviourist/learning approach, the biological approach believes that nature is most important when it comes to understanding human behaviour. It looks at how genes, biological structures (in particular the brain), and neurochemicals affect behaviour. Therefore, while other approaches focus on mainly external factors that influence behaviour or on the internal mental processes that deal with information, biological psychology is concerned with the role that your **physiology** plays in human behaviour.

Key concepts

The influence of biology and the role of genetics in behaviour

At the point of conception, the human embryo receives 23 **chromosomes** from each parent. Each chromosome is made up of many genes (there are around 20,000 in the human genome). Genes contain important information that determine your physical development. Specifically, they contain instructions for building proteins and it is this that determines physical characteristics, such as eye colour, hair colour, and so on. Biological psychologists are interested in the role genes play in your psychological development through the way that they affect brain development and brain chemistry.

> **Key terms**
>
> **Physiology** – how human's and animal's bodies and plants function.
>
> **Chromosomes** – structures containing genetic material.
>
> **Y chromosome** – sex chromosome associated with masculine development provided by father's sperm which may contain either an X or a Y chromosome.
>
> **X chromosome** – a sex chromosome (in humans and other mammals) normally present in female cells, provided by the mother.
>
> **SRY gene** – gene responsible for initiation of male developmental process.
>
> **Testosterone** – male sex hormone.

For example, at conception the egg and sperm join up to give a total of 46 chromosomes. If the sperm contains a **Y chromosome**, the baby's sex will be male. If it contains an X chromosome, the baby will be female. The egg contains only **X chromosomes**. Contained on the Y chromosome is a gene known as the **SRY gene**; the presence of this gene initiates the development of male genitalia in prenatal development. Therefore, if a person possesses the gene, they are genetically male and their body will develop to be masculine. This is an example of physical development.

The SRY gene also causes the release of **testosterone** into the womb which masculinises the developing baby's brain causing some differences in psychological development.

> **Discussion**
>
> Why is this an example of the nature side of the nature vs. nurture debate?
>
> If a male chromosomal pattern is XY – what is the female one?

The **genotype** is your genetic makeup that is present at birth. However, your environment also plays a role in shaping who you become. The expression of genes is affected by our experiences, and this creates your **phenotype**. Your phenotype is based on your genotype but it is what you end up being after exposure to the environment.

Genotype – genetic makeup of a person present from birth.

Phenotype – the observable differences between people that develop as their genotype interacts with the environment.

Monozygotic twins – siblings that develop from the same fertilised egg, therefore sharing exactly the same genetic makeup, also known as identical twins.

Dizygotic twins – siblings who develop from two separate fertilised eggs but at the same time, born together but sharing only 50 per cent of the genes as any other sibling pair (non-identical twins).

Siblings – brothers and sisters within a family.

Case study

Praneet and Parvinder are **monozygotic (identical) twins**. Sadly, their mother died shortly after giving birth and one of the twins was adopted. Praneet went to live with a rich family who were able to afford good food for him throughout his childhood. Parvinder remained with his biological father who struggled to provide good quality food for him. When they were later reunited, it was observed that Praneet was two inches taller than Parvinder.

1 Using your knowledge of genotype and phenotype explain the height difference between the twins who were genetically identical.

2 What other differences might you expect to see between the twins, for example in terms of their health?

Neuroanatomy

Neuroanatomy concerns the physical structures of the nervous system. Neuropsychologists are particularly interested in the role of brain structures in determining behaviour. The brain has different regions or areas. The most obvious of these is the distinction between the left and right **hemisphere**, and into the four **lobes** each hemisphere contains.

Certain functions are controlled by different areas of the brain; this is known as **localisation of function**. For example, it is believed that different functions are dominant in each hemisphere: the left hemisphere (see Figure 1.7) is generally responsible for language, while the right hemisphere deals with non-linguistic processes like face recognition.

▶ **Figure 1.7:** Left hemisphere of the brain showing all four lobes

One important area of the brain that affects how you react to your environment is the **limbic system**. It is situated underneath the cortex in the middle of the brain and is responsible for, among other things, your emotional response. For example, in the fight or flight response a small area of the limbic system called the amygdala (see Figure 1.8) will activate the fight or flight mechanism when it detects a threat. This is quite a primitive area of the brain that works below the level of conscious awareness.

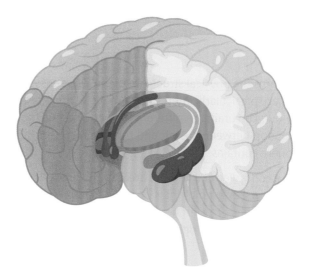

▶ **Figure 1.8:** The brain, showing the amygdala and the prefrontal cortex

This explanation can account for differences in male and female behaviour. There are some sex differences in brains, for instance female brains tend to have stronger **neural** connections between the two hemispheres, whereas male brains have stronger connections within each hemisphere. This leads to changes in the way males and females process information: females may do better in analytical and intuitive processing (like understanding what people are telling them verbally and non-verbally), whereas males may do better at linking perception and motor skills (they tend to have better spatial awareness in relation to objects in the environment).

Link

Go to page 44 and read the case study about Phineas Gage. This study shows how damage to the brain can result in changes in behaviour.

Research shows that damage to the prefrontal cortex (an area at the front of the brain behind the forehead) is associated with violent and impulsive behaviour.

> **Theory into practice**
>
> "I have really bad anger problems now. I can be fine one second and when the slightest inconvenience happens I'd be throwing and breaking things," said Chelsea.
>
> Chelsea fell onto a hard, wooden floor in her first week at college. She had a seizure and her brain was without oxygen for several minutes. Before this she had no anger problems, but now she falls into a rage easily and has physically attacked both her parents.
>
> Explain what might have caused the change in Chelsea's behaviour.

Neurochemistry

Another physical influence on behaviour lies in the chemicals that operate the brain. There are over 100 different chemicals in your central nervous system, each with different effects. Changes in the levels of these chemicals known as **neurotransmitters** (some are also **hormones**) will result in changes in behaviour.

Testosterone, found in males and females (but in much higher amounts in most males), is the male hormone that has an effect on prenatal brain development and has been associated with aggression.

Another hormone that has an effect on behaviour is **cortisol**. This is produced by the adrenal gland in response to stress (review the fight or flight mechanism earlier in this section) and it has been linked to various behavioural problems. For example, too much cortisol can lead to aggression and/or mental health disorders.

Serotonin is a neurotransmitter which is associated with many functions within the body including mood. It is sometimes called the happy chemical as low levels are associated with depression and also aggression, although this relationship is not that simple.

Dopamine is also a neurotransmitter and is involved in rewards, among other functions. Dopamine pathways in the brain are activated when a rewarding activity is instigated. It is proposed to be an important factor in addictive behaviour and in mental health issues such as schizophrenia.

> **Link**
>
> Go to Unit 3 in the Extended Certificate to learn more about cortisol and dopamine.

> **Link**
>
> Go to Unit 6 in the Extended Certificate to learn more about serotonin.

> **Key terms**
>
> **Neurotransmitters** – chemical molecules that are used in transmitting nerve signals across the nervous system.
>
> **Hormones** – chemical molecules that are released into the blood stream that have an impact on organs of the body including the brain.
>
> **Cortisol** – hormone released from adrenal gland in response to stress signals from the brain.
>
> **Serotonin** – neurotransmitter found in the brain and the body that is associated with mood. Note that some hormones are also neurotransmitters.
>
> **Dopamine** – neurotransmitter involved in many functions in the brain including reward.

Evolutionary psychology

The role of genes in determining physical and psychological development arises from Charles Darwin's theory of **evolution**. This suggests that, over time, individuals who are better adapted to their environment (through having genes that by chance program for useful physical or behavioural characteristics) are more likely to survive longer, be fitter and therefore have healthy offspring. In this way, they pass on their useful genes to the next generation. Genes that give the organism an **adaptive advantage** are those that fit the organism for the environment that they live in. Darwin called this the 'survival of the fittest' because they will do better than other organisms that do not have these genes.

The same advantages will be found in the next generation where those with the useful genes are more successful than those without them. Evolutionary theory also proposes that **sexual selection** enhances this process. There is an evolutionary drive to pass on genes. This must be done through **procreation**, and those organisms with the good genes will be more attractive as mates because their genes will improve the chances of their offspring being successful. The organism, whether human, fish or bird, will prefer mates that will provide their offspring with a greater chance of survival. The theory of evolution therefore suggests that organisms are genetically programmed to choose mates with certain adaptive characteristics. As genes change only very slowly in comparison to the environment, the genes that developed in one environment are the genes that exist today. This is called genome lag and it means that behaviours that were advantageous in the past, because they are genetically programmed, are still present even though no longer advantageous.

> **Key terms**
>
> **Evolution** – the process of change through genetic mutations interacting with the environment over successive generations.
>
> **Adaptive advantage** – in evolutionary terms, any characteristic of an organism that increases its chances of survival.
>
> **Sexual selection** – evolutionary pressures operating to select a mate based on characteristics that would benefit the mating couple's offspring.
>
> **Procreation** – the act of sexual reproduction.
>
> **Environment of evolutionary adaptation (EEA)** – the conditions that existed during the period of evolutionary change.
>
> **Traits** – characteristics.

Environment of evolutionary adaptation is a phrase used in biopsychology which refers specifically to the conditions that applied when your **traits** evolved. Genetically programmed psychological traits that served to increase survival in your evolutionary past are passed through the generations and persist in your genome. For example, males that show more aggression would be better hunters and protectors than males that do not and so the aggressive gene in males would be successful in conditions where food is scarce and the situation contains threats. Successful females, however, are those that can get pregnant, give birth and raise children to maturity, not those that risk their reproductive abilities through aggressive behaviour. Prehistoric females would choose males that had the characteristics of a protector, and males would choose females that had the characteristics of a mother.

Case study

One type of behaviour that is thought to have an evolutionary source is what happens when you are faced with an emergency situation. Your body goes into 'fight or flight' mode. This means that you are physically prepared for action, your heart rate increases as does your respiration. This ensures that there is a good supply of oxygen to the brain, blood supply is focused on the internal organs and there is a release of glycogen into the blood supplying energy. This whole process is triggered by an area in the brain that detects threat.

Consider the environment of evolutionary adaptation. Humans did not have any of the technology that is now available. For example, when it was dark you could not just switch on a light, nor could you see danger clearly (for example from large animals or from poisonous animals). Humans had no protection like weapons to use when confronted with danger.

1 Why would a human that was genetically programmed to detect threat quickly and act on it immediately be more successful than one who did not detect threat nor react quickly?

2 How might this affect sexual selection?

Genetic makeup takes many thousand years to change, so the genes you have now are more or less the same as those your ancient ancestors had. This means that you can explain differences in behaviour between genders as a product of evolutionary development. However, your environment now is completely different from the environment of evolutionary adaptation. This can often cause problems as modern humans possess psychological traits that are not suited to current environments.

Biological approach key studies

The theory of evolution proposes that male and females evolved differently because they had different evolutionary pressures. According to the theory, males evolved to be more competitive whereas women were more nurturing. One hormone associated with typical male behaviour is testosterone and it is known to be higher in males and in females that have more masculine traits.

Buss et al. (1992) Sex Differences in Jealousy: Evolution, Physiology, and Psychology

Evolutionary psychology suggests that males and females will employ different strategies when selecting a mate. Males will look for fertility, and their genes would be best served by impregnating as many women as possible so that they could have a lot of offspring in the next generation bearing their genes. Women employ a different strategy; for them to pass their genes on successfully they have to invest a lot of time and resources into each child. They therefore want a partner who is able to provide resources for her and her children and who will provide a stable home. This leads to different types and levels of jealousy between partners.

Aim: To investigate the hypothesis that men and women differ in which form of infidelity (sexual or emotional) causes them the most distress.

Procedure: 202 undergraduate students were presented with a dilemma regarding serious, committed, romantic relationships they have had in the past, currently have or would like to have. They then had to imagine that their partner became interested in somebody else and decide what, of two options, would distress them most: the partner forming a deep emotional attachment or the partner enjoying passionate sexual intercourse with that other person.

They were then given a number of other questions to answer where they had the same instructions followed by a different choice, either to imagine their partner trying different sexual positions with that other person, or to imagine their partner falling in love with that other person.

Findings: In response to the first dilemma, 60 per cent of the male sample reported greater distress over their partner's potential sexual infidelity. Only 17 per cent of female sample chose this option, with 83 per cent reporting they would experience greater distress over a partner's emotional attachment to a rival.

The second dilemma relating to love and sex revealed similar results: 32 per cent more men than women reported greater distress over a partner's sexual involvement with someone else.

Conclusion: Men and women view sexual infidelity differently. Women will be more distressed over emotional infidelity, men over sexual infidelity. This is consistent with the predictions of evolutionary theory as males would be more worried about the paternity of their offspring, unfaithful females might present their mate with a child that did not have his genes, so he would waste resources raising that child. Females would worry more about the stability of the relationship as they need a mate to provide resources over a long period of time in order to raise their offspring and pass on their genes successfully.

> **Discussion**
>
> Can you think of any other reasons why the males and females in this study answered in the way they did, that might reject the idea of this reflecting evolutionary development?
>
> Could you use social psychology to explain their responses?

▶ Evaluation of the study

Strengths	Limitations
Used a large sample so will have gathered a lot of data, thereby increasing the reliability of the conclusions drawn because one or two extreme or unusual results will have little impact on the outcome.	May lack population validity because sample were all undergraduate students who might have different attitudes to relationship problems than other people in society. For example, they might be more or less prone to jealousy because they are mostly not in a long-term stable relationship yet.
The data gathered was from questionnaires. These were the same for every participant so you can be sure that the questions asked were consistent therefore the test can be replicated quite easily, enabling a check on reliability to be carried out. The researchers went on to do further research using different methodology and finding similar results, therefore the reliability of these conclusions is high.	As a measure of jealousy, the study might lack validity because of the use of questionnaires. People might not know how they would react in the case of infidelity, so the differences between men and women found in this study might be due to social expectations about how they should feel, rather than how they actually would feel if the situation happened to them.
	This study may suffer from issues of temporal validity, which means that the results they obtained were specific to the time period in which the test took place, participants now might react differently to the scenarios due to changes in perceptions of appropriate gender or sexual behaviour.

Deady et al. (2006) Maternal personality and reproductive ambition in women is associated with salivary testosterone levels

Aim: To investigate the role of testosterone in the expression of maternal personality traits in female adults.

Procedure: 27 female university students were recruited from the University of Stirling, Scotland. No participants had menstrual abnormalities.

All participants were given the BSRI (Bem Sex Role Inventory) and additional questions based on their maternal personality and reproductive ambitions. The BSRI is made up of 60 questions assessing masculine, feminine and non-gender traits. Participants had to rate themselves on a Likert scale of 1 (almost never true) to 7 (almost always true). Additional questions included: how broody they felt; how many children they would ideally like to have; how important it was to have children; and the importance of having a career.

> **Research**
>
> You can do the Bem Sex Role Inventory. It was developed in the 1970s by Sandra Bem who was interested in gender, how this links to biological sex and how it relates to other areas of life. It is available online. Look for versions that will score it for you because this can be quite time consuming.
>
> What do you think about the statements Bem used? Are they a fair way of measuring gender? Do you think the test has validity for today's population?

Measures of testosterone were taken by having participants chew on sugar-free gum to stimulate saliva production. The gum samples were then sent to a special lab able to measure the level of testosterone in female saliva.

Findings: It was found that high levels of testosterone were **negatively correlated** with the BSRI item 'loves children' and 'maternal broodiness' this means that as the scores on these items on the questionnaire rose, the level of testosterone decreased. There was also a strong **positive correlation** between the level of testosterone and the ideal age of having their first child. This means that as the level of testosterone increased, so too did the participants' views on the ideal age to start a family.

The levels of testosterone in the saliva of those who rated high for masculinity was on average around a third higher than in those who rated low for masculinity.

> **Link**
>
> If you do not know what a correlation is, look at Unit 2. This will help you to understand what a positive and negative correlation are in more depth.

Conclusion: This suggests that females' maternal drive is affected by testosterone. High levels of testosterone are associated with a low maternal personality.

▶ Evaluation of the study

Strengths	Limitations
Used a good level of controls, especially in the measurement of testosterone which was not open to interpretation as it could be accurately and independently measured through the test on saliva. This means that the conclusions drawn are likely to be reliable.	Lacks ecological validity in terms of the way it measured maternal ambition: the use of a questionnaire might not reflect actual behaviour, so people could answer in ways that do not accurately represent how they might feel when confronted with issues regarding motherhood.
The BSRI is a widely used and well-validated measure of gender which therefore lends credibility to their measures of maternal ambition.	There is a **correlation** that testosterone levels and maternal ambition are linked, for example it may be that low maternal ambition actually raises the testosterone levels in women, or that another uninvestigated factor causes both these things.

Discussion

Do you think that the findings of this study disadvantage men in any way? Consider which gender generally has the most testosterone and consider the effect that testosterone is supposed to have on nurturing behaviour. What about single dads or gay fathers?

Harlow, J. M. (1868) Passage of an iron rod through the head – the case study of Phineas Gage

The brain does not seem to have any obvious structures that can be clearly linked to function. Until relatively recently, the only way to investigate where functions happened in the brain was through cases of brain damage. One of the first recorded cases of research into brain injury was conducted by Phineas Gage's physician. It lacks a lot of detail that would be necessary in modern cases of this type but does show a 'before and after' effect of traumatic brain injury on behaviour.

Aim: To investigate the effect of traumatic brain injury to the brain's left frontal lobe.

Procedure: Phineas was a railway foreman when, at the age of 25, he suffered massive head trauma as the result of an accident in which a metal rod used for putting dynamite in holes drilled in rocks in order to blow them up, passed through his left eye emerging through the top of his skull, damaging his left frontal lobe. Amazingly, Phineas did not die.

Before the accident Phineas was described as possessing considerable 'energy of character' and 'temperate habits' (he was disciplined and had self-control). He was regarded as a favourite foreman among his men at work.

Phineas' physician documented his recovery in a letter written to the Boston Medical and Surgical Journal, where he describes a day-by-day account of Phineas's behaviour.

Though blinded in his left eye, Phineas seemed to be able to carry on working as normal. Neither his speech nor his movements had been affected.

Findings: As a result of damage to the left frontal lobe, Phineas's behaviour appeared to change dramatically. A month after his accident, although his memory and intellectual abilities appeared unaffected, his temperament had changed. He was described as acting childishly and irritably, he refused to follow instructions and would leave the hospital regularly despite being told not to.

 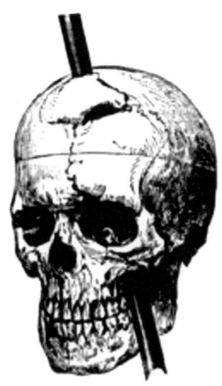

▶ Why do you think this story is still relevant today?

Later, his behaviour would be described as unreliable, that he was partial to swearing and often made inappropriate remarks. His friends said he was 'no longer Gage'.

He lived for 12 years after the accident and although some of these changes persisted, he did show some improvement in his social functioning, for example managing to hold down a job driving coaches.

Conclusions: Damage to the brain can have an effect on behaviour and personality. The case study not only prompts theories that favour localisation of function, but also that it is possible for some people to recover from severe brain injury. This would suggest that the brain is adaptable to some degree.

Research

Relate this case study to material discussed earlier about impulsive aggression.

Are the results from Harlow's study consistent with more modern findings about where aggressive impulsive behaviour is located in the brain?

Link

Look back at page 7 for information about the 'warrior gene' MAOA and how it is associated with impulsive aggression.

▶ Evaluation of the study

Strengths	Limitations
Has ecological validity because it is a case that really happened, so the conclusions drawn from the study are valid as they are based on actual damage and actual behaviour.	Lacks population validity as it is a sample size of one person. You do not know if every person with the same injury would suffer the same behavioural outcome as Phineas did. You must rely on further cases similar to this showing the same results to be able to generalise to the population effectively.
Has useful application to the real world, benefiting people as it shows the potential implications of head injuries. This has led to increased awareness of health and safety, for example wearing protective helmets. It has also helped to explain changes in behaviour following head injury, which in turn has produced better therapies.	Lacks scientific credibility necessary to have full confidence in the conclusions, because this is an early study carried out by a physician rather than a psychologist. For example, at this time there were no brain scans to assess the exact location and amount of damage Phineas suffered, and the changes in his behaviour that were observed were gathered from hearsay from those who knew him, rather than by careful and reliable observations of his behaviour.

Ⅱ PAUSE POINT

Now that you have finished this section, review all of the studies you have learned about and think how they relate to the key concepts you have studied.

Hint

For each study you should be able to write a sentence directly linking it to a key concept. For example, the Phineas Gage case study supports the idea that your brain structure affects your behaviour because when his brain was changed through being damaged, his personality also changed.

Extend

Finally, you could go back over the key concepts and use the key studies to provide some evaluation. For example, the concept of neuroanatomy affecting behaviour is supported by the case of Phineas Gage. When his brain structure was changed by damage, he underwent a major change in behaviour.

C Application of psychological approaches

Psychology is a scientific subject that aims to understand and improve people's wellbeing. This means that the knowledge you have studied so far has to be usefully applied to help people in some way. For example, understanding the chemistry of the brain helps you to understand differences between people and suggests that if you changed the chemistry in some way, you could help people that wanted to change. This section of the unit puts the knowledge you have learned in sections A and B into an applied context. You will examine three issues of relevance to society and explain how the concepts and research from all four approaches can be applied to them. There is very little new knowledge to learn here, so your focus is on application to real-world behaviour.

Use of psychology to explain the contemporary issue of aggression in society

Aggression is a serious problem for society. According to statistics taken from the **Office for National Statistics** (ONS) the police recorded 1,167,426 'acts of violence against the person' in the year ending March 2017. This included 723 homicides. Besides the obvious impact this has on the victims of violence and their families, it also places a burden on society as those convicted of violence will often be sentenced to prison.

Most people do not commit such acts, so what is different about those who do? Psychology aims to explain this.

Aggression can be defined as harmful social interaction with the intention of inflicting damage or harm on others.

> **Key terms**
>
> **Office for National Statistics** – government body that compiles statistics on the population and their behaviour. It is open to search on the internet.
>
> **Hostile aggression** – reactive, often angry aggression in response to a perceived threat. It has an emotional basis.
>
> **Instrumental aggression** – aggression that serves a purpose. It could be described as cold-blooded; it is rational in order to accomplish an aim.

Aggression can be either **hostile** or **instrumental** depending on the motives behind it. Angry aggression would be classed as hostile, whereas aggression that is used to obtain a specific outcome for the offender would be classed as instrumental.

Cognitive approach

Remember, the cognitive approach proposes that behaviour is influenced by the way you process information, so this approach would suggest that aggressive people would process information differently, or that acts of aggression are the result of faulty thinking.

Link

Look back at page 11 to remind yourself about the concept of priming.

Priming for aggression

The simple act of being exposed to aggressive objects or behaviour can cue aggression in the observer. This can be through the media or by direct experience. It is argued that by watching aggression in others, the observer develops cognitive schema and scripts that are then used in situations that are similar. People who are aggressive have lots of scripts and schema for aggressive behaviour.

For example, in Bandura's study the children who were exposed to the aggressive model showed much more aggression than those that were not. This was not just imitation of what they saw; they engaged in new aggression. It could be argued that having watched an adult be aggressive primed them to use the same, and other objects, aggressively.

Hostile attribution bias

For some people, aggression can be explained in their thinking style. Their automatic reaction to other people's behaviour is to become aggressive, even if that behaviour is open to interpretation. Some people are more aggressive if, as a child, they have been exposed to many hostile situations. In childhood, they would develop schema which include hostility so when they are in a situation that cue these schema, they interpret what they see as threatening and respond with aggression. They have misunderstood the intention of the other person. So, if they were used to their parents becoming angry with them and shouting at them for no real reason, they assume that in other situations (such as when a tutor is asking where their homework is) the tutor is about to become nasty towards them, they perceive a hostile intent and react with hostile aggression.

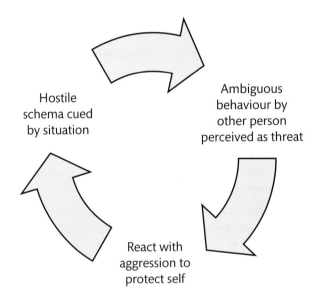

▶ **Figure 1.9:** The relationship between having a hostile attribution bias and aggression

Social approach

Social psychologists argue that the social situation in which behaviour occurs is an important influence on how you behave. So, some people are aggressive because of the situations they are in. This includes the norms of the groups they belong to and the attitudes of people in those groups. It also includes the stereotypes you hold.

Conformity to group and social norms

This means that if you are a member of a group that has norms of aggressive behaviour and attitudes, then, through the process of normative and/or informational social influence you are likely to conform to those norms and display aggressive behaviour in situations where those norms are most relevant to you. Behaviour is changed to fit the group the person is with currently.

This switch to aggression will happen at different levels: it may be superficial (compliance); it may be strong but only when with the group (identification); or it may be widespread and permanent (internalisation).

> **Exam tip**
>
> If you are struggling to understand the terminology used here, you need to go back to the section on conformity and revise it more thoroughly. If you can use terminology well you will show the examiner that you have a good understanding of specific areas in psychology.

> **Case study**
>
> Jake joins a new school after moving home. He soon learns that there are two 'gangs' in the school, each one supporting a different football team. As a supporter of United, Jake soon joins that gang. Nathan and Tao have been in the gang longest, Harry and Alex joined last year. Tao suggests that they attack a member of the City gang. Nathan immediately agrees and starts to plan the attack. Next day they make their attack but they are caught. Nathan and Tao say that the victim deserved what happened and were not sorry. Harry and Alex said that they can see now that it was wrong to do this but felt that it was reasonable at the time, whereas Jake said that he knew it was wrong but felt he ought to join in with the attack.
>
> 1 Explain the difference in attitude between the three groups of boys.
>
> 2 Which group would be most resistant to changing their attitude? Explain why.

This explanation can link real-world aggressive behaviour to group membership. When someone joins a group, the group can become an important part of their identity. In order to maintain that identity, they conform to the group's beliefs and behaviour; in some cases this leads to aggression. Recent statistics from the Office for National Statistics show that in England and Wales in 2017, 6.9 per cent of children aged 10–15 and 4.4 per cent of adults aged 16–24 knew someone in a gang.

Stereotyping

Having a stereotype of the kind of person who is likely to be aggressive will influence how you interact with them and can lead to a hostile reaction with no real provocation.

For most people, having a stereotype of a violent criminal will not affect how you behave, but for some people, in some circumstances, it can lead to aggression. For example, there are suggestions that **implicit bias** might be a factor in the amount of violence shown by the police towards suspects of crime. Officers fearing for their lives, or for the safety of others, might be influenced by their stereotype of a violent person to respond in a more hostile way to that person than to someone that does not fit their stereotype.

> **Key term**
>
> **Implicit bias** – unconscious and non-deliberate attribution of specific qualities to a member of a social group.

The American Community Survey of 2016 estimated that 12.6 per cent of the population of the USA was African American. The census in 2014 estimated that 50.7 per cent of adults in the USA were female. Statistics on police shootings in 2015 show that 95 per cent of those shot by the police in the course of their duties were male and 22.6 per cent of those shot by the police were black African Americans. This shows that there seems to be a bias towards regarding males, and especially black males, as most threatening. Other statistics also suggest that black males are the group most likely to be killed by police even though they were not actually engaged in an attack on the police.

1 Use your knowledge of social psychology to explain these statistics.

2 Explain why women are much less likely to be killed by police in similar circumstances.

Learning approach

The learning approach suggests that how you behave in any circumstance is the product of learning from the environment. The consequences of being aggressive are positive for you, so the aggressive behaviour is reinforced and repeated. Or, you are exposed to models in your environment that commit acts of aggression and because they are rewarded (and you want to be like them) you internalise that behaviour and replicate it when an appropriate opportunity arises.

Operant conditioning

If aggressive behaviour is somehow rewarded, then you are much more likely to display it in the future. Either the aggression leads to a reward (positive reinforcement) or it leads to the removal of something you do not like (negative reinforcement) so you learn that to get what you want, or to avoid what you don't want, you should show aggression. In this way, aggression becomes a conditioned behaviour.

Theory into practice

Isaac has just started secondary school. On his way home another student calls him a name and he turns around and pushes the student over. The other students walking home the same way cheer and slap Isaac on the back. The next day Isaac pushes over another student.

Explain Isaac's behaviour using concepts, theory or research drawn from learning theory.

Social learning theory

Aggression results from seeing other people behave aggressively, especially those you see as a role model. Models are usually those with whom you share some similarities and that you look up to in some way. If your models routinely show aggression, then it is likely that at some point in the future, in a similar situation, you are also likely to show aggression.

Exam tip

Review the key terms associated with conditioning and with social learning. Being able to use them effectively to explain the behaviour in cases of aggression given in the exam will demonstrate your clear understanding of the theory and how it works. It would be a good idea to have a glossary for all the key terms.

Biological approach

The biological approach would propose that the biggest influence on behaviour is biological. It is part of your physical makeup which is shaped by genes that have evolved over hundreds of thousands of years. This approach suggests that this evolution has affected brain structure and neurochemistry in a way that causes aggressive behaviour to be more or less likely in those with the genes, brains or neurochemistry that predispose them to aggression.

Evolution

Any behaviour that is programmed in your genes must have had, at some point in your evolutionary history, an adaptive advantage. Aggression, therefore, must have been a desirable trait that was selected for. Aggressive people (but especially males) would have been more successful in prehistoric social groups. As they gained more resources, they became more attractive as a mate and were able to successfully pass their genes on.

Genetics

Genes are the blueprint to build your physical body. As your body includes the brain (which is the organ of behaviour), some genes build brains that are more likely to produce aggression.

Brain structure

Brains are the organ of behaviour, and as aggression is a behaviour therefore aggression must involve processes in the brain. You could be born with a brain predisposed to aggression (your genotype) or your brain could be changed by environmental experiences (your phenotype), making you more prone to aggressive responses.

The prefrontal cortex in the brain is associated with (among other things) decision making and control of impulses. The limbic system is the area of the brain that is associated with many aspects of mental life including emotional responses. The two areas constantly interact in order to regulate behaviour.

Case study

Charles Whitman was a 25-year-old ex-marine sharp-shooter. He shot his wife and mother and then climbed a tower at the University of Texas and proceeded to shoot 14 strangers. He then killed himself. His suicide note said that he had been experiencing headaches and did not feel himself lately. He even requested that a post mortem examination be carried out on him after his death to look for abnormalities to explain his symptoms.

1 Use your knowledge of social brain anatomy to explain what might have happened.

2 Should biology be taken into account when sentencing aggressive criminals?

Neurochemistry

Your brain works through the action of neurochemicals (neurotransmitters and hormones) creating connections between the cells. Too much, or too little, of particular neurochemicals can lead to changes in behaviour because it affects how the brain works. Biological psychologists would contend that aggression could be caused by a surplus of some chemicals and/or a deficit of others.

Testosterone is a masculinising hormone. During prenatal development, testosterone interacts with genes to masculinise the embryonic brain and body. At puberty, males experience a rush of testosterone. Testosterone is known to have an effect on the areas of the brain that control aggression (for example, the limbic system).

Theory into practice

Data from the Office for National Statistics shows that 47 per cent of the crimes of violence committed by males were committed by offenders aged between 10 and 24.

Use your knowledge of biological psychology to explain these statistics.

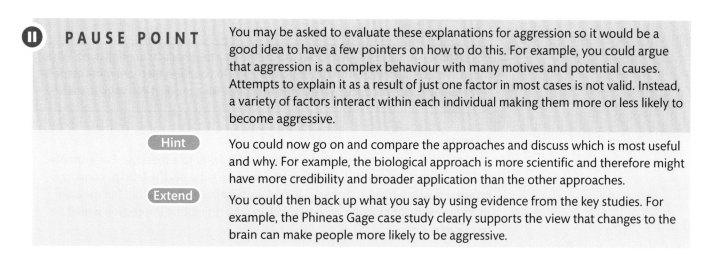

PAUSE POINT   You may be asked to evaluate these explanations for aggression so it would be a good idea to have a few pointers on how to do this. For example, you could argue that aggression is a complex behaviour with many motives and potential causes. Attempts to explain it as a result of just one factor in most cases is not valid. Instead, a variety of factors interact within each individual making them more or less likely to become aggressive.

Hint   You could now go on and compare the approaches and discuss which is most useful and why. For example, the biological approach is more scientific and therefore might have more credibility and broader application than the other approaches.

Extend   You could then back up what you say by using evidence from the key studies. For example, the Phineas Gage case study clearly supports the view that changes to the brain can make people more likely to be aggressive.

Use of psychology in business to explain and influence consumer/employee behaviour

Behavioural economics is the study of psychological processes in economic decision making by individuals and institutions. It includes ideas like 'nudge' which is persuasion by indirect means such as positive reinforcement and priming. Psychology is used across different media platforms to persuade people to buy a product through advertising and is used to encourage employees towards being more productive.

How cognitive psychology influences behaviour

Cognitive psychology can be applied to all areas of life; it is about how you process information continually. In this section, you will be exploring some of the ways cognitive psychology is used deliberately to change behaviour in order to achieve another person's goal or an institution's goal. It is used extensively in retail to influence buying behaviour but also in other areas of life such as improving public health and safety.

Biases in information processing

Many of your decisions happen below your level of conscious awareness, which means you do things without thinking about them. The brain recognises patterns and responds to those patterns without having to think it through, thereby taking mental shortcuts when it comes to interacting in the environment. These mental shortcuts profoundly influence what you do. For example, in choosing a product from a range of similar products, retailers know that products that are at eye level get more attention than those on the bottom shelf. They can also influence which product you buy through pricing it appropriately. In a range of similar types of products, some will be expensive and some will be cheap; your automatic preference is to choose one in the middle. The buyer automatically assumes that price is an indicator of quality and avoids the cheapest as they believe it to be the worst.

Restaurants know that diners hardly ever choose the cheapest wine on the list but opt for those that cost a little more, but rarely choose the most expensive unless they have a reason for doing so.

Advertising is the way that companies sell their products. You are exposed to many adverts in different media every day. Marketing is big business, and it aims to affect how you process information about the products being marketed. Adverts therefore aim to manipulate how you think about a product; they make it more likely that you will pay attention to the product, remember it and desire it.

Schema

Activation of a schema can help to increase receptivity to a message. For example, subliminal perception is the exposure to information below the level of conscious awareness which triggers a change in feeling or behaviour. It is a hidden message that conveys an impression of something. In advertising that impression would be favourable.

More direct forms of subliminal messaging are regarded as brain washing, such as flashing messages below the level of conscious awareness. Using subliminal messages such as these to directly sell a product is illegal in many countries. This is because it is altering how you think without you being aware of it.

Greenwashing is a legal subliminal technique used by advertisers to trigger schema, by using green in their adverts such as grass, trees, and so on. It might even be simply using the colour green suggest to the viewer that the product is ecologically friendly whether this is true or not, and this may encourage them towards a particular product.

Case study

Police in Oxford have been using cardboard cut-outs of police officers around the town centre and have found a 2/3 drop in bike thefts in the city since the cardboard officers were deployed. Two life size cut out cops are being used in other town centres in an attempt to reduce shop lifting.

1 Explain why the cut outs have had this effect using your knowledge of cognitive psychology.

2 What sort of effect do you think it will have had?

3 Why do you think that thieves might have been affected by these cut outs?

Priming

Advertising uses priming very effectively. Associative and repetition priming are often used. Repetition makes a product more memorable. For example, naming the product often and then pairing it with the type of product means it is primed for the name by association.

Further examples can be found in the use of colours. As you have already learned, green carries associations of being environmentally friendly. Other colours prime for different reactions as well. For example, bright red is associated with energy; it is sometimes used in fast-food restaurants to encourage people to eat quickly and not take up space other customers could be using.

Research

Watch a few adverts on TV and look for evidence of greenwashing and priming. Think about how you could develop an advertising campaign for a product (for example, a shampoo) by using cognitive concepts.

Exam tip

Although this book has separated biases, schema and priming to look at how they influence behaviour, they are actually all linked and are quite similar. Remember, schema are at the root of information processing; they guide attention and affect how you recall information. Priming leads to the activation of schema, and biases are also based on basic schema. So, if a question asks about the application of cognitive psychology to a problem you should be able to refer to schema in some form.

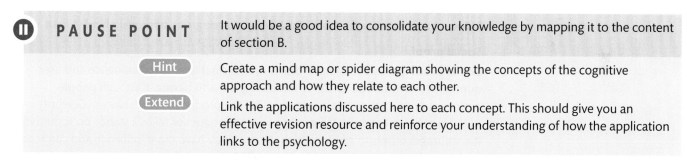

⏸ PAUSE POINT   It would be a good idea to consolidate your knowledge by mapping it to the content of section B.

> **Hint**   Create a mind map or spider diagram showing the concepts of the cognitive approach and how they relate to each other.

> **Extend**   Link the applications discussed here to each concept. This should give you an effective revision resource and reinforce your understanding of how the application links to the psychology.

How the social approach is applied to business and consumer behaviour

The social approach focuses on how the real or imagined presence of others, and social norms, affect behaviour. Conformity research shows how you change your behaviour to fit into groups; some changes may be long lasting (internalised), but some may be very transient (compliance). You do this simply to be liked by others (normative social influence) or in order to do the right thing (informational social influence). Knowledge of these processes can be applied to business and especially consumer behaviour.

Advertising uses social influence to influence buyer behaviour. Two ways they do this is to use the bandwagon effect and social proof.

The bandwagon effect

The **bandwagon effect** draws on social influence in order to persuade people to buy a product. It happens when people want to be part of a larger group and they change their behaviour to be part of a perceived majority. If they think something is very popular, they want to feel part of it and so change their behaviour accordingly. You can link this to normative social influence.

Key terms

Bandwagon effect – changing behaviour to be similar to that of an increasingly popular movement.

Social proof – using information from other people to judge the quality of a person, product or event.

Theory into practice

There was a 30 per cent increase in people joining the cycle-to-work scheme towards the end of 2012, accompanied by a surge in the sale of bikes.

The British cycling team won more medals at the London Olympics than any other team.

Explain how these two events might be connected.

Reflect on your answer. How long lasting do you think the surge in cycling will last? Explain why you think this.

The bandwagon effect is also observed in politics. As a candidate gains popularity, other people without strong political views begin to support them simply because others are seen to do so. This is evident on social media platforms as the number of followers a person has is visible and it is easy to see group approval of individuals.

Social proof

Social proof also applies here. It draws on informational social influence and uses numbers to convince people that something is worth having. If enough people endorse a product then this is evidence that the product is worth having. Celebrity social proof is an example. If a celebrity uses a product or takes a stance on something, it encourages others to go along with them as they have more influence and can reach a wider audience than most other people. This is why celebrity endorsements matter to political campaigns.

Theory into practice

A study in the USA tested the effectiveness of messages aimed at reducing the environmental costs of laundering towels in a major hotel chain. They used a variety of messages including:

- a general one about helping to save the environment
- one that stated that almost 75 per cent of their hotel guests were now reusing their towels
- one that emphasised that people who used that specific room in the hotel had mostly reused their towels.

Use your knowledge of social psychology to predict which message would have been the most successful and explain why.

Other campaigns also use these techniques by inviting people to be one of the group. For example, activities for charities emphasise the social element such as joining in with those who do fun runs for good causes. In this way, people participate to be part of a group that has a positive social identity; they do it to fit in with that group. Additionally, by emphasising how many people have already supported a cause, they can use social proof which indicates to the donor that the cause is worthy (because if it wasn't, then why would so many people have given to it?). This is clearly informational social influence at work.

> **Exam tip**
>
> Although the focus has been on normative and informational social influence here to show how conformity operates through the bandwagon effect and social proof, it is possible to apply stereotyping to some examples of how social psychology can change consumer behaviour, so if it makes sense to do this in your exam, you should do so.

How the learning approach can be applied to business and consumer behaviour

The learning approach suggests that behaviour is influenced by the environment, the association of events (classical conditioning), the provision of reinforcement (operant conditioning) or indeed through observation of the behaviour of **role models**.

> **Key terms**
>
> **Role model** – a person who is regarded as a suitable example for an observer, perhaps due to higher status and some shared similarities with the observer.
>
> **Covert sensitisation** – a form of **aversion therapy** using words or images to change behaviour.
>
> **Aversion therapy** – therapy aimed to stop a particular behaviour using classical conditioning to associate the behaviour with negative feelings.

Classical conditioning

Classical conditioning is used to change people's attitudes. A good example is through something called **covert sensitisation** which is a technique that pairs something negative or positive with something else. A good example is cigarette packaging. Changing the packaging so it has a disturbing image on it is designed to make smokers associate smoking with the disturbing image. The image should trigger negative feelings like disgust and fear, so by pairing these things together the cigarettes should automatically make the buyer feel disgust and fear which would make them want to smoke less.

> **Link**
>
> Go to Unit 3 (Health psychology) to learn more about fear arousal theory of persuasion.

Using this technique to increase the likelihood of product use would simply try and evoke positive feelings when the product is presented. Try the questions in the next box to test your understanding.

The Chocolate Company is launching a new chocolate bar. They have approached a marketing company who suggest they use covert sensitisation in their adverts. They decide that puppies and kittens automatically make people happy and say that the adverts should include them. Turn this into a conditioning process you will need to include puppies and kittens, the chocolate bar and positive feelings.

1 What is the unconditioned stimulus and response?

2 What is the neutral stimulus?

3 How is this paired with the unconditioned stimulus?

4 When does it become a conditioned stimulus and response?

Operant conditioning

This form of learning takes place as a result of experiencing the consequences of your own behaviour. The goal of those that want to change your behaviour is therefore to make the desired behaviour rewarding for the person and other behaviour either neutral or punishing.

Think again about the example of smoking. Banning smoking inside public buildings means that the smoker has to leave the social setting they are in and go outside whatever the weather, in order to smoke. This should act as a punishment and make them want to stop smoking.

Theory into practice

Using the above example of stopping smoking, how could negative and positive reinforcement be used to help people quit?

Social learning

Social learning proposes that you learn your behaviour through the observation of others and what happens to them when they do certain things. You imitate the behaviour of those you regard as role models because you identify with them and want to be like them. This depends on you remembering what they did and how they did it and whether or not you have an opportunity to imitate the behaviour.

Using celebrities in adverts is one obvious use of social learning.

Theory into practice

Imagine you are tasked by The Chocolate Company to design an alternative campaign for their new chocolate bar. The company want it to appeal more to adult male consumers. You suggest using social learning and propose a celebrity to head up the campaign.

Who will you choose and why will you choose them? What should they be doing in the advert?

Social learning is also used in changing public attitudes and behaviour. For example, showing characters on TV giving up smoking or engaging in healthy behaviour is a form of role modelling. You identify with the character and will imitate their behaviour if you are motivated to do so and are capable of it. Characters that are punished for the positive behaviour will not be imitated, but those who receive rewards are more likely to be copied. This is due to vicarious reinforcement.

Research

Some have proposed that the portrayal of gay and lesbian characters in TV programmes has led to greater acceptance of people in society. The characters are portrayed as friends with other characters, so by modelling yourselves on these other characters your acceptance of people with these types of sexuality increases.

❚❚ PAUSE POINT

There are similarities and differences between the social approach and the learning approach. Start by looking at the key assumptions for each approach. For example, both suggest that external influences affect your behaviour rather than internal influences only.

Hint

You could then look at the applications for each one and work out how they share ideas and how they differ in the way they explain behaviour. For example, aggression is most likely caused by environmental factors but these are different. The social approach suggests that social norms are influential whereas the learning approach proposes that aggressive behaviour depends on the consequences for the person of being aggressive.

Extend

Turn this into a Venn diagram in order to demonstrate your understanding fully. It will also make a useful revision resource.

How the biological approach can be used to influence consumer behaviour

This is a fast-growing area of applied psychology in which methods of investigating the brain are used in order to detect changes in response to particular products. In doing so, it uncovers how people genuinely react to products which enables businesses to produce the most appealing products and the most effective adverts.

Neuromarketing techniques

Understanding the reaction of the brain to information helps you to manipulate the brain by changing the information. In this way, you can use biopsychology to develop more effective ways of influencing behaviour. For example, in advertising it is possible to wire up a person to an EEG machine and observe the effect of different adverts on the brain. Psychologists can then link the pattern of brain activity to whether the advert truly engages the person or not. Studying a brain's responses to marketing stimuli like this is known as neuromarketing.

Effective advertising design has drawn on **eye-tracking** techniques. The direction and duration of gaze at specific aspects of a scene indicate which aspects are receiving the most attention. By testing adverts to see what kind of stimuli gains the most gaze, it is possible to design adverts which will get maximum attention to the parts that are important.

Theory into practice

Humans have an innate preference for baby faces, so will focus their gaze on them. However, research has found that you also focus on what a baby is looking at. This means that a good advert for baby products would feature a cute baby but also have the baby looking at the product.

Drawing on your knowledge of the concepts associated with biopsychology, explain why people might have an innate preference for looking at babies.

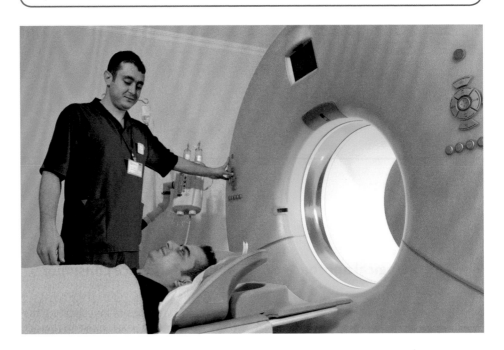

▶ How ethical are neuromarketing techniques?

Case study

The marketing team for a savoury snack company produced an advert where one person played a prank on another by putting the product (cheesy orange-coloured snacks) into a washing machine with a white load. The focus group rejected the advert feeling it was unpleasant, but the ERA showed a much more positive response to it.

1 Explain the difference between the focus group and the ERA group's response to the advert. You should refer to social psychology as well as biopsychology in your answer.

2 Which of the two methods of measuring reaction to the adverts is the most reliable and valid?

By using advanced brain scanning methods such as **functional magnetic resonance imagers (fMRI)** and **electroencephalographs (EEGs)** it is possible to see a brain actually working. In this way, it is possible to locate the function of a particular mental activity in a particular location in the brain. If you know which areas of the brain indicate a positive emotional response, then you can test your advert and/or product to see whether it has a positive impact.

Emotional response analysis (ERA) is used where data from the scans allows the researcher to understand how the person actually feels about the product or advert. This has been used effectively to choose a particular advert from a range of options and has been shown to be more effective than using a **focus group**.

> **Key terms**
>
> **Functional magnetic resonance imager (fMRI)** – large machine that detects changes in oxygen use across the brain showing areas currently being most used when doing a specific task.
>
> **Electroencephalograph (EEG)** – machine that measures the electrical activity in the brain producing a visual pattern of brain activity.
>
> **Emotional response analysis (ERA)** – using data from brain scans to assess the emotional impact of something.
>
> **Focus group** – technique for gaining opinions about things. A group of people is assembled and they are then asked to discuss the topic being investigated. Their responses are analysed in order to draw conclusions.

By using ERA, it is possible to choose the most appealing packaging, the most effective advert and the best design for your product. It does this because it removes the effects of superficial social influence.

Other factors that have arisen from brain research include the effect of complex pricing. By having a product priced at £3.99 rather than £4.00 it makes the brain work harder to understand the price. This means that the buyer pays more attention to it and thinks it is more cost-effective which, in turn, makes the buyer more likely to pay for it. Another example is when businesses offer multiple products for a single price, making the offer seem more attractive, for example two for £4.00.

> **Research**
>
> How ethical do you think this technique is? Is it acceptable to access hidden mental processes in this way and then use the findings to manipulate consumers?
>
> It is possible to use similar techniques in a criminal justice setting, for example in determining whether someone is telling the truth about their involvement in a crime. Studies have found that this is a much more effective way of detecting lies than the use of a polygraph test (such as you might see used as lie detectors).
>
> Is this acceptable? Justify your answer.

Application of psychology to explain gender

Gender is the psychological feeling of **masculinity** or **femininity**. **Typical gender** is where your gender matches that of your biological sex. **Atypical gender** occurs when people do not feel that this is the case. Traditionally, in western cultures gender has been a **binary** choice, either male or female, however in recent years there have been changes as gender is now regarded as more **gender-fluid** and on a spectrum rather than limited to male or female. It has therefore become **non-binary.**

There is an increase in **gender dysphoria** and **transgender** cases. Gender dysphoria is a condition where the person feels that their gender does not match their biological sex. In some cases, this can lead to the person becoming transgender, where they identify as the opposite gender to their gender at birth.

In this section, you will learn how each approach explains both typical and atypical gender identities and the shift towards multiple identities. You will also explore gender dysphoria and apply appropriate knowledge to the understanding of this and of transgender.

How the cognitive approach explains gender

> **Key terms**
>
> **Masculinity** – psychological characteristics associated with being male.
>
> **Femininity** – psychological characteristics associated with being female.
>
> **Typical gender** – gender that reflects a person's biological sex.
>
> **Atypical gender** – gender that does not reflect a person's biological sex.
>
> **Binary** – a forced choice to one or other position, for example masculine or feminine.
>
> **Gender-fluid** – taking the view that gender is not fixed throughout life but can change.
>
> **Non-binary** – view that there are multiple possible outcomes rather than the fixed two.
>
> **Gender dysphoria** – a condition where the person feels that their biological sex and their gender do not match.
>
> **Transgender** – (also referred to as trans) moving from one gender to another.

The cognitive approach assumes that gender stems from the way you process information, what you think about and what you remember, how this affects your beliefs, and how it influences your sense of gender. Information about gender is biased by your beliefs and this affects your gender.

Gender schema

The cognitive approach explains gender as a set of schema that develop during childhood through observation of others; it combines elements of cognition with social learning. Through observation of others children develop gender-related schema where they organise information about gender. They learn about their own gender first and then develop a schema for the other gender. These schema get more complex as children get older. The content of the schema guides a child's interaction with others of the same and opposite gender, and affects what is recalled and what is forgotten. Gender-consistent behaviour is remembered better than information that does not fit their schema.

Cognitive biases

Confirmation bias works to reinforce the schema you have for gender as you ignore, distort or forget data that doesn't fit with your schema. If young girls are shown a woman behaving gender atypically, she will probably either simply forget that information, or will distort it to make it consistent with her views on gender.

How the social approach explains gender

The social approach explains typical gender development within a social context, through conforming to group norms and through the influence of stereotypes. Stereotyping has similar concepts to the cognitive approach, especially gender schema theory, because it is all about picking up the norms of gender within the culture you are socialised into and conforming to those norms.

Normative and informational social influence guide gendered behaviour, especially in children because peer pressure has an impact on who you choose to play with and how you express your gender. Young girls and boys conform to the groups they belong to and try to fit in with the group by behaving like them.

Link

Look back at pages 18–20 for information about key concepts in conformity.

International trends show changes to female gender. Females are now typically expected to spend longer in education and aspire to high-ranking jobs. This can also be explained within the social approach as the norms of society change away from the old stereotypes of women as carers and men as wage-earners. There has been an increase in **androgyny** as both males and females take on behaviour that was previously associated with the opposite sex.

How the learning approach explains gender

The learning approach emphasises the role of environmental learning through direct and indirect experience. The learning approach suggests that nurture is the major force that leads to gender.

Conditioning

Operant conditioning explains gender through reinforcement. When a child displays specific behaviour for which they are reinforced, then that behaviour is likely to be repeated. A parent might selectively reinforce gender-appropriate behaviour while ignoring or even punishing gender-inappropriate behaviour. The child, therefore, becomes gendered as a result of direct experience.

Theory into practice

Adults asked to interact with a baby are filmed and their behaviour is analysed. Some adults play with a baby wearing a blue Babygro and some play with the same baby wearing a pink Babygro. The analysis showed that when the baby wore the blue Babygro the adult engaged in more physical play and when the baby wore pink it was spoken to more softly and cradled more.

Explain how the adult behaviour is shaping the child's gender development.

As gender norms change, then so too would the way in which gender is reinforced in children. This approach can explain the change in trends from binary gender to more gender-fluid identities or to androgynous identities.

Gender dysphoria would be learned in the same way. Children experience reinforcement for expressing dysphoria (or for acting as if they are dysphoric) and so they become dysphoric.

Social learning

Social learning explains gender through indirect experience; children observe the behaviour of models as they act in the environment. Children imitate the behaviour of important people especially if that person is rewarded for behaving that way. A young girl might model her behaviour on her mum or her older sister, copying what they do and, in this way, she takes on the gender-appropriate behaviour of being female.

Current changes in male and female behaviour can be explained through the changes in the behaviour of models, especially in the media. Young people who are developing their identities now have a range of models available to them including those who are more gender-fluid. The gendered behaviour of these models is reinforced by society as they achieve celebrity status. People may identify with these models and change their gender behaviour and identity to be less typical.

Atypical gender development is also much more public than before. Members of the trans community have a high-media profile now although many still do face discrimination. People who feel that they do not fit into the typical gender will observe them and their behaviour and through identification with the trans person will model their gender on them.

How the biological approach explains gender

Typical and atypical gender can be explained by physiological factors like brain anatomy and biochemistry. These physiological factors are shaped by evolutionary pressures that rewarded masculine behaviour in males and feminine behaviour in females. Gender differentiation made prehistoric humans more successful. The genes which code for these differences are still present in modern humans.

Role of evolution

Evolutionary theory suggests that gender differences are adaptive. Having two genders with each suited to different tasks was useful. Successful humans were those that lived long enough to produce and raise offspring to maturity and so passed on their genes to the next generation. Females had to go through pregnancy and birth, and then had to breastfeed the baby for an extended period. To do this successfully, they needed to be nurturing and caring with good emotional skills; they were more expressive. If they went out hunting, they put their reproductive success at risk, so they required a partner who would provide resources and who would protect them. Male reproductive success was therefore improved by having skills in protection and hunting; they were more instrumental. This then can explain the typical gender identities that occur across the world.

Role of sex hormones

Testosterone is a male hormone. Its release is triggered prenatally by the presence of the SRY gene (contributed by the Y chromosome) so is only present in biological males. The default developmental pathway is female, so without testosterone the foetus will become female. Testosterone affects the brain organisation of the developing foetus as well as the sexual and reproductive organs.

> **Link**
>
> Look back at page 7 and page 40 for information about evolution.

Case study

The case study of David Reimer illustrates this point. While still a baby, David suffered an unfortunate accident in which his penis was badly damaged. Doctors at that time recommended that the penis should be removed and David be brought up as a girl. They reasoned that he was young enough for this transition to be successful. David's parents went along with this, renamed him Brenda and treated him as a girl. At first it seemed like it was OK, but David showed a preference for his brother's toys and masculine behaviour. As a young teen, he was very isolated at school because he did not fit in with either the boys or the girls and he was deeply unhappy; he even threatened suicide. At this point, his parents told him the truth about his gender and he immediately reverted to male taking the name David and rejecting Brenda completely.

1 Take some time and think about this case, what his parents were trying to do when they changed him to Brenda. Consider whether his experiences support the view that nature is the more important influence or whether nurture dominates.

2 Which approach would suggest that it is possible to change a child's gender in this way?

3 Explain why David rejected the female gender.

4 Which approach best explains his behaviour?

There is a rush of testosterone at puberty when secondary sexual characteristics develop; this has a further effect on brain development and therefore on gender. Masculine behaviour is therefore explained through the action of testosterone on the brain both before birth and at puberty. Feminine behaviour is explained as resulting from a lack of testosterone.

> **Exam tip**
>
> There is an overlap between gender and aggression here. The biological explanation of gender implies that males will be more aggressive because of testosterone. This hormone masculinises the body and brain but it also has an effect on aggression. This means that it is used in both cases, so do not be afraid that if you need to answer a question on aggression you cannot use it again when asked about gender. Just make sure it is appropriate in the context of the question.

Atypical gender identities can be explained as a malfunction in this system, female foetuses exposed to too much testosterone prenatally will have a masculinised brain, so will be more masculine and in some cases may feel gender dysphoric. The reverse is true of males, a lack of testosterone at the appropriate times of development causes the default feminisation of the brain so the individual will not feel a strong masculine influence.

> **Research**
>
> There is an area in the brain called the sexually dimorphic nucleus; this is different in males compared to females. Studies on transgender male to female people show that the sexually dimorphic nuclei is more similar to that found in female brains suggesting that in some cases at least there is a biological explanation for gender dysphoria.
>
> How might an understanding of this difference be of use in helping someone who feels dysphoric and is considering gender reassignment?

PAUSE POINT

Now you have four competing explanations for the development of typical and atypical gender, it would be a good idea to revise them all by creating a mind map.

Hint

You could put gender in the middle and then in each corner have one of the approaches. For both typical and atypical gender you could list the concepts and research from the approach that best explains gender.

Extend

Check your mind map by using it on its own to write outline explanations for both typical and atypical gender development.

> **Further reading and resources**
>
> **Books**
>
> Raine, A. (2013) *The Anatomy of Violence: The Biological Roots of Crime.* Allen Lane.
>
> **Documentaries**
>
> 1992 documentary *Quiet Rage: the Stanford Prison Experiment.*
> https://www.youtube.com/watch?v=RKW_MzREPp4
>
> 2015 documentary *The Stanford Prison Experiment.*
> https://www.youtube.com/watch?v=L_LKzEqlPto

Getting ready for assessment

This section has been written to help you to do your best when you take the examination. Read through it carefully and ask your tutor if there is anything you are still not sure about.

About the examination

This unit is assessed as an examination. You will have to sit a paper asking you questions about what you have learned in this unit. The questions will consist of a variety of question types, including extended open-resource questions about psychological approaches to behaviour, and scenario-based questions relating to vocational contexts. Remember that all the questions are compulsory and you should attempt to answer each one.

Once you understand what you need to do then you should make sure you understand what psychological content you are being asked to use. Often, this will be signposted for you, for example 'using concepts drawn from the biological approach', but it is crucial that you select the most appropriate knowledge to answer the question. This is a key skill and it stops you wasting time providing the examiner with information that does not answer the question.

Sitting the examination

Before you start to answer a question, you should check how many marks are being offered. This will indicate the scope of your answer. Most questions contain command words. Understanding what these words mean will help you understand what the question is asking you to do.

It is always a good idea to plan your answers before you start and to check them at the end of the exam. This means that you must be aware of timing. It is good practice to read the whole paper first and then go back over your answers at the end, so if you calculate one mark per minute then you will have time for this and you can work out how long to spend on each question.

▶ **Table 1.3:** Definitions of the command words used in the exam questions

Command word	Definition
ANALYSE	Learners present the outcome of a methodical and detailed examination, either by breaking down: • a themed topic or situation in order to interpret/study the relationships between the parts and/or: • information or data to interpret and study key trends or interrelationships.
ASSESS	Learners give careful consideration of varied factors or events that apply to a specific situation and identify which are the most important or relevant. They make a judgement on the importance of something and come to a conclusion.

COMPARE (OR COMPARE AND CONTRAST)	Learners look for the similarities and differences of two (or more) things. This should not require the drawing of a conclusion. Answer must relate to both (or all) things mentioned in the question. The answer must include at least one similarity and one difference.
DESCRIBE	Learners give an account of something. Statements in the response need to be developed, as they are often linked, but do not need to include a justification or reason.
DISCUSS	Learners identify the issue/situation/problem/argument that is being assessed in the question. They explore all the aspects of an issue/situation/problem/argument. They investigate the issue/situation, and so on by reasoning or argument. A conclusion is not required.
EVALUATE	Consider various aspects of a subject's qualities in relation to its context, such as strengths or weaknesses, advantages or disadvantages, pros or cons. Come to a judgement, supported by evidence, which will often be in the form of a conclusion.
EXPLAIN	Learners' explanations require a justification/exemplification of a point. Their answers must contain some element of reasoning/justification to satisfy the definition of 'explain'. The mark scheme must have marking points that are linked. The mark scheme should be clearly laid out so that, to gain full marks, there must be a minimum of one mark for some element of reasoning/justification to satisfy the definition of 'explain'.
GIVE	Recall from memory a feature, characteristic or use.
GIVE A REASON (WHY)	When a statement has been made and the requirement is only to give the reason why.
IDENTIFY	Select the correct answer from the given stimulus/resource.
INTERPRET	Recognise a single or multiple trend(s) or pattern(s) within a given stimulus/resource.
JUSTIFY	Give reasons/evidence to support a statement given in the question.
NAME	Recall from memory the correct object, process, law, and so on, using the correct terminology.
STATE	Recall from memory facts, dates, legal implications, and so on.

Sample answers

For some questions you will be given some background information on which the questions are based. Look at the sample questions that follow and the tips on how to answer them well.

Answering short-answer questions

- Read the question carefully.
- Highlight or underline key words.
- Note the number of marks available.
- Make sure you make the same number of statements as there are marks available. For example, a two-mark question needs two statements.

Worked example

Describe what a gender stereotype is. [2]

A gender stereotype is an assumption we make about someone based on their gender. For example, we assume that boys will like to play with cars more than girls.

Look carefully at how the question is set out to see how many points need to be included in your answer.

This is a good answer which clearly answers the question and would get both marks. The use of an appropriate example to illustrate a concept is a good way to demonstrate your knowledge.

Answering scenario-based questions

- Read the stimulus (source) material carefully, to identify the content of the answer, also there are likely to be further questions based on it so make sure you understand.
- Check your answer to make sure it is detailed enough and answers the question and relates to the source.

Worked example

Amy and Tom are having a baby. They decide that the infant will be raised as gender neutral; this means there will be no attempt to make the child adopt a stereotypical gender. They inform family and friends of their decision, telling them that they will not let them know which sex the baby is. They call the child Alex and provide clothing of all colours and styles. Alex's favourite toys are dolls and cars. Although it is difficult, Amy and Tom maintain the secret of Alex's gender.

Explain why Amy and Tom clothe Alex in all different colours and styles. Use your knowledge of social psychology to answer this question. [2] (A02)

- Go back to the stimulus material and see if there are any clues to help you with the material.

- The command 'Explain' means you have to give a reason. Using the words 'because' or 'so' will encourage you to do this.

- This means that you have to give an elaborated response (include more detail).

Alex is clothed using lots of colours and styles to avoid social categorisation so other people cannot group Alex into one or other gender. This is because they do not have any way of grouping the baby.

Worked example

Alex is a happy and contented child but at the point of starting school Amy and Tom realise they have to reveal Alex's gender. They tell the school that Alex is male, but insist that he is exposed equally to male and female type activities and that he be allowed to wear skirts, dresses as well as trousers to school. At first Alex wears dresses, but soon starts to reject them in favour of trousers. When Amy asks Alex why, he says that the 'other boys wear trousers'.

Explain why Alex no longer wants to wear dresses. Use your knowledge of social psychology to answer this question. [3]

- The command 'Explain' means you have to give a reason. Using the words 'because' or 'so' will encourage you to do this.
- This is a three-mark question which means that you have to give an elaborated response (include more detail).

Alex does not want to wear dresses because of normative social influence. He has identified a social group for himself and changes his behaviour to be more like the group, so he wears what they wear to fit in with them.

Worked example

As Alex grows up, Amy complains to her mum that Alex is not as sensitive as he used to be and refuses to play with his dolls. He chooses to watch different TV programmes from before and Amy thinks this is because he is being stereotyped by his school. But Amy's mum thinks it has more to do with social learning.

Describe what is meant by social learning and explain why Amy's mum thinks this is what is responsible for Alex's change in behaviour. [4]

- The first command is 'Describe'. There are four marks available so it is reasonable to split the question into two markers. Start by describing social learning. You will need to be quite brief; you know a lot about this so limit your response to the basics.
- The second section is 'Explain' which means you have to relate what you have said about social learning to Alex.

Social learning is learning through observing the behaviour of other people and imitating those that are regarded as models.

Alex may regard other boys as models so he imitates their behaviour and because they do not play with dolls, neither does he.

- The first section has a reasonable amount of detail; it says what social learning is and shows how it changes behaviour.

- The second part explains why Alex changes and refers directly to the stimulus.

Worked example

Amy notices that the adverts used to market children's toys are different. Toys for boys are advertised on blue or red backgrounds and girls are advertised on pink ones. The TV adverts for masculine toys are often louder and show boys running around more. Alex automatically pays attention to the 'boy' adverts but seems to ignore the 'girl' ones.

Cognitive psychology explains behaviour as a result of information processing. Priming affects how information is processed.

State what is meant by priming. [1]

Identify the type of priming that Alex is showing and justify your answer. [3]

- The first command is 'State' which means you need to give a basic definition.

- The second command is asking you to 'Identify' which means you need to select and name something.

- 'Justify' means to say why you selected the last answer. This needs to be done in relation to the stimulus.

Priming is where an event or item in the environment automatically triggers a schema.

Alex is showing associative primed behaviour because he associates the colours in the adverts with toys associated with boys, his schema for boys' toys is activated by the colours.

- Priming is clearly defined, without unnecessary detail.

- Associative priming is most relevant (although you could argue for repetition); this is the most likely option.

- The justification is appropriate and linked to the stimulus.

Answering long-answer questions

For a question that uses the command word 'Discuss', you must consider all the relevant knowledge you have about the topic using a reasoned argument.

Amy has a second child, Emma. She cannot believe how different Emma's behaviour is to Alex's. She says that looking back Alex always showed more masculine behaviour than Emma shows. Emma was always dressed in female clothes and been given female toys.

Discuss the role of nature and nurture in the development of gender.

In your answer you should refer to the experiences of Amy and use knowledge drawn from biological psychology and at least one other approach. [9]

The biological approach would propose that nature is more important than nurture in gender development. It suggests that gender is programmed by genetics so males and females behave differently. It says that this is due to evolutionary pressures where males and females had to have different skills in order to be successful. A nurture explanation would come from the learning approach which suggests that gender is learned through conditioning and social learning, we are reinforced for behaving in gender-consistent ways and choose to focus on same sex models to imitate.

Alex is a biological male and his brain will have been programmed to be masculine because of the release of testosterone before he was born. This means he has natural tendencies towards spatial skills and aggression. Emma is a biological female. She was not exposed to testosterone to the same level, therefore her brain and behaviour are different. However, both Alex and Emma have access to male and female role models and they could develop differently because they copy the actions of the models.

It is difficult to decide whether nature is more important than nurture because they work together to affect development. There is evidence to support both sides of the argument. For example, Bandura showed that males are more ready to imitate a male model, but he also showed that despite being exposed to the same amount of modelling, girls were less willing to show aggression, perhaps because they are biologically less aggressive.

- Each paragraph focuses on a different skill. The first one is AO1 describing the two approaches and how they explain gender. There is enough detail without it being too long.

- The second paragraph focuses on the stimulus material but links it to both explanations in an appropriate way.

- The final paragraph introduces some evidence to support nurture, but questions whether it is clear evidence excluding the role of nature and argues that both have impact and it is difficult to separate them.

Conducting Psychological Research

2

Getting to know your unit

Assessment

You will be assessed by a series of assignments set by your tutor.

Being able to take an evidence-based approach in applied psychology is a fundamental element of a psychologist's practice. In this unit you will gain understanding and skills of how research is carried out and how it benefits advancements in treatments and practice. Whether you intend to move towards higher education or work-related practice, this unit will provide you with the skills to undertake a piece of research relating to the field of applied psychology.

How you will be assessed

This unit will be assessed by a series of internally assessed tasks set by your tutor in the form of written reports that:

▶ discuss the importance of research in informing and improving practice and provision (for example, in mental health services)
▶ provide a research proposal for a pilot study in an area of applied psychology
▶ present any procedures followed and the findings and successes of the pilot study together with its implications on practice and provision.

Throughout this unit you will find assessment activities that will help you gain the knowledge and skills that will help you complete your assessment. To be able to fully understand how to conduct research, the activities within this unit will help you identify the best research methods for conducting specific research projects.

The skills you learn throughout this unit are designed to specifically help you to complete the synoptic assessment tasks in this unit. They will also help you with all units within this qualification where you will have the opportunity to plan and carry out your own research project.

In order for you to achieve the tasks in your assignment, it is important to check that you have met the grading criteria below.

Assessment criteria

This table shows what you must do in order to achieve a **Pass**, **Merit** or **Distinction**, and where you can find activities to help you.

Pass	Merit	Distinction

Learning aim **A** Understand research methods and their importance in psychological inquiry

Pass	Merit	Distinction
A.P1 Explain the principles for conducting psychological research. **Assessment activity 2.1**	**A.M1** Assess the principles and processes involved when undertaking psychological inquiry. **Assessment activity 2.1**	**A.D1** Evaluate the importance of conducting research and the research process in psychological inquiry. **Assessment activity 2.1**
A.P2 Explain the research process and key terms used when undertaking psychological inquiry. **Assessment activity 2.1**		

Learning aim **B** Plan research to investigate psychological questions

Pass	Merit	Distinction
B.P3 Plan for a pilot study using appropriate methods. **Assessment activity 2.2**	**B.M2** Assess different research methods when planning research proposals in psychological inquiry. **Assessment activity 2.2**	**B.D2** Evaluate use of different research methods when planning research proposals in psychological inquiry. **Assessment activity 2.2**
B.P4 Explain proposal for own pilot study. **Assessment activity 2.2**		

Learning aim **C** Carry out a pilot study to explore current issues in psychology

Pass	Merit	Distinction
C.P5 Perform a pilot study in one area of psychology. **Assessment activity 2.3**	**C.M3** Analyse findings from conducting own research using appropriate formats. **Assessment activity 2.3**	**CD.D3** Evaluate findings, and the effectiveness of own research, using appropriate formats, self-reflection and feedback from others, and the implication for future practice, provision and professional development. **Assessment activity 2.3**
C.P6 Explain findings using appropriate formats. **Assessment activity 2.3**		

Learning aim **D** Review implications of research into psychological inquiry

Pass	Merit	Distinction
D.P7 Discuss success of own research using self-reflection and feedback from others. **Assessment activity 2.4**	**D.M4** Analyse own research findings using self-reflection and feedback from others for future practice, provision and professional development. **Assessment activity 2.4**	
D.P8 Explain implications of own research on future practice, provision and professional development. **Assessment activity 2.4**		

Getting started

Research is an important tool that allows you to understand the complexities of the world. Without it, you would be forced to rely on feelings, opinions and luck. Through research you can answer questions and theorise over events. Make a list of things you are interested in knowing more about. How could research help you to understand things better?

A Understand research methods and their importance in psychological inquiry

Purpose and value of research in applied psychology

Research is something that you do every day, often without knowing you are doing it. For example, when you open the curtains each morning you look at the weather and question what clothes to wear, or when you brush your teeth you have probably tried different toothpastes before deciding on the one you are using. Research provides you with a tool to understand your world more effectively, to seek out solutions and find new and better ways of doing things. Research has far-reaching effects on improving outcomes for individuals, helping shape the way policy and practice is developed and used, as well as identifying ways to fill gaps in practice or provision.

Issues researched in applied psychology span a wide field and are driven by a number of factors. For example, many charities sponsor research in order to find cures for specific diseases and illnesses. Some research is sponsored by government departments to find effective ways for support services to carry out their functions. Research provides society with a way of justifying and promoting approaches, treatments and interventions to support the health and wellbeing of a society.

Definitions and terms

There are many terms used in research to describe the ways that psychologists conduct research, the methods they use and the tools they use to interpret the data they collect. In this unit you will cover the main key terms you will come across when conducting your own **pilot study**. It is important that you are familiar with these terms so you are able to select and use the right tools for any research you undertake.

Types of reasoning

The concept of reasoning means the way that you would develop your thoughts and make a 'rational argument'. You do this every day. For example, you get up in the morning and see it is snowing so you would choose to wear a thick jumper rather than a summer T-shirt. The snow may turn to rain later, so you may decide to take an umbrella. In this short scenario you are considering the options, developing a rational (reasonable) argument that helps you decide the best outcome. This is the same when you conduct research; you weigh up all the possibilities to come to the best solution. By working through the question in this way (weather > to clothes choice > to appropriate clothing) you are conducting a disciplined exercise to address the initial question of 'what should I wear in this weather?'. Researchers use this same disciplined exercise to conduct research from their initial question (hypothesis). This means they use an approach following set procedures.

Key term

Pilot study – a small-scale study that researchers use to evaluate or test whether doing a bigger study into an area is feasible given the time, cost and other factors a researcher has available. It is also useful for assessing the approach and so potentially adapting it for the main study.

Link

This unit introduces you to the process of research. When choosing a subject to conduct a pilot study you will find it useful to refer to other units within this qualification to help you identify an area to research.

There are many different ways that you can answer questions and solve problems, such as:

▶ **Inductive reasoning** – this is often referred to as 'bottom-up' reasoning. Your conclusion comes from your observations. You can see patterns and regularities in your environment and you can formulate a hypothesis to explore. From these investigations you can formulate theories. For example: I have seen that Sajit eats a lot of green jelly beans, therefore Sajit does not like other coloured jelly beans.

▶ **Deductive reasoning** – this works the other way around and is referred to as 'top-down' reasoning. You arrive at a conclusion which is based on a hunch, or an idea. You may begin by thinking up a theory about a **phenomenon**. You can narrow it down to more specific hypotheses and these can then be tested through observing the phenomenon. During the observation you are testing the **hypothesis** and confirming (or disproving) the original theory. For example: Sajit will only eat green jelly beans. I have reached this conclusion as I have seen him eat only green jelly beans.

The collection and analysis of **primary data** means collecting information about something by using different methods, such as questionnaires or experiments, and analysing or interpreting this information to see if it will answer your questions. With these answers you can then generalise, or make a best guess as to whether the findings of your research could be applied to the rest of the population. In other words, you can predict the possible reason for a phenomenon.

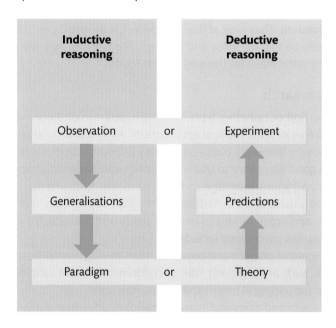

▶ **Figure 2.1:** Inductive and deductive reasoning

Scientific process

The scientific process is one where you identify a problem, you gather data that is relevant to that problem and you then form a question (or hypothesis) from this data. Your hypothesis is **empirically tested**, analysed and interpreted, so it is a way that you learn things about something specific. The scientific process has been developed over time and is highly respected as a method due to its reliability and validity. The reason why this form of research is used so frequently is that psychologists systematically work through a set process of:

Key terms

Inductive reasoning (from specific to general) – drawing conclusions from the facts and examples that you observe.

Deductive reasoning (from general to specific) – starting with a conclusion and then presenting facts and examples.

Phenomenon – a term used to describe something that may exist or may happen but the cause cannot easily be explained.

Hypothesis – a prediction about what is (or could be) happening.

Primary data – is a term to describe the data collected by a research which comes from first-hand sources e.g. surveys, interviews or experiments.

Empirically tested – tested using information obtained through observation or experimentation.

- asking a question
- collating information or otherwise observing something, for example, behaviours
- developing a hypothesis (guessing the answer)
- conducting the research and testing the hypothesis
- interpreting or analysing the results
- presenting a conclusion.

The scientific process therefore follows a set pattern and defines exactly the methods used to collect the data (questionnaires, experiments, procedures involved) so it can be easily **replicated** by others who want to extend and test the conclusions. So, although there is a basis of theory in this approach, theories are tested, and data emerges which validates any questions asked. The following are a few more terms you may come across in understanding the scientific process and these will be discussed in more detail throughout this unit.

- Controlled variables – these are any items, factors or conditions that can be controlled or changed by a researcher. There are three types of variable:
  - the dependent variable (DV): the variable that is tested and remains the same. For example: the time taken to run a race.
  - the independent variable (IV): the factor or thing that is changed during an experiment. For example: a drug dose.
  - controlled variables: the variable that is kept the same during an experiment. Any change in this would invalidate the results. For example: level of blood sugar.
- Cause and effect – this is a common term used to describe the way that a researcher explores a question. They look at the cause which is the producer of the effect. An example would be that of Pavlov and his dogs. The bell ringing is the cause and the dog salivating is the effect (as the dog expects food).

Purpose of research

Research aims to find out whether a pre-existing hypothesis or theory about a phenomenon is true or false. From observations of the world around you, you ask questions about why things are happening. Every phenomenon has a reason behind it. Research is a good way to try to understand and evaluate what is happening so that you can extend your knowledge and understanding. Research can help improve outcomes for individuals and can help to identify gaps in provision. It can also be used by governments and organisations to improve policy and practice. For example, issues researched in applied psychology include:

- the improvement of practice and provision, such as with mental-health issues
- health trends, such as the growth rates of children in different locations
- strategies for supporting ill health and mental functions
- establishing cause and cures of disease, behaviours, advancement in treatments and medication, and technologies.

As you can see, conducting a good piece of research can have many positive outcomes and its purpose is to try to find something new or to extend a current piece of research, not just to replicate it. Researchers often use the phrase an 'original' piece of research, which is research that produces new knowledge rather than just saying what is already known in a new way. There are many ways to produce new knowledge: through observations, experiments, or testing new approaches. An easy way to think about originality is through the following example.

Imagine you are on a remote island where the land has not been explored before. Because the land is arid and dry and you see no wildlife, you hypothesise that nothing can live here. Yet you come across a species of bird with an extraordinarily long, thin

Key term

Replicable – a research study should produce the same results if repeated exactly. If a researcher follows all the procedures and uses the same methods as another study and their results were very different, this means that the original study was not very replicable, or it was not clear enough.

Link

See Unit 1, page 26, for more information on Pavlov's experiment.

Link

See page 84, for more information and definitions of variables.

beak and see it driving its beak into the soil to extract bugs and water. You develop, conduct and write up your findings detailing your hypothesis that this bird is likely to survive in this climate due to the length of the beak and the ability to drive down under the surface of the ground to find food (something other species may not be able to do), the methods you use and an explanation of the results. This forms an original piece of research.

Types of research

There are a number of research processes you need to understand that are important if you want to conduct a research study, as well as understanding the techniques used to collect data to answer research questions or hypotheses. Some are included here and you will explore other processes when you start to design your own pilot study.

The best way to plan a piece of research is to decide on the type of study that would answer your research questions most effectively. In this unit you will be developing a pilot study but it is important to know the advantages of using a number of different types of research.

Pilot study or experiment

As assessment of this unit will be based on a small pilot study, it is useful to understand the purpose of this type of study. Pilot studies or experiments are the first step to designing a good piece of research. Pilot studies are small studies that would help to inform a larger study or experiment. They are a way to test out an idea without going to too much expense or time. The purpose of a pilot study is to test out procedures and identify any areas that need to be improved. It is a cost-effective way of finding out whether your research is worth carrying out on a wider scale. It is usually carried out with a small number of participants and will help you to identify whether:

▶ the design of your research is appropriate
▶ your data-gathering methods and standardised instructions to participants and procedures are robust
▶ any coding (for qualitative data), or measuring (for quantitative data) strategies you use (for example, observations, tests) are appropriate.

The pilot study is a good way to identify whether your questionnaire or interview schedules are appropriate for your target population. Testing these methods on a small sample allows you not only to ensure that the study will run smoothly, but also potentially to identify any further interesting ideas.

A pilot study allows you to practise carrying out your research; in particular, it provides an indication of how long the actual study will take. These timings can be used to brief your participants about the timeframe and the amount of input required of them. You must always inform your participants that they are taking part in a pilot study and you should ask them to raise any issues they find when they take part in the trial.

Laboratory and field experiments

Experiments are probably the most popular method used in scientific research and they are often carried out using strict laboratory conditions. Conducting experiments in a laboratory allows the researcher to control the environment to make sure that nothing interferes with what they are trying to study. The key principle of experiments is to control the variables and through careful measurement, establish 'cause and effect' relationships. Variables will be covered in detail later in this section.

A field experiment is the opposite of this; it is a study that is carried out in an everyday natural setting. A good example of a field study is Hofling (1966) in which nurses were asked to administer a drug to patients, in a typical hospital setting.

Other types of research

Other types of experiment or study you may come across	
Field experiment	• Carried out in real-life environments • Independent variable is manipulated • Difficult to control extraneous (unrelated) variables or other factors that could affect the outcome of the experiment
Natural experiment	• Carried out in a natural environment • Little or no control over the independent variable
Quasi-experiment	• Where people are selected on the basis of common features for example, age, height, gender, culture • Quasi means 'similar', so the experiment will be similar to a real experiment but participants cannot be randomly assigned to conditions
Correlational research	• Measures two variables and investigates their relationship • Different from an experiment which isolates and manipulates the IV and establishes cause and effect • Often displayed visually by drawing a scattergram

Key term

Manipulate – used where variables are changed on purpose. It can be termed as an independent variable.

A correlational study is not (strictly speaking) a research method like an experiment; it is a way of interpreting data that has been gathered. However, it is useful to use if you want to see whether there is any relationship between two variables. For example, this could be used if you want to study whether taller men are always heavier than shorter men.

An experiment isolates and **manipulates** the independent variable, establishing cause and effect (if one causes the other), while the correlation explores the relationship. A correlation can be displayed by using a drawing called a scattergram. This scattergram plots the figures for one variable against the other variable on a graph. It can show a positive or negative correlation, or no correlation at all (see Figure 2.2). Some examples can be seen later in this unit.

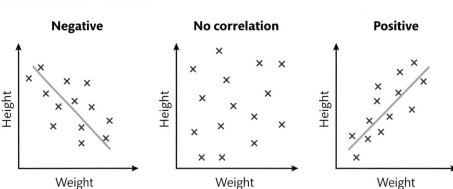

The points are close to a straight line which shows a decrease (negative). This shows that as one variable increases the other decreases, e.g., as a person is taller they are lighter.

There is no pattern here to points. There is no relationship between the two variables, e.g., some taller people are heavier while others are lighter.

The points are close to the straight line which shows an increase (positive). This shows when one variable increases so does the other. There is a relationship between height and weight, e.g., as the person grows taller they are heavier

▶ **Figure 2.2:** Correlation displayed on scattergrams

Primary and secondary research

Approaches to research can be either primary or secondary.

▶ Primary research involves gathering new data that has not been collected before. You collect the data yourself. You might conduct interviews with elderly people about their favourite television shows or send out questionnaires to understand the causes of stress and links to ill health.

▶ Secondary research is also known as 'desk-based research' as it often involves gathering data that has already been produced. It may be searching the internet, journals or company reports. For example, if you wanted to know how many people died in a five-year period you would explore national statistics relating to this on a government site. You may then look at other research that has been conducted in this area and write your own report based on these findings.

Link

How you write up your research findings will be covered later in this unit.

▶ What is the value of gathering people's opinions on research questions?

Self-report techniques

Self-report techniques, such as questionnaires, interviews and diaries, are used to gather data. Participants in a study will provide information without the experimenter being present. A set of questions is developed. For example, the questionnaire or interview could ask about the way a participant feels in different situations. A participant could keep a diary of the differences in their temperament at different points of the day. An advantage of using self-report techniques is that you can develop a deeper understanding of participants' thoughts and feelings. A disadvantage is that it can potentially be difficult for participants to disclose certain information, or they may try to amend their responses to what they think researchers want to find out.

Case studies

Case studies are detailed investigations of one person or small groups of people. They are often used when a researcher is interested in learning about events of a person over time and are sometimes called biographical events. A small sample enables researchers to conduct an in-depth analysis of the people involved. Case studies are commonly used in psychology. For example, Sigmund Freud conducted very detailed investigations into the private lives of patients so that he could have a better understanding of their underlying conditions and therefore treat them more effectively.

Although case studies create opportunities for the researcher to gather rich data there is little control over the number of variables involved in a case study, so it is difficult to establish whether any **causal relationship**s exist between variables. Also, because of the small sample size, it is unlikely that the findings can be generalised to a whole population.

Content analysis

Content analysis is a means of analysing data by breaking the content of media (books, films, media news items, or research articles) into categories. For example, categories could be a particular word, phrase, sentence or a theme. Researchers quantify (count) and examine the relationships between the different content and make inferences (suggestions) about what they might mean.

Research

Find two articles about the same topic (for example, school bullying or Alzheimer's in the ageing population) and produce a short summary on the following:
- What the research study was exploring (what were the research questions)?
- What were the results of the research?
- What conclusions did the researchers make?

Organisations

There are a number of professional organisations involved in research. They offer advice and guidance on conducting research in their specific areas. This could involve guidelines for conduct within a research study, or even guidance on how to submit a report in an expected style. The main UK organisations are given below:

▶ Office for National Statistics (ONS) – this is a non-ministerial department which reports directly to the UK Parliament. They are the largest independent producer of official statistics covering a wide range of data. This is a useful website to find out specific information about different aspects of the UK population.

▶ British Medical Association (BMA) – the BMA is a trade union for doctors in the UK. They have a very large resource bank where you can find books, journals and research information.

▶ British Psychological Society (BPS) – the BPS supports the development and application of psychology. They set the standards for research, education and knowledge in the field of psychology. They also set down a code of ethical principles that must be followed by anyone conducting research on human/animal subjects. You can find a copy of the BPS Code of Human Research Ethics on their website.

Research

Go to the BPS website and familiarise yourself with the Code of Human Research Ethics. What is the main aim of the document? How will it help you in conducting research?

Now go to the BMA website and see what they say about ethics. Look up their 'Ethics: A to Z' and explore the different ethical issues they explain.

Professional and personal skills

You probably have many skills already that are valuable to the research process. You may have a naturally enquiring mind and are curious about the way that things work. You may have developed systems for note-taking that aid revision when studying for examinations.

> **Discussion**
>
> In groups, discuss the skills and competencies needed to conduct a research study. Compare your answers with others and find similarities. Identify key areas where you think you have good skills and try and identify areas that you think you need to develop. Write down the skills and competencies you believe you already possess. Identify those that you think you do not possess or that you need to improve.

A good starting point is to identify those skills and competencies you already possess. From there you can identify those you need to develop to be a skilled researcher. Examples of the skills and competencies you need can be seen in Table 2.1.

▶ **Table 2.1:** Personal and professional skills

Personal skills	Professional skills
<ul><li>Possessing an enquiring mind; being curious</li><li>Working autonomously (being able to work alone)</li><li>Good time-management skills, for example, being able to plan and take account of unexpected delays or disruption to research or research processes</li><li>Organisational skills</li><li>Non-judgemental attitude or behaviours, for example, the ability to remain objective</li><li>Discretion, or the ability to behave in a way that will not attract negative attention</li><li>Having the ability to ensure information is kept confidential</li></ul>	<ul><li>Critically analysing information</li><li>Note taking and record making</li><li>Academic research skills, for example, paying attention to detail; IT skills; statistical and mathematical skills</li><li>Promotion and maintaining health and safety, for example, ensuring participants and yourself are free from risk of physical or psychological harm</li><li>Being aware of the importance of confidentiality and data protection measures</li><li>Mastering various reading techniques, for example, skimming and scanning</li></ul>

From this initial reflection, you can set goals to develop these skills. You may be able to achieve these by working your way through the research process. Alternatively, you may need to set yourself goals along the way.

Key terms in research

There are many key terms used in psychological research. You have already learned about some of the terms. This section will cover some more that will be useful for your pilot study.

Hypotheses

Hypotheses are statements that attempt to explain the possible expected outcome of an experiment or study. In psychological research there are a number of different types of hypotheses and ways you use them.

▶ Directional hypothesis (one tailed) – this predicts the nature of the effect of the IV on the DV. For example, children will accurately identify four animals found in a zoo.

▶ Non-directional hypothesis (two tailed) – this predicts that the IV will have an effect on the DV but the direction of the effect is not stated. For example, there will be a difference in how many animals from a zoo that a child can identify.

▶ Null hypothesis – this predicts no relationship between the two variables (one does not affect the other). For example, children can remember a number of animals from the zoo but this is due to chance as some children may have been to the zoo more than other children.

▶ Alternative hypothesis – this is what the researcher predicts will be found. It is also known as the research hypothesis when the research method adopted is experimental.

Variables

Variables in research refer largely to the **independent variable (IV)** (the cause) and the **dependent variable (DV)** (the effect). The IV is manipulated and the DV is measured. For example:

Aaron is conducting an experiment that will test the theory that drinking fizzy drinks will increase energy levels substantially more than drinking flat drinks.

The *independent variable* here is the amount of fizzy drinks given to the participants in a study. This is controlled by Aaron.

The *dependent variable* is the variable affected by the independent variable (energy levels).

An advantage of experimentation is that it provides an objective explanation for a phenomenon (not the researcher's opinion) and is an observable fact. This means the data produced is more valid. The example provided would likely be a laboratory experiment. For dependent and independent variables, the principles are still the same. The experimenter manipulates the independent variable but, as in any real-life situation, they cannot control every variable. These other variables are known as **extraneous variables**.

> ### Theory into practice
>
> Work out which are the dependent and independent variables from the following two experiments:
>
> 1 Peter conducts an experiment on how many marshmallows a person can eat before they feel sick.
>
> 2 Naila conducts an experiment on the length of time a learner sleeps and how this affects their attention in class.

Another term used for extraneous variables you may come across is **confounding variables.** Normally in an experiment the researcher will put in place a number of controls (assigning participants by age, sex, height) in order to minimise any risk of another variable affecting the results. However, sometimes there are other factors that influence the experiment, for example, although you have the same age group, participants act in a different way.

Look at the statement and discussion below which exemplifies a confounding variable.

'As the death rate rises, so does the sale of houses'.

One possible answer for this could be that the relationship is as simple as it seems: as death rates rise, so does the sale of houses. This is unlikely. It may be that selling houses makes people die. This is also unlikely.

> ### Key terms
>
> **Independent variable (IV)** – the variable the experimenter manipulates or changes. This is something the researcher thinks will have a direct effect on the dependent variable.
>
> **Dependent variable (DV)** – the variable the experimenter measures. This is the result of a study.
>
> **Extraneous variable (EV)** – a variable that is not an independent variable but could affect the results (the DV) of the experiment.
>
> **Confounding variable (CV)** – a variable that affects both the independent and dependent variables and causes the appearance of an association that may not necessarily be correct and could influence the results of a study.

It may be that it is the weather that is causing this effect: the weather being the third confounding variable. In cold weather there are more deaths in the older generation and therefore more houses are sold. The weather is the variable that confounds the relationship between the death rate and the sale of houses.

Operationalisation is a term that can be applied to the IV, DV or other variables and describes the level or frequency or measure of the variable. For example:

▶ Aggression from a clinically depressed teenager is the variable. To operationalise the variable, the researcher could observe the frequency of specific aggressive behaviours, for example, fighting.

▶ Anxiety is the variable and it is operationalised by the researcher. For example, introducing different size spiders and observing the size that triggers the anxiety.

Sources of data and literature

When conducting research, you want to find out as much as you can beforehand to ensure that it has not been researched previously, or that you have a different opinion on the subject. You have already explored the value of primary and secondary research; these terms are also used when referring to sources of literature (other research or data) and should not be confused.

▶ Primary sources – these are pieces of original research, books by authors about their own work, and other material that is original and not copied. Examples of primary sources include original theories, such as Piaget's theory of cognitive development.

▶ Secondary sources – this is information that reports on primary sources or discusses other authors' research or data findings. An example of a secondary source is an author referencing Piaget's theory.

Validity

A further consideration when carrying out research is validity. Definitions can vary depending on their purpose and context.

▶ When *collecting* data, validity means ensuring that you actually measure what you intend to measure.

▶ When *analysing* data, validity affirms the robustness (strength) of the interpretation of the results.

▶ There are many types of validity but here you will focus on some of the most common types.

▶ Internal validity – whether the results of any study can be shown to be a result of the manipulation of the IV, that is whether you have controlled everything you could possibly have controlled in the study.

▶ External validity – the extent to which the findings from a study could be generalised to a population (or applied to other people or contexts).

▶ Concurrent validity – the extent to which the results of any new study compare to previously well-established studies.

▶ Ecological validity – the extent to which a study's findings can be generalised to the real world. For example, a study in the UK may not have the same reliability if applied to a country with different cultural practices or beliefs.

▶ Temporal validity – the extent that the study is valid over time. For example, a study from 1955 on people's attitudes to TV programmes, would probably look very different today.

▶ Inter-observer reliability – the degree that observers or participants give a consistent estimate of the same phenomenon. For example, when observing instances of aggression in clinically depressed teenagers, two observers may provide different explanations of this behaviour due to their own **subjective** opinions. This means that the data is unreliable.

Link

See page 81 for information about primary and secondary research.

Key term

Subjective – based on opinion: what a person feels or believes about a subject rather than the facts in front of them.

Valid research

As part of a study investigating whether boys are better at maths than girls, researchers sampled a group of 16 boys and 16 girls from a high-performing private school in England. Children were all given the same ten maths problems. Results of the study suggested that boys were able to score higher on the ten maths problems than girls, gaining an average of eight out of ten.

1 Which type or types of validity would be affected by this study?
2 How would it have been affected?
3 What changes would you have to make to the study to make it more valid?

Link

You can read more about quantitative and qualitative research on page 99.

Reliability and validity

Reliability refers to the consistency or repeatability of a measure or test on results. It is important to remember that reliability can be achieved without validity: you could ask the wrong questions and get the same wrong answers consistently. In this case your work is reliable (the answers you received were consistent and repeatable) but not valid (you did not find out information about the subject you intended to investigate). In quantitative and qualitative research reliability is related to different factors.

There are four types of reliability.

▶ Inter-observer or inter-researcher reliability examines whether different researchers in the same situation would get the same (or similar) results. An example of where inter-observer reliability can cause an issue is during classroom observations. Observations of behaviour can be subjective meaning two different researchers could interpret the behaviour differently making it difficult to achieve inter-observer reliability. A good example of this would be with Bandura's bobo doll.

▶ Test-retest reliability relates to doing the same test on different occasions and getting the same (or similar) results. An example of a test-retest reliability issue is the measurement of blood pressure. Blood pressure can be affected by different factors such as temperature, time of day, diet, sleep patterns, stress, physical activity levels, and alcohol levels. So, if you measured blood pressure on the same person at the same time of day but on different days, you could get different measurements.

Link

You can read more about Bandura's bobo doll research in Unit 1, page 30.

▶ Internal consistency reliability relates to whether the items in a survey or questionnaire all measure the same thing. For example, if you were measuring phobias and had a five-item questionnaire, it would have good internal consistency reliability if all of the questions measured phobias.

▶ Face validity relates to a way of assessing whether something measures what it claims to measure. For example, whether an IQ test is a good judge of intelligence.

Sampling

Sampling is a way of choosing participants for a research study. Sampling as a technique helps you to gain a better understanding of the whole population based on choosing a small group or **target population**. This sounds simple enough but choosing the right **sample** is important as it can have a significant impact on the findings, which may affect the reliability and validity of the research.

For example, if you undertake a study in your home town (which has, for example, a population of 2000) and wanted to sample 200 people, a good way to do this may be to select every tenth person in the phone book. This would be a representative sample of your town, but it would not be representative of the whole population.

Key terms

Sampling – a procedure for selecting a representative group from the population in a study.

Target population – the total number of people/ individuals from which a sample might be drawn.

Sample – the people or 'participants' taking part in the study.

Many people think that sample size in a survey, for example, should be a percentage of the population. This is not true. A population of 2000 and a population of 20,000 could both be described accurately with the same sample size of say, 150 people. The important factor is that your sample is representative of the population you want to describe. Examples of the different types of sampling techniques can be found in Table 2.2.

▶ **Table 2.2:** Different types of sampling methods

Opportunity	• Whoever is around at the time and willing to take part – for example, people walking into a supermarket at the time the researcher is there • Based on convenience • Example: asking shoppers when they enter a supermarket about their choice of butter
Systematic	• Choosing participants in a logical or orderly way • List all the individuals in a population and decide on the sample you want. This gives you the 'n' number. • Example: picking every ninth number in the telephone directory
Random	• Similar to the lottery. Everyone has an equal chance of being selected. • Good for choosing an unbiased or fair representative sample • Very time consuming for large populations • Example: choosing names from a hat
Volunteer	• Individuals that have been chosen using 'self-selection' • Example: an advert seeking volunteers with heart conditions to take part in clinical trials for a new drug
Snowballing	• Used when other sampling methods are difficult to use • Named 'snowballing' as once the ball is rolling it picks up 'snow' on the way and grows bigger • Example: current research participants recruit other participants for a study such as their friends or colleagues
Stratified	• Selecting a sample based on how often that group of people occur in the population • Makes a deliberate attempt to make the sample representative of the population • Example: 5 per cent of children born in 1999 were twins, therefore 5 per cent of the sample must be twins

---

Theory into practice

A researcher is interested in maximum-security inmates in a prison. What sampling procedure is she using in each of the following?

1 She obtains a list of all inmates in maximum-security prisons in the United States and selects every 50th name.

2 She groups inmates by type of crime, determines the percentage of the total in each crime category, and uses that to select a representative proportion randomly from each group.

3 She groups maximum-security prisons by state, randomly selects 10 states and, from those 10, randomly selects three people.

Other commonly used terms

As mentioned previously there are many different terms used in the study of psychology, such as those shown in Table 2.3.

▶ **Table 2.3:** A selection of terms you may encounter

Design flexibility	• This means that, during the course of the experiment, the design of the research changes due to interim or periodical feedback which is used to change the focus of the study.
Grounded theory	• This form of theory uses the inductive method (starts with the facts or examples and then draws conclusions). You generally start with no idea, prediction or hypothesis for an outcome but the theory comes from information gathered from data.
Narrative inquiry	• A qualitative methodology that refers to the process of information gathering using a storytelling approach. An example of a narrative research approach is Huynh and Rhodes (2011), where psychologists explored connections between distressing events and the career choice of mental-health professionals.
Probability	• This is a sampling method that uses a form of random selection (every person in the population has an equal chance of being selected). In contrast, non-probability sampling uses non-random processes.

Research process

Before starting your research you need to understand the steps you must take to produce an effective piece of research.

Many researchers experience anxieties about how best to conduct their research. These may include the following:

▶ The research process is daunting.
▶ Do I have the relevant qualifications required?
▶ Do I have the time?
▶ Statistics = mathematics = fears that this is too challenging.
▶ How do I start?
▶ What do I research?
▶ I am uncertain about how to use different terminology.
▶ Blind alleys: what if my research takes me nowhere (I find nothing new)?

Research is exciting, challenging and worthwhile. Think of research as your way of making a difference, developing and generating new ideas, pushing forward an area of practice or provision or even helping those who are in need.

Key steps to conducting research

Where to start

You may already have a burning issue that you feel passionate about, or you may have an idea of an area but no particular focus. Research ideas can be triggered by your curiosity or interest, by a specific focus in the news, or by an issue in your line of work or study. The following steps will help you to define your research question:

▶ Gather information on your broad topic and then narrow it down to different areas. Have a look for points in the media, news or perhaps from discussions with others in the field and see whether there are any outstanding questions or ideas that you think would be worth pursuing. The internet is a good starting point to find out about research in your topic area. Make notes of what you find and where you found it (webpages, references).

▶ Look out for key authors in your area of study. For example, you may want to explore the ways that Pavlov's theories of classical conditioning have been used in practice, so you would reference his book *In Practice*.

▶ Make sure the topic interests you. There is nothing worse than conducting research on something that does not seem interesting to you. It will make the research process uninspiring.

▶ Consider the potential impact of your research. What would be the effect of your research on the wider population? Would your research help to improve particular practices, develop a new treatment, or provide a better explanation of a phenomenon? Is there a possible negative effect that you need to consider that may provide an unsatisfactory outcome?

▶ Consider your target audience. If you want to explore the effects of television food advertising on eating behaviour, you would use a group of 13-year-old children rather than a group of six-month-old babies.

Once you have identified your research topic, your task is then to refine it down to a research question/hypothesis which is clear, focused and specific. Here are a few sample research questions to illustrate this point.

Clear vs. Unclear

Unclear: How can social media sites be harmful to mental health?

This example is unclear as it does not define a specific social media site so it could be any. The following example demonstrates how this question can be further refined.

Clear: How are online users of 'This is my place' addressing issues of mental health?

Focused vs. Unfocused

Unfocused: What is the effect of drugs on treating Alzheimer's?

Focused: What is the effect of 'mendmymind' drugs on reducing incidences of Alzheimer's in male patients over 50?

Simple v. Complex

Simple: How are psychologists addressing **ADHD** in children?

Sufficiently complex: What are the common traits of primary aged children with ADHD, and how can these traits support tutors in supporting children's developmental needs?

Key term

ADHD – Attention deficit hyperactivity disorder.

Research design

The research design is a report that illustrates the way that you intend to conduct your study. It is an important element of any research report as it will help other researchers replicate your study if they wanted to research further into the area. A research design includes methods and procedures used to collect and analyse data. There are a number of steps within a research design as seen in Figure 2.3.

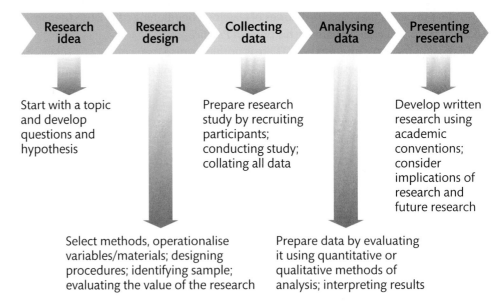

▶ **Figure 2.3:** The research (design) process

Your research should include an explanation of the participants you would use and any specific universal characteristics they may have. For example, you may want to recruit male participants between the ages of 30 and 40. Or you may want to recruit two groups with different characteristics, for example, one group taking warfarin and the other group not taking any medication for clinical trials on prevention of blood clotting. You should discuss your sample size and the method you will use.

Also incorporate a detailed account of the procedure you undertook to find your research topic. These could be the participants you chose, their characteristics, the number of participants, the materials you used to gather your data (questionnaires, observations, experimental tools) as well as the data analysis tools you used (numerical statistical analysis or qualitative interpretive methods such as themes and trends). You will read about these in more depth in the next section, but for now you just need to know about the importance of the research design in reporting your research.

Ethical considerations

As a researcher it is important that you follow a set of principles to ensure that your research meets required standards and adheres to set processes. These are generally known as ethical codes of conduct and they must be followed when conducting research. Following and adhering to ethical guidelines is one of the most important conditions when conducting research as it ensures that all participants are protected. It also makes a research study more robust. Participants should be willing to take part in research and not fear for their own physical or psychological safety.

Ethical codes of conduct

The principles of ethical guidelines and codes of conduct of research were developed following the inhumane experiments of the Nazis in the Second World War. Countries set up their own guidelines when conducting scientific research. In the UK these were created by the British Psychological Society (BPS) and in the USA, the American Psychological Association (APA). Organisations and institutions will also have their own codes of conduct. It is important to check on this before embarking on any research studies.

▸ Physical harm – the BPS state that participants must not be exposed to more risk than they would in everyday life.

▸ Psychological harm – this is a difficult area to be specific about but may involve anxiety, stress, lack of confidence and embarrassment.

▸ Confidentiality – data protection legislation requires that the identity of all participants remains confidential. It also includes safeguarding privacy.

▸ The right to withdraw (from the study) and to withdraw data – participants should be fully informed before any research starts about expectations, the role they are required to undertake, and how they can withdraw from the study and/or have their data removed.

▸ Advance payment – it is not permitted to offer forms of reward to participants to take part in a study as this can place additional stress on participants who may feel obliged to take part.

Key term

Confederate (or 'stooge') – people who are part of an experiment and act exactly how the researcher instructs them. Other participants are led to believe that the confederate is a participant like them, but they are asked to behave/speak in a particular way that the researcher instructs them.

Case study

A study by Milgram (1963) studied people's tendency to obedience towards authority figures. Participants were paired with another person and assigned roles of tutor and learner. The learner was a **confederate**, who had electrodes attached to his arm and the tutor controlled an electric shock generator. The researcher instructed the tutor to apply higher levels of voltage to the learner when they got a question wrong. No electrical voltage was actually used and the learner was instructed to act as if they were receiving a shock. Each time the tutor refused to give a shock the researcher instructed them to 'please continue'. The aim was to see how far the tutor would obey the researcher. Results demonstrated that 65 per cent of the participants (tutors) continued to the highest level of 450 volts therefore conforming to the authority figure (the researcher).

1 What are the ethical considerations in this research?
2 Can you think of any way that this study could have been made more ethical?
3 Refer back to the BPS Code of Human Research. Identify the key areas that demonstrate this type of research study would not be used in the current day.

Research

In Unit 1 you read about the Stanford Prison Experiment. Go back to page 24 and read about the case and consider the ethical implications of such a study. What were the key ethical issues? What is the risk of harm?

Research

The Human Rights Act (1998) is an Act of UK Parliament which incorporated the rights of individuals contained in the European Convention on Human Rights. Research this act online. How do you think the European Convention on Human Rights protects participants in a research project?

Ethics committee – a panel that looks at your research proposal and says whether it is safe and ethical. It will confirm whether you can start work on your project.

Informed consent – consent provided by a participant to take part in a study. Participants have the full knowledge of the possible consequences of their involvement.

When conducting research, to make sure you are working ethically and legally, you need to gain ethical approval from an appropriate person or panel before you start. If you conduct any research as part of your course, ethical clearance will come from your tutor, college or school or school **ethics committee**.

Informed consent

You must gain **informed consent** from your participants to show that they are fully aware of what is expected of them, and what the outcome is expected to be. Having participants sign or confirm consent is important as it also protects the researcher from participants who may wish to complain about their treatment in a study. 'Informed' consent means that you have given the participants full details of the study so you are asking them to sign their acceptance and understanding of the study. Informed consent can be given verbally but it is better to obtain it in written form.

Researchers should ensure that participants have the mental capacity to understand and appreciate requirements fully. Sometimes informed consent may not be available or attainable, for example in health research where research can only be conducted on incapacitated patients, or where providing informed consent to participants may cause unnecessary distress or confusion (patients who are recovering from serious diseases may be focused on their recovery and they may perceive their doctor is unsure which treatment is the best). Informed consent would normally include the following:

▸ a brief introduction to yourself and your experience and interest in the research
▸ a description of the research you are interested in conducting
▸ details of the procedures you will follow and the input you require from the participant
▸ details of any risks to the participant and how you will mitigate against these risks
▸ benefits to the participant in taking part in the research
▸ opportunities for the participant to ask questions
▸ the option for the participant to be able to withdraw at any time without being penalised
▸ an explanation of how the information will be collected, and how it will remain confidential
▸ a section where you, the participant or other relevant individual (such as a parent or carer) signs and dates the consent form.

Obtaining permission

It is very important that the participant fully understands what they are required to do and that they act as a willing participant. In some instances, informed consent will be obtained from others on behalf of participants. For example, where a participant is under 18 it is usual that informed consent is obtained from the child's parent or carer. An elderly or disabled participant may have reduced mental capacity so consent would need to be obtained from a carer.

In some instances, **gatekeeper** consent may be required in order to conduct a research study. An example of this would be a headteacher of a school giving consent for a research study of children in the school. In some instances, the headteacher may provide **blanket consent**.

Data protection

There are various forms of legislation that a researcher also needs to follow, including ensuring they meet all relevant data protection legislation.

Any data collected through a research study is protected under the terms of the Data Protection Act (2018) and General Data Protection Regulation (GDPR). It is important

Gatekeeper – someone who acts as an intermediary between the participants and the researcher. They may also have power to grant or deny access to research participants.

Blanket consent – sometimes given to provide authority to conduct research activity without requiring additional approval. In the case of school children, a headteacher may provide blanket consent where they themselves have already provided information to parents that the school is 'research active'.

to show that all information is kept confidential. To ensure data is confidential it should be stored in a place that no one can access. This could mean physical hard copies in a locked drawer or filing cabinet, or ensuring that any electronic files, whether on a desktop or laptop are stored using a password. If you share a network or computers then you should always ensure that no information about your participants or the study can be seen by other users. Research should also only ever be used for its stated purpose. For example, if an organisation conducted a study to test a new drug on a group of participants, they cannot then use that data to move forward with a different but similar drug.

You should only disclose information important to the study and ensure you do not identify participants. You can do this by changing the identities of participants either by using numbers, codes or **pseudonyms**. For example John Driver could become JD or Participant A. The location of the research participants or research study should also be changed. For example, the researcher might state the research was conducted in a rural location in the south-east of England rather than in a rural location in the north-east of England. If the location is critical to the analysis of the results, say for example 'the percentage of women unemployed in a certain area', then the location would need to be revealed. The location of the actual study should also be hidden in any reports.

Human and animal rights

There are differences in the legal rights of humans and animals in research studies. Human rights are covered by the legislation and acts mentioned previously. In the UK animal rights are protected by the Animals (Scientific Procedures) Act 1986, which banned research on great apes. Since 1998, it is also illegal in the UK for companies to test cosmetics and their ingredients on animals.

However, animals are still often used in research studies in the field of psychology. This can be controversial and many researchers ensure that the rights of animals in studies are protected through carefully controlled measures. Research on animals is permitted if suffering is minimised and there are benefits to humans – benefits that could not be obtained by using other methods. The three Rs are often used in research with animals.

▶ Reduction – reducing the number of animals used by improving experimental techniques and sharing information with other researchers.
▶ Refinement – changing the way the experiment is conducted so the animals are cared for and do not suffer.
▶ Replacement – finding alternative techniques, such as computer models.

> **Key term**
>
> **Pseudonym** – an alias or made-up name used to protect the identity of the participant.

> **Research**
>
> Split your class into two groups. Prepare for a debate with one side in favour of using animals in research, the other against. Ensure you back up all of your points with evidence.

Personal and professional approach

As a researcher it is important that you create the right image and display the professional behaviour necessary for being an effective psychological scientist.

Think about your own personal presentation: how you dress and how you relate to others. Put yourself in the place of the participant. Look at the photos. What impression do you form from them? If you had the choice, which person would you feel more comfortable with when answering their questions?

▶ Which person would you feel more comfortable with?

You must consider the way in which you conduct yourself during the research process. Some of the areas you should consider are listed below:

▶ Keeping participants fully informed – you must ensure participants are aware of what is happening in the study throughout the process, within reason. For example, if you find you are not getting the information you need using some of the methods you introduced and then changed (for example, you changed from interviews to observations) you must ensure that your participants are aware of this and are happy to continue with the research.

▶ Duty of care to report health and safety concerns – you must maintain the highest professional standards and ensure that you do not endanger any participants or yourselves. This is particularly important where you are conducting research with children, or vulnerable adults as well as those with reduced mental capacity. Your school or college will have a policy that outlines how you need to ensure your own health and safety, and that of those around you. You also have a duty to disclose information where you see a safeguarding issue. For example, if carrying out observations in a school setting and you observe a child being bullied, you have a duty to report this to the tutor of the class.

▶ Equality and diversity – you must remain totally unbiased in all actions and practices. You cannot let your own personal opinions affect your work with participants. You must also not allow factors such as race or gender to influence your research or take advantage of any personal relationships you may have.

Research

Find policies and procedures in your school or college or on the internet about health and safety, and safeguarding. Make a list of how this can relate to you in a research situation. Compare your notes with your peers.

It is inevitable that a relationship might develop between a researcher and a participant. Remaining unbiased or objective is one area the researcher needs to be aware of; this is known as **investigator effects**. The researcher may have expectations on the behaviour of the participants or be influenced by their own expectations when interpreting data. For example, steering participants towards the outcome they want to see, or only picking the data that matches that outcome. When a researcher picks elements from the data to produce desired results this is known as 'massaging' the data.

> **Key term**
>
> **Investigator effects** – a participant's behaviour may be affected by the relationship with the researcher. A number of different factors could affect the participant's responses and behaviours including age, gender, ethnic group, appearance, expressions and communication styles.

Researchers need to remain objective. Being able to report data in a factual way is a key skill. As the researcher, you must ensure that you do not offer your own opinions about what people may be thinking; remaining objective means reporting the facts and suggesting links.

Demand characteristics

A demand characteristic is where the participant behaves in a way that they think the research demands of them and not in their normal manner. For example, during a questionnaire a participant may anticipate a question and why the researcher is asking it rather than giving an honest response. They say what they think the researcher wants to hear. This is known as **social desirability bias.**

> **Key term**
>
> **Social desirability bias** – where participants are concerned about how they appear, so do not respond honestly. They may change their behaviour or responses to what they perceive as more favourable.

Here are two more examples of demand characteristics:

- Evaluation apprehension – a participant may change their behaviour because they feel they are being judged or evaluated.
- Faithfulness and faithlessness – a participant could try to guess the purpose of the research and then act in a way that they feel is helpful to the researcher (or to be deliberately unhelpful).

Literature reviews

Earlier we looked at ways that you could define a research question by exploring other research undertaken in the area. The process of conducting a search and evaluation of other literature about the topic you are researching is often called 'a literature review'.

Prior to a research study, it is important to conduct a literature review to show what research has been carried out in your area of interest. It helps you understand what has already been done and is useful in providing insights into areas that still require further exploration. A review of literature in your subject area will allow you to:

- gain knowledge of your subject area
- find limitations and gaps in knowledge
- gain information about existing research to rethink/ focus your own research area
- understand how others have researched areas (questions, methods, data, results) and interpreted findings
- build a body of information to include in your introduction that introduces the purpose of your own research study and the questions you seek to answer.

The literature review will provide a basis for the report you include when you present your research project. It provides a background and rationale (reasons) justifying your research questions. Research you find in the area can be used to confirm points you are trying to make as well as demonstrate differences when comparing them with your findings.

A literature review (or literature search) involves:

- reading and reviewing a wide range of primary and secondary sources on a particular issue, to gain a deeper understanding
- finding out what has been researched previously to inform your own research question
- evaluating how reliable a source is. You need to understand where the researchers gathered their information from
- refining your questions/hypotheses or focus in response to the literature you have found.

An important point to remember is that the research process is a **recursive** exercise which is why your research questions/hypotheses can change the focus and direction of your research at any time. This is true also of the literature review. It is useful to consider the model in Figure 2.4 when conducting a literature review.

> **Key term**
>
> **Recursive** – repeating a process, for example you start with a question and you read something which changes your mind about the question. You then refine your question and search for new literature.

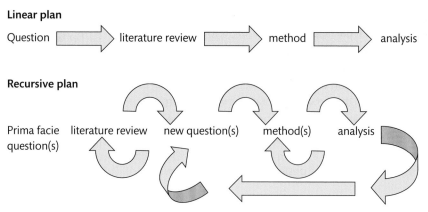

Linear plan

Question ➡ literature review ➡ method ➡ analysis

Recursive plan

Prima facie question(s)   literature review   new question(s)   method(s)   analysis

▶ **Figure 2.4:** A recursive research process

▶ Figure 2.4 illustrates how it is normal that the whole research process, not just the literature search, can be modified and adapted at every stage and your question can differ dramatically between your start and end point.

▶ An important aspect of conducting a literature search is to make notes, and to record and organise the information you gain. Good organisational skills will allow you to work more efficiently and improve your time management.

When conducting a literature search, you should record the key features of the literature you find. The following headings may be of use when noting down the key information and will help you when completing your reference list for your research report.

▶ Title
▶ Author
▶ Source/publisher (for example, journal, government site)
▶ Date of publication
▶ Page number(s) (for books and journals)
▶ Date a webpage was accessed
▶ URL of webpage
▶ Key points (for example what the research was about, methods used, key findings)
▶ Connections to other sources of information and your own research questions

Table 2.4 lists some of the sources of information you may use.

▶ **Table 2.4:** Sources of information for literature reviews

Source	Types of literature	Reliability of source
Internet and library sources, for example, using Google Scholar or your school or college library	Research articles	• Some areas provide full research articles, others provide only links • Good to use as a starting point but you would need to identify whether the information is reliable and valid
Media	Newspapers, specialist magazines e.g., Nursery World, Mental Health Today	• Free resource • May only give summary of research
Journals	British Psychological Society journals	• Reliable source • Need subscription
Statistical information, for example, from the Office for National Statistics	Information on population, e.g., gender, children born in a particular year, instances of obesity or depression	• Generally reliable data provided from authorised sources, for example, government bodies from census

Assessing the validity and reliability

It can be difficult to identify whether the information you have found is valid and reliable. Ask yourself the following questions when assessing the reliability of a source.

▶ Does the website look professional? Where is the site located and are they still current? Currency usually relates to research that has been conducted within the past ten years.

▶ If the information comes from an academic journal, is the source a trusted one? You can check this to see if the articles in the journals are **peer reviewed**.

▶ Who is the author? What are their qualifications or credentials? Are they an expert in their field?

▶ Does the source relate to the topic you are interested in exploring?

▶ How current are the sources (information more than 10 years old may not be relevant or reliable)?

▶ Do the methodologies and results sound convincing and well thought out?

Key term
Peer reviewed – work that has been examined by other experts in the field before it is published.

Academic conventions

You need to be able to know how a research report should be presented and the use of referencing conventions and techniques. The following outlines how a report in psychological inquiry is normally presented.

▶ Title page – includes the author and details of their location, for example, their university, and the date of their publication.

▶ Abstract – a brief summary of around 250 words that provides an outline of the study and its conclusions.

▶ Introduction – background information on the topic. This includes the general theory introducing the topic, narrowed down to the key areas of the literature review. It should end with the key focus of your own research study, and research questions or hypotheses.

▶ Method – you need to assume the reader has no knowledge of what you have done so that if they wanted to replicate your study, they could base their study on what you include in this section. You should write in the past tense.

▶ Design – if you are using an experiment here you would indicate the independent and dependent variables. You would identify any control measures used.

▶ Participants – you need to identify the target population and type of sample you are using in your study. You would report on how you obtained the sample and give details about any specific factors.

▶ Materials or methods of data collection – for this section you would include the types of data collection methods you have used, whether it was a controlled experiment, the equipment you used, questionnaires, surveys.

▶ Procedure – you need to describe the exact procedures you followed when you carried out the research. Again, you need to do this in a way that would allow another researcher to replicate your study.

▶ Results – this is where you report what you have found. You will have conducted a data analysis. You can present results using a range of methods.

▶ Discussion – this is an outline of your findings that compares the background research and information with your research findings. You should discuss how confident you are that the results are reliable. You should also include any suggestions for improving the study and the implications of your findings on research, best practice or future research. Your discussion may also suggest further research that could be triggered from your results.

Link

How to present your results will be covered in more detail later in this unit.

When writing up any report, it is important to follow prescribed conventions when you are acknowledging someone else's work. You must be careful to avoid **plagiarism** (quoting other people's work without giving them credit). You must correctly cite and reference any work that is not wholly your own. You should do this by acknowledging and citing sources as you write. Look at the following example illustrating how you should acknowledge another author's work.

> Whiteman (2011, p. 408) states that 'Chomsky likened the linguistic neural structure to the light receptors of the eye – inborn and not a result of learning.'

A reference list is a list of all the sources you have cited in your report in alphabetical order.

A bibliography is a list of books or research you have used but have not cited in your work. Both the reference list and the bibliography should follow conventions.

Normally for psychology you follow the American Psychological Society (APA) guidelines. However, another commonly used method is the Harvard referencing system. In the text, for both referencing styles you would include the year and page number as above. When the author's name is not mentioned you should also include this in the text as shown in the example below.

> It has been said that 'Chomsky likened the linguistic neural structure to the light receptors of the eye – inborn and not a result of learning' (Whiteman, 2011, p. 408).

Table 2.5 shows how references should be presented in your list.

▶ **Table 2.5:** A brief outline of how references should be set out in a reference list, using the Harvard system

Referencing journal articles: Information appears in this order	Referencing a book: Information appears in this order	Referencing webpages
Author, last name first, and initial	Author, last name first, and initial	Name of author/organisation responsible for the site (if available the date the site was available)
Date	Date	The date you accessed the webpage (year and month)
Title of article	Book title	Any title of the article
Journal title	Place of publication: publisher	URL address between brackets where possible
Volume (and issue number)	Edition	
Page numbers	Page numbers	Page numbers where referred to
Example:	Example:	Example:
Shaw, G. (2017) Exploring experiences of frequent transience on children's psychological welfare. Psychology research in the day Vol 22:12 pp24 - 32	Whitman, D. (2011) Cognition. MA: John Wiley and Sons	Shaw, G. (2017) Exploring experiences of frequent transience on children's psychological welfare. Accessed Jan 2018 [http://www.mywebportal.com]
Note: For multiple authors you would follow these conventions:		
• For more than one author you cite each author. • For four or more authors you cite the first author's name followed by 'et al' (Latin abbreviation for 'and others').		

Assessment activity 2.1

A primary teaching assistant in a special needs school is interested in finding out about the ways tutors support children with autism in joining in with class activities. She wants to find out the views of parents of children with autism and the four class tutors in two local schools.

She needs to consider the impact of any research she conducts in this area and how it can support improving practice and provision.

She also needs to consider the types of research which would be best for this type of study, for example, experiments, desk-based research, case studies and the sample selection methods that might be used. She would also have to consider the ethical considerations in conducting research with children, particularly about gaining informed consent.

Include examples of the ways that this type of research can support practice and/or provision and possible wider implications on policy and training. Think about the best way to gather information. What conventions would you need to think about when preparing a report based on a research study in this area?

Plan
- What is the task? What am I being asked to do?
- How confident do I feel in my ability to perform this task?
- What areas might I struggle with?

Do
- I know what I am doing and my aims.
- I know where I have gone wrong and have adjusted my approach to get myself back on task.

Review
- I can explain the task and how I approached it.
- I can explain how I might do it differently next time.

 PAUSE POINT   Can you explain what an experiment is? Can you give an example of an experiment?

Hint   Think about the difference between dependent variables and independent variables.

Extend   Can you explain any factors that could affect your experiment?

B Plan research to investigate psychological questions

Research methods

There are three main approaches towards research: qualitative, quantitative and mixed methods. There is no one recommended approach to your research and much of the time your decision is based on the type of research questions/hypotheses you are investigating. It is important you understand the different approaches to be able to choose the right method for your research.

Quantitative research methods

Quantitative methods are said to be more **objective** in that they report on the facts and look for the effects of one thing on another (cause and effect). Quantitative data uses measurement and is therefore generally used to generate graphs and charts of **raw data**. The quantitative researcher's aim is to establish general laws, and the purpose of research is to test a theory and support or reject it. It is not concerned with the underlying factors that can be attributed to feelings and emotions.

Key terms

Objective – based on what is seen and reported factually, not influenced by opinions, feelings, or beliefs.

Raw data – data that has not been analysed.

Methods of data collection

Quantitative data is a means of expressing findings in a numerical format. Normally there is a measurement associated with the data, in the form of units such as height, weight or age. Qualitative data describes findings explaining behaviours, feelings and opinions. Quantitive data can be produced using six key methods.

▶ Questionnaires – a questionnaire is a tool used in research which consists of a series of questions seeking to gather information from participants about the research study. Questionnaires can be carried out by post or email, face to face or on the telephone. They are relatively cheap to develop and are a quick way to obtain large amounts of information from a large sample group (participants). Questionnaires can ask both open questions ('Tell me about your experiences when you were ill') and closed questions ('Do you think this drug is right for the experiment?'). In this way they can gather numerical or quantitative data (for the closed questions which elicit yes/no responses) and qualitative data for the open questions.

▶ Experiments (laboratory, field and natural) – experiments taking place in the laboratory are conducted under controlled situations so that any interference that will affect results can be reduced. This is not the case with field or natural experiments as these are conducted generally in the environment where there are many factors that can influence results.

▶ Quasi experiments – the word 'quasi' means 'similar'. This type of research resembles experimental research but is not true experimental research because participants are not randomly assigned to conditions. In this type of experiment, the IV is manipulated before the DV is measured and because participants are not randomly assigned to conditions there is a risk that confounding variables will interfere with the findings.

▶ Controlled observations – these are used to observe behaviours in a laboratory environment. Participants are randomly allocated to groups, with the researcher remaining independent of the group (non-participant). These observations are quick, replicable data that is often generalisable as it can be conducted on large sample sizes.

▶ Interviews – these can be conducted with one individual or a group of individuals. Interviews contain questions that have been designed to draw out information from participants that will help to answer your research question(s). They are normally used as a qualitative method but can be used to gain quantitative data through yes/ no questions, for example.

▶ Checklists – an example of where a checklist could be used is for recording the number of times a person displays a type of behaviour in a timeframe. It could also be used during different times of the day to see whether a participant reacts differently to a set trigger.

▶ Surveys - most commonly used in psychology research. A method aimed at collecting self-report data from participants. You can focus on opinions or factual information about participants and is useful for describing specific factors or characteristics of a large population. This type of method is useful as it can gather large amounts of information from a wide range of the population.

▶ Learning to pick the right method for your research is important.

Some key features of quantitative methods are that:
- ▶ data analysis generally takes the form of descriptive statistics that are used to summarise the data
- ▶ researchers aim to control variables by conducting studies in controlled environments (laboratories)
- ▶ the study is designed and set before it begins
- ▶ researchers seek reality which is objective and exists separately to the researcher, meaning the results can be seen by anyone.

Quantitative research uses closed questions that require answers that do not need further elaboration, for example, only yes/no answers or those that can be answered on a scale:
- ▶ How many people aged 16–20 years old have schizophrenia?
- ▶ What is the frequency of schizophrenic episodes in 16–20 year-olds?

Key features of experimentation

Earlier in this unit, you learned about some of the key features of **experimentation**. Table 2.6 provides a reminder of the key elements of experimental design. Using experimental design is one of the main methods used to gain quantitative data. It can use controlled observations, questionnaires generating closed questions, or rating scales. Quantitative research involves testing of hypotheses and theories. This allows researchers to assess the accuracy of their predictions.

Key term

Experimentation – a design where the researcher manipulates a particular variable and observes the effect of this manipulation on an outcome such as a participant's behaviour.

▶ **Table 2.6:** The key features of experimentation

Independent variable (IV)	The variable the experimenter manipulates or changes, which the researcher thinks will have a direct effect on the dependent variable.
Dependent variable (DV)	The variable the experimenter measures. This forms the result of the study.
Extraneous variable (EV)	A variable that is not an independent variable but could affect the results (DV) of the experiment.
Confounding variable (CV)	A variable that affects both the independent and dependent variables and causes the appearance of an association that may not necessarily be correct and could influence the results of a study.
Directional hypothesis	A (one-tailed) hypothesis that predicts the nature of the effect of the IV on the DV. For example, children will accurately identify four animals found in a zoo.
Non-directional hypothesis	A (two-tailed) hypothesis that predicts that the IV will have an effect on the DV but the direction of the effect is not stated. For example, there will be a difference in how many animals from a zoo a child can identify.
Null hypothesis	A hypothesis that predicts no relationship between the two variables (one does not affect the other). For example, children can remember a number of animals from the zoo but this is due to chance as some children may have been to the zoo more than other children.

Advantages and disadvantages

There are advantages to using quantitative research. Each step in quantitative testing is standardised to reduce bias when collecting and analysing data. As everything is controlled, results are therefore seen to be valid, reliable and **generalisable** to a large population. This method is good for studies that involve numbers, for example measuring difference between groups, assessing effectiveness of new treatments.

There are disadvantages. As quantitative experiments take place in controlled, rigid settings, the researcher may miss essential elements of human behaviour. Also larger sample sizes are required to enable a more accurate analysis, so affecting the ability to generalise across a population. Table 2.7 shows some of the advantages and disadvantages of the different research methods.

> **Key term**
>
> **Generalisable** – a term to describe the extent to which research findings can be applied to the rest of the population.

▶ **Table 2.7:** Advantages and disadvantages of quantitative research methods

Advantages	Disadvantages
Good where systematic, standardised comparisons are required.	Can produce evidence that answers 'what' questions but cannot always explain 'why' something occurs.
Using a larger sample size can make the research more generalisable.	Using fewer people can have the opposite effect as it is then difficult to generalise as the sample is too small.
Emergent not predetermined. Data emerges from tests and experiment. The results of an experiment show clearly outcomes which are not influenced by researcher or participant interpretation.	Data is interpretive and can be influenced by the researcher's interpretation as well as the participant's perception or wish to divulge some information (or data cannot take account of non-numerical data such as human beliefs, thoughts, feelings).
As quantitative research uses statistical methods, it can mean the analysis is considered more reliable.	Survey instruments may be vulnerable to errors, for example mistakes in measurement, or flawed sampling techniques.
Outcomes are easy to measure and results can be clearly shown and easily predicted.	Statistical reports may not give an accurate picture, for example 98% of a sample size of 10 is not an accurate picture of the whole population.

Issues in quantitative research

Generalisability is an issue in quantitative research. Researchers select sample sizes for their studies which could be individuals, or a small or large group. The samples are intended to represent the 'whole population'. For example, a study looks at the effects of a treatment on 15,000 men aged between 18 and 20. Results could be generalised as the sample size was large and results would be considered reliable. However, if the same experiment was conducted on a sample size of 10 men, results could not be representative of the whole population.

Key term

Generalisability – how far we can apply our findings of our research to the target population we are interested in.

Methods of data analysis

There are a number of ways that quantitative data collected can be analysed as you will see below. It can be displayed in simple ways that enable the reader to gain a quick snapshot view of the findings.

▸ Descriptive statistics – the way that data can be described using their basic features. Descriptives provide a simple summary about the sample and the measures involved. Descriptives are just the data found; researchers do not have anything to do with generalising beyond what is in front of them.

Time taken to complete a maze	
Participant number	Time in minutes (seconds)
1	10.03
2	7.24
3	12.05
4	6.55

This analysis provides a breakdown of the basic features in a study. It is useful for providing a simple summary of your findings, including the sample and the measures. Normally, it would be used alongside graphs that show your data in more detail.

▸ Nominal – this is a way of labelling or naming your variables. Some examples could include:

What is your gender?

Male – M

Female – F

What drink do you prefer?

A – Coffee

B – Tea

C – Hot chocolate

▸ Ordinal – this is a way of ordering data, for example, from the highest to the lowest. What ordinal data cannot tell you, however, is the difference between scales. An example of ordinal data is:

How satisfied are you with your treatment?

1 Very unsatisfied

2 Somewhat dissatisfied

3 Neither satisfied or not satisfied

4 Somewhat satisfied

5 Very satisfied

Link

How to complete data analysis will be covered on page 117.

- Interval levels of data – like ordinal analysis, this is a way of ordering (normally numerical) data. The difference is that, in this case, the exact difference between each item is known. For example, a temperate scale like the Celsius scale is interval data, as there are exactly 10° between items.
- Measures of central tendency and dispersion:
  - Central tendency is the central or typical value of your data. It can be measured through mean, median or mode, which will be looked at in more detail later.
  - Dispersion is how much your data is stretched or squeezed. It can be measured through standard deviation, which will be looked at in more detail later.

Case study

In 1958, Harlow separated eight monkeys from their mothers immediately after birth and placed them in cages with access to two surrogate mothers. Both 'mothers' were made of wire, but one was covered with soft towelling. Four monkeys were given milk by the wire monkey and four by the monkey with cloth.

Result: Both groups spent more time with the cloth mother (even where no milk was given).

Conclusion: For a monkey to develop normally they must interact with an object with which they can cling to during the first few months of life (their critical period). Later emotional damage that resulted from this early maternal deprivation could be reversed in monkeys, if an attachment was made before the end of this critical period.

1 What quantitative method do you think was used in this study?

2 How do you think Harlow ensured his results were valid and reliable?

▶ Harlow's monkeys

PAUSE POINT It is difficult to remember some of the key terms used in quantitative research. Check your understanding of the key terms used so far in this unit and compare it with the glossary.

> **Hint**　Think about the way that qualitative research can be used to understand feelings and opinions and quantitative research used to determine what causes something to happen. Can you explain any factors that could affect your experiment?

> **Extend**　Write the key terms onto flashcards so you have a set for your revision.

Qualitative research methods

Qualitative research is subjective. When conducting this type of research you are looking for the subjective meaning that people attach to their actions and events that occur to them. Qualitative research looks at individuals' feelings, opinions and emotions and seeks to explain meaning rather than quantify 'what' or 'how many'. The approach is inductive in that you collect your data and analyse it to develop explanations or theories. Quantitative data can still be used when analysing and reporting qualitative data. For example, you might want to identify the trends occurring within responses.

Some key features of qualitative methods include the following points.
▶ Studies are conducted in real-world situations, in natural settings.
▶ Researchers collect data themselves through observing behaviours, reviewing documents, and interviewing participants.
▶ Researchers collect multiple forms of data including observations, interviews and other documents. They rarely rely on one single data source.
▶ Researchers focus on understanding the meaning that participants give about the problem or issue they are exploring.
▶ Researchers try to devise a complex picture to a phenomenon which involves reporting multiple perspectives. They are not bound by tight cause and effect relationships used in experimental design studies but are more concerned with identifying the complex interaction of factors in any situation.

Qualitative research uses open questions. These allow answers that provide an explanation of people's feelings and emotions. For example:
▶ Tell me what happened when you undertook the programme of treatment?
▶ Tell me your views on whether fizzy drinks affect a child's level of activity?
▶ How do you feel about your recent change in job role?

Methods of data collection

Some of the methods used for qualitative research are listed in Table 2.8.

▶ **Table 2.8:** Qualitative research methods

Qualitative research methods and approaches	Uses
Questionnaires/Surveys	• Common method used in qualitative research methods • Can gather large amounts of data across a range of subjects • Allows participants to explain their feelings, behaviours, thoughts • Can use a mix of closed and open questions • Can be quick and easy to administer • Can collect both qualitative and quantitative data
Interviews	• One of the most common qualitative research methods • Personal interview carried out with individual participants, generally used one-to-one • Can use a mix of closed and open questions, generally conversational method that provides opportunities to get in-depth detail from participant • Provides opportunity to gain precise data about people's feelings, opinions and beliefs • Can be performed face to face, online, via the telephone, or by post • Quick and easy to administer • Can be time consuming to undertake and conduct, as well as to transcribe and collate
Controlled observations (structured)	• Generally a quantitative method, but can be used to gain qualitative data as well • Participants are randomly allocated to independent variable groups and can easily be replicated using the same observation schedule • Data obtained is easier and quicker to analyse (as it is numerical) through means of an observation schedule which monitors behaviours, patterns over a time frame • Fairly quick to conduct so many observations can take place within a short time frame, e.g., an observer can watch a given behaviour every 15 seconds (see Mary Ainsworth)
Naturalistic observation	• Usually unstructured and involves exploring spontaneous behaviour in natural surroundings • Can take the form of **structured** or **unstructured observations** • Researcher records what they see • Studies take place in natural environments • Ability to observe behaviours as they occur in own natural environments results in greater **ecological validity** • Often generates new ideas and may suggest new lines of enquiry • Can be unreliable as other variables cannot be controlled

Key terms

Structured observations – where the researcher gathers data without direct involvement with the participants.

Unstructured observations – where the researcher records everything; there is no plan about what data to collect.

Ecological validity – the extent to which findings can be attributed to real-life settings.

Participant observation	• The researcher joins in and is part of the group they study • Researcher takes a false identify and/or role, for example, posing as a genuine member of the group; alternatively, they can reveal their true identity and purpose of study. (This could be classified as unethical as it is deliberately misleading and misrepresenting the researcher and others.) • Difficult when conducting covert research as it risks identifying the researcher • Researcher may lose objectivity and become biased due to their close proximity to their subjects, for example, their views may be influenced
Non-participant observation	• Researcher sits away from the situation and observes behaviours and events • Researcher can use a range of methods including running narratives of events or behaviours as they occur, time and event sampling to identify triggers and responses to behaviours
Focus groups	• Usually includes a smaller number of participants (5–10) • Aims to answer 'why', 'what', 'where', 'how' questions • Good for market research, such as testing new products and treatments • Can be online or face to face • Can be expensive to administer
Ethnographic research	• Researcher observes participants in their own natural environment • Aims to understand cultures, challenges and motivations as they occur • Relies on experience over interviews and discussion groups • Can last from a few days to more **longitudinal** research • Challenging and requires determination, time and expertise of researcher to be able to observe and infer data
Case studies	• An in-depth study of a situation, person or group • Data can be collected using observations and interviews • Can take place over extended period of time • Widely used in psychology, for example, Sigmund Freud's 'Little Hans' (1909) • Can be costly and time consuming

Advantages and disadvantages

The main advantage of using qualitative research over quantitative research is that it can produce **rich data** and a deeper understanding of the subject. This is because it provides an opportunity to explore a topic in greater depth.

If you wished, for example, to find out about people's attitudes to support services for mental health using a quantitative approach, you would just ask 'Do you think support services are adequate for mental health patients?' The answer would probably be either yes or no, and is therefore a closed response. You would not know the reasons why participants have chosen this answer.

By using qualitative approaches, you can gain more information and find out why participants feel the way they do. You can ask more open-ended questions in order to elicit more information. By using qualitative methods, you can change your question to 'Can you explain how you feel about the level of services provided for mental health patients?'.

> **Key term**
>
> **Longitudinal** – research that takes time to complete, for example, ethnographic research can take years to accumulate the data of a remote tribe's day-to-day culture.
>
> **Rich data** – informative or 'deep' data which provides a deep insight into an idea. Provides a good illustration or explanation of why a person feels the way they do rather than just giving a yes/no answer.

▶ If you are interested in researching something like support services, who would you need to speak to?

Another advantage of qualitative research methods is that it allows the researcher more flexibility to explore a topic from different angles. In the example above, if a participant states they feel the level of one particular service is better than another, the researcher could probe this area further and ask why they feel this.

▶ **Table 2.9:** Advantages and disadvantages of qualitative research methods

Advantages	Disadvantages
Ability to gain rich, in-depth details from participants as they can elaborate on what they mean	Very hard to generalise due to small sample sizes and the subjective nature of the research
Taps into the reasons behind the ways that people behave or think the way they do	Very difficult to draw reliable and valid conclusions. Any conclusions need to be tentative (uncertain)
Very good where a deeper understanding of a phenomenon is required	Unreliable as different results could be found on a different day with different people
Events can be seen holistically (as a whole)	Generally can be more time consuming and expensive
Ability for researcher to explore areas in depth with participants	Lack of anonymity. In some topics participants may not be comfortable responding to some types of questions and prefer anonymous forms of research
Allows for a wide range of data to be reported	A risk of falsification where the researcher may change or omit data in order to achieve a desired outcome e.g., responses that match their own predictions

Case studies

Piaget's theory of cognitive development (1936) is perhaps one of the most classic examples of qualitative research. He was interested in the way children developed through the stages of life. He did this through systematic observation of children in their natural environments spending time observing children of different ages and stages of development to identify their patterns of growth and development.

One of the main disadvantages of case studies is that they can be time consuming. Conducting statistical analysis can be very quick and can take account of larger sample sizes. Qualitative data analysis often involves listening to and re-reading interviews, and it can also be difficult to generalise the results of research.

Methods of data analysis

There are a number of ways that the data that has been collected from qualitative data collection can be analysed.

▶ Thematic – one of the most common forms of analysis. This is a way of drawing out themes from your data. It involves looking at the data collected as a whole and pinpointing any themes across the piece.

▶ Narrative – often used when researching secondary sources, such as diaries or letters. This approach tends to consider the lives of those speaking or writing, as well as the subject which they're discussing.

▶ Content – Widley used research technique and can use a number of approaches (conventional, directed, summative). When using conventional content analysis, coding categories are devised directly from the text data. For summative content analysis the researcher counts and compares (keywords/content) and interprets information. Finally when using directed content analysis the researcher starts with a theory and this guides their initial codes.

▶ Grounded – Data collected is coding and organised around concepts. Categories are formed related to these categories and links made between them. A theoretical explanation is produced from this. The researcher uses a recursive method of going back to the data and development concepts and categories and a theoretical model. The idea behind this method is that theory emerges from what is found in the data.

▶ Discourse or conversation analysis – These forms of analysis explore naturally occurring language in a social context, widely used by anthropologists who analyse written or verbal language. A form of analysis that analyses written or verbal language and can even be of the written form, images and documents. They explore the way that language is used, its meaning and who speaks the language. It is a way of understanding a culture, group or individual in a particularly time and context.

Semi-structured methods
–Are those such as interviews and focus groups that do not rely solely on a predetermined list of features to observe or questions to ask. They allow participants to expand from statements and questions. For example, a researcher may ask a question 'how many times a day do you feel anxious on average'. When the participant gives a number they may expand e.g. 'two but it depends on the circumstances'. The researcher may want to find out more about what triggers these feelings of anxiety so asks the participant to expand.

Reviewing qualitative and quantitative methods

Table 2.10 looks at the differences between these two types of methods.

▶ **Table 2.10:** Consider these differences when choosing your research method

Qualitative research methods	Quantitative research methods
Focus is on describing individual experiences and beliefs	Focus is on describing characteristics of a population
Generally, uses open-ended questions	Uses closed questions
Use of **semi-structured methods** such as in-depth interviews, focus groups, observation	Methods used are highly structured, for example, controlled experiments
Data produced is descriptive and interpretive	Data produced is numerical and factual
Researcher's ongoing questions can be influenced by participants' responses	The responses given by participants do not influence or determine how and which questions the researcher asks

Mixed-methods research

This type of research uses a combination of quantitative and qualitative methods in the same study. It can add a higher level of insight into research that could not be gained from using either one of these approaches on its own. Quantitative data provides information about the strength of feeling and opinions, whereas qualitative data provides the reasons behind these. Each method complements the other and using them together produces more robust conclusions than using just one method. By aiding researchers to identify underlying causes and perceptions, using mixed methods can produce more valid and reliable results.

A simple example of a mixed-method research design would be a trial for a new treatment under controlled conditions with follow-up interviews with participants using a semi-structured approach. This would involve asking their views and feelings regarding their participation in the trial, as well as looking at the medical reports regarding the effectiveness of the treatment. The following examples illustrate how a mixed-methods research design can draw on data that provides valid and reliable data as well as providing the reasons behind this.

Questionnaires and interviews can include questions that elicit information that can be analysed using both qualitative and quantitative data methods.

1 Why do you like the colour green?

This produces the qualitative element because participants explain their reasons behind liking the colour green.

2 How many green clothes do you have?

This produces the quantitative element because participants give an example of how much they like the colour green through their choice of clothes.

Developing your research proposal

A good way of defining your research is to develop a research proposal that identifies the key features and steps you intend to take in conducting your research. The research proposal can be presented to an ethics committee and should provide them with the information they require to enable them to decide whether your research is realistic, achievable and meets ethical conventions.

Identifying and developing good research topic and questions/hypotheses

You may be daunted by the prospect of undertaking research and struggle with knowing where to start. It is quite normal to feel this way and one of the most important things to remember is that there is no 'right topic'. The most important thing to remember is that a piece of research is something that is important and genuinely interesting to you. It is demoralising to study a subject you have no interest in. Consider the following which will help you to identify your research questions.

▶ Brainstorm. Write down as many ideas as you can about the subject area you are investigating.

▶ Ask yourself: 'What am I really interested in?'; 'What do I not understand?'; 'Is the question answerable?'; 'Is my research likely to lead to a valid result?'

▶ Read around the subject area and look at other research.

▶ Explore what already exists in practice and provision. What will be the impact of your current research on this practice and provision?

▶ Explore the possible political implications on the type of research you wish to carry out. For example, would it make a significant impact in changing policy or practices across a particular sector?

▶ Look at the media. What is the news saying? What campaigns are being conducted?

Developing the proposal

A typical project proposal should include:

▶ the title of the research project

▶ the research aim and its academic or scientific rationale – you should decide what the overall purpose of your study is and clearly state this, along with what you hope to identify. For example, you could state that the overall purpose of your study is to identify a new treatment, highlight the importance of a specific treatment, or raise awareness for success or failure of a treatment.

▶ methodology and procedure – a brief description of the methods and/or measurements used. Your study should provide an accurate account of the types of data collection tools you will employ (for example, questionnaires, interviews, case studies), or experimental conditions you assign. You should outline the procedure you will use. Detail is important here because you want to ensure your study is replicable.

▶ target population and sample – you should identify the individuals or groups you intend as participants for your study. You should identify how you will recruit a sample based around the factors that will best produce the results for your study.

▶ research questions or hypotheses – once you have your topic focus and have conducted your literature review you will be able to formulate your questions or hypotheses. The question should be clear and focused and one which is likely to lead to meeting the aims of your study. Questions can be broken down to sub-questions or hypotheses, although avoid having too many as this can complicate your research.

▶ Consent and participant information arrangements, along with **debriefing.**

▶ Ethical considerations raised by the project and how you intend to deal with them.

▶ Estimated start date and duration of the project.

▶ Expected outcomes and impact – this is something you will have thought about when defining your research topic and focus. As with the aim of the study, you are seeking some new knowledge and insight into a phenomenon and should be clear in your proposal what it is that you expect to find, together with the potential impact this could have on your research area.

> **Key term**
>
> **Debriefing** – a process when research is completed to provide an opportunity for the participant to discuss the procedure and findings with the researcher. Participants must be told if they have been deceived and given reasons why. Any questions the participants ask must be answered fully and honestly. The purpose of the debrief is to remove any concerns or anxieties the participants have to ensure they leave the process positively.

Rationale and content of data collection methods

Earlier in this unit you covered all the different types of data collection methods you could use in your research. In your research proposal you should not only identify what type of data collection method you are using (for example whether it is a questionnaire, interview or observation) but also provide a rationale for why you are using it.

If you choose to use questionnaires, then your rationale might look something like this:

> Questionnaires are the best choice for my research study as I can gain both qualitative and quantitative information. For example, I will be able to identify how much participants experience specific episodes as a result of a particular treatment and also ask them to explain these experiences.

The next step in developing your research proposal is to decide on the best methods to collect your data. You may have chosen an experimental design in which case you will be defining your IV and DV and taking account of any factors that could get in the way (control measures). It is likely that for your pilot study you will not conduct an experiment as you would need to take into account strict ethical practice and considerations (for example, psychological or physical harm).

Rationale for research

Earlier in this section you saw how important it is show how you have identified and developed a good research topic; this includes ensuring that you provide a clear and thoroughly explained rationale for the research you are undertaking. One of key ways to do this is by conducting a literature review. The literature review helps you to understand the research problem being studied. It is used to provide a description of the works that will help you build your own arguments and identify any gaps. You will be expected to conduct a brief review of literature when developing your own pilot study and in doing so you will need to consider how you can identify relevant information. The following sections provide you with some ways to identify good sources of literature. Literature in research does not mean just books in a library; it can take many forms including:

▸ books (primary and secondary sources) – you will remember that primary sources are those works that are original, whereas secondary sources are those where authors have referred to other researchers' works

▸ journal articles – you will find journals around specific topics. For example, the British Psychological Society publish many peer-reviewed journals including *Developmental Psychology* and *Clinical Psychology*. Each of these sources provides published research papers and they are a good source of literature for your own pilot study

▸ print and electronic media – news and media channels on the internet and in daily newspapers are another source of literature which will give information on current affairs and issues.

> **Link**
>
> Look back at the explanation of literature reviews on page 95 to remind yourself of what you should cover and how it should appear.

Reliability and validity of sources

There are some important areas to consider when selecting reliable and valid literature or sources. Here are some useful questions to consider:

▸ Where does this information come from? Does the website look authentic? Has the journal article been **peer reviewed**?

> **Key term**
>
> **Peer reviewed** – a process undertaken in professional journal publications where experts scrutinise and review articles before they are published so there is confidence in the reliability of the sources included.

▸ Who gave the information (authors)? Are they experts in their field? Can you find information on their background?

▸ What was their motivation for the research? Does their work give you the impression that they may have been biased in reporting (did they appear to present findings based on their own feelings or expectations rather than what happened in reality)?

▸ Is the source reliable? Some institutions advise against using free online encyclopaedias as information may be given or edited by others. You could, however, look at the links provided on these sites, to lead you to more reliable sources.

▸ Is the research consistent with other research in the field? One study alone does not prove a point. Ensure that you have varied sources of research to show that you have a rationale for your research.

▸ Where was the source published? A reliable source is more likely to be a peer-reviewed journal, not a blog on social media.

▸ Is the internet site provided by an official body, organisation or authoritative source, for example, the British Psychological Society, or a government website?

▸ Is the source contemporary? This means has the research taken place in a reasonable timeframe. Some pieces of research may be outdated. Usually researchers will not use studies dating from longer than 10 years ago.

Electronic media

You may well find key information in your library in the form of books and magazine periodicals. One limitation of research articles is that they often do not allow access to the actual data findings they are based on, so you may only have generalisations to work from based on abstracts or the limited information they provide. You may, however, be able to find some sources using the internet and there are ways to refine your searches by narrowing down the information to a more manageable size. Search engines differ in their protocols for refining using search terms. Some of those you may find useful include those outlined in Table 2.11.

▶ **Table 2.11:** How can you refine your online searches?

Use of quote marks '…'
Example: 'the normochromic system' This method will identify that you want to search for an exact phrase. It does not return every source containing those words in any order.
+ or AND
Example: depression + dementia This will narrow your search to combine terms so it returns information about those elements.
- Or NOT
Example: agoraphobia NOT treatment This will allow you to eliminate words from your search.
OR
Example: agoraphobia OR treatment This will broaden your search and give you information containing either word.
*
Example: friend* – friendly, friendship, friendships Using '*' after a word will bring up all possible extensions to the word.

Think about the sample

Earlier in this unit you explored the different ways you could select a sample or target group for your study. Your literature review will have demonstrated the ways that other researchers have approached this and it will help to guide your own sample size. As you will be working on a pilot study, you will be looking at a small sample size. Your challenge is to ensure that your sample is representative of the target group. Researchers use data from the sample to make predictions about the whole target population. Advantages of sampling include: cost effectiveness (because you are only gathering data from a small sample); speed (because it is quicker to collect data from this small sample); and ease (because it will be easier to analyse data from this small sample to calculate your statistics).

Ethical considerations

Other elements you must include in your research proposal are the ethical considerations around your study. You must include the following:

▶ Consent – include details of the process you will undertake to gain informed consent from your participants. Remember to include any details around gaining gatekeeper and adult consent. When gaining 'informed consent' it is useful to document what you discuss with participants. You could develop a covering letter which highlights the purpose of the research, questions you are looking to answer, the participants' involvement and their right to withdraw, and their need to have sight of any data and research.

▶ Wellbeing and safety – you should show that you have considered how to ensure the physical safety and psychological wellbeing of your participants (safeguarding). You must consider any issues around mental capacity and age of your participants, together with any other factors such as vulnerability.

▶ Data protection and safeguarding principles – include a plan for how you will store data, and in what form, and include details of how you will ensure that data is used only for the intended purpose. For example, electronic data can be stored on a password-protected computer; paper documentation may be kept in a locked filing cabinet.

Link

Ethical considerations were discussed in detail earlier in the unit on page 90. Look back to remind yourself of how to approach them.

Management strategies

Time management

You need to think about how long it will reasonably take you to prepare all the materials you need to carry out your research and write up your reports following data analysis. You should also factor in contingencies that may impact on your ability to meet deadlines. In Figure 2.5 the researcher has provided a good plan of how they will complete their research by plotting each phase of their study. You must ensure you consider when holidays are, and consider any unforeseen events such as illness (you or your participants).

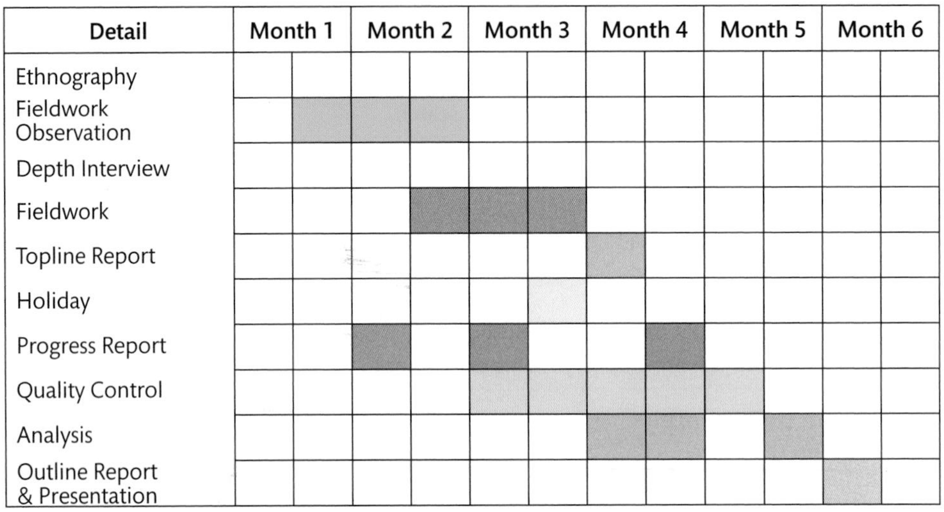

Detail	Month 1		Month 2		Month 3		Month 4		Month 5		Month 6	
Ethnography												
Fieldwork Observation		▓	▓	▓								
Depth Interview												
Fieldwork					▓	▓	▓					
Topline Report							▓					
Holiday						░						
Progress Report			▓		▓			▓				
Quality Control					▓	▓	▓	▓				
Analysis							▓	▓		▓		
Outline Report & Presentation											▓	

▶ **Figure 2.5:** A SMART timeline like this is a good way for you to organise your thoughts

SMART targets

SMART is an acronym for Specific/Measurable/Achievable/Relevant/Time-bound. SMART targets help you structure aims and goals.

Specific – make sure your goal is clear, otherwise you will be demotivated. To identify your goal, answer these questions:
▶ What do I want to achieve?
▶ What is involved?
▶ Why is the goal important?
▶ Which resources do I need?

Measurable – setting some deadlines and measuring your path along the way is an important element to keeping you motivated and on course for your goal.

Achievable – you have to be realistic about meeting your goals.

Relevant – ensure your goal is relevant to the process and outcome of your study. However interesting, you should avoid getting distracted by other avenues of research.

Time-bound – all goals need a target date so you have a deadline to focus on. This helps you to prioritise everyday tasks to fit in with your longer-term goals.

Next steps

Once you have completed the above tasks you are then in a position to present your research proposal to the ethics committee or your tutor for approval. Institutions usually have standard templates for you to complete. Alternatively, you can create your own template that incorporates the information. Table 2.12 is an example of how you could present your proposal. You should also include a copy of your timeline.

Project proposal template

▶ **Table 2.12:** Creating a research proposal template will help you remember what to include

Title	Are reward schemes within a primary school effective in promoting positive behaviour and in providing suitable motivators?
Research question **Hypothesis/es and rationale for research**	Does the school's behaviour policy support the multi-layered reward scheme? What are the effects on children's behaviour when applying different forms of reward? Does using Skinner's theories on reinforcement really work? Findings will be useful in guiding tutors on the best methods to use in managing children's positive behaviour in primary school settings.
Design and data collection methods	Child-centred approach using: • interviews with staff to establish schemes in place and views on effectiveness • interviews with children as to their views on reward systems • questionnaires to parents/carers about their views on reward systems and home/school links.
Analysis	Quantitative and qualitative data from interviews and questionnaires. Review of before/during/after experimentation.
Sample	A sample of 10 children from two primary school classes Children aged 8–9 years old Equal boy and girl distribution Tutors from the two classes Parents of the child participants
Literature reviewed	Shaw, G., (2017) Exploring children's perceptions of the reward system Lovett, P., (2016) The experiences of primary school teacher's application of rewards using Skinner's theories
Ethical considerations	• Gatekeeper consent from headteacher (copy attached) • Consent from parents of child participants (copy attached) • Transcript of verbal instructions to children giving details of the research, what they are required to do, their rights (copy attached) • Questionnaires for parents/carers (attached) • Interviews with staff • Interviews with children • Debriefing transcript (attached) All confidential information including data will be stored in a locked cabinet and on a password-protected computer. Only myself and my research supervisor will have access. I will substitute all the participants names for other names and will change the identity of the school and location.

Assessment activity 2.2

Refine your own research project and questions and develop a project proposal on a pilot study that includes all the factors you have covered in this section. Explore the internet and libraries for research or work on your topic area, try to find out any gaps and areas that interest you. Make notes on literature that would support your ideas. Evaluate the benefits and disadvantages of using qualitative, quantitative or mixed-methods design and decide which methods would be best suited for your study. Develop your project proposal following guidance provided in this section or create your own. Conduct a brief search of the literature available on your topic. Think about your own time management in carrying out the pilot study.

Plan
- What am I learning? Why is this important?
- How confident do I feel in my own abilities to complete this task?

Do
- Am I confident that I know what I am doing and that I know what it is I should be achieving?

Review
- I can explain which elements I found easiest
- I can explain which elements I found hardest

C Carry out a pilot study to explore current issues in psychology

Data collection

Earlier in this unit you looked at the way that questions or hypotheses could be refined or developed from your literature review. This is your first step in developing and refining your questions based on what you find. For example, you might want to find out why children get excited when the school bell rings for breaktime. You could search the internet and come across a study conducted by Ivan Pavlov who studied dogs' behaviours and the effects of ringing a bell (the stimulus) before giving them food (the reward). This research can help you frame your questions and refine them. It can also support your decisions on the methods you choose.

Once you have gathered literature, you can start to think about following the procedure you developed in your project proposal and ethics check to conduct your research. The literature you have found will also help you to refine the methods of data collection and analysis you might use, for example, you may identify that the majority of studies in the area you are exploring have used a mixed-methods approach using semi-structured interviews and questionnaires and each have provided some robust findings. The literature may also include some charts or tables the researchers have developed to help them structure their data collection or analysis frameworks. It is acceptable to replicate a data collection or analysis method in another study, but it is important that you acknowledge this source either in its original format or where you have adapted it to suit the purposes of your own research.

The following is an example of the procedure you might take to work through the data collection process.

Worked example

Refined research question: Are reward schemes in primary school settings an effective tool in promoting children's positive behaviours aged between 8 and 9 years of age?

1 Recruitment of participants.
   • Approach school to seek permission and gain gatekeeper consent. Ask them to identify suitable participants or state the sample you require, for example, five boys and five girls from each class who display unwanted behaviours.
   • Where appropriate, write to parents to request consent for children to take part in the study and invite them to complete questionnaires.
   • Discuss interviews with tutors and gain informed consent.
   • Conduct initial discussions with child participants detailing the research and obtaining further verbal consent.
2 Refine and develop questionnaires and interviews and create SMART targets for the research process.
3 Arrange timings to collect data and conduct interviews with tutors and children.
4 Conduct data collection and ensure debriefing takes place with all participants.
5 Organise your data into numerical or **code** qualitative data to devise themes and trends ready for analysis and interpretation, including defining themes and trends.

Key term

Code – or coding data means that you would arrange data into categories to help analyse the data. So you might identify a common phrase that participants use.

Once you have completed your data collection through your chosen qualitative or quantitative methods, whether they are observations, interviews, questionnaires or controlled experiments, you need to organise your data which means sorting your data ready for data analysis.

Data analysis

Quantitative data analysis methods

There are a number of ways that data can be manipulated or sorted to help you understand and report on your findings and there are a number of reasons for this. For example, sorting data into a chart or figures provides an easy to read snapshot of key findings.

Descriptive statistics

One of the most common methods used is descriptive statistics. A descriptive statistic is a way of summarising features of the data. These are very useful when you want to show numerical data in a clear way. They are useful to demonstrate the strength of opinion of something, for example 92 per cent of participants felt the NHS service was efficient and supported those most in need or the average number of participants preferring not to take therapy was ten. There are four types: measures of frequency (count); measures of dispersion (range, variance, standard deviation); measures of position (percentile ranks, quartile ranks); and measures of central tendency (mean, mode and median).

Example: Using results from a study of the number of times participants sneezed after sniffing pepper. Results were:

1, 5, 2, 10, 6, 7, 5

Mean: This provides the average or 'measure of central tendency' and is useful when describing the most common response or example of something. This means adding the values in the data set together and dividing by the number of values in the set. In our pepper example therefore, there are a total of:

70 values (participants) added together = 36 which would give a mean of 5.1

Median: This is the middle value in the series of numbers. It is useful where a sample size is large and does not include outliers.(a figure that is much smaller or larger than others in the data but have little effect on the mean or median) In the pepper example you would organise the numbers into a logical scale as follows:

1, 2, 5, 5, 6, 7, 10

The median here is 5.

The median here is based on seven values (participants). What if there were eight participants how do you work out the median value here? Let's say that a participant sneezed eight times:

1, 2, 5, 5, 6, 7, 8, 10

You take the two middle numbers (5 and 6), add these together and divide by two.

This gives a median of 5.5

Mode: This is the value that occurs most frequently in your set and is used to identify the most popular or common response. For example, in our set, the mode would be 5 as it appears twice.

Standard deviation: The standard deviation is the number that shows how much each of the values in the set deviates from the mean (or centre). Deviation refers to the distance each value is from the mean. The formula for working out the standard deviation (sd) is:

$$\sqrt{\frac{\left(\sum (X - \bar{X})^2\right)}{n}}$$

Where:

$\sum$ = sum of

x = individual score

$\bar{x}$ = mean

n = number of participants

To calculate use the following steps:

1 Calculate the mean ($\bar{x}$).
2 Take away the mean from each participant's score ($x - \bar{x}$).
3 Square the answers ($x - \bar{x}$)^2.
4 Add up all of the squared scores $\sum (x - \bar{x})^2$.
5 Divide by the number of participants minus 1 ($n - 1$).
6 Take the square root of the answer.
7 An example of how to work this out is shown below.

Records of memory recall failure of schizophrenic patients over two-week period = 38, 26, 13, 41, 22

Number (x)	x − $\bar{x}$	(x − $\bar{x}$)^2	sd =
38	+10	100	$\sqrt{\dfrac{\left(\sum (X - \bar{X})^2\right)}{n}}$
26	-2	4	
13	-15	225	= √ 534/(5 − 1)
41	+13	169	= 11.55
22	-6	36	
140	**0**	**534**	

Range: This is the distance between the highest to the lowest value in the set. The range is found by subtracting the lowest value from the highest value. For example, in our set 1 is the lowest and 10 the highest.

The range is therefore 10 − 1 = 9.

Correlations and distributions

▸ Correlations are studies that demonstrate the strength of a relationship between two, numerically measured variables. You might want to use this type of analysis when you compare a person's height to their weight: the taller a person is, the heavier they will be.

▸ A correlation coefficient is a measure that states the degree to which two variables differ or are associated, whether a relationship exists and the strength and direction (positive or negative) of any relationship between two variables. There are a number of correlation coefficients, the most common being the Pearson product-moment correlation. Another is the Spearman's rank correlation coefficient. An example is shown in Figure 2.6.

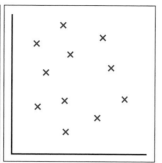

Positive correlation	Negative correlation	No correlation
The points lie close to a straight line, which has a positive gradient. This shows that as one variable **increases** the other **increases** .	The points lie close to a straight line, which has a negative gradient. This shows that as one variable **increases** the other **decreases**.	There is no pattern to the points. This shows that there is **no connection** between the two variables.

▶ **Figure 2.6:** Correlation graphs

Distribution curves are a method often used when working with ranges greater than 21 (r = 21) and with more than 20 participants (n > 20). The term bell curve is used to describe the normal distribution of a data set. A bell curve relates to the shape that is created where a line is plotted using the data points for the set of data. A normal curve is displayed symmetrically which means that the mean, median and mode are all equal.

A normal distribution of data means that most of the examples in a set of data are close to the 'average' or mean, while some other examples are at one extreme or the other.

In a normal distribution graph (Figure 2.7), the curve is bell-shaped with a single peak.
▶ The mean (average) is at the central point of the distribution and the distribution is the same around it.
▶ The tails, or either end of the distribution, tend to get smaller.
▶ The shape of the distribution is determined by the mean and standard deviation.

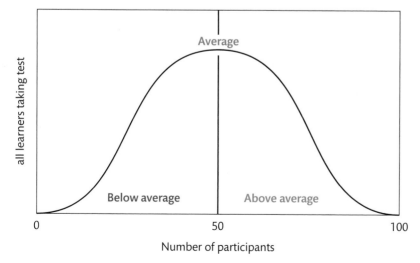

▶ **Figure 2.7:** A normal bell curve graph

Not all graphs show a type of curve in this way. Some have flatter curves, while others will be steeper. Sometimes the mean will lean to one side or the other. The standard deviation shows you how far away from the mean you are. If the shape of the curve is asymmetrical, your data is not distributed normally and is said to be positively or negatively skewed.

▶ In Figure 2.8 the tail is longer on the right of the curve of the positive skew. The majority of the scores appear to the left of the centre.

▶ In Figure 2.9 the tail is longer to the left of the curve of the negative skew. The majority of the scores appear to the right of the centre.

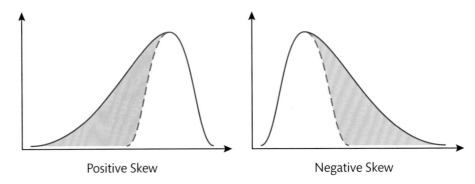

Positive Skew   Negative Skew

▶ **Figure 2.8 and Figure 2.9:** Asymmetrical curve graphs

Displaying this type of graph can give you a pictorial representation of data, particularly the mean or average scores. It is a much more effective way of displaying data, rather than merely stating, for example, participants were found to sneeze on average 5.1 times.

Qualitative data analysis techniques

Thematic and narrative analysis is a means of interpreting qualitative data. Figure 2.10 shows an example of one of the more widely used qualitative analysis tools, thematic analysis. This six-step model was proposed by Braun & Clarke (2006).

Thematic analysis aims to identify patterns of meaning from the data to provide an answer to a research question. Patterns are identified through familiarising yourself with the data and coding it into specific areas. In general, narrative analysis takes the form of a story and focuses on the way in which people use stories to interpret their world. This could be in the form of interview accounts, diaries that provide accounts of events at a time or over a period of time. Coding refers to the process of taking data apart and examining it for differences and similarities. So, it may be a sentence or paragraph of speech, or an observation. The researcher will ask questions about what these phrases and sentences may mean and put them into different categories to identify distinct concepts.

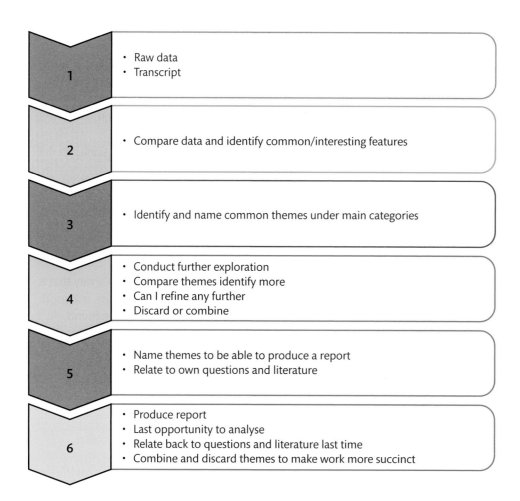

1
• Raw data
• Transcript

2
• Compare data and identify common/interesting features

3
• Identify and name common themes under main categories

4
• Conduct further exploration
• Compare themes identify more
• Can I refine any further
• Discard or combine

5
• Name themes to be able to produce a report
• Relate to own questions and literature

6
• Produce report
• Last opportunity to analyse
• Relate back to questions and literature last time
• Combine and discard themes to make work more succinct

▶ **Figure 2.10:** Braun & Clark Six-stage phases of thematic analysis (2006) (adapted)

▶ Stage 1: You would start with the raw data and transcribe it (write it out if tape recorded).

▶ Stage 2: You would then compare the different data to identify common or interesting features. For example, you might find that a number of participants say that a treatment 'really helped' or they reported similar symptoms from a specific treatment. The main focus is to look for identifying features that might support your questions/hypotheses. You would assign initial codes to these features which could be numbers or letters which could provide a context for the research.

▶ Stage 3: This is your first attempt at identifying common themes that occur in your data. For example, several participants may identify that learning online is better than face-to-face learning because they feel more at ease working at their own pace. This could be themed as 'relaxing in online environments'.

▶ Stage 4: You would conduct a further exploration of the themes and compare them with the questions you are asking and whether any can be refined further, discarded or combined with another theme. This leads to the following step.

▶ Stage 5: Themes are named and defined to enable you to produce a report on your findings, relating them to your own questions and literature you have found in the field.

▶ Stage 6: Producing the report. This provides you with a last opportunity to analyse the data relating back to the literature and research questions.

Presenting your findings to an audience

Once a research study has been completed, you should have your findings in a form that can be interpreted and presented. There are two main ways to present your findings:

1 a summary presentation, usually in the form of a poster presentation to an audience (your class group)

2 a formal written report following the academic conventions covered earlier in this unit.

You should become familiar with developing presentations of your work. Good research can be shared with wider audiences and it is common for many researchers to attend national and international conferences to disseminate their research.

Summarising data

When you write up your report you will want to present your findings in a way that is interesting and engaging to your readership. Using pictorial representation is a good way of doing this and helps the reader gain a good idea of what you have found.

Scattergrams

Scattergrams are useful for identifying whether there is a relationship between two variables. Figures 2.11 and 2.12 illustrate relationships between two variables.

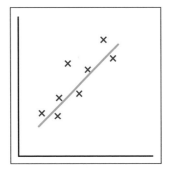

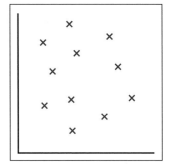

▶ **Figure 2.11:** The closer the items are to a line, the closer the relationship between the two variables

▶ **Figure 2.12:** The more dispersed (spread out) the items are from a central line, the weaker the relationship between the two variables

Tables

Tables or charts are a very simple way of displaying data. It can be useful if you want to show a comparison such as in the following example:

Positive response to treatment (male)	Positive response to treatment (female)
10	14

Histograms

Histograms are another way of representing data and give a good idea of the overall results as well as the mean and range. A histogram can be a good way of displaying data such as the mean, mode and median. There is software that can produce these charts, such as Microsoft Excel® or Minitab®. Your school or college may have access to one of these or other statistical packages you could use.

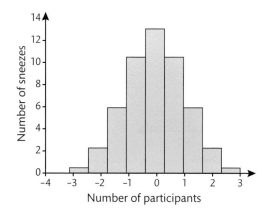

▶ **Figure 2.13:** Data displayed using a histogram.

In Figure 2.13 the y-axis indicates the number of sneezes a participant had. The x-axis represents the number of participants that sneezed that frequency. You can include a distribution curve or bell curve on your histogram. The bell curve indicates where most occurrences take place in the middle of the distribution and taper off on each side; it measures the highest point of the curve see (Figure 2.14).

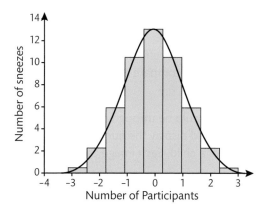

▶ **Figure 2.14:** A bell curve on a histogram

Data will not always appear in this way on a histogram. Data may be skewed either to the right or the left. This does not mean that there is any error but merely shows where the most common occurrences are (see Figures 2.15 and 2.16).

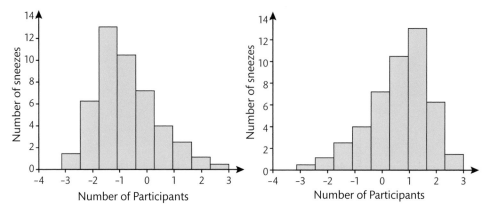

▶ **Figure 2.15:** Negative skewed data ▶ **Figure 2.16** Positive skewed data

Pie charts

Another way of presenting data is through pie charts. Pie charts are good for displaying data and providing an overall view of findings. They are often used to show data sets that are parts of a whole, such as percentages. A pie chart can give you an instant idea of majority views, behaviours, and so on.

Bar charts

Bar charts are another way to display data. They are easy to design and interpret. They give the reader an instant overview of the findings.

Graphs

Similar to bar charts, a line graph is an effective way to display data as it again displays the data at a glance and helps you compare and demonstrate trends and relationships.

Other pictorial representations

Other ways of displaying data could be through using an image of a person or other graphics. For example, you could display the number of children who lived in each location, through an image of a child. Each image could either represent one, five, or 10 children.

Video

You may wish to include video content as part of your findings. This could be video diaries you have recorded yourself, or video of the participants undertaking research (with their permission).

Narrative

You can codify qualitative data through interpreting language data and refining to codes and themes. Presenting this data in a format other than a formal report can be difficult due to its volume. It can be useful to look back at your final themes and trends and highlight the main ones with some brief examples of participants' comments.

\<Theme\>	Treatment worked really well
\<Comments\>	'I felt like a new man'
	'It was as if I had woken from a long dream'
\<Theme\>	Treatment did not work
\<Comments\>	'I thought what's the point, two weeks and no change'
	'They made me feel worse, so I gave up'

Feedback from others

Presenting your research to your class group is a good way to gain **constructive feedback**. Feedback is a good way to gain opinions on the approach you have taken, your findings and the outcome of your research. Receiving feedback can help you think about areas you might have missed or possible future developments in your research. Watching other people's presentations can also give you ideas on how to refine your own research and the way you present your ideas.

> **Key term**
>
> **Constructive feedback** – feedback that focuses on providing insights that someone can use to improve their work and/or behaviour.

Assessment activity 2.3

Under the guidance of your tutor, refine and carry out your pilot study. Ensure you follow the timelines you have set out. Gather your data and analyse it. Produce a report that follows conventions. From this report develop a presentation that you can deliver to your class group which provides your audience with:

1 the research title and focus

2 the reason why you were interested in carrying out this pilot study

3 key background literature that helped you refine your questions (consider one or two key pieces)

4 your research questions and methods for gathering data

5 your participants and how you chose them

6 your key findings

7 your interpretation of these findings. Your report could be in a PowerPoint format with slides and discussion notes, or as a poster (standard size is usually 122 x 91 cm). You could provide your audience with a transcript that explains each of your points on your presentation.

Plan
- What aspects of the task do I think will take the most/least time? How will I balance these?
- Do I have any existing knowledge around the task at hand?

Do
- I am recording my own observations and thoughts
- Am I utilising all of the support available to me?

Review
- I can draw links between this learning and prior learning
- I can identify how this learning experience relates to future experiences (i.e. in the workplace)

D Review implications of research into psychological inquiry

Review research process and findings

Completing your study and developing your conclusion is as important as the rest of your study. It provides you with the opportunity to look back on your research and reflect on its success and consider ideas for the future. Writing the conclusion to your research is not just a summary, it is a **synthesis**. This is an appraisal of your findings compared with the findings of others. It identifies the strengths and weaknesses of your work, its potential impact and how it looks to the future.

Self-reflection is an equally important aspect of any research process as it helps you reflect on your own research skills as well as your personal and professional development. You will explore each of these elements in this section.

Success of pilot study

You will need to review whether your findings answered your research questions or confirmed your research hypothesis. There are two ways you can identify this information. Firstly, compare your research findings to your questions and ask yourself the following questions.

1 Did you find out what you wanted to?
2 Did you have to change your questions as you went through?
3 At what stage(s) of the research process did you come to this conclusion?
4 Did you alter any areas of your research (questions, processes, literature searches)?
5 What were the changes you made?
6 Were they successful? If not, how would you have further refined your research study or process?

You may find it useful to place these questions in a table and answer each one in turn to identify the overall effectiveness of your research on answering the questions/hypotheses.

Interpreting, discussing and presenting

You now need to ask yourself questions about how well the literature you found has supported your interpretation, discussion and presentation of the research findings. Earlier you looked at how the literature review is a recursive process and you may well have changed your focus or questions based on new literature you uncovered.

Consider how these reviews have changed your focus and how they have influenced your interpretations and discussions about your research topic. You should consider whether this process has provided you with further insights into the topic area. For example, has it demonstrated limitations that need to be studied further? How useful is your evaluation in identifying whether you consider the research to be useful?

Issues and the future

Another area to consider is the issues you encountered during the research process. You should reflect on aspects of the research design, the participants you recruited and any issues you experienced with implementing and carrying out the research.

You also need to consider the impact your research has in identifying and promoting change or further insight. In some cases, research goes nowhere and leads the researcher down a 'blind alley'. This is not to say the research was a waste of time.

Key term

Synthesis – a combination of all the elements of the research project brought together to provide the reader with an overview of a document/research project. A written discussion that draws on your research questions, findings and discussion that finishes with a statement as to the current situation and possible implications and future research areas.

Such perceived failure must be taken as an opportunity. Discovering whether research is worth pursing is the main reason why you conduct a pilot study. In these situations, reflection is important as it helps you identify the areas that did not work well, as well as give clues as to how future research could be developed. The important message here is that no research is wasted research.

It is useful to identify factors associated with each of the following that you feel interfered with the research process:

1 Research design – setting your question; designing your methods (qualitative, quantitative, mixed methods, experiments, and so on).

2 Participants – the selection and recruitment of participants; encouraging participation in the whole research.

3 Implementation – researcher or participant effects (whether you or the participants were influenced in any way); experiences when implementing your research, for example accessing your participants, changes made to procedures, questionnaires, interview questions.

4 Findings – difficulties experienced through relating findings to literature and questions/hypotheses.

Review of the research process

Finally, in this section you need to think about the research process as a whole, not just about the subject you were investigating. Consider how research as a process can help in promoting and driving change in an area of applied psychology and also in supporting individual mental health and wellbeing. When you have completed your research it is good practice to follow the steps below and provide a reflection on your own experience of the research practice, the success of your current project in answering the research questions, issues you experience and any changes you feel could have been made.

1 Was this a successful piece of research?
  • Identify any gaps the research aimed to identify and the success in addressing any gap.

2 Explain the success of the project in answering the research question/confirming your hypothesis.
  • Were there any factors that impacted on the research (negative/positive) for example did you find that some of the questions were not easily answered, did participants understand what was required of them?
  • How did it affect your interpretation (were you influenced to change your focus / redesign an aspect of your research?).

3 Were you able to evaluate the research to clearly identify how it could be useful in the future? Explain these factors.

4 What issues did I encounter throughout?
  • Was there an issue with participants (gaining consent, cooperating, guessing what I was exploring)?
  • Gaining access. Did you have difficulty getting permission with your research?
  • Designing and making changes to the research. What were these and what justification did you make for changing these?
  • Ability to meet deadlines.
  • Gaining the data you intended.

5 Overall, how you felt the pilot study was in identifying and promoting change and promoting health and psychological wellbeing.

Implications of research into psychological inquiry

The final aspect of this unit encourages you to explore your own views on how your particular research project can contribute to the field of psychological inquiry.

Identify key elements for future research

You should identify whether the research has answered the questions you set out to achieve and identify any gaps or missed opportunities. For example, you may have asked participants about their view on a particular therapy but failed to explore the reasons why participants made that choice. This may be a focus for a future research project.

Explore how your research could provide insights that might improve life chances or advancement in technologies, treatments or just a better understanding of a phenomenon.

You could review a small sample of literature around the area to see if there are any differences from the literature you found in your original research to now. What questions could you ask and how could this extend your research or create new insights?

The potential impact on practice and provision

You need to consider the impact of your research on practice and provision within the area you are exploring. When you set your research questions you would have had in mind your intention. For example, you may have wanted to understand how new technology has supported the identification of a disorder. Your results may identify some advantages and disadvantages of using a specific technique. This will help future development of technologies and may improve life chances. For example, PET scans identified that psychopath's brains were wired to seek rewards no matter the consequences. Therefore, treatments could be developed around forms of rewards to treat behaviours. Studies such as these provide the platform to advance technologies to understand more into psychopathological disorders, identify treatments and ultimately improve life chances.

How research can be developed in future studies

It follows from the above that by understanding the outcomes of the research you have conducted and its potential impact that you can develop research that will fill any gaps you identified in this current pilot study. Using the example above you may want to explore the forms of rewards that work well and the types of behaviour modification you can encourage. This, in turn, will further support professionals in diagnosing and treating psychopathic behaviours.

▶ You will have lots to think about for your pilot study; try to focus on the most important parts

Self-reflection and personal professional development

▶ Finally, it is useful to conduct self-reflection to explore how this particular project has helped you identify your own strengths and areas for development. For example, did you manage to complete the study in time? Were there any aspects of the study you could have changed?

▶ Reflect on your own research project from start to finish and consider how your research evolved to come to the conclusions you have made. Reflect on the feedback you have received from your tutors and your fellow researchers. Consider how has this feedback helped support you form your own ideas about how your research could be developed further.

▶ Earlier you explored the way you can develop SMART targets in developing your own research skills and conducting your research process. This approach is also useful in developing targets to help you meet your own personal and professional goals. Look back at the skills and knowledge that you felt you had and/or needed to develop when you started this pilot study and answer some simple questions.

1 How do they differ now?

2 Have you developed further skills throughout this process?

3 If so, what are they and how can they support you in future research or in your own professional development?

4 Having completed this pilot study what skills do you want to develop further?

5 You could also identify those areas of applied psychology that have really interested you and those which you may pursue in any career progression.

▸ Finally, even if your questions do not give you this clear idea of future research in your chosen topic area, hopefully conducting this pilot study has given you an enthusiasm for research in many areas of your life.

Reflect

This final section encourages you to reflect on your pilot study. Now look back over this section and your pilot study. Do you have anything you would add to this? Do you think you have achieved any of your list?

Remember that your role as a researcher is valuable. Without research there would be no progression or advancements, without research there would be no new knowledge and understanding. Research is an exciting and rewarding process and you can make a significant difference to people's lives by actively engaging in research.

Assessment activity 2.4

Develop a report based on your reflections of the research process, your findings and success of the pilot study. How has this research provided ideas for a future study? Discuss the implications your pilot study has had on research in that area but also on possible ways it can help support those working in that area of psychology and how it may affect practice and provision.

Reflect on feedback you have received from others and your own reflections. Include this in your report to show how you consider what others have said compared to your own reflections. How will this help you develop as a researcher and influence your own professional development? Will this support you to further study into further or higher education or other career paths? Finally, consider how this has supported you in developing skills and understanding that could be applied in other areas of work and study.

Plan

- What resources do I need to complete the task? How can I get access to them?
- How much time do I have to complete the task? How am I going to successfully plan my time and keep track of my progress?

Do

- I am open to change
- I am recording any problems I'm experiencing and looking for ways/ solutions to clarify queries

Review

- I realise where I still have learning/ knowledge gaps and I know who/how to resolve them
- I can make informed choices based on reflection

Further reading and resources

Bell, J., Waters, S. (2018) *Doing your research project* 7th Ed London, England: Open University Press

Flanagan, C. (2015) *The Research Methods Companion for A Level Psychology (Complete Companion Psychology)* Oxford, England: Oxford University Press

Howitt, D., Cramer, D. (2016) *Research Methods in Psychology* Harlow, England: Pearson Education Ltd

Thomas, G. (2017) *How to Do Your Research Project: A Guide for Students* London, England: Sage

THINK ▶FUTURE

Jessica Faulkner

Psychology learner

I have been working with children in special needs provisions in schools for a year now. During this time, I encountered children with different abilities and needs. I have always had an interest in mental health and at school did well on my psychology qualification. The qualification gave me insight into different areas of psychology and I was amazed at all the roles that could be open to me when I qualified.

Since then I have worked in a number of different job roles but my interest in psychology has always been there. I decided to take a degree in psychology and train to be a clinical psychologist. I could have gone to a conventional university but felt that I needed some work experience so I am now taking an Open University Psychology degree that will give me BPS status and provide me with the opportunity to move on to gain a Masters and ultimately a PhD in this subject.

I was really excited to recently find a job working as a research assistant for studies on PTSD and am finding my studies really useful in my daily practice. I know I will be getting lots of opportunities to put my learning into practice as I will be developing and conducting interviews and studies with groups and will be able to design aspects of the research project under the guidance of an excellent team. Having this background in psychology has provided me with a fabulous springboard and launched me into a career. I'm really excited about my future.

Focusing on your skills

Conducting psychological research

Research is core to continued practice within all areas of psychology and helps to develop knowledge, understanding and skills. Think about the following:

- Before completing any research with participants, make sure you have a clear plan for your research and have their consent.

- Make sure they fully understand what their role will be, and what you expect to find.

- Make sure your own knowledge, understanding and skills are up to standard in all areas of research.

There is no single best approach to research. You have to fit your approach with your questions.

Health Psychology

3

Getting to know your unit

Assessment
You will be assessed by one externally set and marked exam.

What motivates people to pursue either a healthy or unhealthy lifestyle? Addictions and high levels of stress affect many people in society today. Medical and psychological professionals spend a great deal of time supporting sufferers by helping them to change their behaviour. Treatments and persuasive techniques can be used but their long-term impact is often questioned in terms of their effectiveness.

How you will be assessed

This unit will be assessed using a written examination set by the examination board. The examination will be a set period of time and contain questions worth a range of marks.

The paper will consist of a number of short- and long-answer questions that will assess your understanding of health-related behaviour, stress and addictions and the promotion of positive changes in behaviour. You will be expected to apply your knowledge, understanding and critical evaluation to the different approaches, theories and studies of health psychology.

Throughout this unit you will find activities that will help you work towards your final assessment. By completing these you will gain a better understanding of health psychology and they will support you later when completing your final assessment.

This unit has three Assessment Outcomes which will be included in the external assessment. Certain command words are associated with each assessment outcome (see Table 3.1).

▶ **Table 3.1:** Assessment outcomes (AOs) on which you will be tested

AO	Description	Command words and marks
1	Demonstrate knowledge and understanding of psychological approaches, theories and studies used to explain health-related behaviour and behavioural change.	Describe, Give, Give a reason why, Identify, Name, State. Marks: range from 1 to 4 marks.
2	Apply knowledge and understanding of psychological approaches, theories and studies, to explain health-related behaviour and behavioural change in given contexts.	Describe, Explain, Interpret, Justify. Marks: range from 1 to 4 marks.
3	Explore the use and effectiveness of psychological approaches, theories and studies in relation to explaining health-related behaviour and implementing behavioural change.	Analyse, Assess, Compare, Discuss, Explain. Marks: range from 1 to 9 marks.

Getting started

Health psychology covers an array of different areas, including stress and addiction. Through both biological and psychological developments, a range of explanations, support and treatments now exist. From your own experiences write down different psychologically-related illnesses you know about and as a group discuss what sorts of treatment and advice are out there for patients. How do you think treatments and advice for mental illness compare to those for other illnesses, like measles?

 Lifestyle choice and health-related behaviour

Health psychology explores the importance of understanding why people make the choices they do and the impact this has on their health. In this section you will look at the different psychological definitions of health and ill health, stress and addiction.

Psychological definitions of health

Humans have always tried to maintain and improve their health and the health of those around them. Medicine has been hugely influential in this field, but in order to consider health **holistically** you also need to consider the influences of different groups including health workers, health psychologists, complementary therapists and many others. Health itself is not just physical but also needs to be studied in terms of a person's mind and body.

Health and ill health

Biomedical model

One of the oldest explanations of health, the **biomedical** model focused on physical reasons for illness and health problems. A physical upset to the body's systems could be the result of germs, genes, chemicals or diseases. Treatments come in the form of vaccinations, surgery, chemotherapy and medicines that all aim at changing the physical imbalance in a person back to one of balance and good health. The biomedical model considers the mind as a separate part and therefore not influential in the cause or treatment of an individual's health. It also ignores social or economic factors.

Biopsychosocial model

The **biopsychosocial** model developed due to doubts about the biomedical model's assumption that health was just the focus of physical explanations. This model (see Figure 3.1) attempted to integrate biological (for example genes), psychological (for example behaviour), and social (for example employment) elements into a combined model and ultimately an explanation of health.

> **Key terms**
>
> **Holistically** – looking at a person's health in terms of both their mind and body.
>
> **Biomedical** – focuses on physical, medical and biological explanations, for example genetics.
>
> **Biopsychosocial** – an integrated approach to health which involves biological, psychological and social areas.

▶ **Figure 3.1:** Engel's biopsychosocial model

Engel's ideas offered a more holistic approach to health, combining the physical elements of the biomedical model with other explanations (for example psychological and social). He suggested that an individual's behaviour may influence how a person feels which then may result in a physical change. Therefore, to look at physical, social and psychological factors together would give a better explanation of why someone was behaving in a particular way.

For example:

- a psychological treatment for stress might be cognitive behavioural therapy
- which when used with a patient could influence biological responses by reducing their insomnia for example
- which would also improve social responses (friendships or relationships) by allowing them to go and meet people.

Health as a continuum

A **health continuum** recognises the importance of physical health and suggests that mental factors impact on health at all stages. In continuum models the individual can be placed along a range, for example healthy to ill (see Figure 3.2). This reflects the likelihood of an individual working towards changing their behaviour.

Healthy	Reacting	Injured	Ill
• Normal mood fluctuations	• Nervousness	• Anxiety	• Excessive anxiety
• Normal sleep patterns	• Irritability	• Anger	• Easily enraged
	• Sadness	• Pervasive sadness	• Depressed mood
	• Trouble sleeping	• Hopelessness	• Unable to fall or stay asleep
		• Disturbed sleep patterns	

▶ **Figure 3.2:** Mental-health continuum model

The influence of psychological factors can be seen at many different stages, for example 'in order to reduce my stress levels after a busy day at work I will attend a yoga class'. By recognising that stress is making this person feel unhappy and by initiating a behaviour change (such as seeking out exercise), the outcome is likely to be a reduction in stress levels.

Behavioural and physiological addiction

Behavioural addiction looks at the role of the environment in the maintenance and relapse of addictive behaviour whereas physiological addiction has a biological focus.

Discussion

In groups, think about different illnesses that could have more than just a physical explanation. Try and explain them in terms of all three of Engels' influences: biological, psychological and social.

Key terms

Health continuum – a type of scale. At one end of the scale your health is very good and at the other it is very poor. Different factors, for example physical or psychological, will influence where you are on that scale in terms of your health.

Behavioural addiction

Behavioural addiction was influenced by the theories of learning psychologists within the disciplines of classical and operant conditioning and social learning theory.

Within classical conditioning, the addiction will occur as a response to two stimuli being associated with each other. For example, an unconditioned stimulus (UCS) such as cocaine produces an unconditioned response (UCR) such as relaxation. After repeated pairings between the (UCS) and the (NS), the (NS) becomes the (CS) and produces the (CR) of relaxation.

Operant conditioning works on the principles of positive and negative reinforcement in maintaining the addiction. For example, taking the drug cocaine will make you feel relaxed which could be positively reinforced by your friends who are also taking the drug.

Social learning theory suggests that addiction results from observing and imitating a role model who received a reward of some kind for their action. For example, seeing a friend (role model) winning money at a race track might be enough to encourage someone to start betting.

Link

Look back at Unit 1 for more information about conditioning theories and positive/negative reinforcement.

Physiological addiction

This might include the chemical messengers in our brains called **neurotransmitters**, such as dopamine. Biological **predisposition** would suggest that certain individuals are vulnerable in the early stages of addiction due to their biological makeup, for example their genetics. So, an individual's biological structure makes them susceptible (more likely) to be affected during the maintenance of the addiction. During relapse, the individual could be more biologically predisposed to relapsing than others.

Key term

Neurotransmitters – a chemical messenger that carries messages between neurons.

Predisposition – a genetic characteristic you have inherited from your parents that makes you more likely to develop an illness.

Theory into practice

Daniel is a 30-year-old heroin addict. He arrives at his local support centre asking for help and tells the nurse that he wants to give up his habit and is looking for some help. He shows some withdrawal symptoms: he has a runny nose, he is shaking and he has a slight temperature. Daniel tells the nurse that his father died from a drug addiction. He also tells him that he has tried twice before to give up heroin but has been unsuccessful. He explains that his mother has thrown him out after the police brought his sister home from a party where she was suspected of taking drugs.

1   Is there any evidence of a biological predisposition for Daniel's behaviour?

2   Explain how physiological and behavioural addiction would explain Daniel's behaviour.

Griffiths' six components of addiction

Griffiths (1996) characterised addiction into six different features. He said that all need to be present for a diagnosis of addiction.

Physical and psychological dependence (salience)

Physical dependency refers to the withdrawal symptoms that an individual may experience when the drug stops, for example pain, irritability, shaking and sweating. Psychological dependence (salience) is when the behaviour or drug becomes the most important thing in that person's life. Even if the person is not actually taking part in the behaviour, they will be thinking about the next time they will be.

Mood alteration (modification)

People may report the 'buzz' or 'rush' they experience when taking heroin. An addict can bring about different mood alterations by changing their activity. For example, someone with a nicotine addiction will smoke in the morning to wake them up, giving them the 'rush' that they need to start the day. In the evening it can be taken to relax them before they go to bed; one addiction can therefore result in different mood changes.

Tolerance

Tolerance is an addict's need to increase the amount of behaviour, for example ten cigarettes a day to 15 and so on, in order to maintain the same effect. The addict will need a bigger and bigger 'hit' in order to have the same resulting behaviour. For example, a gambler will need to take bigger and bigger risks in terms of the size of the bet they place in order to maintain the effect of happiness that was initially gained from placing a smaller bet.

Withdrawal symptoms

These are the negative effects, both psychological and physical, that result when the addict is prevented from taking part in the activity. Some psychological effects may include moodiness or irritability and physiological effects may include sweating, shaking, insomnia, and so on.

Conflict

Conflict arises between the addict and those around them as a result of their addictive behaviour. Continuing to take part in short-term pleasures can lead to ignoring other areas of life such as family, work and activities such as sports.

Relapse

This is the return to the behaviour after the addict has attempted to give it up. This can occur after months, or even years, in which the addict resumes the full behaviour and pattern of their original addiction. For example, after only a couple of cigarettes an individual addicted to smoking after a period of time will resume their full smoking habit.

> **Discussion**
>
> What other examples of addictive behaviour can you find? Try and come up with at least one for each of Griffiths' points.

Stress

Stress can take many forms, but it is agreed that how someone recognises a stressful situation and how they are able to deal with it is important. Stress can be both good and bad, depending on the individual and the situation they find themselves in.

Psychological stress

Psychological stress is the emotional and physiological reaction shown by individuals when they are in a situation that they don't have the resources to cope with. This involves a **stressor** that will cause or trigger a positive or negative response.

> **Key terms**
>
> **Stressor** – anything physiological or psychological that produces a stress response, for example divorce, examinations, getting married, or moving to a new house.
>
> **Environmental fit** – the degree to which the environment and individual match.

A stressful situation can create a physiological response: an increased heart rate, erratic breathing, or even an increase in the release of glucose. Your body bases its response to the situation on information from your senses and also from your stored memory of how and whether you can cope with the situation. This evaluation process is very important and will vary from person to person. Ultimately its response is designed to help you cope with the situation you find yourself in.

Lazarus & Launier (1978) proposed that stress is 'transactional' between people and their environment. If a person is sitting an exam the degree of stress is influenced by their judgement of the event (Is this stressful?), in addition to what their personal resources are (Will I cope? Is this important?). If the person has a strong **environmental fit** they will cope with the situation but if they have a weak environmental fit, they will not cope and this results in stress.

Theories of stress, behavioural addiction and physiological addiction

In order to understand the area of stress and addiction fully it is important to study the theoretical evidence and research proposed so far. In this section you will look at the different theories of stress, behavioural addiction and physiological addiction. You will apply these theories to different scenarios, selecting and evaluating studies to support the different views.

Models of health

Health theories quite often describe how something might work rather than how something does work. There are different models and theories that suggest explanations for stress, behavioural addiction and physiological addition within health psychology.

Health belief model (Rosenstock 1966)

The health belief model (HBM) was developed by Rosenstock (1966) to investigate health behaviour that could be prevented and to study patients' responses to the treatment provided. This decision-making model has a number of components that suggest the likelihood of whether an individual will take part in a particular health behaviour, for example quitting smoking.

1 **Perceived susceptibility** is the individual's assessment of their risk of getting the condition, for example 'If I smoke, I have a higher chance of getting lung cancer'.
2 **Perceived severity** is an individual's assessment of the seriousness of the condition and what the consequences might be, for example 'Lung cancer is a serious illness'.

3 **Perceived benefit** is the individual's assessment of the positive outcomes of adopting the behaviour, for example 'Stopping smoking will save me money' (cost-benefit analysis).

4 **Perceived barriers** involve an individual's assessment of the influences that support or discourage the behaviour being carried out, for example 'Stopping smoking will make me ill-tempered'.

This model suggests that the best way to change behaviour is to limit barriers by making healthier choices whereas the least effective way is to try and convince people of the seriousness of the situation. If you get rid of the barriers, people are more likely to follow through with following healthy behaviour, such as giving up smoking.

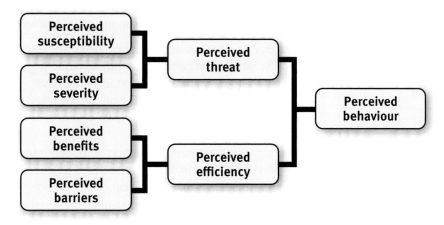

▶ **Figure 3.3:** Health belief model (HBM)

Cues of action

Cues of action are triggers to remind the individual that they need to do something which is consistent with a target they set themselves. This makes the behaviour more likely. Cues to the individual to begin the healthy behaviour can be internal, for example feeling breathless because they are unfit; or external, for example a health promotion leaflet from a health professional.

Demographic variables

Demographic factors like age, gender, culture and social-economic background could also influence whether someone takes part in healthy behaviour. **Demographic variables** can be applied alongside **psychosocial factors** of family, peers and previous contact with a disease. Together these main elements should be used to predict the likelihood that a behaviour will occur. They are a starting point in finding out where an individual's beliefs about their health started from. They modify the 'perceived seriousness', susceptibility, benefits and barriers of the health-related behaviour. For example, older people may be less likely to participate in risky health-related behaviour such as binge drinking, due to an awareness of perceived seriousness. In terms of gender, women are more likely to participate in different healthy behaviour such as yoga, as they may value the perceived benefits. Cultural differences may determine whether they view the perceived severity of an illness with a medical explanation and ultimately seek help.

Strengths

▶ The HBM can help develop effective treatments that patients will be motivated enough to carry out. It has been applied to a wide range of populations and health behaviours, for example Murray & McMillan (1993) successfully used the HBM to predict cancer screening behaviour in women.

> **Key terms**
>
> **Demographic variables** – statistics about people that include information of gender, class, education, family size and age.
>
> **Psychosocial factors** – information combining psychological and social influences.

- It has also been applied to health interventions. Williamson & Wardle (2002) employed the HBM when designing an intervention aimed at increasing participation with cancer screening.

Weaknesses

- The HBM's structure indicates that humans process information in a rational yet unrealistic manner; often humans are irrational in their decisions after an event has occurred.
- Alternative models have been proposed that may offer additional explanations of health behaviour, for example self-efficacy theories and the belief in perceived confidence in being able to achieve a particular behaviour change.

Link

Look later in this unit on page 148 (Bandura's self-efficacy theory 1977) for information on an alternative theory to HBM.

Health belief model – studies

Becker (1978) Compliance with a medical regimen for asthma

Aim: To use the health belief model to explain mothers' adherence to treatment for their asthmatic children.

Procedure: Interviews were used with 117 mothers of children previously diagnosed with asthma who brought their children to the emergency facility at the Johns Hopkins Hospital (in Baltimore, Maryland, US) for treatment of an asthmatic attack. Researchers were seeking a **correlation** between beliefs disclosed in the interviews and their compliance with self-reported administration of asthma medication. The 45-minute interview dealt with the mothers' general health motivations and attitudes; their faith in doctors and effectiveness of medication; their views about their child's susceptibility to illness and asthma; how serious they thought the asthma was; how much it interfered with their child's education, how much embarrassment it caused and how it interfered with the mothers' activities.

Key terms

Correlation – a relationship or association between two variables that can be positive, negative or zero (no relationship).

Regimen – is a prescribed course of medical treatment used to promote healthy behaviour that is suggested people to follow.

In addition, an evaluation of compliance was made by drawing blood from the children to test the presence of a drug that is used in asthma medication – theophylline.

Findings: A mother's belief about her child's susceptibility to asthma attacks and compliance with administering prescribed asthma medication resulted in a positive correlation. Therefore, the more the mother believed her child was susceptible, the more likely they were to comply with treatment.

- The higher the mother's perception of the seriousness of asthma, the more they complied with the treatment and gave their children the medication.
- Mothers who reported that the asthma interfered with their personal activities were more likely to comply with the treatment.
- Mothers who said that the asthma interfered with the child's schooling were more likely to complete the treatment.
- Demographic variables such as marital status and educational level were associated with compliance, with married mothers and those with a higher level of education being more likely to comply.

Conclusions: From the results you can conclude that the HBM was useful in attempting to predict levels of adherence to medical regimes and health behaviour in relation to asthma. Many of the HBM components were helpful in predicting health-related behaviour. Only faith in doctors was different to what the HBM would suggest but even then, children still ended up at the emergency facility getting the treatment they needed.

▶ **Table 3.2:** Evaluation of study (Becker 1978)

Strengths	Limitations
The data gathered came from the mothers' self-reports together with blood samples. The blood samples tested for compliance which allowed for results to be checked against each other. This added to the reliability of the findings.	The asthmatic study was correlational and so showed only a relationship between variables. A cause and effect could not therefore be achieved.
Validity could be achieved as the HBM model allowed for predictable behaviours. It was therefore a realistic measure as it predicted the behaviour of the adherence of the mothers of asthmatic children.	Self-report interviews may have social desirability effects as the mother may not have wanted to give fully correct answers for fear of embarrassment or repercussions on how they looked after their asthmatic children.
The study showed that the HBM could be used by health professionals like these in hospitals to show how serious a disease like asthma is to sufferers and their carers. The hope was that it might improve health behaviour.	Only mothers of the children admitted to the emergency facility were used in the study. It did not include information about the child's health condition from their fathers, therefore it may be biased.
Ethically the mothers were asked for their consent to take part in the interview about their child's health in terms of asthma. Mothers were given the ethical right to withdraw and from the final sample size it was clear this was the case, as there were fewer participants in the final sample.	

Exam tip

During your exam, you can be asked about any part of what the researchers did. When revising, therefore, make sure you know the key areas in detail.

If asked to explain the results of any of studies, you will need to show clearly that you understand the results of the study in terms of its aims. Be careful not to confuse this with the conclusions from the study which can be asked as a separate question.

Research

Think of an illness, for example HIV, diabetes, and so on, and apply the HBM to this illness. You need to consider the decision making the person with the health problem may make.

Carpenter (2010) A meta-analysis of the effectiveness of the health belief model variable in predicting behaviour

Aim: To analyse the effectiveness of the HBM in predicting behaviour.

Procedure: This was a **meta-analysis** in which Carpenter looked at longitudinal studies to see their effectiveness at predicting behaviour and analysing their results to determine whether the HBM was a good predictor of health behaviour. He suggested that the length of time between measurement of health belief model variables and the measurement of behaviour could fade over time due to more knowledge being gained – so maybe these could influence a person's health beliefs after they had

been measured. The studies selected had to meet certain requirements, including measuring at least some of the HBM variables. They had to be longitudinal and those studies that used HBM variables to design an intervention but did not measure the variables were excluded. 18 studies, conducted between 1982 and 2007, totalling a sample of 2,702 were chosen.

Link

Look back at Unit 1, page 14, for more information about longitudinal research.

Coding of the studies (measurements)

▶ Length of time between the measurement of the HBM variables; measurement of the health behaviour.
▶ Whether they looked at a treatment outcome or a preventative behaviour; whether this was drug-taking behaviour (prescribed) or some other behaviour.
▶ Percentage of people who changed their behaviour.
▶ Correlation between HBM variables (susceptibility, severity, barriers and benefits) and the behaviour.

Key term

Meta-analysis – involves researchers using studies and results that already exist and drawing overall conclusions from their findings.

Findings

Severity: This resulted in a slight positive correlation between subjects' estimates of the severity of an outcome and whether they would adopt the behaviour. The more severe, the more likely that they would adopt the health behaviour. This was highest for prescribed drugs and so the consequences of not taking them were seen as important. In addition, they found that the longer the length of time, the less severity has an effect on the behaviour.

Susceptibility: There was no relationship between susceptibility beliefs and preventative and treatment behaviour. The longer the time between HBM measurements and behaviour outcome measurements, the weaker the relationship. A positive relationship only occurred when it measured the likelihood of a subject complying with the drug-taking regime.

Benefits: There was a positive correlation between a person's perceptions of the benefits of adopting a health behaviour and them being more likely to do it. Negative health outcomes showed the smallest positive correlation. The amount of time that passes between measurements is a strong moderator of the effect of the time a person benefits, indicating that longer periods of time are associated with weaker effects.

Barriers: The higher the participants perceived the barriers to be, the less likely the behaviour would be. Barriers were a weaker predictor of behaviour when the behavioural outcome was treatment than when it was prevention. Time between measurements and behaviour outcomes had little effect.

Conclusion: The findings suggest that you can conclude that the HBM model is varied in its effectiveness, with benefits and barriers being the strongest predictors of behaviour. This would suggest that only two of the four variables are completely effective in predicting behaviour.

▶ **Table 3.3:** Evaluation of study (Carpenter 2010)

Strengths	Limitations
Meta-analysis allows for lots of information to be collected and analysed. This information is already published by other researchers on the effectiveness of the HBM and eliminates practical issues surrounding time and cost of doing research of this size from the beginning.	Meta-analysis uses secondary sources and so there is no guarantee that the studies were carried out reliably and that results were interpreted in the same way. This reduces validity.
Application of the importance of benefits and barriers in predicting health behaviour can be used within both future studies and campaigns to ensure that higher levels of these elements are focused upon when educating people on health issues.	16 of the 18 studies relied upon convenience samples that may have reduced generalisability.
Ethically the studies used in this meta-analysis have not been named so confidentially was maintained.	Meta-analysis to an extent assumes that the ethical considerations were adhered to when the original studies were carried out, however it is impossible to be completely certain of this.

 **PAUSE POINT**   Can you explain the four components of the health belief model?

Hint   Close your book and draw Rosenstock's health belief model.

Extend   Think of an illness that you have experienced and analyse your experience in terms of the health belief model.

Locus of control theory

Rotter's (1966) theory of **locus of control** (see Figure 3.4) involves the idea of perceived control by the individual. Rotter believed that you cannot consider personality based on one factor alone, but rather on an interplay between internal influences from within the individual and external influences from their surrounding environment – so personality is interchangeable.

People with a strong internal locus of control feel responsible for themselves, meaning success or failure is due to their own efforts and actions. Those with a strong external locus of control consider external factors (such as luck, chance or other people) are responsible for their efforts or actions – so success or failure is outside their control.

Key terms

Locus of control – the extent to which people believe they have power over the events in their lives.

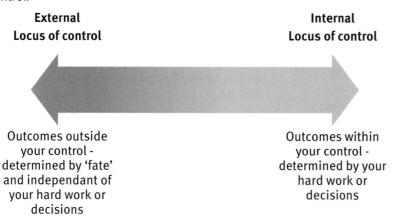

▶ **Figure 3.4:** Locus of control

If people feel that they have no power over their lives and that an external locus of control dominates, they are less likely to take part in health protective behaviour because it is beyond their control. This is known as 'generalised expectancy'. The opposite is true of those with an internal locus of control; they are more likely to look after their health by avoiding addictive behaviours and following health advice.

Link

Look back at Unit 1 for information on behavioural theory.

Attribution theory has four main dimensions of causality.
1 Internal or external
2 Specific or global
3 Controllable or uncontrollable
4 Stable or unstable

If a person attributes their situation to an external force then the possibility of controlling the situation is unlikely. For example, if a person who drinks too much alcohol attributes their situation to an external force (such as a group of work colleagues who drink four to five nights a week) they are then less likely to control the situation and give up drinking alcohol. The same is true of the opposite but with more of a chance of the person influencing their outcome. So, it can be assumed that internals are more responsible for their own health than externals, which in turn means that they are more likely to lead to adopting healthy behaviours.

However, external factors can play a role because these, combined with internal traits, can also lead to healthy behaviours being adopted. In addition, the internal locus of control may not always be positive in relation to healthy behaviour. Kaplan et al. (1993), for example, found that the burden of self-responsibility correlated with increased depression in those with a renal transplant.

You need to consider different factors in whether someone takes part in healthy behaviour, in addition to the importance of outcome to the person and their belief in whether they can take part.

Research

Go online and look at Rotter's I–E (internal–external) scale. What sorts of questions did he ask? Have a go at answering some of them. Can you determine which ones are measuring internal behaviour and which external behaviour?

Strength

▶ Supporting evidence from studies including Kaplan et al (1993) regarding depression and Abouserie (1994) regarding stress have shown how the locus of control theory can be used successfully in understanding health-related behaviour.

Weakness

▶ It has been suggested that the locus of control scales suggested by Rotter in his theory lack coherence, at times they have been judged confusing which makes measuring difficult. This undermines the credibility of the theory as an explanation for health behaviour.

Locus of control – studies

Rotter (1966) Generalised expectation for internal versus external control of reinforcement

Aim: To investigate the effects of internal and external locus of control on behaviour through the review of articles which focus on the topic in question.

Procedure: Rotter used several pieces of research focusing on individuals' perceptions of their ability to control outcomes based on reinforcements. Rotter's I–E (internal–external) scale was used in all of the studies and people were asked to choose between two pairs of internal and external items about their daily situations. For example, on one item someone may respond that a person's misfortune is due to their own mistakes (internal) or just bad luck (external). Those involved were told to select one statement in each pair that they strongly believed more than the other. Once all pair combinations had been answered a score was totalled from their responses. This indicated the type of locus of control (internal or external) that the individual was most likely to have. The research gathered from this study looked at a variety of situations to see if the scale could predict a number of behaviours.

Findings:
1 Rotter found that individuals identified as internal tended to prefer gambling on certainty, i.e., 'sure things' and did not like betting on situations where they were unlikely to win. Externals, on the other hand, preferred risky bets.
2 Internals were more resistant to influences from others, which could mean that they were more likely to avoid the temptations of drugs, alcohol and other risky behaviour.
3 Internals also tended to have more control. For example, they were more likely to quit smoking after a health warning than externals.
4 Internals were also less likely to conform to the influence from a majority than externals.

Conclusion: Rotter concluded that an individual's locus of control affected behaviour differently. He suggested this came from cultural factors, **socioeconomic** differences and parenting styles. He found enough consistent results across the research to conclude that people will behave differently in situations depending on whether they are external or internal.

Key term

Socioeconomic – looks at how social and economic factors affect individuals.

▶ **Table 3.4:** Evaluation of study (Rotter 1966)

Strengths	Limitations
Rotter's study suggested that a personal locus of control, especially in internals, can be used in health-related treatment programmes like cognitive behavioural therapy (CBT). CBT can be used to change negative health behaviour.	Rotter's study gathered its findings from secondary sources. This is an issue as it is unclear how reliable other researchers' interpretations of the I–E scale were.
Rotter used secondary sources that were cheaper and more practical to use than gathering data.	Rotter determined that our health behaviour is determined by our locus of control, but it ignores the concept of free will and the impact of individual differences.
	To an extent you can assume that the ethical considerations were adhered to when the original studies were carried out. However, it is impossible to be completely certain of this.

Abouserie R. (1994) Sources and levels of stress in relation to locus of control and self-esteem in university students

Aims: To identify academic sources of stress and consequent stress levels in university students. To investigate gender differences, if any, in sources and levels of stress. To examine the relationship between sources, levels of stress and locus of control.

Procedure: Questionnaires were given to 675 (202 males and 473 females) second-year undergraduates at the University of Wales, Cardiff.

1 **Academic Stress Questionnaire (ASQ)**: This looked at apparent causes of stress, such as examination results, conflict with lecturers and financial problems. The questionnaires invited respondents to indicate the degree of stress experienced in response to each item on a scale of 0–7 (no stress to extreme stress).

2 **Life Stress Questionnaire (LSQ)**: This covered different aspects and symptoms of psychological stress which led to a total stress score that was categorised as low, moderate, serious and very serious.

3 **Locus of Control Questionnaire:** This looked at locus of control in relation to academic learning at university level. The scale consisted of 12 items that related to stress, and 12 items that related to failure.

4 **Self-esteem Scale -** Likert scales.

Findings:

1 **Sources of stress** showed that the highest sources of stress were examinations and results (Mean=5.56), with essays or projects (Mean=4.36) being the lowest.

2 **Students' life stressors** showed that the majority of students were in the moderate stress category, with only 10.4 per cent being in the serious stress category. There was no one in the very serious category and only 12 per cent had no stress problems.

3 **Gender differences in academic stress and in life stress** showed that female stress levels were higher than male stress levels (females 102.99 compared to a mean of 93.25 for males).

4 **Stress in relation to Locus of Control and Self-Esteem** found a significant relationship between stress and students' locus of control and self-esteem, suggesting that personality variables are important factors in the response to stress.

Conclusion: Abouserie concluded that, from the order of the stressors, academic-related activities are the biggest cause of stress in students. In addition, most students suffer moderate levels of stress, and an external locus of control is associated with higher levels of academic stress. This suggests that students who believe they have control over

their situation are less stressed than those who believe things happen by luck or external forces.

▶ **Table 3.5:** Evaluation of study (Abouserie, R. 1994)

Strengths	Limitations
A total of 675 students were used from the University of Wales which increased generalisability to students and representativeness of sources of stress as the sample size was quite large.	The study suggested a correlation between academic stress and locus of control which meant that other factors could have been an influence, as correlations only show a relationship between variables, not that one causes the other.
The results from the study can be applied to help counsellors support students suffering from academic stress.	Students completed self-report questionnaires which can be prone to bias if participants do not tell the truth.
	Participants may have been distressed by the content and completion of the questionnaires.

Krause (1986) Stress and coping: reconceptualising the role of locus of control beliefs

Research has mostly concluded that internals cope better with stress than those with an external locus of control in terms of the samples selected. More recent research has extended this to include older populations and to look at the possibility that extreme internal and extreme external locus of control are different.

Hypothesis: The effects of stressful life events on depressive symptoms are stronger among older adults with extreme internal and external locus of control beliefs than among elderly people with moderate internal and moderate external locus of control.

Procedure: A total of 351 retired participants (who were over 65 years old, not living in an institution and who lived in Texas) were sampled through a random community survey. They were all interviewed and paid $10. 66 per cent were women and 34 per cent were men. The majority of them were white, although there was ethnic diversity.

The Centre for Epidemiologic Studies Depression scale (CES-D) was used to measure depressive symptoms. Three factors were measured on this scale:

1 depressed effect: for example sadness
2 somatic and retarded activities: for example sleeping problems
3 positive effect: for example happiness.

77 life events were used as a checklist for stressful life events based on different categories, for example children,

friends, some miscellaneous events, and so on. A total was obtained by adding up the number of life events which involved the participants as the main figure.

A summarised version of the Rotter I–E locus of control scale was used, based on two factors.

1 **Effects of chance** was based on how much a person believed external forces (chance) were affected by outcome, so a high score showed an external locus of control.

2 **Mastery beliefs** involved their beliefs about how much they could control a successful outcome, so a high score showed an internal locus of control and a low score an external locus of control.

Findings: Both extreme internals and externals felt the effects of stress on depressive symptoms more than moderate externals and internals. This demonstrated that extreme cases are vulnerable to effects of negative stressful events. The effects of stress on feelings of sadness, loneliness and depression were stronger in those elderly adults who believed in the effect of chance (externals) than among those elderly adults who did not believe in the effects of chance (internals). Extreme externals reported an average of 2.20 events that caused them stress, compared to 1.53 of extreme internals, which means extreme externals have a coping behaviour that helps them avoid stressful situations.

Conclusions: Extreme internal elderly adults may be vulnerable to the effects of negative stressful situations. This extreme internal locus of control can help in terms of coping strategies and avoiding stressful events. So having an extreme internal locus of control has its positive and negative aspects.

▶ **Table 3.6:** Evaluation of study (Krause 2016)

Strengths	Limitations
Measurements were gathered using established scales therefore ensuring valid results were gathered from participants.	The sample size was from one area in the USA, which is not generalisable to the rest of the population.
Using a random community survey to sample participants would have reduced bias compared to alternative sampling techniques.	Using **self-report methods** to measure the effects of stressful life events are prone to bias as participants may not tell the truth as they do not want to be embarrassed.
The study can be used to recommend that increasing the level of control the elderly have over their lives is useful to help reduce stress in everyday situations.	Participants were paid to take part in the research, which ethically may have influenced their right to withdraw as they may have felt obliged to complete the research.
	The research methods were focusing on stressful events, which may have distressed some participants.

Theory of planned behaviour (Ajzen 1985)

The theory of planned behaviour (TPB) included the factors: behavioural intention, attitude and subjective norm. The model was based on the idea that a person is likely to do what they intend to do. So, a person's behavioural intentions are influenced by a person's attitude about the behaviour and their subjective norms.

Intentions are influenced by three factors.

1 **Attitude towards a behaviour:** This involves the likely consequences of the behaviour. For example, if an individual believes exercise is good for them then

they are more likely to take part in it because they know they will benefit from the result.

2 **Subjective norm:** This involves beliefs about the normative expectations of others. For example, 'People important in my life will approve of me exercising as I will lose weight and I want their approval'.

3 **Perceived behavioural control:** These are beliefs about factors that may encourage or prevent the performance of the behaviour. For example, if the individual knows that they can lose weight through exercising then they are more likely to try it.

Within the TPB people do not always have control over their behaviour and there could be obstacles in their way,

---

Theory into practice

1 Eleanor drinks alcohol even though she knows her dad does not like her drinking. She believes that if she stops drinking, she will get stressed out over her exams again. She feels that she cannot control the withdrawal symptoms that would come from giving up drinking alcohol.

2 Jacob has put together a plan to stop drinking alcohol. Jacob's family and most of his friends drink alcohol. His school counsellor is very supportive and has helped Jacob put together a plan to give up alcohol which involves steps that Jacob knows he can achieve.

1 Why is Eleanor unlikely to give up drinking alcohol according to the TPB?

2 Why is Jacob likely to stop drinking according to the TPB?

---

such as unsupportive friends and family. Being able to assess a person's perceived behaviour control can be used to put in place intervention strategies that support them overcome health problems like smoking, drug addiction and drinking.

Strength

▶ The TPB can be used to explain the process of addiction and other health-related behaviour. It can therefore be applied to develop appropriate treatments to try and reduce the long-term effects of health problems like addiction.

Weaknesses

▶ The TPB does not take into consideration individual differences, such as personality, age, or social

environment that may also influence a person's perceived behavioural control. However, it has been used with some success. Penny (1996) found that those who failed to quit smoking several times believed that they would not succeed in the future if they tried again so were less likely to try and stop again. This supports the idea that past experiences are important.

Theory of planned behaviour – studies

Louis et al. (2009) Stress and the theory of planned behaviour: understanding healthy and unhealthy eating intentions

Aim: To research the domain of healthy- and unhealthy-eating intentions by adding stress as a factor.

Hypotheses: (1) Stress moderates the relationship of attitudes, perceived control, and subjective norms to unhealthy eating. (2) The extent to which life stress impacts on healthy eating, independent of body-image discrepancy, (a psychological stressor that has been shown to play a role in unhealthy eating decisions).

Procedure: A sample of 154 students (106 females and 48 males), aged 17 to 33, were selected from a large Australian university. They were mainly first-year psychology students who could exchange participation for partial course credit. Participants were asked to complete a questionnaire measuring demographic data, life stress, perceptions of their body image, and planned behaviour variables in relation to healthy eating. They also recorded their height and weight.

▶ **Life stress:** This was measured subjectively using questions such as 'How is your living situation?' which participants had to score on a 7-point scale ranging from –3 (extremely stressful) to +3 (extremely relaxing).

▶ **Body-image discrepancy:** This was measured using the Body Image Inventory which measures differences between participants' perceptions of their own body image and participants' perceptions of ideal body image for their gender. The former was measured by the item 'Which drawing looks most like your current figure?', given a score on a 9-point scale. The latter was measured by the item 'Which figure do you most want to look like?'. Again, a 9-point scale was used.

▶ **Attitudes, subjective norms and perceived behavioural control:** These were assessed using scales with three items of each – attitude items, subjective norm items and perceived control items.

▶ **Eating intentions:** These were measured on a scale from past healthy-eating research. The frequency of 30 food choices over a two-week period was reported using a weekly scale. An 8-point scale was used from 0 (never) to 7 (every day).

▶ What affects whether you eat healthily?

Findings:

Healthy-eating intentions	Unhealthy-eating intentions
Attitudes towards healthy-eating were found to be positive. Positive healthy eating attitudes were associated with healthy intentions.	Those with acute body-image discrepancy intended to eat more unhealthy foods while those with higher life stress intended to eat less unhealthily.
Females intended to eat healthy food more often than males.	Perceived control was linked to lower unhealthy-eating intentions, but those who perceived more social pressure to eat healthily (subjective norms) actually had greater intentions of eating unhealthily.
Perceived control and subjective norms on healthy eating were not found to relate to healthy-food intentions.	Attitudes did not affect unhealthy intentions.
No interactions between life stress and planned behaviour variables was obtained.	Stress moderated the effects of subjective norms and of perceived control, therefore high levels of stress subjective norms were ignored.
When other variables were controlled there was a slight trend between perceived control and healthy-eating intentions.	At low levels of stress subjective norms favouring healthy eating were associated with higher unhealthy-food intentions.

Conclusions: The results supported, to an extent, the theory of planned behaviour model in relation to healthy-eating choices. However, stress influenced the impact of planned behaviour variables on unhealthy-eating intentions, especially in relation to subjective norms and perceived control.

The results indicate therefore that perceived control is most important in getting students to eat healthily. Interventions focusing on highlighting unhealthy foods and getting rid of barriers to healthy eating (for example access to cafeterias and affordable pricing) would be a good key focus.

▶ **Table 3.7:** Evaluation of study (Louis et al. 2009)

Strengths	Limitations
The study collected information on stress and the planned behaviour model using multiple variables of demographic data in addition to weight and height, which provided a more realistic picture of how effective the model was in terms of those sampled.	Student participants were taken from one university in Australia which meant that the results may not have been representative of the wider population. The sample may have been too narrow to cover all types of people in society.
The results can be applied to suggest planned interventions for young adults in terms of stress and uncovering barriers to healthy eating, increasing long-term good health.	Students completed self-report questionnaires which can be prone to bias if participants do not tell the truth.
	Participants may have been distressed by the content and completion of the questionnaires when referring to their life stressors.

Cooke et al. (2016) How well does the theory of planned behaviour predict alcohol consumption? A systematic review and meta-analysis

Aims: To provide a comprehensive and up-to-date review and meta-analysis of the applications of the TPB to the area of alcohol consumption.

Procedure: A search generated 166 studies that measured intention to drink alcohol, drinking within certain limits or abstinence (not drinking at all), of which 40 were reviewed. Studies included direct measures of attitudes, subjective norms and perceived behavioural control. Perceived Behavioural Control (PBC) was measured using items which looked at perceived control and self-efficacy separately. These were coded separately. Perceived control questions included 'It is up to me whether or not I engage in binge drinking in the next week' and self-efficacy 'For me, to engage in binge drinking in the next week would be easy'.

Alcohol consumption was standardised in terms of amount of alcohol (ethanol) consumed: 56g. From these, five categories were used, (1) getting drunk, (2) heavy episodic drinking (binge drinking), (3) light episodic drinking, (4) quantity of drinks consumed, (5) not drinking at all. All studies were coded for gender of participant and mean age of participant. Study sample sizes ranged from 49 to 2814.

Findings:

▶ **Intentions to drink:** This unsurprisingly resulted in a strong positive correlation with actual alcohol consumption.

▶ **Attitudes and intentions:** This had the strongest positive relationship ($r\pm=.62$).

▶ **Subjective norms:** This had a stronger relationship with intentions to drink than PBC.

▶ **Stronger perception of control (PC):** PC over alcohol consumption did not always lead to high intentions to drink – in fact a weak perception of control often led to higher consumption.

▶ **Higher confidence (self-efficacy):** This meant that their ability to consume alcohol was associated with stronger intentions to drink alcohol, and higher consumption.

Conclusions: The results from the study indicated that TPB was useful when looking at the intention to drink alcohol. The TPB had the strongest correlation from the results with attitude and subjective norms and intentions to drink. A medium correlation was found with PBC (Perceived Behaviour Control). This was influenced heavily by self-efficacy, which resulted in the strongest relationship with intentions to drink. This might suggest that PBC may have less of an effect on health-risk behaviour than health-promotion behaviours. Also considering episodic drinking with TPB variables must also be recognised as more than just getting drunk – there seems to be more to it than this conclusion.

▶ **Table 3.8:** Evaluation of study (Cooke et al. 2016)

Strengths	Limitations
A total of 40 studies were selected to complete the review. These provided a great deal of data on which to assess the applications of the TPB to the area of alcohol consumption thereby making the study conclusions more valid.	The studies were collected by a range of researchers over time on alcohol consumption and TPB. There is no guarantee that the collection procedures and how they were analysed are completely comparable. Inaccuracies may have occurred which may have affected the overall credibility of the studies in terms of their conclusions.
The theory of planned behaviour could be used with different people to analyse their drinking intentions and advice on healthy-drinking consumption once people are targeted.	From the research pieces analysed you can assume to an extent that the ethical considerations were adhered to when the studies were carried out. However, you cannot be completely certain of this.

Self-efficacy theory

Self-efficacy is your belief in your ability to succeed in specific situations or accomplish a task. It reflects confidence in the ability to exert control over your own motivation, behaviour and social environment. This means that higher levels of self-efficacy may result in a greater motivation to change behaviour as people feel they have the confidence to succeed. This means that people with higher levels of self-efficacy may be more likely to try health-related behaviour change. In addition, they are more likely to keep going, which should result in a more positive outcome.

Key term

Self-efficacy – your belief in your ability to succeed in specific situations or accomplish a task. It reflects confidence in the ability to exert control over your own motivation, behaviour and social environment.

Bandura (1986) proposed four different influences that would affect self-efficacy, as shown below.

1 **Enactive (mastery) influences:** These involve a person's past experiences of success and failure. For example, a person who has tried to give up alcohol in the past and failed several times may be less likely to try again than someone who has not experienced this type of failure. Someone who has experienced success will be more confident about succeeding in the future.

2 **Vicarious influences:** These consist of comparing yourself with others and judging your own competence according to them. One application of this is to present someone with another person who has succeeded. For example, meeting someone who has given up smoking can result in gaining confidence as if they see that one person can do it, then so can they.

3 **Social persuasion influences:** These can be increased when others encourage the person that they can be successful. If family and friends encourage a person that they can stop gambling, their persuasive comments will help the person see that they can do it.

4 **Emotional influences:** These relate to an increase in anxiety when the person believes that they cannot do it. For example, a person reduces the number of cigarettes they smoke daily but are worried about the physical side effects. This can cause the person to lack confidence in their ability to reduce the number of cigarettes they smoke daily.

Self-efficacy can play a major part in influencing our day-to-day chances of being successful. This can be used in treatment programmes to help set goals and to ensure our self-efficacy beliefs are in line with what health behaviour change is trying to be achieved.

Theory into practice

Mahika is a 19-year-old learner who is struggling to fit into her new college and make friends. She finds the work on her new course difficult and feels that both her college life and her social life are a challenge.

Mahika is developing high levels of stress thinking about and attending her lectures; she is now finding sleep difficult. She starts missing lectures because she is too tired and stressed to attend. Mahika is referred by her lecturer to the college counsellor to get help.

1 How could Mahika's college counsellor use self-efficacy to explain her behaviour?

2 Using self-efficacy ideas, what might the counsellor suggest Mahika could do to deal with her behaviour?

Strength

▸ Self-efficacy has been used to reduce stress and depression in lots of people, encouraging their resilience and improving their mental health. It is therefore a good coping strategy for intervention from counsellors and other health professionals to try.

Weakness

▸ High self-efficacy can sometimes lead to an individual applying less effort as it can lead to overconfidence in your own attitude, thinking that you know more about the health-related behaviour than they do, which results in less effort being applied.

Self-efficacy theory – studies

Bandura & Adams (1977) Analysis of self-efficacy theory of behavioural change

Self-efficacy is the amount of self-belief you have in your competence to complete a task successfully and produce a favourable outcome. This study looks at **systematic desensitisation** (SD) as a treatment for behaviour change (treating a phobia) and how it can raise self-efficacy. This study considers how SD changes behaviours through its interaction with self-efficacy because it lessens emotional arousal. (Emotional arousal is one of the four areas that might lower self-efficacy in an individual.)

Key term

Systematic desensitisation (SD) – a treatment for phobias in which the patient is exposed progressively to more anxiety-provoking behaviour. The behaviour is then paired with relaxation in order to cope with the anxiety caused by the phobia.

Aim: To assess the self-efficacy of patients undergoing SD in relation to their behaviour with previously phobic objects.

Hypotheses: (1) Eliminating emotional arousal alone would enhance self-efficacy but the levels of attainment could vary. (2) The higher and stronger the self-efficacy expectations installed by the SD, the greater the reduction in avoidance behaviour.

Procedure: The participants all had a chronic snake phobia which is why the study was a quasi-laboratory experiment. Bandura could not have randomly assigned people to groups: either participants had a fear of snakes or they did not. Therefore, there was no control group. Participants were ten patients who replied to an advertisement in a newspaper. Nine females and one male aged 19–57 years old.

Prior to treatment there were three measures taken.

1 **Behaviour avoidance:** This required participants to complete a series of tasks involving a boa constrictor. Those who could not enter the room scored 0, while those who could lift the snake from a cage were considered not-phobic enough and eliminated from the sample.

2 **Fear arousal:** This was the degree of fear shown when a situation was described and then actually performed. The participants' score on the 10-point scale were averaged between the two.

3 **Efficacy expectations:** These were taken after they had performed the avoidance tasks, so they would have some idea of what was expected. This included whether they thought they would be able to perform a series of tasks. On a 0–100 scale (10-point units) they rated their expectation of success, from high uncertainty to compete certainty. So, the **self-efficacy level** was the number of tasks rated higher than ten and the **self-efficacy strength** was the scores across tasks, divided by the number of tasks.

Treatment: SD was given by a therapist. A standardised procedure was administered to each person that involved relaxation techniques (they provided them with relaxation tapes and so on to practise at home), which were then paired with imaginary, increasingly threatening situations involving snakes. The least threatening situations would be, for example, looking at toy replicas of snakes, to the more threatening, holding live snakes. Each image would be presented until there was no anxiety, then participants would move to the next increasingly threatening image, until the subject anxiety was eliminated. The average duration of the desensitisation treatment, not counting relaxation training was 4 hours 27 minutes.

Post-treatment measures: The same assessments in the pre-treatment phase were re-administered within a week of completing the treatment. The subjects were initially tested with a corn snake and then the boa constrictor was used again. The same female tester was used to conduct both pre- and post-treatment measures.

Findings: In post-treatment results, self-efficacy was higher. This correlated positively with higher levels of snake interactions and less avoidance behaviours. So, the higher the self-efficacy, the more they would interact with the snakes. This result indicates that the high levels of self-efficacy in the subjects led to less fear arousal at the prospect of performing tests they had previously avoided. So, fear arousal was reduced by the treatment approach.

Conclusion: Systematic desensitisation enhanced levels of self-efficacy. This, in turn, led to a belief that the subject was able to work with their snake phobia and interact with snakes. So, levels of self-efficacy may be important in behaviour change, which could inform future treatment programmes.

Table 3.9: Evaluation of study (Bandura & Adams 1977)

Strengths	Limitations
Having the same female tester in pre- and post-treatment groups being 'blind' to who was phobic or non-phobic would eliminate investigator effects. Meaning that the experimenter would not accidentally influence the subjects, thereby avoiding bias and enhancing the validity of the results.	The sample was made up of nine women and one man, so was unequal in terms of gender. It may be that males with a similar phobia may behave differently, so an equal sample would have been better to demonstrate this and make the results more generalisable.
The study can be applied as it highlights the importance of self-efficacy for behavioural change. Therefore health interventions can use it to target phobias.	Self-report methods were used to gather the data at different stages of the treatment, which may have been problematic as participants may have committed social desirability (the tendency to report an answer in a way they deem to be more socially acceptable than their 'true' answer).
The standardised procedure employed for all participants would have ensured that the extraneous variables were eliminated and did not affect the treatment.	Anxiety was induced by the treatment programme which ethically may not be acceptable in terms of the distress participants may have experienced.
The use of SD allows participants to take control of their fear hierarchy, which is ethically more acceptable than having it imposed on them.	

Marlatt et al. (1995) Self-efficacy and addictive behaviour

This review focuses on the role self-efficacy plays in preventing the onset of addiction (resistance self-efficacy) or having the ability to quit (coping self-efficacy).

Review: The review did not have a formalised procedure but rather focused on articles that analysed current understanding of self-efficacy and addiction, in addition to looking at research already completed. The review looked at the different ways self-efficacy theory was applied to change addictive behaviour.

How self-efficacy is involved in the initiation of, or resistance to, drug use

From the review, addictive behaviour patterns were identified as involving two phases.

1 **The initial use:** Research has shown that low resistance to self-efficacy combined with pro-drug social influences can predict intention and actual use of alcohol and tobacco in adolescents. So, prevention programmes should be aimed at training adolescents to resist social pressures and internal temptations.

2 **The reduction of self-harm of the addictive behaviour:** Promoting drinking in moderation or abstinence. Intervention programmes work best if harm-reduction goals are set that are achievable for adolescents, which will raise their harm reduction self-efficacy as they will believe that they can moderate their behaviour.

Self-efficacy for change, treatment and relapse prevention

Self-efficacy seems to be very important in changing behaviour. This begins with a commitment for action, coping efficacy and then recovery efficacy.

Coping efficacy is the ability to cope with high risk situations such as negative emotional stages, conflicts and social pressures without relapsing. Evidence from research suggests that relapse prevention techniques like CBT aim to raise self-efficacy and prevent relapse. This suggests that coping efficacy is important when looking at potential for change, successful treatments and when trying to prevent relapse.

It involves looking at how people bounce back in terms of their reactions to a setback. Research shows that a helplessness reaction to the first setback, attributed to internal factors such as lack of willpower, can lead to a greater chance of relapse. Recognising a setback is vital to restoring self-efficacy. When a client is able to recognise their trigger, they can be taught coping strategies to reverse the course of that behaviour – helping them not to be overwhelmed with that one failure.

Conclusions: The review findings suggest that self-efficacy is very important in all stages of alcohol and smoking addiction, indicating that it could be used successfully in treatments. Treatments using self-efficacy can target personal effect to gain better outcomes. It can be used to identify people at risk, for example those who are most likely to relapse. Training using self-efficacy can be targeted at those who need it, especially when it poses a greater risk to the individual.

▶ **Table 3.10:** Evaluation of study (Marlatt et al. 1985)

Strengths	Limitations
Articles were used to provide a current understanding of self-efficacy and addiction which would have provided a current and valid overview.	You cannot guarantee that the articles used met methodological and ethical criteria.
You can assume that the articles used met the ethical requirements in terms of the participants used and reported on.	The articles were gathered by someone else and analysed within this study. There may have been subjective interpretation which could have influenced the findings.
The findings can be applied to recommend criteria for intervention programmes for smoking and alcohol addiction.	

Ⅱ PAUSE POINT   Can you explain what the learning aim of this section was about? What elements did you find easiest?

Hint   Close the book and draw out a concept map about the four different theories.

Extend   Looking for strengths and weaknesses of these theories is important especially in terms of different human factors (often called individual differences). Make a list of all the individual differences that you have covered. Are there any others not considered or taken into account by these theories?

Assessment questions

Scenario

Miguel is 19 years old and started his business apprenticeship three months ago. He got the results from his first assignment and he has not done very well. In his work placement he is also underperforming. He has made many mistakes and his manager has set him more targets to achieve over the next four weeks. Miguel is feeling overwhelmed and decides to go and see his GP who diagnoses depression. The GP suggests that his apprenticeship may be one of the factors affecting him being depressed.

Rotter's Locus of Control theory suggests that behaviour is influenced by internal and external locus of control.

1   Define what is meant by internal and external locus of control. (2 marks)

2   Explain Miguel's behaviour in terms of internal locus of control. (2 marks)

3   Explain Miguel's behaviour in terms of external locus of control. (2 marks)

Self-efficacy is the amount of self-belief you have in your competence to complete a task successfully and produce favourable outcomes. Bandura (1986) proposed four different influences that could affect self-efficacy.

4   Explain how two of these influences could be used to explain Miguel's behaviour. (4 marks)

5   Explain one strength and one weakness of the self-efficacy theory. (4 marks)

Stress, behavioural addiction and physiological addiction

Stress

It is important to study the causes of stress, including a person's physiological response to **stress**. You will also be making judgements on the importance of these different causes and the problems with looking at stress from a physiological point of view. You will then be able to apply your knowledge about the causes of stress and the physiological response to different health scenarios.

Causes of stress

A person may feel their health is compromised or threatened in some way. Stress is influenced by a person's perception of what is stressful and how they perceive their ability to cope with this situation. Stress therefore usually occurs when a person feels that they cannot cope with the situation they find themselves in.

Life events

Life events involve looking at daily life factors and how they affect how someone becomes stressed. Certain events in people's lives are going to cause them stress and the more of these events that occur, the more stress they will experience.

Holmes & Rahe (1967) created the Social Readjustment Rating Scale (SRRS) which is a self-report scale that uses a questionnaire to measure life events and stress. They asked a large sample of people to rate the degree of social readjustment required to adapt to 43 stressful **life events**, including death of a parent, personal injury, and illness. Those items that they judged more stressful were given more points (**Life Change Unit – LCU**), for example divorce was 73 points, compared to son/daughter leaving home which was 29 points. The level of stress was measured by asking participants how many stressful life events they had experienced in the previous 12 to 24 months, then the points from these responses were added together. So, a person with fewer than 150 LCU has a 30 per cent chance of suffering from stress compared to a person with a score of over 300 LCU, who has an 80 per cent chance of developing a stress-related illness.

Key terms

Stress – a state which occurs when the perceived demands of a situation exceed the perceived ability to cope.

Life events – major changes in the circumstances of an individual such as death, moving to a new house, or getting married, which require the person to readjust in some way.

Life Change Unit (LCU) – refers to the number of points awarded on an item on the SRRS.

Research

Do you think this scale would be completely relevant to society today? Research and find out about the sample used and have a look at the different scaled life stressors.

There are resources in the Further Reading at the end of this unit to help you.

In groups, critique the scale in terms of how the items may be ranked today. Is it inclusive of different cultures? Does it take into account individual differences?

Rahe et al. (1970) Prediction of near-future health change from subjects' preceding life changes

Aim: To investigate whether scores of the Holmes & Rahe SRRS correlated with the onset of illness.

Procedure: The sample group comprised 2664 males from three US Navy cruisers: two in Vietnam and one in the Mediterranean. There was a range of educational and maritime experience and the sample involved different ranks. They were given the SRRS prior to a tour which was to last around six to eight months. They were asked how many life events they had experienced in the previous six months and the total score on the SRRS was given for each participant.

Over the next six months records were kept on illness (for example number and severity) for over 90 per cent of the sample who had completed the original questionnaire; this totalled around 2500 men. The correlation between Life Change Units (LCUs) and frequency of illness was recorded.

Findings: There was a positive but small correlation +0.0118 between life change scores and illness scores across all three ships. Therefore, as frequency of illness went up so did Life Change Units.

Conclusion: There is a relationship between life events and the development of stress-related illnesses. So, the higher the number of life events, the greater the chance of stress-related ill health. However, the correlation was not perfect, which suggests other factors may have led to the illnesses.

> **Key term**
>
> **Daily hassles** – minor events from everyday life such as misplacing your shoes or missing the train to work.

Daily hassles

Daily hassles as a cause of stress was developed as an alternative to the life events explanation by Kanner et al. (1981). Kanner suggested that it was the frustrating and distressing everyday events that were more closely related to stress. These were referred to as 'daily hassles' and based on this Kranner et al. developed a scale to measure stress by asking people to rate how irritating or annoying these hassles were.

They recognised that certain everyday events can have a positive effect on stress, referred to as 'daily uplifts'. The hassles scale used consisted of 117 hassles, including losing things, pollution, concerns about owing money. The uplifts scale consisted of 135 items, including being lucky, getting a present, getting on with people. On both scales participants were asked to circle which items had happened to them in the previous month. Once completed they rated each of these on a 3-point scale relating to severity (hassles) and frequency (uplifts). The scale has been used in many studies.

Kanner et al. (1981) Comparison of two modes of stress measurement: daily hassles and uplifts versus major events

Aim: To compare the hassles and uplift scale with the SRRS as predictors of psychological symptoms of stress, such as ill health.

Procedure: There were 100 participants (52 women and 48 men), aged 45–64, who participated in a 12-month study on stress, coping and emotions. They were white, generally well educated, on an adequate income and were from the Bay Lake area in California. The study used the daily hassles scale (117 hassles) and the uplifts scale (135 uplifts).

The tests were sent to each participant one month before the study began. They were asked to fill it out beforehand and a month later they would have an assessment via interview.

The schedule was as follows: completion of the hassles and uplift scale, the SRRS and a self-reporting symptoms checklist.

Findings: The hassles and uplifts scores were generally consistent from month to month. They found that men's life events were positively correlated with hassles (the more life events, the more hassles) and negatively correlated for uplifts (the more life events, the fewer uplifts). For women life events positively correlated with both hassles and uplifts. Finally, daily hassles were a significantly better predictor of psychological symptoms, for example stress/illness than life events.

Conclusions: Daily hassles are a better predictor of stress than major life events. Hassles seemed to be associated with outcomes that involved well-being and social functioning, rather than life events in general. Daily uplifts may be more useful in measuring stress in women than in men. The findings suggested that hassles contributed to psychological problems no matter what the life event was.

Strengths and weaknesses of self-reporting

Self-reports are a common way of measuring stress and rely on participants themselves providing information on their own levels of stress. Quite often these involve scales that allow participants to rank their stress, stressful events and other stress-related factors.

▶ **Table 3.11:** Strengths and weaknesses of self-reporting

Strengths	Weaknesses
Self-report measures ask participants directly about their lives and stress. They are, therefore, a valid measure.	Social desirability may occur when you ask participants to report on their stress and daily lives. For example, they could be embarrassed which could cause results to be biased.
Lots of qualitative and quantitative data can be gathered about stress and its influences from participants in order to analyse patterns of what is influencing stress in society.	Self-report questionnaires generally have a low response rate as people do not always have time or take them seriously, so results of what influences stress may be limited.
Self-report questionnaires and scales of stress are often standardised which makes replication with other samples of participants possible.	

Role of the workplace in stress

Workplace stress has become a key focus of a lot of research in recent years, mainly due to its increase in people's lives and the impact it has on health in the work environment. Knowing about types of stress is very important as it not only affects the individual but also their performance at work, which ultimately affects the company and people they work with. It is important for organisations and employers to reduce stress in the work environment and help individuals cope with their daily work routines.

> **Key terms**
>
> **Work-life balance** – refers to ideal situations where workers have time for both work and family, for example.
>
> **Neuroendocrine stress response** – a physical reaction to stress in the body that affects homeostasis involving the endocrine system.

There are areas within different work environments which can affect stress levels in employees.

- ▶ **Environment effects:** Heating, lighting and physical arrangement of the workplace are all potential sources of stress on employees. Factors such as increased temperature can lead to frustration; additional noise and crowding can also aggravate a workplace. Glass et al. (1969) asked 60 participants to complete cognitive tasks such as word searches under one of four conditions and concluded that you can adapt to high noise levels, but it is more difficult if the noise is not constant or is unpredictable.
- ▶ **Organisational factors:** Areas such as opportunities for promotion can cause stress, involvement in decision-making, and relationships with other workers. For example, if a job is advertised internally, lots of workers may get stressed over the pressure to apply, the application process and ultimate outcome when someone is appointed. Many workers feel that they need to impress employers and work longer hours believing that this will put them in a better position for promotion.
- ▶ **Home-work effects:** Many people nowadays have to balance work and home life. A **work-life balance** suggests that an individual should have time for both, which would result in less stress and better psychological wellbeing.

Johansson et al. (1978) Social psychological and neuroendocrine stress reactions in highly mechanised work

Aim: To investigate the psychological and physiological stress response in two separate categories of employees in a Swedish saw mill.

Procedure: The sample was made up of two groups: the high-risk group (made up of 14 sawyers, edgermen and graders), and the control group (made up of ten stickers, repairmen, maintenance workers, and so on). All the workers were on performance-related pay (those who did well in their work got more money) and worked shift work (different time periods were worked).

Differences between the groups included the high-risk group having better lighting but were exposed to more dust and noise. They also had a higher risk of accidents from cuts compared to the control group who had more slipping, stumbling incidents. High-risk jobs were boring, with no control, were isolating and had higher targets for production levels.

All participants provided a urine sample in addition to rating themselves on mood and wakefulness by selecting words like sleepiness, irritation, and so on (scale from none at all to maximum).

Findings: The adrenaline levels of the high-risk group were two times higher than their baseline (which was measured at home); these levels continued to increase throughout their working day. The high-risk group had higher irritability ratings and reported being more 'rushed' than the control.

Conclusions: Repetitive, machine-paced and attention-demanding work in a Swedish sawmill contributed to a high stress level in the high-risk group; this was a risk to their wellbeing. In addition, the high-risk group were on performance-related higher pay which may have added to the stress for them as their family may have depended on it.

> **Exam tip**
>
> Identify and explain one strength and one weakness of the study by Johansson et al. (1978). (4 marks)
>
> For this type of question make sure you both identify and explain what is asked of you; you will lose marks if you don't fully explain what has been asked. Always make sure that you read the question fully before you start and take a look at the number of marks available as this will guide you on how in-depth your answer needs to be.
>
> Within this question you will need to identify knowledge from within the study that can provide context for your strength/weakness, questioning whether the study is reliable, valid, generalisable, can be applied to the health profession, supporting theory, are among some areas that are quite often used.

Role conflict

Role conflict occurs when an individual is put in a position that requires them to behave in a way that they know and believe is not in their best interests. For example, working lots of overtime may mean that you do not have much time to spend with family. Those in middle management may feel stressed at having to balance the needs of a team and the targets set by their boss. Pomaki et al. (2007) found that role conflict was responsible for emotional exhaustion, depressive symptoms and even some physical illnesses in a study of hospital doctors.

Level of control

The amount of work that an individual has to do can increase their workplace stress; having too much or too little can have similar effects. Breslow & Buell (1960) found that employees working more than 48 hours a week were twice as likely to develop coronary heart disease (CHD) than those working 40 hours a week. Being in control is an important element of workplace stress, high levels of control lead to lower levels of stress, while low levels of control lead to higher levels of stress. Karasek's (1979) model (Figure 3.5) illustrates this well.

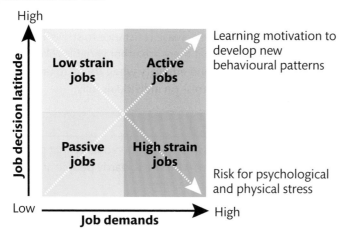

▶ **Figure 3.5:** Karasek's model, identifying the level of control in stress

Therefore, stressful jobs involve high demand and low control and least stressful jobs involve low demand and high control. So, a sense of control is needed in the workplace if stress is to be avoided.

> **Key term**
>
> **Role conflict** – involves an individual being put in a position that requires them to behave in a way that they know is not in their best interests.

Case study

Laura works long hours in a restaurant, more than what she is contracted to work, and her boss seldom pays her for this overtime. He says that she is too slow and that she needs to clear up before she goes home late at night. Laura has made suggestions about how to improve the menu as some of the items never sell, and customers complain about the lack of variety. This means that every week there is a lot of food thrown away. But Laura's boss says that this is not her problem and that she just needs to get on with taking orders and waiting tables.

Laura once rearranged some of the tables to get more customers in, but her boss told her to put the tables back as he did not want them that way. They had to send customers away that night as the restaurant did not have enough tables and her boss yelled at Laura and said it was her fault.

Laura's friends tell her to quit the job, but it pays well, and as her father is out of work, she has to contribute to buying food for the whole family.

Using workplace research, explain why Laura might or might not have workplace-related stress.

Personality

Individual differences, such as our gender, class, ethnicity, or personality can have an influence on stress. People will respond to stress differently depending on these, especially if they make a person vulnerable. This also means that their coping mechanisms to try and relieve stress may be different from others, so some treatments may work better than others.

> ### Key terms
>
> **Type A Behaviour (TAB)** – shows patterns of behaviour associated with hostility, competitiveness and impatience, which are aspects linked to stress-related illness.
>
> **Type B Behaviour (TBB)** – relaxed, non-competitive style behaviour, which is generally non-aggressive.
>
> **Type C Behaviour (TCB)** – behaviour characterised by patience, cooperation and a minimal negative emotional reaction.
>
> **Type D Behaviour (TDB)** – behaviour in people who are prone to stress, anger and tension, and who generally have a pessimistic outlook.

In the 1950s two researchers Meyer Friedman and Ray Rosenman came up with different personality behaviour types.

▶ **Type A Behaviour (TAB):** this refers to patterns showing hostility, competitiveness and stress-related aspects. For example, in terms of hostility, Type A people will be easily irritated, impatient with co-workers, easily angered and direct emotions inwards.

▶ **Type B Behaviour (TBB):** this is behaviour which shows non-competitive, non-aggressive patterns of behaviour.

As personality theories have developed so too have the additional personality types.

▶ **Type C Behaviour (TCB):** this was identified by Tremoshok (1979). People with Type C behaviour are those who are patient, cooperative and show little emotional negativity. They are more concerned with others than their own well-being, and they tend to be self-sacrificing and unassertive.

▶ **Type D Behaviour (TDB):** people with Type D behaviour show more vulnerability to stress, they are angered easily and show tension. They have a pessimistic outlook and have low-self-esteem.

Hardy personality

Kobasa (1979) introduced the idea of **hardiness**, which involves individuals who are less likely to see stressful events as being stressful. Her research on 800 workers involved them completing a measurement of stress (Holmes & Rahe's SRRS) from which she selected her final sample.

Kobasa then administered a range of measures to assess personality differences, including a locus of control scale and a commitment scale. She found that the group who did not suffer stress-related illnesses scored a lot higher on these dimensions. They showed higher levels of commitment to their jobs, had a strong internal locus of control and saw stressful events as a challenge to embrace and overcome. So, these three aspects – 'control, commitment and challenge' – make up the hardy personality.

However, the tests used within this study have flaws. For example, self-report questionnaires have an element of subjective bias. In addition, Klag & Bradley (2004) suggested a gender difference after sampling 130 mixed-gender university staff. They found that hardiness acted as a buffer between stress and illness for the men but not the women sampled.

High levels of control, commitment and challenge seem to protect against stress for some people, even to the point where they increase resistance to stress. However, you must consider that there are other variables like gender, coping strategies and ethnicity when trying to understand the effects of stress on individuals fully.

> ### Key term
>
> **Hardiness** – a type of personality that shows resilience when faced with stress; hardy people are controlled and embrace a challenge.
>
> **Adrenal medulla** – inner part of the adrenal gland controlling hormones that initiate the fight-or-flight response.

Physiological responses to stress

Stress involves a biological and psychological response that occurs when you feel that you do not have the resources to deal with a situation. If a situation is judged stressful our hypothalamus is activated. The hypothalamus is found in the brain and is responsible for dealing with a stress response. When a stress response it activated the hypothalamus will send signals to two other areas of the body: the pituitary gland and the **adrenal medulla**. The pituitary gland will aid the release of **hormones** to help deal with the stressful situation. The adrenal medulla (which is part of the **autonomic nervous system)** will aim to regulate body systems like breathing and heart rate which could be elevated in a stressful situation. These developments have led to lots of physiological responses to stress being provided as alternatives to other explanations.

General adaptation syndrome (GAS)

Selye (1947) developed a three-stage model (Figure 3.6) of how the body responds to stressors, calling it the general adaptation syndrome. This is shown in Table 3.13.

▶ **Table 3.13:** The general adaptation syndrome

1	Alarm	The body's mechanisms to deal with stress are activated. The brain receives the perceived stressor and sends signals to the hypothalamus. Stress-related hormones increase, so the heart rate and blood pressure go up and the body's energy reserves are activated.
2	Resistance	The body holds this level of response, but after a while the response systems begin to show signs of strain. Stress-related illness then occurs as the immune system is unable to cope. This means the situation becomes long term.
3	Exhaustion	The long-term stress level can make the body very tired as it uses up its reserve of energy and tries to maintain the circulation of high levels of the stress hormones. It is at this point that stress-related illnesses are most likely to occur.

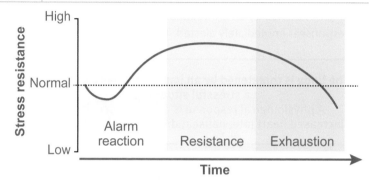

▶ **Figure 3.6:** Seyle's diagrammatic representation of GAS

Seyle's work was the first attempt at developing a description of the body's response to stress, illustrating a link between chronic stress and illness – a link that potentially could be developed further in terms of new treatments. However, Seyle did not consider individual differences such as gender, personality and ethnicity which are very important when you are perceiving and reviewing stressful situations.

Theory into practice

Naila is a newly qualified doctor who has just finished her first month in an A&E department. Naila found the work very stressful. She spent most of her evenings reading up and studying the different illnesses and ailments her patients were showing in addition to studying for her end-of-year examinations.

Naila then worked for another two months before getting a week off. She fell ill almost immediately; she fell ill almost immediately, she had a cold which developed into flu. Naila had two more weeks extra off work before she was able to return.

1   Use your knowledge of the general adaptation syndrome to explain Naila's experience.

2   Using the GAS's three stages, identify behaviour that Naila is showing at each stage.

Sympathomedullary (SAM) system

SAM is a system that responds to immediate danger and gets the body ready for its **fight-or-flight** response (acute stress). The autonomic nervous system (ANS) is a regulatory system that keeps the body calm, stable and under control. It is made up of two parts that oppose each other:

1 **Parasympathetic nervous system (PNS)** involves slowing down the heart rate, lowering blood pressure, reducing breathing and increasing digestion. It is the state of balance that you exist in most of the time.

2 **Sympathetic nervous system (SNS)** involves increasing the heart rate, blood pressure and breathing. It is part of the fight-or-flight response that is activated when you are stressed.

The SNS originates in the brainstem with nerve pathways travelling via the spinal cord to different organs in the body. One of these pathways leads to the adrenal medulla which, along with the **adrenal cortex,** make up the **adrenal gland.**

When the body is threatened by an immediate danger (such as a stressful situation), a physiological response is immediately alerted. This process is shown in Figure 3.7.

Link

Look back at Unit 1, page 8, for more information on 'fight-or-flight'.

Key terms

Fight-or-flight – a physiological reaction that occurs when a person feels under attack or perceives a threat to their survival.

Parasympathetic nervous system – part of the involuntary nervous system, that slows the heart rate, increases intestinal and gland activity.

Sympathetic nervous system – part of the autonomic nervous system that influences the body to become aroused.

Adrenal cortex – the area of the brain that surrounds (and is immediately adjacent to) the adrenal gland.

Adrenal gland – produces hormones to help the body function; can help control heart rate, blood pressure and stress reactions.

Adrenaline – a hormone which works on the heart and respiratory systems to increase the heart rate and blood pressure.

Noradrenaline – a hormone which activates the body into action when it is threatened, increasing arousal, for example.

> The body is threatened by an immediate danger (such as a stressful situation).
> A physiological response is activated causing an increased heart rate, nausea, dilated pupils, and so on.

> The hypothalamus in the brain detects the stressful situation and then activates the SNS.

> The SNS then stimulates the adrenal medulla to release the hormones **adrenaline** and **noradrenaline**.

> This increase in the response of the body's organs is maintained by the hormones.

SO

> This combined effect from the SAM system ensures that our body is ready to deal with the stressful situation by either fighting or taking flight. When the situation decreases the parasympathetic system comes into effect. Adrenaline stops being released so and the body organs begin to go back to their normal functioning.

▶ **Figure 3.7:** The physiological response to danger

Hypothalamic-pituitary-adrenal (HPA) system

If a stressful situation continues the hypothalamus will release a chemical CRF (cortico-trophin releasing factor) which stimulates the **pituitary gland** into action. These glands then pump the hormone adrenaline into the bloodstream which produces a number of physiological changes. Figure 3.8 demonstrates this process.

The HPA deals with the long-term effects of stress (**chronic stress**). It has a slower reaction and occurs only if the stress situation continues for a sustained period of time. The pituitary gland can be found just beneath the brain and is connected to the hypothalamus which is responsible for releasing lots of different hormones into the bloodstream.

The main stress hormone is adrenocorticotrophic (ACTH) which is released from the pituitary gland into the bloodstream. It travels to the adrenal cortex (located in the adrenal gland) which stimulates the release of cortisol. Cortisol influences an increase in glycogen (needed for energy), lowered sensitivity to pain, lower immune response, impaired cognitive functions like concentration and slowing of the digestive system. The system self-regulates with both the hypothalamus and pituitary glands working together, monitoring cortisol levels, increasing or decreasing their levels when necessary. This will help the body deal physically with the stress situation.

Key terms
Pituitary gland – the main gland in the body which directs other glands to release hormones.
Chronic stress – the emotional response to stress over a long period of time involving continuous arousal.
Acute stress – the immediate response to a traumatic or stressful situation which produces a strong emotional response.

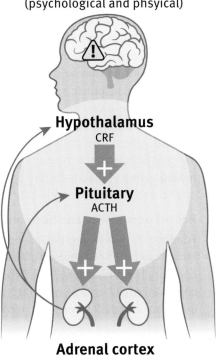

Stress
(psychological and phsyical)

Hypothalamus
CRF

Pituitary
ACTH

Adrenal cortex
Cortisol

▶ **Figure 3.8:** The HPA process

By measuring stress hormones within the body, you can get an objective scientific measure of how the body reacts to stressful situations, providing evidence of how to deal with stress as a health issue. Physiological explanations of stress show both short-term increases in the immune response as explained by **acute stress** and long-term immunosuppression in response to chronic stress.

Adrenaline and stress response

In times of stress, the hormone adrenaline prepares the body for fight or flight, resulting in physiological changes such as an increase in heart rate, sweating, blood pressure and pulse rate. Adrenaline activates the sympathetic nervous system into arousal and reduces the role of the parasympathetic nervous system to prepare the body for action. When the stress situation stops the nerve impulses to the adrenal glands are reduced and the production of adrenaline ends.

Limitations to the view of stress as physiological responses

Gender differences in physiological responses

Most of the early research into fight-or-flight was carried out on men so applications to women is limited, there was an assumption from this research that women will behave in the same way to stress as men. New research has suggested that women adopt a more 'tend and befriend' response to being in a stressful situation. The physiological stress response to a threat in both genders is the activation of the SNS and the HPA. Research suggests that in women, the stress response is influenced by care-giving attachment principles which influences their arousal levels. They are more likely to befriend the enemy or seek social support. This results in an increase in more endorphins, which makes them feel good and motivates them to behave in a friendlier manner. Tayler et al. (2000) suggested that women are more likely to protect offspring and befriend others, instead of fighting or going into flight, therefore their responses are different and early research can be challenged on its findings.

More than two responses

Within stress research there are additional responses to stress other than the physiological and psychological ones discussed so far. There is a contemporary add-on to the fight-or-flight response in humans; the same physiological principles occur but an additional element of freeze has been added.

The freeze response to stress occurs when you are confronted with a stressful situation that your coping mechanisms cannot handle; the resulting response is, in essence, paralysis. This occurs in a situation in which the individual does not see a way out, they do not know what to do and no matter what they consider it will not get them out of the stressful situation. Situations which may cause this level of indecision could include car accidents or witnessing criminal acts in which the individual falls into a **cognitive paralysis**. The stressful situation reduces cognitive resources and stops how the person can interact with their environment, leading to paralysis. The stressful situation therefore prevents cognitive functioning and a freeze response occurs. This response is seen more in children as their cognitive processes are not as sophisticated as adults and they do not have the experience to deal with these new stressful situations. However, certain stressful situations, even as an adult, can trigger unresolved childhood memories which are traumatic or upsetting for the adults' cognitive processing – therefore resulting in this freeze response idea.

> **Key terms**
>
> **Cognitive paralysis** – involves over-thinking a situation resulting in paralysis so the situation cannot be dealt with.
>
> **Maladaptive behaviour** – involves things that a person does that stops then from adjusting to healthy situations.

Maladaptive fight-or-flight response in modern society

The fight-or-flight response has been a survival mechanism for humans for a very long-time. In the past, threatening situations such as being hunted by a predator, meant that the fight-or-flight response was essential for survival. However, such a reaction nowadays may not apply due to the absence of similar situations. Stressors activate the fight-or-flight response more regularly which can have physical implications for our body in terms of using up energy and putting continual strain on vital organs like the nervous system. This means that the fight-or-flight response may not be healthy for humans in modern society; it is **maladaptive** in that its current reaction is not a healthy one for those who are continually stressed.

Role of personality and hormone release

Friedman & Rosenman (1959) conducted research to understand the link between a Type A personality and coronary heart diseases (CHD). Type A personalities are competitive, self-critical, have high work involvement, are impatient and easily aroused in terms of aggression. From their research they found that twice as many people with Type A compared to Type B developed CHD. Such people are a lot more likely to have their fight-or-flight response activated by stressful situations within their environment and as a result they are more likely to have stress hormones present for longer periods of time. This means that this personality type has an increase in hormones released. This heightened hormone release can lead to a range of stress-related illnesses.

The link between stress and ill health

As stressful situations put a body on alert it is the action of hormones like corticosteroids, such as cortisol that suppress the activity of our immune system (lowering lymphocytes for example), resulting in people becoming vulnerable to illness. Eczema, gastric ulcers, coronary heart disease, irritable bowel syndrome, among many other conditions have been associated with stress.

> **Key term**
>
> **Antigens** – any substance foreign to the body that produces a response such as creating antibodies to fight the foreign (harmful) invader.

Immunosuppression

The immune system is our first defence at dealing with infection and illness. Any agents that stimulate the immune system are called antigens, for example bacteria, viruses and fungi, (familiar **antigens**). The immune system is made up of various cells and circulating proteins which are designed to deal with these agents. The main immune cells are white blood cells called lymphocytes and phagocytes.

You have two immune systems in place:

1 **natural immunity** involves a primitive system made up of blood cells (leucocytes) in the bloodstream. These attack and absorb pathogens that invade the body, for example viruses and bacteria

2 **specific immunity** is more complex and involves cells (made of different lymphocytes) which recognise invading pathogens and then produce antibodies to eliminate them.

Together these systems defend the body against infection.

However, there is a suggestion that stress suppresses the immune system (immunosuppression) which results in an increase in illnesses and infections.

Kiecolt-Glaser et al. (1984) Psychosocial modifiers of immunocompetence in medical students Some studies have suggested that stress affects the immune system. However, many of these used animals, which limits their generalisability. This study looks at a natural occurring stressor i.e., exams and its impact on stress in human participants.

Aim: To look at natural life stressors and their impact on the immune system function.

Procedure: Volunteer participants were gathered from first-year medical students from Ohio. There were 75 in total (26 females and 49 males), with an average age of 23. She took blood samples one month before their examination and on the first day of the examination. The BSI (Brief Symptom Inventory), the SRRS and UCLA loneliness scale were then all used. The SRRS was used to detect life changes and from this data the students were divided into high or low stress groups. A lower level of natural killer cells (NK cells) in the blood would mean a compromised immune system.

Findings: There was a significant decrease in NK cell activity from the first measure prior to the final exams and the second sample during the exams. The high stress/high life events groups also had lower NK activity than the low stress. The high loneliness scores had lower NK than the low scorers.

Conclusion: The stressed condition had significantly fewer natural killer cells. A connection was found between life events, loneliness and problems such as depression and a weakened immune system.

> **Case study**
>
> Manon and Ava have been asked to research and present to their class a summary of the links between stress and ill health. They researched Kiecolt-Glaser et al. (2005) who looked at the effects of marital arguments on the immune system and wound healing. Manon and Ava found that Kiecolt-Glasser et al's (2005) research concluded that stress can slow down the immune system and delay healing, which has implications for recovery from operations, for example. However, Evans et al (1994) got students to give talks to other students which caused acute stress. Evans measured the student's levels of a particular antibody. After the talks the level of this antibody had increased - suggesting increased and not decreased immunity. Therefore, Manon and Ava could conclude that not all stress causes lowered immunity.
>
> 1 Describe what Manon and Ava could put in their presentation to explain the influences of stress on ill health.
>
> 2 Identify one problem that Manon and Ava might find when trying to come to a final conclusion about how stress influences ill health.

Cardiovascular disorders

The fight-or-flight response activates an increase in blood pressure which can cause long-term damage resulting in a heart attack or, in terms of the brain, can cause a stroke.

Coronary heart disease has contributing risk factors including gender (men are more susceptible), age, cholesterol, high blood pressure, genetics, diabetes and so on. Coupled with any of the stress factors, such as divorce or work stress, there is a high chance of coronary heart disease.

Ⅱ PAUSE POINT Briefly explain five factors that have an influence on a person becoming stressed.

(Hint) Find evidence to support each factor.

(Extend) Analyse the strengths and weaknesses of this evidence.

Think about how you could extend your analysis of the causes of stress within a longer response answer.

Assessment questions

Scenario

Alicia has just got a new job in an office. She shares her office with two other people, Sian and Marta. They play loud music and talk to each other throughout the day.

1 Identify one workplace stress factor that Alicia may be suffering from. (1 mark)

2 Describe one physiological response to stress. (4 marks)

3 Describe what is meant by life events in terms of stress. (2 marks)

4 Describe the procedure from Kanner et al's. (1981) daily hassles study. (3 marks)

5 State one conclusion that Kanner et al. (1981) made from the results of his daily hassles study. (3 marks)

Scenario

Benito must complete his tax return ahead of the deadline otherwise he is fined. Benito has to do this every year which coincides with him always getting a bad cold.

6 Explain why Benito may be prone to getting colds around the time when he is completing his tax forms. (4 marks)

Physiological addiction

Link

Look back at learning aim A on page page 133 for an overview of behavioural and psychological addiction explanations.

In order to understand physiological addiction fully, it is important to find out about addiction in terms of **initiation**, **maintenance**, and **relapse**. Being able to make judgements on the effectiveness of approaches that explain addictive behaviour can give you a better understanding of the unhealthy behaviour itself, in addition to being able to question the credibility of the different approaches. In so doing, you will be able to apply your knowledge about physiological addiction to different health scenarios.

Smoking

Key terms

Initiation – refers to the beginning of the addiction.

Maintenance – how the addiction keeps going.

Relapse – when the addict has resumed their addictive behaviour.

Currently around 19 per cent of British adults smoke, which has led to smoking being classified as a substance-related disorder by the DSM-5 classification system (disorders are diagnosed according to a manual published by the American Psychiatric Association called the Diagnostic and Statistical Manual of Mental Disorders. The fifth edition of this manual is often referred to as simply the DSM-5). Nicotine is thought to produce an addictive behaviour and researchers have spent a great deal of time looking at biological, environmental and personality explanations to smoking-related behaviour.

▶ What environmental explanations can you think of for smoking-related behaviour?

Biological approach

Biological addiction involves a substance, in this case nicotine (smoking) which has been incorporated into the normal functioning of an individual's body. Most smokers want to stop but the addictive nature of nicotine makes it very difficult. Their body has been altered and is expecting the nicotine to fulfil certain requirements.

Initiation

Nicotine is a psychoactive drug which has a stimulating effect on the brain and its activity. It can also have a calming effect especially when you are in a stressful situation such as moving house or getting divorced. Smoking nicotine causes the pleasure centres in the brain to be activated, acting on this **reward pathway** to give the person pleasure. Nicotine affects the dopamine **receptors** in the area of the brain that is the reward pathway. **Dopamine** is a neurotransmitter which is released by **neurons** in the brain that are involved in giving pleasure. Nicotine copies the actions of acetylcholine, another neurotransmitter in the body, and binds to the acetylcholine receptors (ones specific to nicotine, not all of its receptors). When nicotine and the correct acetylcholine receptor bind together the response is to excite the neuron causing a release of the neurotransmitter dopamine, which then results in pleasure (see Figure 3.9).

> **Key terms**
>
> **Reward pathway** – a specific limbic circuit within the brain that creates feelings of pleasure.
>
> **Receptor** – part of the nerve that receives and reads signals from other nerves, helping transfer information around the nervous system and brain.
>
> **Dopamine** – a neurotransmitter that helps control the brain's reward and pleasure centres.
>
> **Neuron** – a specialised nerve cell that receives, processes and transmits information to other cells in the body.

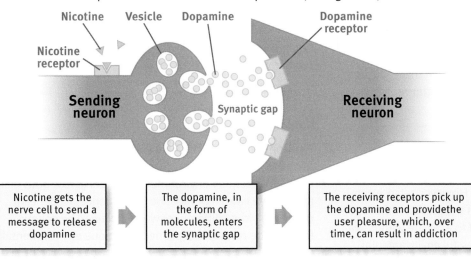

▶ **Figure 3.9:** Dopamine synaptic functioning and nicotine

Maintenance

Over time this binding of nicotine to the acetylcholine receptor results in a decrease of dopamine receptors. This is because the dopamine is not needed to provide pleasure as the nicotine does this instead. Addiction occurs when the natural dopamine is not there to stimulate the pleasure feelings, so nicotine needs to be taken to maintain the same effect. **Desensitisation** (tolerance) occurs when more of a substance, for example nicotine, is needed to get the same effect or feelings, in this case pleasure. Addiction results as more nicotine is needed to provide the normal functioning that the brain no longer does, as the nicotine has caused a physical change.

When asleep or after a period of time without a cigarette, the unchecked nicotine receptors become unregulated, as there is limited dopamine present in the brain to keep them working correctly. Sensitivity occurs in the person and results in negative feelings, for example feelings of anxiety and restlessness (withdrawal). The smoker can regulate these feelings by having a cigarette. This releases nicotine into the synaptic cleft that deals with the (nicotine-based) acetylcholine receptors by releasing the dopamine once again. Pleasure again results from this and withdrawal symptoms decrease. This explains why smokers often have a sense of great relief from their first cigarette of the day.

Tolerance develops when there is a greater need for the drug (in this case nicotine). If the nicotine level is not maintained the negative effects will occur once again and are a sign of withdrawal. Withdrawal symptoms can by psychological (such as a low mood) or they can be physical, such as vomiting, shaking or headaches. These symptoms will continue until nicotine is taken again.

> ### Key terms
>
> **Genetic predisposition** – the increased chance of developing a disease or pattern of behaviour based on our inherited genes.
>
> **Desensitisation** (tolerance) – a treatment that reduces emotional responsiveness to a stimulus after repeated exposure to it.

Relapse

Many people who have smoked will undergo treatment to eliminate these negative effects. However, relapse can occur if they return to the source of the pleasure (the cigarettes). There is a physical need to alleviate withdrawal symptoms and, if there are also stressful environmental factors, this can lead to relapse in many smokers.

A **genetic predisposition** (susceptibility) is the likelihood of developing a particular disease due to a person's genetic make-up. This involves looking at genetic variations that are inherited from a parent that then contribute to the development of the disease. For example, some people will have a genetic predisposition to becoming addicted to smoking, but others won't. So, it is also important to consider other factors that contribute to addictive behaviour. Often the person with an addiction to smoking will be in a situation with environmental stressors, for example a bad day at work triggers the need for a cigarette. Their genetic vulnerability makes them more likely to take part in the behaviour and have a cigarette compared to others who will not follow this pathway. Comings et al. (1996) showed a genetic link between A1 allele (a variation of the DRD2 gene) and the likelihood of a person being a smoker, suggesting that a genetic predisposition for smoking may exist.

Vink et al. (2005) Heritability of smoking initiation and nicotine dependence

Aim: To look at genetic influences in nicotine dependence as previous research had not addressed this area adequately.

Procedure: This study was part of an ongoing study on health-related behaviour. The twin/family method used the Netherlands Twin Register, assessing families with adolescent and young adult twins every 2–3 years from 1991. A total of 1572 Dutch twins were used in the study. The sample consisted of 868 monozygotic (identical) male and female twins, and 413 dizygotic (non-identical) male and females twins, with 291 dizygotic opposite sex twins.

The longitudinal method collected smoking data every 2–3 years between 1991 and 2000, with 61 per cent of the twins participating more than once. Classifications consisted of non-smokers who reported that they had never smoked or had tried smoking a few times but never reported being a regular smoker. If an individual reported to having smoked regularly they were classified as an 'ever smoker'.

In 2000, the survey used only those classified as smokers or ex-smokers (they filled in the FTND – a test of nicotine dependence).

Findings: In terms of individual differences in smoking initiation, 44 per cent could be explained by genetic factors and 56 per cent by environmental factors across both male and female twins. For nicotine dependence, 75 per cent of the individual differences were explained by genetic factors. The rest were explained by unique environmental factors.

Conclusion: The study summarises that there are two routes to non-smoking. Either an individual can be a non-smoker due to genetic and/or environmental factors that influence initiation, or because that individual is low on the nicotine dependence dimension.

> **Exam tip**
>
> Describe dopamine's involvement to nicotine addiction. (4 marks)
>
> For 'Describe' questions you need to ensure that you are providing enough detail so consider including an example. For a question like this, you would need to refer to the dopamine reward system. You could describe dopamine's role in addiction to nicotine in addition to including an example from research to clarify your answer.

Learning approach to smoking

Another explanation of nicotine addiction is that it is a learned behaviour, which involves smokers being rewarded through positive reinforcement. Positive reinforcement is where the individual gains pleasure and enjoyment from the behaviour of smoking, which results in the individual repeating the behaviour. Learning operates during the initiation phase when the person first begins to smoke, the maintenance phase where the behaviour of smoking becomes a habit, and then the relapse phase when they try to give up but because their learned behaviour is now associated with pleasure, they find it difficult.

> **Link**
>
> Look back at Unit 1, page 28, for more information on conditioning, including the idea of negative and positive reinforcement.

Initiation

Social learning theory suggests that the rewards associated with smoking do not have to be immediate but could involve the positive effects of the actions of others. Therefore, when a child observes an adult or role model (parent or celebrity) smoking they are more likely to associate these positive role models with the behaviour of smoking (initiation phase).

Operant conditioning also plays a role, as the initiation of smoking might be encouraged by peers, so the person begins to smoke to get the reward of popularity; this is a form of positive reinforcement. They will imitate the smoking behaviour as they now associate the smoking

behaviour with this positive reward. Brynner (1969) showed that the media often portrayed smokers as being attractive and tough – desirable traits that the smoker may also want.

Classical conditioning can also add to the initiation process by explaining that an association has now been made between smoking and an increased good mood.

Maintenance

Maintenance of the smoking behaviour is continued with the idea of operant conditioning. The reward element of smoking is responsible for both its initiation and also for maintaining the behaviour. Negative reinforcement can be seen in withdrawal symptoms. However, these provide a strong influence on the smoker to continue so as to avoid the negative effects of smoking occurring.

> **Key term**
>
> **Cue reactivity** – external environmental cues can trigger initiation of an addictive behaviour.

Cue reactivity can increase maintenance of the smoking behaviour through ritualised behaviour. For example, some smokers tap their cigarette on the table before lighting it. Cues then come in the form of having a coffee in the morning or a meal at a pub, which are cues that trigger a desire to have a cigarette. There is now an association between these places and the smoking behaviour. The classical conditioning stimuli related to the addiction becomes associated with a positive outcome.

Finally, self-efficacy will determine maintenance of the smoking behaviour as it involves the confidence that someone has in their ability to control their need for a cigarette. Adults who smoke a lot have low self-efficacy and they don't believe they have the drive, determination or ability to give up cigarettes.

Relapse

Cue reactivity (classical conditioning) and operant conditioning account for smoking relapses. After quitting smoking, these cues that the smoker has still exist, so many years later, meeting with an old friend or visiting a certain place can trigger the craving for a cigarette. This psychological craving is also accompanied by physiological changes within the body, particularly the autonomic nervous system and results in increased heart rate, breathing and so on, as the craving for a cigarette is once again initiated. In terms of operant conditioning therefore the individual relapses to avoid the unpleasant consequences of nicotine withdrawal such as shaking.

Evaluation of biological and learning approaches

Biological explanations for explaining smoking behaviour are seen to be reductionist as they only consider certain aspects, such as genetics. This may be an oversimplified approach as it does not consider personality, situational factors or cultural differences in its explanation of smoking as an addiction. Treatment methods have been successfully developed to try and alleviate addictions like smoking. An example is aversion therapy which involves replacing the positive associations with something negative in order to reduce the smoker's cravings. Alternatively, cognitive approaches suggest that smoking is based on the irrational thought processes of the smoker, for example believing that smoking improves concentration and therefore does not support either learning or biological explanations.

Alcohol

It's estimated that in England 2.5 million people report drinking over 14 units of alcohol on their heaviest drinking days. As drugs go, alcohol can be viewed as being socially accepted in certain areas and if taken in moderation there is evidence that it may have some positive health benefits. However, when it turns into an addiction, it can cause major health issues.

Cognitive approach

The cognitive approach to addiction focuses on the way in which events are perceived and interpreted. Faulty cognitions are seen as responsible for the initiation, maintenance and often relapse of addictive alcoholic behaviour.

Initiation

Gelkopf 2002 developed the cognitive **self-medication model** that states individuals use drugs like alcohol to treat psychological problems. Therefore, drinking alcohol is chosen to relieve anxiety, stress or nervousness. Those who drink alcohol persist in their behaviour because they are under the impression that the drug is working. Drinking alcohol will alleviate nervousness as it stops the withdrawal symptoms of increased breathing and anxiety that the individual would have been experiencing otherwise.

People often become reliant on alcohol for other issues like anxiety, nervousness and stress in their lives. The alcohol is used as a coping mechanism which if overused can lead to overreliance, resulting in the addictive behaviour. So, the alcohol is used to relieve a person's current life problems. However, alcohol in the long term increases nervousness and anxiety, as shown in Figure 3.10. Overall this suggests that the initial decision to start drinking alcohol is conscious and deliberate and is an attempt to relieve stress, nervousness or some other negative psychological symptom.

Maintenance

There is an expectation that drinking alcohol will lead to positive outcomes. However, once drinking alcohol becomes established it becomes part of the person's thinking – their **automatic processing**. In terms of the self-medication model, the reason for initiated drinking was to relieve nervousness and stress for example. Continued drinking realistically can lead to an increase in nervousness and stress, not a decrease as the drinker believes. There is an assumption that they are managing the problem when in fact they are not, and actually are potentially increasing it. The drinker continues to believe that the act of drinking is causing stress relief when in fact the real increased stress just encourages the person to drink more. So, individuals believe that the alcohol is managing their problems when in fact it is not.

Relapse

Relapse involves a person's ability to exert control over their actions, in this case stopping drinking alcohol. When a person is addicted to a drug like alcohol, the symptoms they are trying to treat, for example stress, anxiety, and so on, often also become the withdrawal symptoms that occur when they have not taken the drug for a period of time. While trying to alleviate these symptoms they may find it difficult to deal with everyday life, so they will relapse and drink alcohol again. This means that taking alcohol may reduce their worries and stress in the short term only.

However, it is counterproductive as the withdrawal effects make them drink again and produce a loss of control over their behaviour. It is this loss of control that adds to their stress because as they attempt to solve the problem they cannot, as they do not have the control required. So, people often drink alcohol as a reason to relieve anxiety, for example when they stop they experience withdrawal symptoms which makes copying with daily life difficult without the support of the alcohol so they relapse and take alcohol again, so trying to 'solve' the problem causes the relapse.

Learning approach

Operant conditioning suggests that if a behaviour is to be repeated there needs to be a reward of some kind. Rewards can be positive or negative.

Initiation

Positive consequences of drinking alcohol can be that it makes you feel good and relaxed, reducing stress – this is the positive reinforcement associated with it. Other positive consequences could be friendship from others and being socially popular; this reinforces the drinking behaviour.

Further positive reinforcement can come from role models, like parents or celebrities, who the individual will see drinking, especially those in the media. They are famous, popular, seem to have great lives and they are drinking alcohol, so the individual will imitate such role models and drink alcohol themselves. This is positive reinforcement in the hope of gaining the same rewards. For a behaviour to be repeated it is also rewarded through negative reinforcement, for example removing unpleasant consequence such as withdrawal symptoms.

The physiological effects of taking alcohol are powerful. Alcohol stimulates the release of dopamine into the prefrontal cortex which produces happiness and provides stress relief for the individual; it has activated the reward pathway in the brain. They will want to feel like this again, so they keep drinking. Therefore, reward behaviour also has a physiological focus.

Maintenance

Maintenance of alcohol consumption will involve ensuring that the negative side effects associated with drinking, such as headaches, shaking, seizures and hallucinations, will be prevented by drinking again. When the individual stops drinking, they have these negative withdrawal symptoms as a result of these biological changes. So, having an alcoholic drink acts as a powerful form of negative reinforcement as it immediately removes all the unpleasant feelings. Negative reinforcement can also be delivered via peer groups and social situations where the individual may feel uncomfortable not drinking alcohol. The addictive behaviour brings rewards (positive reinforcement) such as a reduction in anxiety, friendship from others and so on. This will make the behaviour more likely to be repeated.

Person drinks to relieve nervousness

The person becomes nervous thinking that they have not had a drink, urging them to maintain this behaviour

If a person has an alcoholic drink they quickly become nervous again due to the fact they are drinking

The behaviour is then repeated

▶ **Figure 3.10:** The cycle of alcohol addiction

Relapse

Often the negative symptoms associated with the alcohol make it very difficult for the individual not to relapse. Taking the alcohol again will stop the negative symptoms of shaking, nausea and feeling low, therefore negatively reinforcing the behaviour to start drinking again.

Evaluation of cognitive and learning approaches as an explanation of alcohol

Faber et al. (1980) found a difference in alcohol use through negative reinforcement (escape drinking) and positive reinforcement (social drinking) suggesting that learning theories are linked to explaining alcohol as an addictive behaviour. The cognitive explanation for addiction in alcohol focuses on expectation and beliefs in cognitive processes but it does not consider biological factors associated with addiction in terms of dopamine production and its effects on the reward pathway. Cognitive explanations for addiction have been successfully implemented into treatments like cognitive behavioural therapy (CBT) suggesting that addiction must have at least some cognitive element.

Link

Go to page 183 later in this unit for more information on cognitive behavioural therapy.

⏸ PAUSE POINT

Can you explain physiological addiction in terms of smoking and alcohol?

Hint   Recap on the two physiological approaches to explaining smoking as an addiction and the two approaches to explaining alcohol as a psychological addiction.

Extend   Summarise all these approaches in terms of initiation, maintenance and relapse.

Look at the evaluation points: do you see any similarities or differences?

Add additional evaluative points and think of alternative explanations, supporting evidence or applications to therapies as starting points.

Assessment questions

Scenario

Max is a successful businessman in the highly stressful world of corporate finance. He is usually professional, honest and objective in his work life. He is sent to you through the business welfare team after several reports from co-workers concerning work-related incidents of unprofessionalism.

Max explains that he only intends to have one or two glasses of wine with dinner each night but in fact usually finishes the bottle. He says that this is the only way that he can unwind from the pressures of work and it helps him sleep. At a recent executive business lunch, it was reported to his manager that he drank a whole bottle during the meal and bought a round of shots for the clients he was entertaining. Max admits that he drinks at work, usually in the afternoons after the midday meeting when he is given targets to complete for the next day. Max says that a lot of his co-workers go for drinks with him after work.

Recently Max has been very abrupt with several co-workers, especially in the morning and has been reported as being rude and uncooperative in terms of helping them with their work. When questioned Max admits this is probably true but he cannot remember. He is remorseful and says that these allegations have made him sad and upset as he is usually a helpful and supportive co-worker.

1   Using the cognitive approach and the learning approach explain Max's alcohol addiction. (6 marks)

2   Explain one strength and one weakness of the learning approach as an explanation of smoking. (4 marks)

Behavioural addiction

As with physiological addiction, in order to understand behavioural addiction fully, it is important to find out about addiction in terms of initiation, maintenance, and relapse. Being able to make judgements on the effectiveness of approaches to explaining addictive behaviour can give you a better understanding of the credibility of the different approaches in addition to looking at its impact on the health of different individuals. In so doing, you will then be able to apply your knowledge about behavioural addiction to different health scenarios.

Link

Look back at learning aim A on page 133 for an overview of behavioural and psychological addiction explanations.

Gambling

DSM-5 places gambling under its impulsive disorder category because those who suffer from this addiction are usually preoccupied with the disorder, have repeated attempts to stop, and continue the habit despite losing financially and suffering other effects like damage to family relationships and support. Gambling can take many forms such as slot machines, betting on horses and online games such as bingo.

Cognitive approach to gambling

The cognitive approach to gambling suggests that the cause of the addition is down to irrational beliefs. Addictive behaviours like gambling are caused due to a person's expectations being based on irrational and illogical thought processes. According to the cognitive approach's expectancy theory, addictive behaviours are often selected over healthy ones and the pros and cons of the addictive behaviour outweigh the pros and cons of the healthy behaviour.

Initiation

When a person expects the pros and cons (**cost-benefits**) of addictive behaviour like gambling to outweigh the pros and cons of healthy behaviour, they have chosen the addiction. For example, gamblers have the irrational belief that that the odds are not stacked against them and overestimate the extent to which their behaviour can affect the outcome of them winning. Generally, they underestimate the amount of money they put in and overestimate the amount of winnings they get back. The addiction is created due to the individual's expectations of the costs and benefits of taking part in the gambling. They consider the cost (money lost) minimal compared to the benefit (money won), even though they often have a biased view of how much they have won. The more control they think they have over the gambling environment, the more likely they are to become addicted.

Key terms

Cost-benefit – an evaluative process that judges and compares the situation to determine if it is worth doing.

Cognitive or distorted bias – a type of thinking that allows people to make quick decisions which are drawn on expectations based on past experiences; these can be biased and lead to false information.

Maintenance

Irrational thoughts play a role in the maintenance of gambling as, despite the probability of failure when gambling, frequently a person's irrational perception regarding their ability to influence the outcome of their gambling takes over. As the addiction becomes more dominant there are fewer conscious expectations and more unconscious ones (or irrational thoughts) that result in a lack of control by the addict. The irrational beliefs about their ability to influence the outcomes of their gambling is therefore biased. Gamblers therefore have a number of **cognitive or distorted biases** related to their gambling behaviour. They tend to overestimate the amount of control they have.

The illusion of control can be illustrated with the example of fruit machines. On these the gambler has a feeling of control as they are using features such as 'nudge' and 'hold', even though very little skill is involved in playing. Gamblers overestimate this control. They look back, for example, at past gambling situations to try to justify their control, even over random gambling like the lottery or tossing a coin. Superstitious behaviour is also associated with gambling and gamblers believe that they can manipulate the event in their favour. For example, they may wear a lucky item of clothing or sing a particular song. Gamblers also exaggerate their ability through high levels of self-confidence in their own ability to 'beat the system'. The gambler therefore believes that they can exert influence or control over the outcomes of the gambling activity because of their belief in their skill at winning and not to the randomness of the game itself.

Griffiths (1994) *The role of cognitive bias and skill in fruit machine gambling*

Aim: To compare the behaviour of regular (RG) and non-regular (NRGs) fruit machine gamblers. Three hypotheses were measured:

1 there were no differences between both groups in terms of skill
2 RGs produce more irrational verbalisations than NRGs
3 RGs are more skill orientated in subjective measures of skill than NRGs.

Procedure: 60 participants, 30 regular gamblers (at least once a week) and 30 non-regular gamblers (once a month or less) were selected. The regular gamblers consisted of only one female compared to 15 females in the non-regular gamblers group. This may show a gender imbalance, but you must remember that statistically more men gamble than women. Recruitment was through posters displayed at a local British university, with a number of RGs being recruited via a gambler known to the researcher.

A real-life arcade was used, and each participant was given £3.00 to gamble on a fruit machine which equalled about 30 free plays. Griffiths hoped that using someone else's money may lessen the risk to the gamblers and allowing them to keep the money would compensate for this.

Each participant was tested individually according to seven variables, for example total plays, end stake, and so on. Half the participants were randomly allocated to the 'thinking aloud' condition. This group had to say aloud every thought that came to mind, even if irrelevant. This led to an additional hypothesis that the thinking aloud group would take longer to finish the task than the non-thinking aloud group. Skill judgements were tested by semi-structured interviews where the participant was asked their opinions on the level of skill needed to play a fruit machine.

Findings: In terms of the seven (dependent) variables, regular gamblers had a higher rate of eight gambles per minute compared to six for NRGs. RGs who thought aloud had a lower win rate and made fewer gambles.

Non-regular gamblers made significantly more rational verbalisations, which supports hypothesis two, whereas the thinking aloud group did not statistically take longer than those who were not thinking aloud – this difference therefore was not significant. Hypothesis three was supported as, in their interviews, RGs suggested that an equal amount of chance and skill would be needed for playing compared to NRGs chance option.

Conclusions: Regular gamblers did not behave differently to non-regular gamblers as there were no overall differences in the seven measures. RGs thought differently in terms of producing more irrational verbalisations than non-regular gamblers. Therefore, they had different cognitive thought processes – a form of cognitive bias. Finally, regular gamblers were more skill orientated in the self-report ratings, suggesting that they thought that there was more skill involved than there was.

▶ What do you think of when you hear the term 'gambling'?

Relapse

Gamblers often suffer from a **recall bias** which is the tendency to remember and overestimate wins while underestimating or rationalising their losses. This means that a number of losses in a row does not act as a deterrent to stop gambling. The gambler believes they will eventually be rewarded for their efforts. This motivates them to continue to gamble because of their biased belief that they deserve to win as they have lost so many times in the past. This is known as the 'just world hypothesis'.

This is further elaborated by cognitive cycles that prevent a gambler from recovering. The gambler believes that their low mood is created from having financial problems and that this is offset by a return to gambling and the belief that a win will be enough to pay off their debts.

Learning approach to gambling

Learning approaches suggest that gambling behaviour is acquired through reinforcement and rewards, in the case of gambling this will be wins and rewards from money or prizes. In addition, social learning theory would explain this through imitation of others. The person imitates the gambling behaviour of role models who are gambling already.

Initiation

Seeing others rewarded for their gambling behaviour acts as a form of **vicarious reinforcement** which then may influence a similar desire in others. There is an association between buying a lottery ticket or scratch card and winning, so you must buy one in order to win. The behaviour might be triggered by an earlier win, for example £10.00, and this acts as a powerful reinforcer (operant conditioning). A cash reward could lead to addiction. These small wins give the individual pleasure and excitement, which again act as a reinforcer to play again so that the individual can receive similar feelings of happiness. These reinforcers lead the gambler to repeat the gambling behaviour to get a win.

Maintenance

Gambling behaviour is maintained through the excitement of the early wins, they act as their own positive reinforcer. However, what keeps a person gambling when these initial wins are outweighed by the overall long-term cost?

Schedules of reinforcement have differing reinforcements and can provide an answer to why a person continues to maintain their gambling even if they are not winning each time. Partial reinforcement involves giving a reward on some occasions. For example, fruit machines work on the principles of a variable ratio schedule of reinforcement in which a reward (money) is obtained after a variable number of responses (number of plays on the slot machine). The next attempts at the slot machine might lead to the jackpot and it is this incentive (reward) that keeps the person gambling and putting their money in. Even smaller winnings can offer reinforcements to maintain the gambling behaviour.

Schedules of reinforcement can be very powerful in maintaining the gambling addiction as they help the gambler resist extinction. Extinction is the gradual reduction of a conditioned behavioural response because the removal of the reward that has become associated with that response. So, if you get rewarded by a win every time you play then this ceases to become a reward, it become normal behaviour, so you will then stop gambling. Only winning occasionally and not knowing if the next play is the big pay-out keeps the person playing and an occasional win is the reward that keeps them interested – avoiding extinction of the gambling behaviour.

Relapse

Environmental factors are key to the success of learning theory and in explaining gambling behaviour. Therefore, the environment is very important in maintaining the gambling addiction. Cue reactivity helps explain this in terms of a recovering gambler who is trying to avoid relapse and may be continually reminded by friends who gamble or social areas they used to gamble in acting as cues to their original gambling behaviour. Television can provide cues through adverts on gambling, such as bingo sites that can be accessed online or walking down the street and seeing advertisements in the window of a betting shop. In supermarkets the national lottery machines and advertisements may be a cue reminder of a person's gambling addiction and how easy and accessible gambling behaviour is. This increases the likelihood of a relapse as, when presented with the renewed stimuli, the addict will anticipate the associated pleasure making them more likely to gamble again.

Evaluation of cognitive and learning approaches as an explanation of gambling

Both theories of gambling have lots of evidence to support their explanations, however often sample sizes within these studies are limited or they only focus on one type of gambling, such as Griffith's fruit machines. The generalisability of the results, therefore, may be limited. Cognitive and learning approaches to gambling provide good explanations.

However, there are alternative suggestions from biological approaches that say that genetic inheritance to gambling as an additional explanation may be a possibility.

Shopping

With an ever-increasing access to credit cards, the number of people in recent years with a spending addiction has increased considerably. It is now estimated that ten per cent of adults in Western countries are believed to have a compulsive spending disorder.

Learning approach to shopping

The learning approach suggests that you imitate and copy role models within society. These role models are often rewarded and reinforced for their behaviour in society by, for example looking good, wearing the most fashionable clothes and driving the best cars. People in society set their standards by what they see and copy, also wanting the desired rewarded behaviour.

Initiation

Social learning theory would suggest that you continue to behave in a certain way depending on the rewards you receive. Rewards, such as getting complemented on wearing fashionable shoes, can happen immediately by someone who happens to stop you in the street to complement you. On the other hand, it can be done vicariously; vicarious reinforcement involves observing the positive effects of actions for others. Seeing others rewarded for their excessive shopping acts as a vicarious reinforcer and triggers the desire in others. Being complemented on having fashionable shoes and being seen as a fashion role model may trigger the desire in others to go out and shop for the best clothes and shoes – it will make them feel good.

A shopping addiction can be seen as a symptom that there are negative feelings you are trying to avoid, indulging in excessive shopping helps to numb these negative feelings. The addiction temporarily allows the individual to alleviate these feelings and allows the addict to feel they are in control, when realistically they are not.

This is further reinforced by society's emphasis on appearance in relation to areas like success, which is further reinforced by celebrities who play a role in setting acceptability standards in the world of fashion. This could be in relation to designer handbags, the most up-to-date technology, a specific type of limited-edition car and even desirable areas where a person should aim to live. Social media also plays a role here, with 'influencers' on various sites promoting various products, and a particular lifestyle. The fact that these influencers are often portraying themselves as 'normal' people provides yet more pressure to conform to their lifestyle. Therefore, the accessibility to credit cards, online shopping and the continual positive reinforcement of celebrities and role models adds to the initiation behaviour of the addict.

Maintenance

Rewards from the feelings, comments and behaviour associated with continual shopping can also be responsible for maintaining the behaviour. Compulsive shopping and repetitive purchasing are quite often followed by a loss of control over buying behaviour. Those addicted to shopping will keep buying merchandise regardless of whether they want or need it. You would expect that, coupled with debt, guilt, disappointment with themselves and a negative influence on relationships, these would influence the buyer to stop – but it does not. This compulsive buying coupled with poor credit management and a belief that the new purchases will make them happier seems to encourage the buying behaviour to continue. Shoppers have an association that buying items will give them an adrenaline rush and so reward them with a better mood – so the behaviour is strengthened. They believe that these purchases will change their lives, for example make them look better, give them self-confidence and have successful relationships. They believe the purchases will take them away from their problems and self-confidence issues. In terms of appearance, looking good and having the most up-to-date material objects gains positive comments from others, so the behaviour is not only rewarded but positively reinforced.

Relapse

It is very difficult for the addict to avoid the cues associated with their shopping addiction. Watching television provides cues from advertisements on the best cars, clothes and mobile phones to buy. Walking down any shopping high street will be a continual reminder of what people are wearing, using or buying. These constant reminders could initiate a relapse in the addict as they want the positive outcomes that shopping provides. There is a need to shop, from the process of shopping to the maintenance of the pleasurable mood gained from purchasing the items. The shopping behaviour substitutes for factors such as low self-esteem, guilt or frustration, which, in addition, to the guilt felt at spending so much money can lead to a relapse to alleviate the symptoms again. So, the individual will take part in the shopping behaviour repeatedly to reduce the negative effects of the withdrawal symptoms – this is negative reinforcement.

▶ How often do you go shopping?

Cognitive approach to shopping

Cognitive approaches to shopping as an addiction involve irrational beliefs; the normal cognitive processing associated with daily behaviour has become distorted in some way.

Initiation

The self-medication model suggests that those addicted to shopping will select the addictive behaviour of shopping as it will help them with a problem they may have. For example, the individual may feel very unhappy about their appearance or may be bored with their daily lives. They engage in the shopping behaviour to distract themselves from their real psychological problems, for example depression, anxiety or eating disorders. The individual will believe that the excessive shopping is helping their problems in making them feel better, for example improving self-esteem, taking their minds off their distress and giving them excitement through alleviating the symptoms of depression for a period of time. When those addicted to shopping buy something their brain is stimulated, providing feelings of pleasure and excitement. Even from the early process of planning the shopping event the addict has feelings of anticipation. They become preoccupied with buying and in doing so become excited at the thought; there is a build-up to the buying of the product. The normal rational thought processes of shopping in terms of, say, sticking to a budget are replaced by irrational thoughts that shopping is important. This then results in an attempt to alleviate those negative feelings.

Maintenance

Individuals then begin to think that the shopping is really helping their problems, that shopping is a way of giving them self-confidence about their appearance. They therefore continue to do it. Cognitive bias will occur where the shopper will continue to shop despite, for example getting into more debt. As they become more anxious and have lower self-esteem they will return to shopping to make them feel good. Often addicts have an urge to shop, they make decisions about which credit card to use and where to shop. They will feel intense excitement, euphoria and happiness once the items are bought but this will be followed by guilt and disappointment. This can result in further shopping to eliminate this guilt and disappointment, so the behaviour is maintained.

Relapse

Relapse involves the shopping addict's inability to stop the shopping behaviour. To succeed, the addict needs to realise that their self-worth and self-esteem are not related to the items they buy – so dealing with the underlying issues is very important for success.

The shopping addict will find that withdrawal symptoms of boredom, lack of excitement and financial worries occur when they have not taken part in the addictive behaviour for a period of time. It is these withdrawal symptoms that the addict will find difficult to deal with. Their coping strategies – for example having a budget, only using cash, not having any credit cards – can contribute to the situation as they are added pressures the addict cannot deal with in their vulnerable state.

In addition, the shopper thinks that their addiction will incur debts, cause relationship problems when partners find out and they feel guilt at putting the lives of their family in difficulty when there are money issues. Their self-confidence, for example, can relapse and they will return to the shopping behaviour to make themselves feel better. Withdrawal symptoms can cause boredom and increased anxiety due to worrying about financial debts incurred by the original shopping. The addict may only be able to take so much and then lapse into shopping again to alleviate the negative withdrawal symptoms.

Evaluation of cognitive and learning approaches as an explanation of shopping

Leaning suggestions for shopping as an addiction are rather simplistic in terms of not considering biological explanations for the addiction. There could be possible genetic explanations for gambling and shopping behaviour and neurotransmitter changes that may also lead to the development of addictive behaviour, which have not been considered by either cognitive or learning approaches. Treatments have been developed from both approaches, for example cognitive behavioural therapy. This is effective for some in terms of replacing negative thoughts with positive ones to ensure addictive behaviour like shopping is not returned to.

> **Reflect**
>
> Think about family and friends who might have an addiction.
>
> Can you relate any of the theories you have learned about to their behaviour?
>
> Are there examples of what they have done, said or do that you can explain from what you have learned from the different approaches?

Assessment questions

1   Describe the cognitive explanation of a shopping addiction. (4 marks)

2   Explain one strength and one weakness of the learning approach as an explanation of gambling. (4 marks)

Promotion of positive behavioural change

Theories of persuasion

In order to understand persuasion theories fully, it is important to study their key concepts, strengths and weaknesses, especially in terms of their effectiveness in predicting behavioural change. From this learning you will then be able to apply theories to scenarios, selecting and evaluating studies to support these theories.

Persuasion is a powerful force that can be used in everyday life. Many areas – including for example politics, the media, health, advertising and so on – use persuasion to get certain messages across. Persuasion is very subtle and how you respond depends on lots of different factors.

Persuasion involves the ability to communicate to others in a way that encourages them to believe, behave or act in the way that is desired. They are ultimately persuaded in some way to change their behaviour.

Hovland-Yale theory of persuasion

Hovland was recruited to investigate how propaganda could be used to help support the American war effort in the closing stages of the Second World War. From the research carried out, Hovland suggested that the most important factor in discovering when a communication was likely to be persuasive was understanding the characteristics of the person presenting the message (source; the role of the communicator), the contents of the message itself, and the characteristics of the receiver of the message (audience; the recipient of the communication).

Hovland wanted to find out what factors were most likely to affect a change in **attitude**. From testing one variable at a time they concluded that there are a number of components to persuasion.

| Key term |

Attitude – a predisposition towards an object or situation.

▸ **The role of the communicator:** this suggests that people are more likely to be persuaded when a source presents itself as credible, for example trustworthiness, expertise (a doctor) and attractiveness to the persuader.

▸ **Message:** this involves several different types of messages, including the number, strength, order and emotional appeal of the argument. They found that two-sided messages influence attitudes more than one-sided messages, especially when the two-sided argument eventually leads to a solid conclusion. Repetition of messages are also seen as more effective. It is generally accepted that messages need to be repeated several times if they are to have an impact; the additional exposure to a person or object increases familiarity and liking. Fear-induced messages are more effective if the message causes low to moderate fear, as higher fear levels may hide the key information the message is trying to get across.

▸ **Audience (the recipient of the communication):** the audience strongly affects how likely someone is to be persuaded. There are several traits that determine how easily they are influenced by persuasive communication, including how good people in the audience feel about themselves. They found that more intelligent audiences are more likely to be persuaded by valid arguments, for example medical treatments that have been tried and tested. There are cultural variations in audiences with, for example, Chinese audience members preferring products portraying togetherness, compared to American audience members who preferred separateness.

▸ **Situation:** this involves whether it is formal or informal and whether the message is actually relevant or not.

Hovland-Weiss (1951) The influence of source credibility on communication effectiveness

Aim: To investigate if source credibility (trustworthiness of sources) affect an audience and whether this effect lasts over time (retention).

Hypotheses: (1) Students' opinion would change towards the direction supported by the communicator when the communicator is perceived to be trustworthy (so students would be more persuaded by a source with high credibility). (2) After four weeks of presentation, students would be more likely to take the position presented by the low-credibility source than they did immediately after the presentation because they will have disassociated the source from the content after a period of time (sleeper effect).

Procedure: A sample of history students from a class at Yale University were presented with the same information on a certain topic area. There were two groups of students. One group received the information from a high-credibility source and the second from a low-credibility source. Using questionnaires students' opinions on the topics were taken five days before presentation, immediately after presentation, and then four weeks after presentation. Questionnaires included questions from three categories; the students' evaluation of the credibility of the source, facts and arguments presented by the sources (recall) and their own opinions about the issue. All students were given positive and negative articles about four topics: anti-histamine drugs; the steel shortage; atomic submarines; and the future of movie theatres (controversial topics). The information provided was said to be either high-credibility sources (first group) or low credibility sources (second group) but the information was generally identical. Sources varied with the high-credibility sources being journal articles and the low-credibility sources coming from a tabloid newspaper.

Findings: In 14 out of 16 of the possible comparisons, the low-credibility sources were seen as being less justifiable or fair than the high-credibility sources. Opinion approval ratings for high-credibility sources were much higher and people changed their mind more often with high-credibility sources. There was no difference in retention.

Conclusion: Information tended to be forgotten and remembered to the same extent. A higher-credibility source did change the opinion of the person reading the information, but this did not last over time. It could be that those reading the high-credibility source forgot where it came from or vice versa in terms of those reading the low-credibility source – resulting in an opinion change.

> **Research**
>
> Devise a leaflet on the healthy impact of smoking using the key components of the Hovland-Yale theory.
>
> Deliver your leaflet to a group to see whether it changes their attitudes about the impact of smoking.
>
> Remember to measure the group's attitude before and after.

Fear-arousal theory of persuasion

Exposure to messages aimed at persuading your behaviour comes in many different forms. These may have a real fear aspect within them – persuading you that whatever you are doing is bad for your health. These may be to do with the fears associated with unprotected sex, drink-driving, drug taking or smoking.

Janis & Feshbach (1953) were able to show that high-fear messages may not be as effective as many had assumed. If a message is so frightening, then it creates a degree of emotional tension which the individual cannot deal with through changing their behaviour. This can result in ego defence mechanisms. For example, if you show drivers who have been caught drink-driving images of graphic death caused by drink-drivers, this will give them additional stress and they may initiate avoidance of giving up alcohol. They might demonstrate suppression, for example by messing around and not paying attention to the video they are watching because they cannot cope with the excessive fear attached to the images. This means their behaviour will not be changed due to the high levels of fear-arousal incited by the stressful images; the fear-arousal level is too high to change the behaviour.

Individuals may not pay attention to low levels of fear either, so the behaviour is not changed as there is insufficient motivation. As the level of fear content increases, so too does the attention of the audience. But too high and the message may be obscured by the panic, anxiety and stress produced by the images themselves, so behaviour change (such as levels of fear which are too low or too high) is limited.

It has been found that the strength of the fear is correlated with the level of arousal and behaviour change. Therefore, low levels of fear elicit some behaviour change that increases to medium levels as the fear gets higher. However, when moving from moderate to high levels the persuasion decreases, not increases. The higher levels of fear tend to produce defensive reactions, so behaviour change is restricted.

Fear appeals – messages that are often used to influence attitudes and behaviour in terms of making people aware of the potential harm to them if they do not accept what the message is saying.

Janis & Feshbach (1953) Fear arousal and dental hygiene

Aim: To investigate the consequences on emotions and behaviour of **fear appeals** in communication.

Procedure: A laboratory experiment using 200 students from a large Connecticut High School, who were divided randomly into four groups. Groups were similar in age, sex, education level and IQ, with roughly equal numbers of males and females.

A standardised lecture lasting 15 minutes was prepared in three different forms, but all contained the same essential information about the causes of tooth decay and the same recommendations concerning oral hygiene. The same speaker was used for each one. The only difference across the three lectures was the amount of fear-arousing material presented.

▸ Group 1 – strong fear appeal showing strong consequences of tooth decay and dangers.

▸ Group 2 – medium fear appeal showing more mild description of dangers and more factual.

▸ Group 3 – minimal fear appeal which rarely mentioned consequences of tooth neglect.

A control group was given a similar lecture on the functioning of the human eye. Data was collected via a questionnaire one week before the lecture (asking them about dental hygiene), a second questionnaire immediately after the lecture (asking about the immediate effects of the communication), and a third questionnaire approximately a week later (asking whether their oral hygiene behaviour had changed).

Findings: All three groups had the same amount of knowledge about dental hygiene. The strong fear group said their lecture was 'interesting' and also demonstrated more anxiety about tooth decay (42 per cent) than the minimal fear group (24 per cent). The strong fear group also thought that the lecture was more "horrible and disgusting" and suggested that the slides were too unpleasant.

Conclusion: The overall effectiveness of a health promotion communication is likely to be reduced by the use of a strong fear appeal. Janis & Feshbach proposed that when fear is strongly aroused but is not relieved by reassurances in the message the audience tend to

be motivated to ignore the message or minimise the importance of the threat.

Central route – involves being persuaded by the arguments or the content of the message.

Peripheral route – involves not being persuaded by the arguments or the content of the message, but could be based on who the speaker is in a debate, attractiveness of speaker, and so on.

Elaboration–likelihood model of persuasion

Petty & Cacioppo (1986) suggested the idea that persuasive messages are processed through the central and peripheral routes, with a change in attitude occurring as they process the information, and persuasion being dependent on the degree of elaboration of the messages. When given a persuasive speaker people usually pay attention, but not always deeply because sometimes it will involve a lot of mental effort. If the persuasive argument is important to them, then in certain situations people are sufficiently motivated to analyse the content of the message, which can be further supported by the context of the argument. There are two main routes to persuasion.

1 **The central route to persuasion:** this is when individuals having both the motivation and ability to think about messages. The central route involves listeners caring about messages and understanding them. Central route messages have persuasive communication in which messages are credible, grabbing the receiver's attention and convincing them of the benefits. Individuals will have the motivation to process messages if they are relevant; when they are pitched at the correct level the ability to process them is higher. Finally, the nature of the argument must be strong, clear and convincing.

2 **The peripheral route to persuasion:** this is when individuals cannot fully concentrate on messages due to conflicting demands. The peripheral route is quite often used when messages are uninteresting or listeners are distracted. But persuasion and attitude change can still occur if peripheral cues are present, for example consistency, persuasiveness of messages, and past thoughts.

The elaboration–likelihood model attempts to explain the process that can lead to an attitude change, something advertisers take very seriously. Television and media are factors of influence that use persuasive arguments to get their political, health and advertising messages across to the audience. Persuasion models have been used to try and get these messages across in the best way possible, for example celebrities are often selected to advertise products, quite often they do not need to be famous, they just need to be recognisable. Therefore, advertisers can tap into the peripheral and central routes of persuasion by activating mental images, for example a famous model advertising a beauty product, or a celebrity known to have an illness advertising a treatment. This may be likely to increase the motivation of the audience to process the message more deeply as the argument they are putting forward (about the benefits of the product or what they are recommending) may be motivation enough for attention to be paid and acted upon.

Research

Research and identify different adverts that use a celebrity to persuade the audience. What is the product? What are the benefits? What is the argument in terms of who the celebrity is and what are their links to the product? Would you be using your peripheral, central or both routes?

Now focus on the health-related adverts and compile some examples that you could use to support your understanding to persuasion arguments from health promotion.

Individuals may differ in the degree of need for cognition, some have a greater need and enjoy thinking about information they receive and analysing problems they encounter. Those with a high cognitive need search out, criticise and reflect on information in order to fully understand the world around them. Those with low cognitive needs rely on the credibility of others when making decisions.

Evaluation

The elaboration-likelihood theory is an accurate model of persuasion in that it considers that an audience at times might be active and at other times may be passive therefore providing different routes for specific behaviour. Supporting evidence comes from Benoit (2008) who found that receivers can think deeply about messages at the same time as perceiving the communicator as a likeable expert. This suggests that the central routes and peripheral routes can be used side-by-side as well as on their own.

Petty, Cacioppo & Goldman (1981) Personal involvement as a determinant of argument-based persuasion

Aim: To test the argument that when individuals are highly involved with an issue, the central route is more important, whereas the peripheral route may be more important when individuals do not feel any personal involvement.

Procedure: They used 145 male and female undergraduates from the University of Missouri, which involved students getting extra credits for their introduction to their psychology course. Undergraduates were told the university was undergoing an academic revolution and that the new chancellor was looking for recommendations about policy changes. The participants were told that the chancellor had asked several groups and individuals to prepare policy statements to be considered. The participants were also told that the statement had been recorded for possible broadcast and that the psychology department had been involved in rating them for quality.

After reading these background comments, the participants heard a message (same male speaker used) suggesting that all seniors were required to take a comprehensive new exam in their major area and that all students needed to pass this to graduate. After listening they had to rate the concept proposed, such as how favourable they were to the idea.

Three independent variables were manipulated:
1 message strength (strong or weak arguments)
2 source expertise (expert or non-expert)
3 personal relevance (high or low).

The participants were told that because their personal views might influence the way they rated the broadcast, measures of their own opinion were needed. First, they were asked to rate the concept 'comprehensive exam' and second, to rate the 'extent to which they agreed' with the proposal about the comprehensive exam. The scores were averaged.

Findings: Results indicated that students' attitudes towards the concept, in the high personal-involvement condition, were not particularly influenced by the expertise of the source, with their attitude being relatively neutral. Those in the low personal-involvement condition were significantly affected by the expertise of the source. This meant that when the source was an expert, they were more favourable compared to being negative when there was a non-expert source. Low personal-involvement condition students were only slightly influenced by the quality of the argument compared to the high personal-involvement condition, who were significantly affected. As expected, strong arguments produced favourable attitudes towards the concept.

Conclusion: When an issue is important to students, they engage in thoughtful processing of the message itself. When irrelevant messages were put forward, the students used the expertise of the source to support their attitude rather than the content of the message itself.

PAUSE POINT | Briefly explain the three different theories of persuasion and how they relate to health psychology.

> Hint | For each theory identify key terminology to help you remember the information.

> Extend | List ways that health professionals could use these theories to try and get the general public to be healthier.

Assessment question

Marina wants to design a leaflet for her school which informs the learners and staff there of outcomes of skin cancer due to not using sun cream. She takes her first leaflet to her headteacher who says that the information contained in it is very upsetting.

1   Using your knowledge of fear-arousal theory explain why this type of leaflet may not be effective on the staff and learners at Marina's school. (4 marks)

Treatment and management of addiction and stress

In order to understand the treatment and management of addiction and stress fully, it is important to understand key physiological and psychological methods together with the professional approaches to managing stress and addiction. This will include looking at how effective these approaches are in treating and managing stress and addiction, and the ethical and practical factors that may occur. You will then be able to apply theories to scenarios, selecting and evaluating studies to support and contradict these theories.

There are two different approaches in treating and managing stress and addiction.

1   **Physiological approaches** for stress focus on drug therapy and biofeedback, and for addiction they focus on drug therapy and aversion therapy.
2   **Psychological approaches** for stress focus on stress inoculation therapy and social support, and for addiction they focus on CBT and skills training.

Physiological and psychological stress management techniques

Drug therapy

When people are stressed, they have feelings of anxiety and are in need of treatments to reduce these symptoms and help them manage their daily lives. **Benzodiazepines (BZ)** were developed in the 1960s and act on the brain by increasing the action of the neurotransmitter **GABA**. GABA works by dampening down the activity of other neurotransmitters in the brain and relieving the anxiety symptoms. BZ drugs include chlordiazepoxide and diazepam, which are often prescribed to relieve symptoms of stress and anxiety. They work by making the person feel calmer and more able to manage their day.

BZs were seen as a better alternative to earlier drug therapies such as barbiturates which, although a good option at the time, if not accurately taken could result in an overdose. With most drugs there is always an addictive element, as physical dependency develops as the drug creates a physical change. When a person stops taking a drug, withdrawal symptoms result, in the form of sweating, tremors and elevated heart rate, among other symptoms. For ethical reasons, patients, or those supporting them (carers or family) need to be informed of the side effects of taking such drugs.

> **Key terms**
>
> **Benzodiazepines (BZ)** – anti-anxiety drugs which increase the amount of GABA in the brain.
>
> **GABA** – a neurotransmitter which suppresses the activity of other neurotransmitters in the brain.

Beta-blockers act directly on the heart and circulatory system by stabilising heart rate and blood pressure, drowsiness and memory problems brought on by high stress factors. They act fast which is an advantage for those with heart and blood pressure problems and do not have major side effects. However, like most drugs, beta-blockers do not target the causes of stress but only the resulting symptoms. This means that they are an incomplete stress management technique on their own.

Beta-blockers include drugs such as propranolol and atenolol. They are used mainly to treat high blood pressure and heart problems. They are also given for high anxiety levels sometimes caused by addiction and stress. They work by blocking the effects of norepinephrine – a stress hormone that is associated with the fight-or-flight response. They control the physical symptoms of shaking, shallow breathing and increased heart rate.

Biofeedback

Biofeedback is a technique involving both psychological and physiological methods to manage stress. It involves the participant being wired up to equipment that tracks physiological responses, for example the pulse rate when faced with stress triggers. As the participant practises relaxation techniques, images or sound stressors are shown. The machine will show heightened levels of pulse rate which will indicate that an image or sound is a stressor. The individual then practises relaxation techniques and sees immediately the result of whether it works. This means that positive feedback should reinforce the individual to apply this technique to real-life situations.

Evaluation

Research from Attanasio et al. (1985) suggests that biofeedback works well for tension headaches, especially in children, therefore it is an effective technique. In comparison to drugs there are fewer side effects and the technique has been proved to be successful long-term in reducing blood pressure. In this way, it may be seen as being more ethically acceptable. However, individuals taking part need to be motivated and committed to the training programme which can take several sessions. This can impact on how practical it is for some participants to complete the training. In addition, as the training takes place in a laboratory, applying this to real-life situations may prove difficult for some people.

Key terms

Beta-blockers – drugs that reduce activity in the sympathetic branch of the autonomic nervous system.

Biofeedback – a technique that involves feedback about a person's physical stress reaction to a situation and how this can be managed.

▶ Can you think of any examples where biofeedback would be an appropriate treatment?

Stress inoculation therapy

Stress inoculation therapy is a cognitive behavioural method designed to prepare individuals for stressors they may come across in their lives; its aim is to manage stress levels. After learning about stress people are then taught different coping strategies that they can use in dealing with that stress. They are then exposed to different challenges so that they can practise these newly learned skills. This is done gradually and allows people to learn effective coping strategies by inoculating themselves against potentially stressful situations in the future – they are made more resilient. There are three phases to the therapy.

1 **Cognitive preparation:** this involves reliving stressful events and identifying, with help from a therapist, the sources of their stress

2 **Skills acquisition:** this involves being taught specific and non-specific coping strategies, such as relaxation techniques. Some people find examinations highly stressful for example, so the coping strategy might be exam practice. Being prepared for what might be on the paper will help to avoid feelings of stress about the unknown.

3 **Application and follow through:** this is when, after practice in the therapeutic setting, the participant is then encouraged to apply their strategies to the outside world. This is supported with further therapy sessions to ensure that the coping strategies are working. Recognising what works and does not work is key to development. Additional training and rehearsal may be needed which adds to the participant's eventual coping abilities.

Key term

Stress inoculation therapy – a cognitive behavioural method which looks at reducing stress through a conceptual skills training method that applies to the real world.

Evaluation

Stress inoculation therapy allows clients to have some control over their treatment so ethically they may feel less stressed about having it imposed on them. Practically it can be expensive and time consuming as the training programme needs to be put in place and supported over a long period of time. When they consent, clients need to be motivated and clearly informed that the therapy will be intensive and long-term.

Theory into practice

List different stressful events that you have encountered in the last year. Talk to others in your class; have they had similar events?

Now research different relaxation techniques; there are lots of examples from the NHS and other websites.

Find techniques that you think you would be able to do and, with the help of your tutor, research how it would work in terms of stress inoculation therapy for one of your stressful events.

Social support

Social support involves a network of people known to individuals, for example friends, family and co-workers, who can be relied upon when stressful situations arise. Support can come in many forms and in many different types.

▶ **Instrumental support:** this is usually concerned with practical support, for example a friend who gives you a lift home or helps you with your homework.

▶ **Emotional support:** this usually involves listening, expressing concern over problems or the causes of stress, giving reassurance as to what the person is going through. This can be in person, by email, on the telephone, or through another social network platform.

▶ **Esteem support:** this involves people who can support the situation and boost the person's self-esteem in their ability to cope.

▶ **Informational support:** involves providing knowledge and facts about different stressors. This could be advice acquired from a doctor, leaflet or the internet and can help to provide strategies on how to cope.

Uchino et al. (1996) completed a meta-analysis of social support studies and suggested that social support is effective in reducing physiological responses like increased heart rate and blood pressure. However, you cannot be sure which type of **social support** is more effective in reducing stress symptoms or whether combinations could be more effective. In addition, individual differences cannot be accounted for. For example, women tend to rely more on social support than men, and some personality types may need more support than others.

Key term

Social support – comes from friends, family, co-workers, or any other form of social network who can involve themselves in practical, emotional support and help boost self-esteem.

Physiological and psychological treatments for addiction

Aversion therapy

Aversion therapy involves **behavioural techniques** to reduce addictive behaviour like smoking, gambling or alcoholism. It is based on classical conditioning principles and involves the person creating a learned association between an **aversive stimulus** (something unpleasant) and their addictive behaviour, for example smoking, drug taking and so on. Figure 3.11 demonstrates this idea.

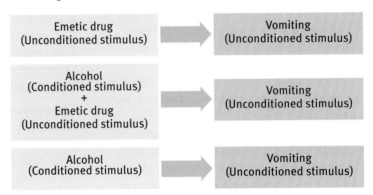

▶ **Figure 3.11:** Aversion therapy

Aversion therapy involves alcohol being paired with an **emetic drug** that makes you vomit. Vomiting therefore becomes a conditioned response to alcohol. Between the conditioning trials, patients sip soft drinks to prevent **generalisation** to all drinking behaviour. Aversion therapy can also be performed using electric shocks and has been used successfully to treat gambling addiction.

Evaluation

The success of aversion therapy to treat addiction is supported by Danaher (1977) who found success with those addicted to smoking. In addition, Meyer & Chesser (1970) found 50 per cent of alcoholics were able to stay off alcohol for a least a year following aversion therapy, which suggests it is mostly successful. Aversion therapy is ethically distressful as it instils unpleasant behaviour that, although in the addict's best interests, could be both painful and distressing.

Discussion

There are lots of different physiological and psychological treatments for addiction. Discuss the differences between physiological and psychological treatments with a partner.

Drug therapies

Drug therapies work by replacing the addiction, with a drug that has similar effects. The principle of the therapy suggests that the drugs will take care of the physical dependence, while the patient seeks other support or therapies to reduce the psychological dependency.

In terms of smoking, nicotine replacement therapy (NRT) includes the use of nicotine patches, gum tabs placed under the tongue and nasal sprays. These provide the body with an immediate hit of nicotine to relieve the withdrawal symptoms. Additional forms of drug therapy for smokers involves antidepressants, bupropion and varenicline, which both increase dopamine activity and reduce the number of nicotine receptors; if the person smokes, the cigarette will be less pleasurable.

Key terms

Aversion therapy – a therapy designed to extinguish (remove) the addictive behaviour, for example gambling, drug taking, and so on, by pairing it with something unpleasant.

Behavioural techniques – a broad term that refers to different treatments for mental health disorders.

Aversive stimulus – an unpleasant event that when presented with a consequence that is negative will reduce the likelihood of the behaviour happening again.

Emetic drugs – used in medicine to induce nausea or vomiting.

Generalisation – the tendency to respond in the same way to different but similar stimuli, for example liquids.

In terms of alcoholism, benzodiazepines (BZs) such as diazepam work by reducing alcohol intake by providing a relaxation effect to deal with the withdrawal symptoms that occur.

Over time these are then gradually withdrawn by reducing the dosage, so the person is able to cope with the withdrawal symptoms on their own.

Evaluation

Drug addictions like heroin have involved the use of methadone, which produces less of a high. Warren et al. (2005) found methadone to be effective in treating heroin addiction in 900 prisoners. Those who received methadone used heroin less than those who did not.

Overall drug treatments have proved effective with many different types of addictive behaviour. However, many of the drugs prescribed have side effects and are addictive in themselves, so addicts may find themselves having additional unpleasant symptoms in addition to becoming addicted to the treatment drug – ethically they should to be made aware of this.

Cognitive behavioural therapy (CBT)

Faulty thinking processes have led to the addictive behaviour of smoking, drinking, taking drugs, and so on. CBT (**cognitive behavioural therapy**) involves the patient and the therapist working together and clarifying how the addictive behaviour occurred in the first place. They will look at the motivational factors, feelings that occur when doing the addictive behaviour and how they feel afterwards. The therapist will then teach the patient skills such as coping strategies. These coping strategies will focus on unlearning the negative thought patterns and replacing them with new ones that eventually eliminate the addictive behaviour. Alongside this the patient is encouraged to think positively to ensure that self-esteem is high, and to encourage a belief that they can beat the addiction.

Evaluation

Support for CBT comes from King et al. (2012) who found it to be effective in successfully treating internet addiction in children. In addition, it is cost-effective as it takes approximately 10–15 sessions and can be done on an outpatient basis – keeping costs low. However, it may not work for everyone as the addict needs to be motivated and committed to changing their faulty thought patterns, so alternatives may be more effective in some cases.

Skills training

Skills training involves the addict learning new coping skills that will help them deal with their addiction. These can come in many different forms but ultimately they will support the recovering addict to deal with the addiction and subsequent withdrawal symptoms. Relaxation training is a skill that involves the release of stress and tension. People are taught to relax when stress arises, for example breathing exercises and meditation which they can use when put in a stressful situation that reminds them of their addiction, or even when withdrawal symptoms are beginning to occur. Teaching drug addicts to refuse others who are pressuring them in social situations is another skill that can be taught. This involves confidence, tone of voice and using body language.

> **Key term**
>
> **Cognitive behavioural therapy** – a therapeutic technique which gets a person to change their thinking, resulting in changing the addiction behaviour.

Assertiveness skills support addicts in expressing their own needs to others. This quite often occurs in those who cannot communicate well and who need to be taught to be more assertive in their approach to dealing with their addiction. Problem-solving skills can help the addict focus on dealing with everyday life without the drug to get them through.

Evaluation

Providing addicts with a variety of specific skills can then support them to deal with situations that may cause them to relapse. Many CBT programmes use coping skills embedded within their therapy programme, however it is still unclear how effective these are in the overall recovery of the addict. It may be that, combined with other treatments like drugs, a combination may be more effective that one therapy on its own.

Ⅱ PAUSE POINT	Briefly explain two ways of reducing stress and two ways of reducing addiction.
Hint	For each of the ways of reducing stress provide one example of a stressful situation they can be applied to.
	For each of the ways of reducing addiction provide one example of an addictive behaviour that they can be applied to.
Extend	List as many strengths and weaknesses of the ways of reducing stress and addiction you have identified as you can.

Assessment questions

1 Explain how drug therapy can be used to manage stress-related behaviour. (4 marks)

2 Describe and evaluate two ways of reducing addiction. (8 marks)

Scenario

Ellie is addicted to smoking and has been told by her doctor that she needs to give up as it is affecting her health, especially as she suffers from asthma.

3 Identify one therapy that Ellie could use. (1 mark)

4 Explain the process that Ellie might go through when beginning her therapy for her smoking addiction. (3 marks)

Maintenance of behavioural change

An understanding of how behaviour change can be maintained involves being aware of both adherences and non-adherences and how they work in terms of health behaviour. This will involve looking at how patients adhere to medical advice, therefore improving or maintaining a healthy behaviour and whether what has been suggested is effective for individuals.

Adherence involves following the advice given to a patient or individual by health professionals. Adherence is also complying to the wishes of the medical professionals and following the support they are being given. This can involve lots of different measures including taking preventative actions, for example attending medical appointments, taking medication at certain times and taking the correct dose of medication. **Non-adherence** is a failure to follow advice to the extent that it could cause harmful effects to the health of the patient or reduce the effectiveness of the treatment.

Key term

Non-adherence – the extent to which patients do not follow the instructions they are given by medical professionals in following their recommended treatment programme.

Rational non-adherence

Rational non-adherence involves a patient refusing to continue with their recommended health treatment, but unlike adherence their act is deliberate; they do it intentionally. The patient believes their choice is rational and justified, for example not taking medication because they do not want to experience the side effects. In addition, patients may believe that their diagnosis is incorrect, therefore the logical and rational argument for this is that the treatment offered is not the correct one.

Cost-benefit analysis

The costs associated with non-adherence can be high if the illness is prolonged; the patient may need lots of visits to the doctor or continuous care and this can be expensive on the individual, family and support network. Supportive family members can be a great help in ensuring that a patient adheres to medication and advice from doctors. This support is invaluable and can provide benefits that other patients may not have. An example of a cost-benefit analysis can be seen in Figure 3.12.

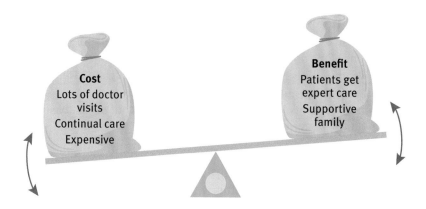

Key term

Rational non-adherence – involves the patient directly refusing to follow their recommended health treatment.

▶ **Figure 3.12:** A cost-benefit analysis

Research

Using Figure 3.12, imagine that you are working with a patient who is recovering from an alcohol addiction. Consider further costs and benefits that this patient may have and create a cost-benefit anaylsis for your patient.

Bulpitt & Fletcher (1988) Importance of wellbeing in hypertensive patients
Aim: To review research on adherence in patients with **hypertension**.

Procedure: Involved a review of articles focusing on different studies of non-adherence in hypertensive patients. They focused on articles that looked at the problems experienced by patients in taking hypertensive drugs, for example high blood pressure medication. The research articles looked at the physical effects associated with the drug treatment in regards to the individual's everyday life, for example their work, their physical and psychological wellbeing, hobbies, and so on.

Findings: The researchers found that medication for hypertension had several side effects like sleeping, dizziness, impotence and weakened cognitive functioning.

Conclusion: They found that patients are less likely to adhere to side effects if the costs outweigh the benefits of treatment. This was prominent in the problems that they were treating – hypertension had very few symptoms most of the time.

Key term

Hypertension – is another name for high blood pressure which involves a state of high physiological arousal.

Financial barriers

There may also be financial barriers to individuals not continuing with treatments. For example, some may have to take time off work, have extended stays in hospital, and even additional supported care. Some of these will be covered by the NHS and work insurance, however patients may have to add to this financially if the cover they need is not fully provided for. These are both causes and effects of non-adherence. Individuals may not be able to afford to have time off work, but non-adherence may actually cause them to have more time off work. Ley (1997) found that non-adherence may lead to as much as 10–20 per cent of patients needing a second prescription, 5–10 per cent needed a second doctor visit, in addition to days off work and hospitalisation. Therefore, non-adherence is counterproductive in that the patient might actually need additional time off due to their illness not being dealt with in the first place.

Patient-practitioner relationships

A doctor's style of treatment can influence a patient's adherence to treatment for example, a patient might be more likely to adhere to treatment if their doctor takes an interest in their case. There are three different types of patient-practitioner relationships.

1 **Doctor-centred:** this involves an active doctor and a passive patient who submits to the decisions of the doctor.
2 **Co-operative:** this involves the doctor being flexible enough to take into account the needs of the patient but still having control.
3 **Patient-centred:** this involves negotiation, with the patient being able to accept or reject the treatment offered.

Lack of understanding

Using technical language which the patient does not understand can undermine adherence, in addition to patients forgetting what the doctor has said. If the patient cannot remember the instructions given by the doctor then non-adherence will occur.

Ley's cognitive model (1988) and adherence

Ley's cognitive model (1988) of adherence shows clearly that the patient's understanding and memory of the consultation directly affects his or her satisfaction which, in turn, affects adherence. The model (Figure 3.13) provides a successful doctor-patient relationship as the main element of whether a patient follows the instructions and advice of the doctor. Therefore, the patient's satisfaction with the consultation process, the extent to which they understand the information and the patient's ability to remember is key to their adherence.

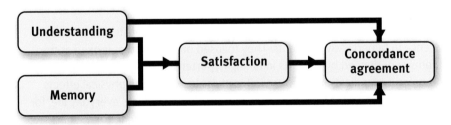

▶ **Figure 3.13:** Ley's cognitive hypothesis model of communication

Therefore, there must be satisfaction in terms of how the treatment progresses. So, having sufficient time to spend discussing the treatment with a doctor is important, ensuring that there is full understanding of terminology and outcomes. In addition, access to repeat visits to the same professional to ensure consistency in care is useful.

Access to other health professionals and support systems, however, can help with the progress of the treatment. This will be supported through carefully memorising important information early on in the treatment and then later on during time with health professionals.

Methods used to improve adherence

Physiological measures

Physiological measures of adherence include blood tests, urine tests and outcomes in terms of patient health, such as an improvement in blood pressure levels. In addition, looking at blood results, weight control, as well as indirect methods of counting pills, checking refill records and how many times the service is used, can also contribute to non-adherence and adherence measures.

Non-adherence to anti-depressants is a significant barrier to the successful treatment of depression. Research has highlighted that non-adherence comes about due to a number of reasons including discontinuation of anti-depressant medication and a lack of consistency in the prescribed medication. Approximately one-third of patients discontinue medical treatment for depression against medical advice, which results in poor recovery rates and risk of relapse. Inadequate adherence to treatment may be due to fear of becoming dependent on the drug, rather than to its undesirable side-effects in the long term. In addition, over a long period of time patients question whether they are ill which may result in non-adherence to long-term depression medication.

> **Key term**
>
> **Double-blind procedure** – neither the participants nor the experimenters knows who is receiving a particular treatment.

Lustman et al. (2000) Fluoxetine for depression in diabetes: a randomised double-blind placebo-controlled trial

Aim: To assess the efficacy of the anti-depressant fluoxetine in treating depression by measuring glycemic control. This idea begins by looking at whether treating depression with fluoxetine can improve adherence and therefore the life of diabetic patients.

Procedure: A randomised control **double-blind study** was carried out. 60 patients were recruited who had either type 1 (26) or type 2 (34) diabetes, and also had had a major depressive disorder. Participants were from the Washington University Medical Centre community. Volunteers were excluded if they had a history of suicidal behaviour, bipolar disorder, psychotic disorder, current alcohol or substance abuse disorder, or were taking psychoactive medication.

Participants were then randomly assigned to either a group receiving daily fluoxetine tablets for eight weeks. Participants were then randomly assigned to either a group receiving daily fluoxetine tablets for eight weeks or a control group receiving a placebo. The fluoxetine group started at 20mg per day, rising to 40mg per day depending on the clinical response and side effects.

Neither the researchers nor participants (double-blind study) knew which patients were given the fluoxetine or the placebo. The levels of depression were measured using self-reports and psychometric tests. In addition physiological measures, for example blood sugar levels, were taken through blood tests. This was used as a measure of self-adherence to their diabetic medical regime.

Results: 54 patients completed the study and from this the participants who were given fluoxetine were significantly less depressed than the control group. In addition, improvements in mean glucose levels were greater in the fluoxetine group than in the control group. However, this was not a significant improvement.

Findings: Diabetic patients had better control over their blood sugar levels after treatment probably as a result of improved adherence to their treatment. Adherence, therefore, can be improved by reducing their level of depression using fluoxetine.

There are problems with measuring non-adherence to medication in terms of medical professionals underestimating how many patients do not regularly take their medication. Continuous relapse rates are high, especially in terms of mental-health issues like depression and there still seems to be a misunderstanding of many illnesses, in addition to a fear of long-term addiction. Though many studies to date have some objective measures in terms of blood tests and urine samples, they also rely on self-report evidence which patients may often provide false information for, so a realistic measure is difficult to determine in terms of outcomes.

Psychological measures

There are lots of different suggestions as to how to improve patient adherence to medical treatments; quite often success will depend on the patients and lots of other factors. Behavioural explanations come in a range of formats from memory aids, reminders, email or similar techniques to monitoring, feedback, support, skill building and rewards. The involvement of family and friends can support adherence to health medication in addition to enhancing the knowledge of the patients, with clear and simple instructions so that there is no confusion. Many treatment packages recommend a combination of different techniques to ensure that adherence is maintained and that behaviour change is maintained in terms of a healthy outcome.

Use of reinforcements and financial incentives

Reinforcements involve giving rewards (positive reinforcement) in the form of, for example, encouragement as a form of feedback which reinforces the behaviour to be carried out again. For example, approval from family and friends for remembering to take medication, a reward of a trip from a support group when adherence is maintained for a period of time. The more regular and frequent the reinforcement, the more significant the adherence to medication for example. This is, of course, an advantage in getting patients to take their medication.

Financial incentives can be used as one of these reinforcements and there are suggestions that monetary rewards can help patients adhere to medication and medical treatment programmes in addictions like smoking. These types of rewards work well when the reinforcement is immediate and consistent. The patient will feel motivated to continue to adhere to the medication and treatment programme as they can use the monetary reward and it is regular. However, if there is confusion in administering financial incentives as positive reinforcement, the patient may become confused and this can be counter-productive and adherence may stop.

Volpp et al. (2009) A Randomized, controlled trial of financial incentives for smoking cessation

Aim: To find out if financial incentives for smoking cessation (stopping smoking) in work settings has an effect on smoking cessation rates.

Procedure: A total of 878 employees of a multinational company in the US were recruited via surveys. Employees could take part as long as they were at least 18 years old and if they smoked five or more cigarettes a day. Participants were tracked for 12 months and when biochemical tests confirmed they had given up smoking, an additional six months followed. They were randomly assigned to either a group that received information about smoking-cessation programmes (442) or to receive information about programmes plus financial incentives (436). At different stages participants were given financial incentives, for example $400 was given for abstinence over an additional six months. Biochemical testing confirmed cessation at all stages.

After three months participants were contacted and asked if they had stopped smoking. Those who said yes were interviewed at least seven days later and assessed. Those who did not report abstinence were contacted another three months after for a follow-up assessment.

Measurements included enrolment in a smoking-cessation programme, completion, rate of smoking cessation and rates of cessation.

Findings: The incentive group had significantly higher rates of smoking cessation than the information-only group nine or 12 months after enrolment (14.7 per cent compared to 5 per cent), and 15 and 18 months after enrolment (9.4 per cent compared to 3.5 per cent).

Conclusion: Financial incentives for smoking cessation significantly increases the rates of smoking cessation.

Evaluation of improving adherence

Improving adherence can have its benefits if the patient begins and continues to take their medication. However, practical applications of many treatments can provide issues for the health industry in terms of additional money required to initiate support for patients and the time that many doctors may feel that they cannot give. In addition, training to ensure consistency takes time and money to ensure all medical professionals and support workers are qualified to ensure adherence programmes are properly delivered. These individuals will ultimately be the ones supporting patients and their support network, friends, family and relatives to ensure patients take their medication and continue with their treatment programmes.

 PAUSE POINT   Identify the difference between non-adherence and rational non-adherence.

> **Hint**   For both adherence and rational non-adherence identify and explain barriers to adherence.

> **Extend**   List additional factors from your psychology learning that could add to the barriers discussed in this unit. From this, suggest ways to improve adherence that may relate to removing these barriers. Ensure that you justify your decision-making process to support improving adherence.

Assessment questions

1   Define the term adherence. (2 marks)

2   Describe psychological methods to improve non-adherence. (4 marks)

Scenario

Barnaby is learning about health psychology on his course and decides to design a programme that involves using financial rewards as a way of getting patients to take their medication.

3   Explain some of the key factors that Barnaby will need to consider when designing his programme. (5 marks)

Further reading and resources

Castella, T. (2011) *Is stress good for you?* BBC News Magazine.

Holmes, T. H. & Rahe, R. H. (1967) *The Social Readjustment Rating Scale. Journal of Psychosomatic research* 1192, 213–221.

Moss, C. and Dyer, K. (2010) *Psychology of Addictive Behaviour* London: Palgrave Macmillan.

The British Psychological Society:
https://www.bps.org.uk
https://thepsychologist.bps.org.uk/volume-26/edition-5/why-it-so-hard-quit-smoking

American Psychological Association:
www.apa.org

NHS:
https://www.nhs.uk
https://www.nhs.uk/common-health-questions/lifestyle/why-is-smoking-addictive

Mind:
https://www.mind.org.uk/information-support/guides-to-support-and-services/addiction-and-dependency

THINK ▶FUTURE

Adam Masters

Health psychologist

When I started my Level 3 Applied Psychology course, I took a keen interest in how stress and addiction affected people's lives. I took part in some voluntary work experience with my local hospital, firstly shadowing different medical professionals and then working with the hospital's health team. I knew that when I finished my course, I wanted to become a health psychologist, so I continued my education and completed a BPS accredited psychology degree and then a postgraduate training programme.

The most rewarding part of my job is seeing clients succeed in overcoming heath issues; even a little progress made makes it all worthwhile.

Being a health psychologist is my dream job which was inspired by my Level 3 Applied Psychology course. My choice of qualifications has been key to my success and I would not change anything.

Focusing on your skills

Supporting clients by understanding their addiction

- Using your knowledge and expertise to understand the addictive behaviour of your new patient to find them a relevant treatment programme.

- Gathering key information about the patient, their medical, psychological and environmental information is key to putting together their addictive behaviour and background.

- Collaborating with colleagues from different disciplines to ensure that you have considered all possible avenues in the treatment programme.

Treatment implementation for addictive behaviour

- You must follow the correct procedure when treating patients for addictive behaviour.

- Speak to the patient about their current behaviour and what recent events that may be contributing to their addiction being ongoing.

- Explain to the patient which damaging health behaviours are contributing towards their health issues, reassuring them that treatment programmes are available.

- Explore current patient behaviour and identify possible psychological interventions that could support the patient in their treatment programme.

- Implement a treatment programme that is focused, relevant and tailored to your patient.

Getting ready for assessment

This section has been written to help you to do your best when you take the examination. Read through it carefully and ask your tutor if there is anything you are still not sure about.

About the examination

This unit is assessed as an examination. You will have to sit a paper asking you questions about what you have learned in this unit. The questions will consist of short- and long-answer questions relating to three different unseen contexts. Each context will relate to one of the specific health behaviours discussed in Learning aim B: stress, physiological addiction and behavioural addiction. The questions will assess applied knowledge, understanding and critical evaluation of psychological approaches, theories and studies that explain or predict health-related behaviour and behavioural change.

Remember that all the questions are compulsory, and you should attempt to answer each one.

Once you understand what you need to do then you should make sure you understand what health psychological content you are being asked to use; the scenarios will give you a good indication of the area being focused on. This is a key skill and it stops you wasting time providing the examiner with information that does not answer the question.

Sitting the examination

Before you start to answer a question, you should check how many marks are being offered. This will indicate the scope of your answer. Most questions contain command words. Understanding what these words mean will help you understand what the question is asking you to do. It is always a good idea to plan your answers before you start and to check them at the end of the exam. This means that you must be aware of timing.

Your exam will be a set period of time and will contain different sections. Each section will be worth a set number of marks. It is good practice to read the whole paper first as the scenarios can be lengthy. Reading time has been added into the length of the paper; the first two sections will require less time than the third as they are worth less marks.

▶ **Table 3.23:** Definitions of the command words used in the exam questions

Command word	Definition
ASSESS	Learners give careful consideration of varied factors or events that apply to a specific situation and identify which are the most important or relevant. They make a judgement on the importance of something and come to a conclusion.
DEFINE	Learners state the meaning of something using the correct terms.
DESCRIBE	Learners give an account of something. Statements in the response need to be developed, as they are often linked, but do not need to include a justification or reason.
DISCUSS	Learners identify the issue/situation/problem/argument that is being assessed in the question. They explore all the aspects of an issue/situation/problem/argument. They investigate the issue/situation, and so on by reasoning or argument. A conclusion is not required.
EVALUATE	Consider various aspects of a subject's qualities in relation to its context, such as strengths or weaknesses, advantages or disadvantages, pros or cons. Come to a judgement, supported by evidence, which will often be in the form of a conclusion.
EXPLAIN	Learners' explanations require a justification/exemplification of a point. Their answers must contain some element of reasoning/justification to satisfy the definition of 'explain'. The mark scheme must have marking points that are linked. The mark scheme should be clearly laid out so that, to gain full marks, there must be a minimum of one mark for some element of reasoning/justification to satisfy the definition of 'explain'.
IDENTIFY	Select the correct answer from the given stimulus/resource.

Sample answers

For some questions you will be given some background information on which the questions are based.

Look at the sample questions that follow and the tips on how to answer them well.

Answering short answer questions

Matthew works for an advertising company and is told by his boss to get some help for his stress. Matthew is worried about keeping deadlines and as his firm attracts bigger and bigger contracts he has had more deadlines for which he has to come up with creative advertising products. The deadlines are also becoming tighter. He is working longer hours and rarely sees his wife and children.

At weekends Matthew works on different work products, which means time with his family is reduced. His wife has complained that he is always tired and never helps around the home or with the children. His youngest child Erin got upset recently when Matthew did not attend her school show. Matthew felt guilty about this and became irritable with his boss the next day.

Matthew feels anxious about going to work every morning. He continually worries that he isn't doing enough and that he will lose his job. His sleep pattern has become erratic, he feels lethargic all the time and is irritable towards both his family and his boss.

Matthew's doctor asks him to complete a stress questionnaire to measure his stress levels and discovers that lots of factors are causing his stress, but that the most dominant factor is his job.

Worked example

Question 1

Explain how workforce stress can explain Matthew's behaviour. [2]

Role conflict causes workforce stress and involves Matthew behaving in a way that goes against his best interests. Matthew therefore puts his job before his family and spends very little time with them.

Look carefully at how the question is set out to see how many points need to be included in your answer.

This answer gives an explanation of Matthew's workforce stress in relation to role conflict, in addition to extending this explanation with the conflict between Matthew's work and his family. This answer gains two marks.

Worked example

Question 2

There are different ways of measuring stress like Matthew's. Many of these use self-report methods to gather information on stress levels and what influences people to become stressed.

Explain **one** weakness of using the self-report method to measure stress like Matthew's. [2]

Self-report methods involve questionnaires that ask people what makes them stressed; in Matthew's case this is workforce stress. Self-report methods might involve some people not telling the truth as they may be embarrassed by what makes them stressed. So, the information given on the self-report may be biased, which will reduce the validity of the results as they may not be a real indication of what influences stress.

This answer explains one weakness of using self-report methods to measure stress. There is a clear and accurate identification of the method which is related to stress. It is well explained and linked clearly to the idea of providing false information through embarrassment, resulting in a second mark for clear elaboration in terms of validity and unrealistic results.

Worked example

Question 3

Seyle developed the General Adaptation Syndrome (GAS) explanation of how the body responds in times of stress.

Describe how the General Adaptation Syndrome (GAS) can explain Matthew's behaviour. [4]

GAS involves three stages, alarm, existence and exhaustion. Exhaustion is when the body is very tired, and all reserves have been used up.

This answer involves a description of the General Adaptation Syndrome explanation to stress. The listing of the three terms is correct but there is no description of any of them in the first half of this answer. To gain full marks for this question, the learner would need to provide more information about each of the stages and apply it to Matthew's behaviour.

Answering long-answer questions

Question 4

Ian is a 43-year-old heavily addicted smoker who has several ongoing problems that are hindering him giving up his addiction. Ian has a heart condition and is currently undergoing treatment for mild depression. He has attempted to give up cigarettes in the past but relapsed shortly afterwards.

When discussing a new treatment programme with this therapist she discovers several additional factors that may be influential in Ian failing to give up his addiction the first two times he tried. Ian's wife Melissa is also a smoker and is not very supportive in helping Ian give up. Ian also lost his job three months ago and has been unable to get another one which had made him irritable, angry and feeling low.

Using **two** different explanations discuss Ian's smoking behaviour. [9]

The biological approach would suggest that Ian's reward pathway has changed because of his smoking. His reward pathway naturally is there to give pleasure, but if it has been changed it will not do this anymore. The nicotine in Ian's cigarettes have replaced the dopamine in his reward pathway which has led to his body no longer producing it. This means that Ian does not have natural pleasure from the dopamine coming into his system and making him happy; this may explain why he is feeling low.

On the other hand, social learning theory, a psychological explanation to addictive behaviour, would suggest that Ian has observed his favourite celebrity on television smoking which he is then copying; he sees them as a positive role model. He sees them getting pleasure from smoking; they are happy, famous and popular. Ian is motivated to be like them so keeps smoking because he observed them also smoking and being rewarded, which he then thinks he will get as well.

Both theories can explain why Ian is feeling low and angry, however there are other explanations of addictive behaviour that may also be beneficial to explaining his smoking behaviour. If you know what causes Ian's addictive behaviour, you can also use these explanations to suggest treatments that will help him stop such as using positive role model celebrities who do not smoke or providing him with drugs or patches that will reduce some of the withdrawal symptoms when nicotine is reduced in his system.

The answer clearly identifies two explanations of addictive behaviour and they are well linked to Ian's smoking addiction throughout. The first explanation is a biological one and refers to the reward pathway and dopamine in terms of addictive behaviour, which also links to aspects of Ian's behaviour. This could have been developed further by reference to acetylcholine which is another neurotransmitter important in causing the addiction.

In the biological explanation if the learner had added reference to another neurotransmitter, for example Ian's acetylcholine was not working sufficiently therefore preventing him giving up smoking, they would have gained an additional mark.

This could have been supported further by reference to positive and negative reinforcement, and classical conditioning. For example, Ian's wife could have been more supportive in encouraging him verbally when he had given up cigarettes for a whole day, using positive reinforcement of a verbal praise to reinforce his behaviour – this would have gained an additional mark.

The second explanation of Ian's addiction involves learning theories, focusing on social learning theory and positive role models. Explanations of learning include role models but also emphasise positive and negative reinforcements in addition to classical conditioning. These areas (although not compulsory in this answer) would have provided additional context in terms of understanding Ian's addiction for this second explanation. The answer ends with some discussion elements in terms of treatments and alternative explanations, which adds to the overall answer. Again, these could have been developed further, especially in terms of the course and Ian's smoking addiction. This answer would be awarded 5 marks.

Question 5

(a) Identify and explain two reasons why Ian is finding it difficult to give up smoking [4]

Ian is finding it hard because he has low self-efficacy; this means having no confidence in his ability that he can actually give up smoking as he has failed twice before. Research suggests that people with low self-efficacy believe that they do not have the ability or determination to give up smoking and because of this Ian's smoking behaviour will be maintained.

Ian also has lots of other problems in his life, for example he lost his job which is an external stress factor that might be contributing to him not giving up smoking.

This answer requires two reasons to be identified which they are, implicitly. These should be made more explicit, ensuring that the learner directed the answer more clearly to what the question is asking.

The first part of the answer identifies low self-efficacy as a reason and goes on to explain it in the context of the source of Ian's addiction – 2 marks are awarded. The second reason is not as clear, but it is identified with some elaboration, so 1 mark is awarded. This answer gains 3 marks.

Criminal and Forensic Psychology

4

Getting to know your unit

Assessment

You will be assessed by a series of assignments set by your tutor.

Understanding the rationale behind why people commit crimes helps to influence the ways in which criminals are managed within the criminal justice system. Some treatment or punishment options are more effective than others. We also need to have a reliable way of catching suspected criminals, in order to be able to prevent further offences from taking place.

How you will be assessed

This unit will be assessed by a series of internally assessed tasks set by your tutor. Throughout this unit you will find assessment activities that will help you work towards your assessment. Completing these activities will not mean that you have achieved a particular grade, but you will have carried out useful research or preparation that will be relevant when it comes to your final assignment.

In order for you to achieve the tasks in your assignment, it is important to check that you have met all of the Pass grading criteria. You can do this as you work your way through the assignment.

If you are hoping to gain a Merit or Distinction, you should also make sure that you present the information in your assignment in the style that is required by the relevant assessment criterion. For example, Merit criteria require you to analyse and discuss, and Distinction criteria require you to assess and evaluate.

The assignment set by your tutor will consist of a number of tasks designed to meet the criteria in the table. This is likely to consist of a written assignment but may also include activities such as the following:

▶ creating a report that details different theories and research used to explain criminal behaviour
▶ reviewing and analysing case studies of profiling
▶ exploring sentencing options available to offenders
▶ developing offender profiles based on crimes reported in the media.

Assessment criteria

This table shows what you must do in order to achieve a **Pass**, **Merit** or **Distinction**, and where you can find activities to help you.

Pass	Merit	Distinction

Learning aim **A** Understand different psychological approaches to explaining criminal behaviour

Pass	Merit	Distinction
A.P1 Explain the use of psychological approaches to examine criminal behaviour. **Assessment activity 4.1**	**A.M1** Discuss explanations of criminal behaviour using psychological research. **Assessment activity 4.1**	**A.D1** Evaluate the use of psychological approaches and research to explain criminal behaviour. **Assessment activity 4.1**
A.P2 Explain research supporting psychological explanations of criminal behaviour. **Assessment activity 4.1**		

Learning aim **B** Investigate punishment strategies and behaviour modification of criminal behaviour

Pass	Merit	Distinction
B.P3 Explain the use of behaviour modification methods on criminal behaviour, using psychological theories. **Assessment activity 4.2**	**B.M2** Assess the effectiveness of behavioural modification and punishment methods on criminal behaviour, using psychological theories. **Assessment activity 4.2**	**B.D2** Evaluate the impact of behaviour modification and punishment of criminal behaviour on the individual and society. **Assessment activity 4.2**
B.P4 Explain proposal for own pilot study. **Assessment activity 4.2**		

Learning aim **C** Apply different methods to create an offender profile

Pass	Merit	Distinction
C.P5 Produce an outline offender profile using different profiling methods. **Assessment activity 4.3**	**C.M3** Produce a detailed offender profile using different profiling methods. **Assessment activity 4.3**	**C.D3** Produce a comprehensive profile using different profiling methods, giving full justification for effectiveness of techniques used, and supporting theories. **Assessment activity 4.3**
C.P6 Explain techniques applied in own offender profile, with reference to their use and limitations, and supporting theories. **Assessment activity 4.3**	**C.M4** Assess own offender profile, with reference to techniques applied, their use and limitations, and supporting theories. **Assessment activity 4.3**	

Getting started

You develop skills and behaviours from many different places. Sometimes they develop due to the people you spend time with or where you live (nurture). Sometimes they develop because of who your parents are and the genes that they pass onto you (nature). What have you learned from your environment? What have you inherited from your family?

A Understand different psychological approaches to explaining criminal behaviour

In order to understand criminal behaviour, it is important to recognise some of the reasons why people commit offences. In this section you will look at some of the theories that can help to explain this. Psychologists are interested in understanding why someone may commit a crime. This knowledge can help to try and prevent, treat or manage the risks associated with criminal behaviour.

Biological explanations of criminality

The 'nature–nurture' debate considers whether criminal behaviour is the result of genetics, hormones and other biological factors, or whether people experience outside influences that lead to criminal behaviour. Biological theorists argue that criminality is due to *nature*. They believe behaviour is determined before you are born, and therefore it is difficult to change such behaviour. They believe that people commit crimes because of who they are as a person: their genes, hormones or brain structure. The biological approach suggests that it may be difficult to prevent becoming a criminal, or to stop offending, if a person's genes, hormones or brain structure are such that it makes them vulnerable to committing crime.

Inherited criminality

You inherit many things from your parents, including eye colour, hair colour and height. Biological explanations of criminality say that criminality can also be inherited, passed down in the genes you inherit from each parent. You inherit an equal number of genes from each parent. Each person has 46 chromosomes (a type of gene), 23 from each biological parent. This suggests that there is an equal likelihood that each parent can biologically influence any future criminal behaviour.

As genes (and so chromosomes) are inherited, this means that researchers can look at families, and in particular twins, to investigate criminality.

Twins and family studies

Families are all different sizes and are made up of different relatives. Families that live together all share the same environment. This means that it is likely that members of the same family also share many of the same experiences, and are also likely to have many things in common. This could include crime and it is not uncommon to see a number of members of the same family involved in crime.

When looking at the effect of families on criminal behaviour, it can be difficult to be sure why a person shows the same behaviour as their family members.

Link

Look back at Unit 1: Psychological approaches and applications for more information on genes and how behaviour is inherited.

There are two possible explanations:

1 they share the same genes (nature)
2 they share the same environment and interests (nurture).

The most helpful way to try and find out which of the above two reasons may lead someone to become a criminal is by carefully choosing how you research the effect of the family on behaviour. One way to investigate crime within families, and the reasons for it, can be to use twin studies.

These studies look at the behaviour of sets of twins (or other multiple births) and compare the behaviour of these individuals to each other. Twins can be known as identical (**monozygotic**) twins or non-identical (**dizygotic**) twins depending on the similarity in their genes.

If a pair of identical twins, who were raised in the same environment, were to show similar levels of aggression, and a pair of non-identical twins, who were also raised in the same environment, were to show very different levels of aggression, then this would suggest that aggression is due to genes (nature) and not because of the environment they were raised in (nurture). Both sets of twins share the same environment and so the only difference is the amount of DNA they share with their twin. From this you could conclude that it is their shared genes that make the identical twins act with the same level of aggression.

However, as twins are usually brought up in the same environment, it can be difficult to be certain if similar behaviour, such as similar levels of aggression, is due to their genes or because of their environment.

Key terms

Monozygotic (MZ) – twins who are identical. They are always the same sex – both boys or both girls who will look the same as each other. Their DNA is 100 per cent the same.

Dizygotic twins (DZ) – are non-identical. They may be either the same sex, or a boy and a girl. They will look slightly different. They share 50 per cent of their DNA.

Link

Look back at Unit 1, page 14 for more information on longitudinal research.

Case study

Brendgen et al. (2005) aimed to investigate whether social and physical aggression is the result of genetics or the environment. They used 234 pairs of twins, including identical and non-identical, male and female six-year-old twins, and used a longitudinal method. Peers and tutors rated each child on their levels of aggression.

They found that identical twins were twice as likely to both show physical aggression than non-identical twins. There was a greater genetic influence for physical aggression, suggesting this may be due to genes rather than the environment, though with some environmental influence. Social aggression was influenced more by environmental factors than inherited factors.

1 How does this study relate to the nature–nurture debate?

2 Are there any limitations to the study based on the research methods used?

Adoption studies

A common way of trying to reduce the influence of the environment can be to look at adoption studies, where children are brought up in environments which are different from the environment of their biological family.

Adoption studies help to clarify the effect of genes on behaviour. They look at the effect of genes on children who are not raised by their biological parents. This means that the environment the child grows up in will be different from that of their biological parents; this makes it easier to see whether genes or the environment affect a child's behaviour.

Case study

Mednick, Gabrielli & Hutchings (1984) wanted to explore if criminal behaviour is caused by genetics. They looked at the court convictions of adoptive and biological parents of over 14,000 Danish male criminals.

There was a significant relationship between adoptees and their biological parents for committing instances of property crime. They did not find any relationship for violent crime. The criminal behaviour of the adopted parent had no relationship on the adoptee's criminality.

They concluded that there is a biological influence that predisposes individuals to criminal behaviour.

1 What do the findings of this study tell you about the influence of the environment on those with family criminal backgrounds?

2 How do the findings of this study and that of Brendgen et al. (2005) help crime prevention, if at all?

The biological explanation of crime argues that an individual's future criminal behaviour is pre-determined, and therefore not an activity that someone *chooses* to take part in. It suggests that it is difficult for people to avoid crime, as it is in their genes. It also suggests that it is then more difficult for them to stop offending, as people can't change their biology.

Diathesis-stress model

While a person may have biological tendencies towards criminal behaviour, an environmental trigger is also often needed in order for the person to actually take part in any criminal behaviour.

Theory into practice

One evening when Jerome was walking home from work, he was shouted at in a threatening way, by someone he did not know. He reacted by shouting back at them, telling them to leave him alone, and then trying to hit them.

In this example, Jerome's biology may have made him react in an aggressive way, but it would not have happened if he had not been threatened. His biology made him more likely to react aggressively when put in a position where that behaviour could happen.

A person who has greater vulnerability to criminal behaviour can be considered to have a **predisposition** to crime. This could be due to genetics or other biological influences. The diathesis–stress model in relation to criminal behaviour is shown in Figure 4.1.

Key term

Predisposition – a tendency to behave in a certain way or have a certain attitude, due to genetics or other biological influences.

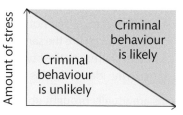

▶ **Figure 4.1:** The diathesis–stress explanation of crime

Figure 4.1 shows that a person who has greater predisposition to crime would require less exposure to stressors than someone who does not have the same biological predisposition. Alternatively, without any predisposition to crime, it is possible that a person would need much higher levels of stress in order to engage in criminal behaviour.

Theory into practice

In Jerome's case, being shouted at was enough to make him become aggressive himself. Using the diathesis-stress model, what does this suggest about his level of stress in that situation and his predisposition to crime?

One way to try and reduce the likelihood of the behaviour occurring (in this case, aggression) is to develop what are known as protective factors. These are skills, personal beliefs or environmental situations that would keep someone away from criminal behaviour.

In the example above, Jerome could introduce protective factors such as learning not to hit someone when he gets angry, trying to ignore the person, or not walking home on his own where possible. This could reduce the likelihood that he will react aggressively when exposed to stressors, such as someone shouting at him.

The diathesis–stress model suggests that criminal behaviour may not be completely explained by biology (nature). While people can be pre-determined to act in a criminal way, the environment can also have an influence (nurture). For example, a child raised in a hostile environment is potentially going to display more anger and aggression, and be quicker to react to **stressors**, than a child raised in a content, loving home.

> **Discussion**
>
> Think about situations in which you have felt under pressure or 'stressed'. What effect does this have on your ability to manage the situation well? Are you a person who works well under pressure, or makes quick decisions that don't always help the situation? Discuss your thinking within a group and compare your thoughts.

Low genetic activity

All genes have specific jobs within the body. Any faults within the genes can lead to changes in the way the genes work. These faulty genes can also lead to changes in the behaviour of the person. Not every criminal will have a faulty gene, but they have been found among some prisoners.

Tiihonen et al. (2015) gathered DNA information from almost 800 Finnish prisoners, who had given consent to take part. They compared the DNA of the prisoners against whether the prisoners had committed a violent crime, and also noted the severity of any violent crime. They found that violent prisoners in Finland commonly have two specific faults within their genetic code. These are faults with the MAOA gene, and the gene CDH13. Those convicted of violent crime had low activity MAOA and variations in CDH13. A fault in these two genes is thought to be a potential reason for the violence these prisoners have committed.

What is MAOA?

Monoamine oxidase A (MAOA) is an enzyme that breaks down important neurotransmitters in the brain, including dopamine and serotonin. Dopamine helps to control behaviour motivation and hormone secretion. More dopamine is secreted during activities that make you feel good, such as winning a competition, which reinforces people acting in the same way again. Serotonin helps to regulate appetite, sleep and mood. Low serotonin is found among those with depression, sleep problems and anxiety disorders. It is also linked with impulsive and aggressive behaviour.

There is a specific MAOA gene that makes sure the enzyme is working properly. The gene MAOA therefore helps to regulate serotonin and other neurotransmitters in the brain.

> **Key term**
>
> **Stressor** – An event or experience that causes stress to the individual

Some people will have a form of the gene that results in low levels of MAOA activity (known as MAOA-L) and so produce less of the enzyme. This leads to dopamine being used up in the body at a slower rate. As a result, the person may have high levels of dopamine in their body.

High levels of dopamine have been found to increase aggression. So people with the MAOA gene may show higher levels of aggression than those who do not have this gene.

It is not known how many people have the MAOA gene and do not become aggressive. The total number of violent people who have the MAOA gene is also uncertain. This is because genetic testing is not usually undertaken for everyone who is aggressive. Some studies have been undertaken on this subject; Brunner (1993) found that in a Dutch family with a history of serious aggressive crime the men had abnormally low levels of MAOA, supporting this explanation.

> **Research**
>
> MAOA-L has been called the 'warrior gene'. Research online to find out why this is and consider its links to criminality.

What is CDH13?

CDH13 is a molecule that helps in the development of the pathways in the brain. It works specifically on the transfer of messages within the brain.

The presence of CDH13 increases the messages being sent in the brain. This can lead to increased frequency of brain activity in the **hippocampus**. It is this effect on the hippocampus that can lead to heightened aggression.

It is suggested that the CDH13 gene also contributes to factors other than aggression, such as attention deficit hyperactivity disorder (ADHD) and depression.

> **Key term**
>
> **Hippocampus** – a small organ within the limbic system, responsible for the processing and storage of short-term memory.

Amygdala – a set of neurons that forms part of the limbic system, responsible for emotions, including anger.

Limbic system – a set of brain structures that controls many things in the body, including instincts and the processing of emotion.

Link

Look back at Unit 1, page 8 for more information about fight or flight responses, and Figure 1.7 in Unit 1, page 37 to remind yourself of where the amygdala is in the brain.

Role of amygdala and aggression

The **amygdala** is part of the brain's **limbic system**. It controls, among other skills, how you experience and control emotions. It helps the brain to recognise potential threat situations. When the brain feels under threat, the body will prepare for fight or flight reactions, by changing breathing and heart rate to be able to respond to a possible threat situation. It therefore drives survival instincts.

Damage to the amygdala can affect how well a person manages their emotions. It can lead a person to interpret a situation as more or less threatening than it actually is. A smaller size amygdala has been found among those with psychopathic personalities. These people are often less likely to care about others and lack empathy.

Case study

Raine et al. (1997) found a difference in the functioning of the amygdala of murderers when compared to a control population. They studied 41 murderers who had pleaded 'not guilty by reason of insanity' (NGRI).

They found lower levels of amygdala activity for murderers than for the control group. It was concluded that the low amygdala activity might make it difficult for a person to control their violent impulses.

1 What may be some of the challenges of applying the findings of this study to other criminals?

2 Brain scanning is a very scientific method. What are the benefits of a scientific approach?

The study done by Raine et al. shows that the amygdala can have a significant impact on behaviour. The effect of the behaviour can be so noticeable that it is often diagnosed by professionals as problematic. There may be many diagnoses that a person may be given if they are often aggressive. Two of them include:

▶ intermittent explosive disorder
▶ reactive aggression.

Intermittent explosive disorder (IED)

IED is a mental health condition that is diagnosed by psychiatrists. The condition includes the person:

▶ having frequent episodes of serious violence or property damage
▶ being unable to manage thoughts of anger
▶ acting more violently than would be appropriate in the given situation.

The person does not have any other mental health conditions that may explain the violence, nor are they using drugs or alcohol.

IED often develops in teenage years. There is evidence that biological causes of IED are due to the malfunctioning of the amygdala, or it may be genetic and passed through generations. Treatment of the condition may be through medication to address the imbalances within the brain, and therapy with a psychologist to help them deal more effectively with situations without resorting to violence.

Reactive aggression

Reactive aggression is a response (or reaction) to a perceived threat. It occurs when people consider themselves to be in a situation in which they feel under high levels of threat, such as when they fear for their own safety.

People who display reactive aggression believe that in that situation, aggression would be the best way to deal with the threat. This theory suggests that the aggression would not occur if the threat were not present.

People may be more vulnerable to reacting with aggression as a result of the amygdala not working effectively, due to its effect on emotional control.

| | PAUSE POINT | Design a poster that describes the different theories of biological criminality. |

Hint Try and remember why these theories affect a person's behaviour.

Extend Considering the nature–nurture argument, what other explanations could be used to explain why people may turn to crime?

Individual differences explanations of criminality

Link

Look back at Unit 1, page 48 for more information on conditioning.

Every person is an individual with different interests. You may think about situations in a different way from your closest friends or family. It is these individual differences, specific to each person, that can explain the difference between someone engaging in crime or not. The ways in which you are different can include:

▸ your personality
▸ your morals.

Both of these factors can be explored further using theories from well-known psychologists: Hans Eysenck and Lawrence Kohlberg.

Eysenck's theory of criminality

Key term

Conditioning – conditioning relates to the way in which a person learns a specific behaviour. The response that happens after you behave in a certain way makes it more or less likely that you will behave in the same way again.

Personality is the term used to describe a person's characteristics and behaviours. Hans Eysenck, a German psychologist, believed that personality was influenced by biology, such as hormone levels and the environment, including behaviour learned through **conditioning**. He believed that each different personality type could be linked to a different biological cause.

In 1947, Eysenck produced a questionnaire while working at the Maudsley psychiatric hospital in London that was designed to identify personality traits, and give information about the nature of the person's reported personality. He gave his questionnaire to 700 soldiers being treated for neurotic disorders within the hospital. He asked questions such as:

▸ 'Do you stop and think things over before doing anything?'
▸ 'Are your feelings rather easily hurt?'

This early version of his questionnaire, and his theory, focused on extroversion and neuroticism. The inclusion of psychoticism came in 1966.

Eysenck identified three personality traits, which help to explain human behaviour:

▸ **extroversion:** characterised by outgoing, energetic interactions and behaviours
▸ **neuroticism:** characterised by heightened negative moods, such as anxiety, loneliness and anger
▸ **psychoticism:** characterised by aggression or hostility towards others.

Extroversion

Extroversion is measured on a **continuum**. People will range from high level of extroversion (those who become known as extroverts) and low levels of extroversion (known as introverts). Eysenck believed that extroversion is due to low levels of arousal within the 'thinking' part of the brain: the cortex. As a result they try to find arousal for their cortex by engaging in activities that would excite this part of the brain. Introverts have a high level of arousal in the cortex, making them want to avoid any further arousal. The differences between the two are covered in Table 4.1.

Extroverts may be more likely to commit offences with others and may even be influenced to commit crime from encouragement by those around them.

▸ **Table 4.1:** The differences between extroverts and introverts

Extroverts	Introverts
• are usually very sociable, talkative and comfortable in groups of people • often enjoy being the centre of attention • may have a wide group of friends and will choose to engage in activities that surround them with other people.	• are quieter than extroverts; they will feel less comfortable when in larger groups, particularly if they do not know people within the group • are often more comfortable working on a task or activity on their own, or with limited interaction with others • may have a much smaller social group.
Job choices may include: human resources, solicitors or event planners.	Job choices may include: research analyst, accountant or computer programmer.

Neuroticism

Eysenck refers to neuroticism as a person's level of emotional stability. This is referring to how well they are able to manage their emotions and whether they become easily emotional.

Those with high levels of neuroticism tend to feel high levels of stress. Their ability to manage stressors in life would be lower than those with lower levels of neuroticism. Their reactions to the same situation may therefore be more exaggerated than someone with lower levels of neuroticism. They also try to achieve perfection in everything they do. This adds additional stress to their lives and can lead to anxiety and disappointment if they do not achieve perfectionism. They display heightened anger or frustration, which can present itself through aggressive behaviour.

A person with a low level of neuroticism would have a greater ability to manage stress. They put fewer pressures on themselves and therefore do not feel as disappointed if they do not succeed. Such people could be described as more emotionally resilient in their ability to be less affected by stressors.

Theory into practice

Exam times provide an opportunity to observe who may be more neurotic than others. Studying for exams can be a very stressful time for learners. This time of the academic year is likely to be more emotionally difficult for those with higher levels of neuroticism. As a result they may display more emotions at this time than others, or show emotions that appear less expected in the situation.

As you move into the assessment for this or other studies you are doing, consider how best to manage some of the high emotions you may experience.

Psychoticism

The word 'psychotic' is often used in mental health terms to relate to someone with a specific mental health issue. Eysenck's use of the word psychoticism has a different meaning to that used within the mental health world. Eysenck described someone with high levels of psychoticism as showing aggression, impulsivity and antisocial behaviour. Their behaviour may be more inclined to be irresponsible or criminal. Those with lower levels of psychoticism would be considered more law abiding. A person with low levels of psychoticism is more likely to show an ability to control their behaviour and would not act in an impulsive manner.

Eysenck believed the level of psychoticism a person presented within their personality was influenced by their hormone levels, particularly in relation to testosterone. Testosterone is a hormone found in higher levels in males than females. It is the testosterone which appears to contribute to greater aggressive behaviour in men.

He argued that those with high levels of psychoticism were less open to the influence of conditioning, unlike those with lower levels of psychoticism. As a result they did not significantly change their behaviour in the presence of reward or punishment. This helps to explain why they may be more likely to be involved in criminal behaviour, with little regard for, or fear of, possible punishment.

Figure 4.2 below shows the relationship between Eysenck's three personality types. It is possible to identify some of the behaviours that contribute to criminality within this.

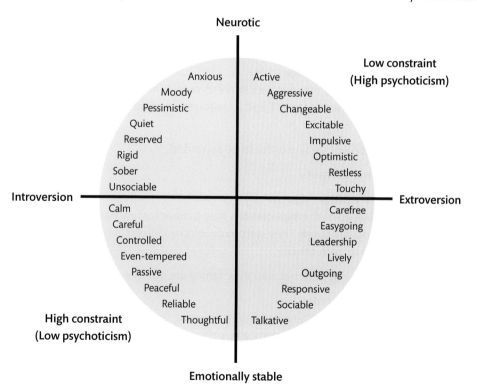

▶ **Figure 4.2:** Diagram of Eysenck's personality types

 **PAUSE POINT**

Think about characters from your favourite TV programme. What personality types are shown among these characters?

Hint

Some characters may show a mixture of personality types, though there may be ones that appear more often on television.

Extend

Is there a relationship between the behaviour of the characters that you see and their personality type?

Cognitive factors and criminality

Your thinking in a situation has a big effect on how you behave in that situation. Your thoughts are often influenced by how you interpret a situation, based on your understanding of what is right and wrong.

Kohlberg (1984) believed that as people develop cognitive (thinking) skills, all individuals pass through various stages of moral development. He argued that as a person gets older, and their thinking skills develop, their understanding of the world, and their role within it, would develop. He identified six different stages of moral development, which fall under three different levels.

Level 1: Pre-conventional morality

Stage 1: Order and punishment
Individuals act in a way that is socially acceptable. Rules are fixed and rigid. Obeying the rules is due to fear of punishment from authority figures.

Example: individuals do not steal for fear of punishment by a parent.

Stage 2: Individualism and exchange
Individuals start to recognise that people's interests may differ from their own. They act in their own best interests. Stages 1 and 2 are found in infants and school-age children.

Example: individuals do not steal in order to be rewarded.

Level 2: Conventional morality

Stage 3: Interpersonal relationships
Individuals want to live up to the expectations they believe society has of them, known as the 'good boy–good girl' stage. They start to develop an interest in approval from others and being nice to each other.

Example: individuals do not steal because their family are not thieves.

Stage 4: Maintaining social order
Individuals recognise the importance of right and wrong, and the role of the law and rules. If someone is punished for breaking a law, this encourages obedience among others.

Example: individuals do not steal because that is not what good people do.

Level 3: Post-conventional morality

Stage 5: Social contract and individual rights

Individuals look for the rules of society to be based on morals and do not go against human rights. They want laws, to ensure that justice prevails.

Example: individuals do not steal because it is not in the interests of everyone for them to do so.

Stage 6: Universal principles

There is a universal principle of justice and respect. There may be a need to disobey unjust laws in the attempt to achieve justice.

Example: individuals do not steal because that does not lead to a 'perfect' world.

Kohlberg believed that individuals would typically progress through these stages chronologically. Many individuals remain at Stage 4, and do not progress through to the post-conventional level. If progress is not made through the stages, their level of moral maturity is impaired. He believed that criminals display significantly reduced moral development. The higher moral stages are less likely to fit within a criminal lifestyle.

It is suggested that criminals tend to display a level of moral development consistent with the pre-conventional level. In particular, this would include the premise that the 'right' behaviour is what is in the individual's own best interest.

An assessment of moral development is not routinely carried out with people convicted of a crime. As a result, it is not possible to be clear on exactly what level of moral development a criminal has reached.

Case study

Palmer & Hollin (1998) wanted to compare moral reasoning among young delinquents and non-delinquents. They found that young people within a Young Offenders Institution showed less mature moral reasoning. Delinquents showed a greater focus on engaging in behaviour that was beneficial to themselves, which could explain them engaging in criminal behaviour.

Some psychologists have suggested that a way to treat criminality is to try and increase people's level of moral development. This builds on the work of Kohlberg, and specifically the idea that higher levels of moral development are not suited to a criminal lifestyle.

Treatment programmes for offending therefore include elements of moral development. These treatment programmes (such as the Thinking Skills Programme) have had some positive effect in reducing the reoffending of some individuals.

1 What do you think would need to be included in a treatment that aims to develop moral development?

2 What may be the benefits of addressing moral development through *group* programmes, with other offenders?

Social psychological explanations of criminality

This unit has so far introduced the biological explanation of criminality and the influence of the individual on their decision making. The final explanation considers the influence of the world in which a person lives on their behaviour. Most importantly, it looks at what influence observing criminal behaviour has on an individual's own criminality.

Link

Look back at Unit 1, page 28 to remind yourself of the details of social learning theory and Bandura's theory of behaviour.

Social learning theory

Social learning theory (SLT) explains that people engage in criminal behaviour because they have seen the same behaviour carried out by other people, such as in the media or by watching other people in their community. SLT has been covered previously, so here you will look only at its relation to criminal behaviour.

The four stages of social learning theory are:
▶ attention: a person pays attention to the behaviour someone shows
▶ retention: this behaviour is remembered by the observer
▶ reproduction: the observer has the ability to act in the same way
▶ motivation: the observer wants to carry out the behaviour they have seen.

An individual cannot learn offending behaviour through SLT, without observing someone commit a crime. This observation can happen in two ways:
1 directly observing a peer commit a crime
2 indirectly watching crime committed in the media, generally in fiction.

Without the observation taking place the later stages of SLT cannot occur, so the behaviour would not be reproduced. An individual may reproduce the behaviour some time after they have observed it, not necessarily straightaway.

Albert Bandura (1977) outlined three factors that are important in determining whether an individual will choose to copy criminal behaviour – that is, whether a person will move from the attention and retention stage, to the reproduction stage.
1 Behaviour is more likely to be repeated if the behaviour is rewarded, providing an **external motivation**. Similarly, if someone is punished for the behaviour, it is less likely to be repeated. This is the principle of operant conditioning.
2 SLT also focuses on **vicarious learning**. An individual observes the consequences of someone committing an offence, before choosing if they are going to act in the same way themselves. A criminal who gets caught when committing an offence is less likely to motivate someone to commit a similar offence. However, a criminal who does not get caught and receives positive benefits for committing the crime, such as attention from peers or financial gain, may make it more likely that an observer will see the benefit in replicating the behaviour.
3 You may choose to copy the behaviour you have seen because of **self-reinforcement**. A crime may cause an individual to have a positive emotion, so they will repeat the crime in order to experience the positive feeling again.

Role models

In order for an individual to copy criminal behaviour in another person, the individual needs to look up to and admire the person acting in a criminal way. This role model may be a family member, friend, or a famous person or TV character. They are more likely to copy their behaviour if they have social status (so that they are well thought of among their peer group). The influence of role models is consistent across genders. A person is more likely to reproduce the behaviour of a role model who is of the same gender as them, with males and females being equally influenced.

> **Key terms**
>
> **External motivation –** wanting to do something because of the influence of someone or something else.
>
> **Vicarious learning –** learning through observing the consequences of others.
>
> **Self-reinforcement –** individuals reward themselves when they achieve a certain outcome.

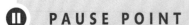 **PAUSE POINT**   What characteristics do you admire in other people?

 Hint   Close the book and recall the characteristics of a role model.

Extend   Reflect on the people in your life that you look up to, and identify which characteristics they display that you admire the most.

Case study

Anderson & Dill (2000) wanted to see if people who played violent video games were more aggressive. They used 210 psychology learners, with half playing a violent video game, and half playing a non-violent one. Both groups played their game for 30 minutes. Rather than the true aim of the study, participants were told the study was about motor development.

They were placed in a cubicle and asked to play the game against an opponent in another cubicle. In reality there was no opponent. After 15 minutes they were asked to play a competitive game with the opponent. This involved completing a reaction test. The person who pressed the button first would be able to set the volume and duration of a noise heard by the opponent as a punishment.

They found that the loudest and longest blasts of noise were given by participants that played the violent game. Women gave greater punishment to their opponents than men.

They concluded that playing violent video games increased aggression levels, particularly in women, compared to those who played non-violent video games.

1 Why did the researchers deceive the participants about the aim of the study?

2 What implications could these findings have for video game manufacturers?

This can explain why some individuals commit 'copycat' crimes. High-profile offences can be widely reported, and people can become fans of the crime or the criminals who committed it. Individuals who admire the offender have been known to commit similar offences.

The media is influential in whether vicarious learning takes effect. Reports that highlight the consequences, or punishment, of offences committed may help to deter people from reproducing the behaviour they have seen others display.

Differential association theory

As with SLT, the differential association theory believes that crime is a learned behaviour, learned from interactions with others. It is a theory heavily influenced by sociology, developed by Edwin Sutherland in 1939.

What do people learn to do? An individual will copy criminal acts, much in the same way as SLT. In learning criminal behaviour from others, the criminal attitudes of that person are also learned.

How do they learn it? Differential association theory states that if an individual is exposed repeatedly to people who have positive attitudes and who encourage criminal behaviour, they are more likely to act in a criminal way themselves.

From whom do they learn it? The exposure comes from many different places, such as anti-social friends or family, or TV programmes and computer games that promote criminal behaviour as exciting. The theory suggests that peers have more influence on behaviour than what is seen in the media.

It is arguably possible to understand a person's risk of being involved in criminal behaviour based on the amount of time they spend in the company of people who have positive views on crime. The differential association theory can help to explain why there may be social groups of criminal activity within a community, and within families.

This theory helped to develop psychology's understanding of the influence of social factors specifically on criminal behaviour. It can be difficult to test this theory, and separate it as an explanation from others, such as social learning and even biological explanations within families. As with other theories, it is difficult to separate what could be nature and what could be nurture.

Upbringing

The direct environment that an individual is brought up in, such as the family home, can influence a person's behaviour later in life. This is because early experiences from childhood, such as exposure to criminality or witnessing domestic violence, can influence how a person thinks about their own future, their current situation and people round them. Children will often replicate the behaviour they observe in childhood, often repeating a cycle of behaviour, including criminality.

Disrupted families

David Farrington is a British forensic psychologist. In 1994, he published an influential longitudinal (over a long period of time) research study looking at how people became involved in criminal behaviour. He interviewed over 400 boys from London when they were aged eight years old. Over 30 years later, he interviewed them again to investigate whether they had displayed any criminal behaviour.

▶ What would the potential impact be on a child growing up in this environment?

His research showed that where parents or an older sibling had criminal convictions the chance of the boys having convictions increased. He also found that poor parental supervision of certain behaviours when the boys were young, also influenced future criminal behaviour. Children who had parents that did not always know where they were playing increased the potential for negative influence from peers. Where parents used harsh physical punishment, it was possible to see that their children demonstrated similar behaviour in their later years.

Families that have parents who demonstrate criminal behaviour are often those who also experience poverty. There may also be numerous children which can mean that there is less time available for each child to have quality interactions with their parents. There is often a greater likelihood of parents in conflict (such as domestic violence), or for single-parent families. This all reduces the level of stability a child can feel in their environment. It can result in a child feeling less safe and emotionally supported. They are also likely to have limited physical resources due to lack of money.

Maternal deprivation

John Bowlby's theory of attachment argues that a warm relationship with a mother figure is needed for an individual to develop positive emotional and psychological health. If a child does not experience the level of emotional warmth that Bowlby states is required, it can have a number of negative consequences for the individual.

▶ It can make it difficult for the person to feel emotionally close to others, and form attachments in the future.
▶ The person may engage in early criminal behaviour, such as delinquency.
▶ There may be delayed cognitive development.
▶ There may be difficulties in feeling remorse for others (known as **affectionless psychopathy**).

Link

Look at Bowlby's theory of attachment in more detail in Unit 5.

Bowlby's (1944) juvenile thieves study demonstrated affectionless psychopathy. Among a group of 44 juvenile thieves, 17 of them had experienced **early separation** from their mother for a prolonged amount of time, before they were five years old.

Of these 17 juveniles, 15 of them showed no guilt or remorse for their criminal behaviour. They were known as affectionless psychopaths. The amount of time separated from the mother was higher than the control group, where only two had been separated from their mother for any amount of time.

Poverty

High levels of unemployment are often noted among individuals with criminal history. Children who are brought up in families with limited money, often due to unemployment among parents, have a higher likelihood of later criminal behaviour. Offence types are often related to stealing, either for items they don't have or to sell items in order to get money. A lack of money in early years can reduce the positive experiences a child has growing up as well as placing additional challenges on their educational choices.

Poverty contributes to the quality of housing environments in which the child grows up. In such environments there is a higher likelihood of criminal activity. As such, poverty results in children being more likely to live in areas with a high crime rate, and therefore have greater exposure to such behaviour.

> **Key terms**
>
> **Affectionless psychopathy** – an inability to show affection or concern for others. Those with affectionless psychopathy have little remorse or guilt for any bad behaviour.
>
> **Early separation** – when a child is separated from his or her mother when the child is young.

 PAUSE POINT   What are the social factors commonly reported in relation to criminality?

 Hint   Draw a diagram that reflects all the different social factors that relate to crime. How
Extend   much detail can you remember on each?

Look at recent news articles that document crime. How many explanations are reported within the news article that may help to explain the crime being discussed?

Assessment activity 4.1

A psychologist is asked to give a presentation to the police that outlines some of the reasons why there may be a high crime rate in their area.

In particular the police are keen to find out why they keep arresting the same people for different crimes, as they want to try and reduce the crime rates.

Produce a presentation that will provide information about all the possible theoretical explanations for a high crime rate in the area.

Within this you should include a consideration of the social environment of your home area, such as the employment level.

Information should be included that would explain why the individual commits a crime, and why they may commit more than one crime while others in the area do not commit any.

You will need to be able to support your theoretical explanations with research from studies you have learned.

Plan
- What is the task? What am I being asked to do?
- How confident do I feel in my own abilities to complete this task? Are there any areas I think I may struggle with?

Do
- I know what it is I'm doing and what I want to achieve.
- I can identify when I've gone wrong and adjust my thinking/approach to get myself back on course.

Review
- I can explain what the task was and how I approached the task.
- I can explain how I would approach the hard elements differently next time (i.e. what I would do differently).

Investigate punishment strategies and behaviour modification of criminal behaviour

An important role of psychologists is to try and prevent an individual committing more offences in the future. This can be done by giving a negative consequence to anyone caught committing a crime or by working with the criminal to try and change their behaviour.

Punishing criminal behaviour

The principles of operant learning suggest that a person is less likely to demonstrate a certain behaviour again if an unpleasant negative consequence is the result. In the case of criminal behaviour, the punishment can vary from a police warning to time in prison.

Imprisonment

Imprisonment relates to the sentencing of an offender to a prison, either an adult prison, young offender institute or a secure training centre, dependent on the age of the offender. In 2018, the prison population was approximately 92,500 prisoners across England, Scotland, Wales and Northern Ireland.

The number of prisoners has been steadily increasing in recent years. Criminals who are considered to be too dangerous to be in the community are sent to prison when they are found guilty of their crimes. Some people will also be sent to prison after getting caught, even if they have not yet been found guilty; they will await their trial in prison or, if under the age of 18, in a young offender's institute.

Why use prison?

The reason for sending individuals to prison, thereby incapacitating them, is to keep the public safe from the crime that such people have been committing, or have been accused of committing. **Incapacitation** is a form of punishment, for breaking the rules of society. It is used as a form of punishment in the hope that the experience of prison will prevent people from wanting to come back to prison in the future. It is also a way of removing people who do not obey the rules of society from the general population, so that they cannot commit more crimes. Prisons have typically been very **punitive,** with a primary focus on punishment.

In recent years prisons have tried to rehabilitate those in prison, to reduce the likelihood of them committing more crime in the future.

Rehabilitation has been attempted through teaching skills to prisoners. It helps them:
▶ to get a job when released from prison. This makes their lives in the community more productive and provides them with financial support and structure, meaning they may not need to reoffend.
▶ to change the thoughts and behaviour that lead to their offending through therapy. This will help them to avoid getting into situations that may lead to them commit crime in the future.

Key terms

Incapacitation – aim of preventing future crimes by taking away the offender's ability to commit them (such as placing them in prison).

Punitive – to inflict a punishment on an individual.

Rehabilitation – the belief that individuals who have committed criminal offences can be treated and can return to a crime-free lifestyle.

▶ How do you think prisoners feel when involved in rehabilitation activities?

Does prison work?

Prison aims to act as a deterrent for potential offenders. It is hoped that the fear of going to prison will stop people from committing crimes. It works on the basis that, by avoiding committing a crime, a person avoids going to prison. This in turn helps to reduce the rate of offending, as people do not start committing crimes because they are scared of the consequences.

It is difficult to research the impact of this fear, as it is not possible to identify potential criminals. A more observable way of looking at the use of prison as a deterrent is to look at the numbers of people in prison at any one time, and if this is changing each year.

In recent years the prison population has been steadily increasing. It is now at a significantly high level. This would indicate that fear of prison is not a deterrent for some individuals.

Unfortunately, this data does not tell you any information about the people that are going to prison. A helpful way of understanding the effect of prison on those with a criminal record is to look at **recidivism** rates. This is the number of criminals who go on to commit a further offence. The overall reoffending rate is approximately 25 per cent. This rate has remained fairly stable since 2004.

What is life like after prison?

The length of time a criminal has been in prison can affect how they adjust to life back in the community. Prisons are very structured settings, with specific rules to be followed. While they are encouraged to work to earn money, what they can spend the money on is limited.

If a person has been in prison for many years, they will have not had to pay bills or rent for a long time. This can be overwhelming for them when they are released from prison.

> ### Key terms
>
> **Recidivism** – the tendency for an offender to commit a further offence, or offences.
>
> **Institutionalised** – a developed dependency after a long period of time in an institution.

Some prisoners refer to feeling 'institutionalised'. This refers to an emotional feeling of being overwhelmed by the demands placed on a person in a community setting, and the fact that they need to readjust to the change in their environment. These adjustments may be practical in relation to accommodation and employment, or psychological. This could be related to redeveloping relationships with friends and family and dealing with the response of others in the community to their having been released from prison. For some prisoners, the feeling of institutionalisation is so great that they think returning to prison is the only way for them to respond to their difficulties. This can often result in individuals committing offences with the specific goal of returning to prison.

Discussion

Imagine you have not been into the community for a period of time. What do you think you will find difficult to adjust to?

Do you know of any resources or places that you could go which would help you adjust back into the community?

Mental health in prison

The number of prisoners with known mental health conditions is disproportionate to the number of those with mental-health conditions in the community. Complex social and personal issues such as substance misuse or histories of trauma are more common among the prisoner population. Experiences of trauma and substance use has a direct correlation with mental health issues, with these individuals having a greater likelihood of having difficulties with their mental health.

Self-inflicted death and **self-harm behaviour** is also more common in prison than in the community. Being in prison can make mental health problems worse, through separation from family and friends, boredom and loss of freedom. This means that prisoners, even those who enter prison with good mental health, are vulnerable to developing difficulties with their mood while in prison, in direct reaction to their imprisonment.

Key terms

Self-inflicted death – a person dies as a result of a deliberate action they have done to themselves.

Self-harm behaviour – causing deliberate injury to oneself.

Self-inflicted deaths are any death of a person who has apparently taken his or her own life. It does not matter whether they intended to die. Therefore, this not only includes suicides but also accidental deaths as a result of the person's own actions. This classification is used because it is not always known whether a person intended to commit suicide.

Data relating to deaths in custody is released every three months by the government. In 2017 there were 70 self-inflicted deaths. The number of self-inflicted deaths remains high, and higher than the number of self-inflicted deaths in the general population.

While the number of self-inflicted deaths has reduced over recent years, the number of prisoners who self-harm (intentionally hurting themselves) has increased significantly. According to the Ministry of Justice (MOJ) (2018), in 2017 there were almost 45,000 known incidents of self-harm, undertaken by 11,600 prisoners. This suggests that many prisoners who do self-harm will do so more than once. Figure 4.3 shows data to indicate the rise of self-harm in prisons.

The severity of self-harm can vary depending on the method of self-harm chosen. In 2017, almost seven per cent of prisoners attended a community hospital for treatment after self-harm, due to the severity of the injury (MOJ 2018). This percentage of prisoners requiring hospital treatment has been relatively stable over the years. This suggests that self-harm behaviour is not becoming more serious in what type of injury the individual causes themselves, but that individuals are committing self-harm more frequently than ever before.

Even though there are many more male prisoners than female prisoners, women participate in higher levels of self-harm than men in prison. This variation could be due to a tendency for women to communicate their emotional distress in a different way from men. Men have a greater tendency to engage in serious self-harm, so a greater number of men need to have hospital treatment because of their self-harm.

While the data provides an indication of the levels of known self-harm in prisons, this data does not reflect the actual, higher, level of self-harm taking place in prisons. As in the general population, self-harm in prison is often hidden by the prisoners themselves and may go unreported. Serious self-harm is more likely to be reported in prison because of the increased need for medical treatment, making it difficult for the prisoner to hide this behaviour from staff. This may lead to an over representation in data reports of serious self-harm in comparison to the type of self-harm that does not require any form of medical help.

Self-harm incidents (per 1000 prisoners)

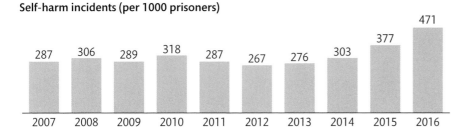

Self-inflicted deaths (in total)

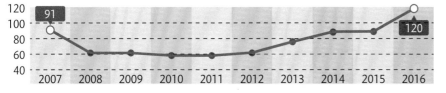

▶ **Figure 4.3:** Number of self-harm incidents and self-inflicted deaths in prisons in England and Wales over 10 years. (Source: National Audit Office)

Thinking about someone's level of distress can be upsetting. It is possible that you know someone who has self-harmed in the past or spoken about wanting to hurt themselves.

If this topic causes you any concern, speak to your tutor or someone else you trust to support you with how you are feeling.

Prisons are taking active steps to try and reduce the number of suicides and to support those with mental health issues in prison. Each prison will have a relationship with a mental health service that provides mental health support, including support in managing anxieties; self-harm behaviour and dealing with any trauma symptoms. Prisons will also be able to access support for any drug use their prisoners may have, to try and prevent further drug use, which can increase the likelihood of prisoners developing mental health issues. A prisoner who has significant mental health issues in prison may be transferred to a secure hospital for treatment instead of remaining in prison where the person may be vulnerable.

Case study

Sweden has adopted a punishment approach to drug use with an aim of creating a drug-free society. They use a zero-tolerance approach. Penalties were increased for those caught with drugs, fines for drug possession became prison sentences, and police had the capability to take blood and urine tests without an individual's consent.

As a result of this policy, the number of convictions for drug offences has more than doubled over the last 10 years; most are for simple drug possession. On the downside, illicit drug use including cannabis is on the increase (although it is still much lower than in other countries) as is other drug use among the general population.

1 What does the outcome of this policy suggest in terms of its effectiveness in tackling drug use?

2 This approach has been criticised as it does not consider how to reduce the harm caused by drug use, instead focusing on stopping drug use completely. A harm-reduction approach may include educating people about the risks of using drugs, and how to inject without the risk of contracting Hepatitis C. How might a harm-minimisation approach have a more positive effect on drug use than the punishment approach adopted by Sweden?

▶ New York in the 1980s successfully implemented the zero-tolerance approach to criminal behaviour

Zero tolerance

Zero tolerance is a strict way of dealing with any criminal behaviour. It works on the basis that people caught committing *any* offences are dealt with severely. The police have no discretion about whether they charge someone with an offence or not; anyone caught committing any type of crime will be charged with it. The zero-tolerance approach aims to deter people from committing any offence.

It is based on the 'broken windows' theory from Wilson & Kelling (1982), which is the idea that minor physical and social disorder, if left unattended, would cause more serious crime in a neighbourhood. This approach believes that people stop caring as much for their environment if one incident occurs, leading to more incidents and a spiral of crime.

The US model

The US model of zero tolerance can be seen from a study of New York in the 1990s. Implementing zero tolerance resulted in a 66 per cent reduction in murder between 1990 and 1997. This was the largest sustained reduction in violent crime in the city for decades. All types of murder reduced in number, though the most remarkable reduction was in the number of deaths as a result of shootings.

This was achieved through policies put in place by New York city Mayor Rudolph Giuliani. He hired a police commissioner to tackle the problem. As a result, police started to use a policy aimed at creating public order. They aggressively enforced laws against quality-of-life offences, such as public drunkenness, littering and other offences that were considered minor. They particularly focused on people who avoided paying when they used the subway. This led to a huge increase in the number of arrests for these offences and led to New York seeing a significant reduction in these behaviours within a few years.

It has been suggested that the reduction in crime rate may have been due to the increased police presence on the streets of New York, as well as the 'broken windows' influence that meant a reduction in low-level crime was having a positive effect on more serious crime.

War on drugs

Zero-tolerance approaches have been used to try and address drug use and the 'war on drugs'. In many countries there are severe punishments for being in possession of drugs. Those who want zero tolerance approaches to be used more widely for drug use suggest that if punishments are not severe for drug offences, then it looks like the law supports the behaviour.

A zero-tolerance approach to drug use has meant that drug addicts in these countries are only ever offered punishment, rather than treatment, which is considered by some to be the better approach to actually change their behaviour.

System abuse

A zero-tolerance approach on drugs and other criminal behaviour can lead to a potentially abusive system in which those in power target individuals based on their race or gender, or unfairly target those who have offended previously or are known to the system. For example, there is evidence to show that police implementing 'stop and search' unfairly target young black men. The focus of a zero-tolerance approach is often influenced by political decisions as a result of public demand. It is important that this approach is driven by evidence of crime rates, rather than by more subjective methods. In this way, potential criticism of unfair targeting of specific community populations is minimised.

Offender disclosure schemes

Serious criminal offences can lead to future changes in the law. There have been a number of high profile offences that have led to the introduction of offender disclosure schemes; laws that allow the public to check on the violent history of people they know.

One example of an offender disclosure scheme is commonly known as 'Clare's Law'. Clare Wood was murdered in February 2009 by a man she had met on an Internet dating site. The man, unknown to Clare, had a long history of violence against women. Prior to harming her, he had previously made threats towards her. She had complained to the police about his behaviour prior to her death.

Officially known as the Domestic Violence Disclosure Scheme, Clare's Law means that people have the power to check the police record of their partners. There are strict rules to how this information can be accessed, and why. It was mainly developed for individuals to check the history of their partners, to learn if their partner has a history of sexual or domestic violence.

Offender disclosure schemes have two functions:

1 'Right to ask': This enables someone to ask the police about a partner's previous history of domestic violence or violent acts.

2 'Right to know': The police can proactively disclose information in certain circumstances if it is in the best interests of the person asking for the information. This could occur if the identified person has a history of such violence and is considered an ongoing risk as a result.

Police will support individuals making a request if the information search suggests they may be in a difficult and potentially unsafe position. They can issue 'Protection Orders' to help support the individual if needed.

The ethics of disclosing information about someone without their consent is very important within disclosure schemes. Though any person can submit a request to a disclosure scheme, the police carefully review the reasons for the request and the information they have on the identified person before any disclosure is made. This is to make sure that individuals who do not have a legitimate reason to know this information do not receive it. There is a need also to consider the protection of the named person from any possible retribution if the wrong person learns of their history.

Community sentences

Not all offences require the offender to go to prison. Where possible the preference will be for the person to remain in the community. This reduces the disruption on the person's family, living situation and employment, all of which are considered important to support a non-criminal lifestyle in the community. A community sentence also reduces the labelling effect of those who have been in prison, thereby reducing stigma against those who have been in prison. **Stigma** can result in a future challenge for offenders in gaining employment and moving on from a criminal lifestyle.

> **Key term**
>
> **Stigma** – a sense of disapproval directed to someone with a particular characteristic or engages in a specific behaviour, i.e. crime.

Community sentences can be considered an effective alternative to custodial sentences (incapacitation), particularly for more minor offences. These are often used as punishment for crimes such as property damage or minor assault.

There are 13 different community punishments that can be given to an individual. These include:

- unpaid work
- curfews so the offender is required to be in a particular place at certain times
- restrictions on where people can go and live and what they can do, including foreign travel
- treatment for alcohol, drugs, mental health and offending behaviour
- alcohol abstinence and monitoring.

In 2017, eight per cent of the sentences imposed on offenders in court were for community sentences; a small proportion of all sentences. Some of these community punishments, such as the mental health treatment option, are potentially underused.

For many of these treatments to be considered appropriate, the offender must agree to undertake the treatment before they can be given this sentence. If someone fails to stick to this agreement it can lead to other punishments, including prison being imposed instead. The advantage of many of the treatment elements of community punishment is that the person has given their agreement to take part. As such, the offender has greater influence over their sentencing outcome than those sent to prison.

In addition to the previous community sentences, community supervision is also required. This involves working with Offender Managers in the community (historically referred to as Probation Officers). Community supervision is often referred to as **probation**.

> **Key term**
>
> **Probation** – the supervision of an offender in a community setting, either as an alternative to prison or those who have been released from prison. It is more typically known as community supervision.

▶ Ankle monitors can be used to ensure offenders with curfew or location restrictions are not moving outside of an allowed range.

The role of Offender Managers is to ensure the offenders' sentences are adhered to. They play a significant role in delivering much of the treatment and support required for the offender to be successful in their community sentence. They work with offenders who have spent time in prison who were told by the courts to undergo additional community supervision on release from prison.

Recidivism rates within 12 months for those who are given community sentences, compared to short-term prison sentences, is lower than the rates for those sent to prison. In 2013 there was a three per cent reoffending rate for those with community sentences, compared to four per cent for those sent to prison (Ministry of Justice 2013). It was found that three years after the initial offence, reoffending rates were improved for those given community sentences rather than prison. By the five-year stage there was less difference in reoffending rates.

This suggests some effectiveness of community sentences in the short term. However, community sentences are not available for all offences, with more serious offences unsuitable for a community punishment. As such, community sentences only reflect those who have engaged in less serious offences, which may impact on recidivism rates.

One difficulty in using recidivism rates to consider the success of community sentences is that it only reflects offending that has been proven to be committed by that specific offender. If the person who committed the crime is unknown, or the suspect has not been found guilty of the offence, it is not counted within recidivism data. As such, recidivism data has limitations to its use.

Fines and discharges

Other types of punishment that can be used are fines and discharges. These aim to impact offenders on a moral and financial level, rather than giving them a more severe punishment.

Fines are the most common type of sentence given to individuals convicted of what are generally lower-level crimes. These include driving offences and crimes such as littering. The specific amount of the fine to be paid is often decided at court, or there may be 'fixed penalties', which are often associated with speeding offences for example. The fine can be given to a company or a person who may have been a victim of a crime. In 2017, 75 per cent of all offenders received a fine.

Individuals who are unable to pay fines can find themselves serving a prison sentence for non-payment of fines. This results in an additional conviction of non-payment, which is added to the original offence. Fines if applied to those without the means to pay can therefore present the risk of additional punishment. This creates an imbalance in the outcomes of those given fines dependent on their financial situation.

Discharges are reserved for the least serious of crimes. Often a person's character and the type of the offence are taken into account and the decision is made that no punishment would be appropriate. The discharge can be:
▶ Absolute discharge: the experience of going to court is considered enough of a deterrent. The offender still gets a criminal record.
▶ Conditional discharge: the offence goes onto their criminal record. No more action is taken unless they commit another offence within a specified timeframe. If they do commit another crime, they can be sentenced for the first offence as well as the new one.

The option to discharge an offence also serves to ensure individuals are not unfairly stigmatised for criminal involvement.

The options available to a particular offender at a particular time are dependent on the type of offence committed, the offender's motivation to undertake treatment specific to the offence, and the decision made by judges in court.

Modifying criminal behaviour

There are many ways in which psychologists can try to change criminal behaviour to reduce the likelihood of further offending. The treatment chosen will be influenced by the behaviour that needs to be changed.

Anger management

Anger management interventions are offered to individuals either in the community or in prison. These interventions aim to help people understand what makes them angry and how to manage this anger in the future if it occurs again. This includes helping them to manage their anger in the community and/or in prison to reduce prison violence. The treatment may be provided in a group setting or on an individual basis. Anger management interventions are only appropriate for those who commit offences as a result of being angry.

The content of many anger management interventions is based on a cognitive behavioural approach, with two elements to such interventions:
▶ Cognitive skills: understanding and changing angry thoughts.
▶ Behavioural skills: understanding and practising what to do when angry in order to reduce the anger.

These elements are found in the original anger management interventions, based on **stress inoculation training** (Novaco 1975). The presence of stress contributes to heightened emotions. This can then be presented by an individual in an aggressive way.

Key term

Stress inoculation training – a form of cognitive behaviour therapy designed to maximise a person's ability to cope with stress. It involves teaching coping strategies to manage stress.

There have been many new anger management programmes developed since the work of Novaco, but each follows many of the same principles as they continue to be based on a cognitive behavioural approach.

Stage 1: Conceptualisation – people learn to understand what makes them angry

Individuals are introduced to various skills they can use to manage their anger, and to reduce feelings of anger if and when they experience them. Offenders are not taught to be fearful of becoming angry, as it is an emotion everyone experiences. Instead they are taught to *control* their anger.

Those with anger management difficulties may have a hostile attribution bias. This is a tendency to interpret the behaviour of other people in a negative way and then to react based on this interpretation. For example, if someone walked into a room and people quickly left the room, someone with a hostile attribution bias may interpret this as the people leaving the room *because* they had entered. A person would then react based on their belief that the reaction of others was personal to them. This can lead to aggressive or confrontational behaviour.

This biased thinking can lead to the person thinking about the situation in a way that is not based on any reality; it is an irrational thought. The way to treat this hostile attribution bias, and the irrational thoughts that it leads to, is to help the individual challenge their own thinking. If they can reduce their beliefs that someone is acting negatively towards them, they can reduce the likelihood of them reacting to a situation with aggression.

Stage 2: Skills acquisition and rehearsal – people learn to practise using these skills when angry

Skills such as relaxation techniques may be given to offenders to help to reduce feelings of anger. This can include skills to use in the immediate moment, such as counting to 10 silently when feeling angry. Alternatively, the offender would be supported to think of alternative ways to manage an aggressive situation, such as getting out of the situation or remaining assertive rather than starting to shout at someone.

Individuals are then encouraged to practise the skills they have been given. Practice makes it more likely they will be able to use the skills in the future at times when they are angry.

Anger management only works for those offenders who have problems with anger control. If an offence was not committed due to poor anger control, taking part in an anger management programme would have no positive change on their offending behaviour.

While anger management programmes have been shown to be effective (see Howells et al. 2005), much of this data is based on those taking part in the programme completing questionnaires that ask about how angry they have felt in recent days or weeks. It is possible that the information they give may suggest they have felt less angry than they really have. This is a common concern particularly if they believe this will have a positive effect on their sentence, that is, being released from prison at the earliest point.

> **Theory into practice**
>
> Imagine you had to design a new prison, and you had control about how you would want it to run. The aim of the prison is to reduce reoffending.
>
> What would be the key features you would have in the prison?
>
> It may be helpful to undertake a detailed review of how prisons are run in different countries to help you decide on your final plan.

Restorative justice

Restorative justice starts a conversation between the person who has committed a crime, and the victim against whom the crime was committed. There is an emphasis on communicating the victim's perspective of the offence, for example how it has made them feel, or the impact on their social and work activities.

It aims to provide offenders with a more personal understanding of the effect of their behaviour on others, with the hope that this will encourage them to make amends for their offence and be reluctant to create future victims. This then leads to a reduction in further offending by this person.

It is used at various stages of the criminal justice system, including prior to sentencing and afterwards. It works with youth offenders and with adults. It can involve victims:

▶ explaining to an offender the effect the offence has had on them
▶ seeking an explanation and an apology from the offender
▶ contributing to decisions about the restorative or reparative activity for the offender, for example, paying to repair any material damage, or keeping the victim informed of their progress in getting a job.

Pilot programmes suggest that restorative justice has contributed to an estimated 14 per cent reduction in the frequency of reoffending. It has also found that victims who take part have found the experience a positive one, which helps them to recover from the crime.

Restorative justice is a more recent initiative within the criminal justice system. A challenge to making it more widely available is that specially trained staff are needed to deliver this approach.

Token economy based on principles of behaviourism, used in prisons

Token economy is based on operant conditioning as a means of changing an individual's behaviour. It is used within prisons as a way of encouraging prisoners to comply with the rules of the prison. A desired behaviour is identified, such as not getting involved in fights.

If the offender displays this positive behaviour, they are given a token, which acts as a secondary reinforcer. The token can then be traded for a **primary reinforcer** that meets a basic need, such as leisure time. This helps to reinforce good behaviour, making it more likely this behaviour will continue to be shown.

Prisons operate an Incentives and Earned Privileges (IEP) scheme, which follows the basis of token economy. There are three levels of the regime: Basic, Standard and Enhanced. Prisoners move through these levels dependent on their behaviour while in prison. These levels become the secondary reinforcer. The amount of social activity, frequency of visits from family and the type of work they can do in the prison (and therefore their freedom/primary reinforcers) is directly influenced by their level on the IEP scheme. This forms the economy that prisoners work towards.

The token economy approach in prison provides prisoners with a greater level of influence around some areas of their time in prison, giving them some control over their environment. It can help to improve compliance in prison, and therefore improve prison behaviour, though it has limited effect on future offending behaviour. It therefore has no impact on recidivism.

> **Key term**
>
> **Primary reinforcer –** reinforcement for a behaviour that meets a basic need, including sleep and food.

> **Link**
>
> Look back at Unit 1, page 28 for more information on operant conditioning.

Assessment activity 4.2

A Police and Crime Commissioner (PCC) is worried about the high rates of criminal behaviour, despite having more police on the streets in the local area.

She has to think about where she may need to direct her police resources to try and reduce crime in the future.

She is keen to learn if she should invest more money in treating the offenders in the community or punishing those who commit crime to try and deter them.

Design a poster that would give the PCC information about what she could try in the community to help her with this problem.

In a creative way, document the treatment that she could look at providing within a community setting that may not already be provided in the local area. Remind her of initiatives that may be there already that are particularly helpful.

Plan
- What is the task? What am I being asked to do?
- What do I need to spend my research time focusing on?

Do
- I am clear of the goal for this task and how I can achieve this.
- I can structure my work in a way that shows a breadth of knowledge.

Review
- I can explain what the task was and the reasons for including the information that I did.
- I can explain how I would approach the hard elements differently next time (i.e. what I would do differently).

C Apply different methods to create an offender profile

Psychologists have a thorough understanding of human behaviour, and can help to understand why a person may act in a particular way, and helpfully, consider who that person may be. Through applying theoretical knowledge, psychologists can influence important decisions relating to detection of criminals.

Methods of offender profiling

Psychologists can play an influential role in assisting the police in finding an offender. This is often used when there is a need to understand the reasons for the offender's behaviour, as a way of reducing the number of people who may have committed that offence. This way of looking at the crime and using that to suggest who the offender may be is known as offender profiling.

Top-down techniques (US)

The original method of offender profiling was developed by the Federal Bureau of Investigations (FBI) in the United States.

In the 1970s the FBI conducted in-depth interviews with convicted murderers, many of whom had killed a number of people. From this they developed a picture of 'typical' **offender profiles**. These profiles demonstrated what many of the people who commit such offences were like as individuals, how they committed the crime, and so on.

When a crime is committed, the top-down approach to profiling would look at the crime scene and make decisions about what they find. They would then compare this to the 'typical' profiles previously gathered from research. Using this information they would then build up a profile for the offender of the new offence.

The top-down approach refers to a way of working that focuses initially on the bigger picture (the offence and what is known about offenders in general) and then works to find the smaller details about the offender.

Typology of serial murder

The top-down approach suggests that offenders can be grouped into two categories: organised or disorganised offenders. Table 4.2 shows some of the characteristics of these two groups. This information is from Hazlewood & Douglas (1980) who were FBI agents working in the Behavioural Sciences Unit. The research focused on lust murders, which are offences that have a clear sexual focus. The approach they used is based on the premise that once the type of offender who committed a crime has been identified, it is possible to make predictions about what offences they may commit next.

▶ **Table 4.2:** The characteristics of organised and disorganised offenders

Organised non-social offenders	Disorganised asocial offenders
• Life is ordered, and methodical • Average to high level of intelligence • Self-centred attitude, manipulates others • Crime reflects preference for order and control • Lives away from crime scene • Premeditated /planned offences • Actively wants body to be found • Takes weapon to the offence • Less physical evidence left at scene due to control	• Prefers own company/a 'loner' • Less intelligent/socially competent • Crime is frenzied and less methodical • Lives or works close to the crime scene • Plans the offence /fantasises about it • Offence itself may occur based on opportunity • No attempt to conceal the body • Uses a weapon of opportunity • More physical evidence left at scene due to frenzied attack

Top-down profiling, and particularly the use of two groups of offenders (organised and disorganised) is a somewhat simplistic way to reflect the thinking of all serious offenders. Many offences display both organised and disorganised elements.

As the FBI based their theories around known convicted offenders, all of whom were sexually motivated murderers, it can only be used accurately when attempting to profile a similar offence. It therefore cannot be accurately used for other types of serious offences.

The disorganised/organised classification of offenders was later reviewed by Canter et al. (2004). Using 100 cases of offences committed by serial killers they wanted to test the hypothesis of Hazelwood & Douglas (1980). They found that it was not possible to separate organised and disorganised variables clearly, as most offences have some organised elements within them. The study suggested it would be more helpful to study the personalities of the individuals.

Top-down profiling has been successfully used in Canada and the Netherlands, suggesting that there is some useful application of this approach (Ainsworth 2000). In particular, it is helpful in crimes where the crime scene provides clear information about which type of offender committed the crime.

Theory into practice

Imagine you were a profiler asked to help investigate a number of burglaries in the area.

Discuss with others how you would apply the top-down approach to try and help the police in their search for the serial burglar.

What do you know about burglary (or what does the evidence suggest) that may help you in developing a profile?

Bottom-up behavioural analysis (UK)

An alternative approach to offender profiling places greater emphasis on the personality of the offender who has committed the crime being investigated. It is less concerned about comparing the offence to other offenders in the way the top-down approach does. This approach is based on key psychological theories.

A key psychologist in the development of the 'bottom-up' approach (which was developed in the 1980s) is David Canter. In his approach, there is no attempt to define the offender of the crime into any specific category. Instead, this approach starts with the small details about an offence and aims to create a bigger picture about who committed it. It relies heavily on the use of databases of crimes that have been committed, and applies psychological theories that relate to social psychology.

Within this approach there are five characteristics that could help the police in identifying the offender. These are outlined below.

1 **Residential location:** the location of the crime will be significant to the offender. The location of the offence will reveal information about where the offender lives, known as geographical profiling.

▸ **Significance of place: geographical profiling** is used within a bottom-up approach of profiling. It helps to make some estimates about where an individual may live based on what is known about the offences committed. This can help to track down where the offender may be.

Key term

Geographical profiling – a process of evaluating the location of connected serial crimes, such as murder or burglary to decide the most likely area in which the offender will live.

It works on the theory that offences are often committed in an environment in which the offender is familiar. From the information about the location of the offence, it is possible to work out where the offender may live.

2 **Criminal biography:** clues found within the offence can provide an insight into the offender's criminal history. For example, someone who takes steps to reduce the presence of forensic clues, such as fingerprints at the crime scene, may have a previous history of similar offences. This is particularly relevant as the offender's DNA and fingerprints from previous offences are available. This means that the police can check current information against this historical information. Such behaviour on the part of the offender would suggest a high level of forensic awareness; they understand what forensic experts will be looking for and so attempt to leave no evidence.

3 **Domestic/social characteristics:** different offences are more likely to be committed by those from specific domestic or social backgrounds. For example, sexually sophisticated rape offences may suggest someone who is living with a partner and is currently sexually active, rather than a naive offence that may suggest less sexual experience.

▶ **Significance of time:** the time of day at which offences are committed helps to provide information about the individual. A pattern of the same time of day would suggest a degree of routine for the offender. It may be that they are at work at other times of the day, thereby reducing their opportunity to offend. Variation in times may suggest unemployment or, in the presence of a pattern to the times of day, that the individual is a shift worker.

4 **Personal characteristics:** while this approach does not attempt to categorise offenders into groups based on personality, it is recognised that personal characteristics have an impact on the type and style of offences an offender would commit. This leads to a consideration of 'criminal consistency'.

5 **Criminal consistency:** a consistency in the behaviour of an offender makes it possible to look for similarities between their everyday behaviour and their behaviour when committing a crime. The idea of **interpersonal coherence** plays a key role in drawing conclusions between the crime and the offender. Criminal consistency allows the profiler to understand the behaviour of the individual offender, without needing to place the person into a category regarding the type of their offence. This approach believes that the actions of an offender within a crime can provide information about the person's background, such as experiences or interests.

Key term

Interpersonal coherence – the similarities between a crime or victim and the offender's behaviour within their every day lives.

6 **Occupational/educational history:** elements of the offence can provide clues to an offender's background. For example, planning the offence in detail may be a reflection of high intelligence, and so the offender may be someone with qualifications. Use of a weapon in a particular way may lean towards a profession, for example, butcher.

Of these five characteristics, residential location and criminal history have been found to be the most effective in finding offenders (Boon & Davies 1993).

The bottom-up approach is considered a more objective, and therefore more reliable approach than the US top-down approach. A key advantage to this approach is that it can be applied to many different types of offences, and not just to sexually motivated offences as in the US approach. It does however take a long time to review the data if a lot is available, so it can take some time before a profile will be of assistance to the police.

II PAUSE POINT		Close your book and write down as many features as you can remember for bottom-up profiling. For each feature provide a brief explanation of what it is focusing on.
	Hint	Try and write the points into a numbered list as this may help you remember them.
	Extend	Would the profile for burglary look different using a bottom-up approach rather than a top-down one?

Offender profiling, purpose and techniques

Aims of profiling

There is a close relationship between the aims of the profiler (often a psychologist), and the aims of the police investigating the crime. Their shared aim is to apprehend the individual who has committed an offence. They try to achieve this aim by working to understand the reason why the offender committed the offence (known as their Modus Operandi). There are three main goals of offender profiling:

▶ narrowing the range of suspects
▶ predicting future crimes, for example, times, locations
▶ suggesting police interview techniques.

Offender profiling does not aim to solve the crime in itself but is a way of reducing the number of suspects in a crime, hopefully allowing the crime to be solved.

Narrow the range of suspects

The aim of a criminal investigation is to identify the suspect as quickly as possible. It may be the case that there is no specific suspect for an offence. For example, the only available information may be that the offender is male and in his mid-20s. This means that the police need to be able to find a way of refining their investigation of males in their 20s to a smaller, more manageable number.

Predict future crimes

Reoffending for some offences can be quite high. As a result, it is necessary to try and find the suspect quickly. The severity of some offences, particularly violent ones, means that any more offending will lead to significant negative consequences for the victim and the community.

In understanding why a person may have committed a particular offence, it is possible to look at ways in which the person may commit another, similar offence. It may be that any future offences are predicted to involve the same type of crime, the same area of a town or the same time of day. In knowing this information, the police can actively look for the person with this information in mind, as well as potentially warn the public if it were considered necessary.

Interview techniques

Knowing the personality characteristics of the suspected offender will help to provide information about their thinking and their attitudes. This may include their attitudes to the police. The police can use this information within their interviews to ensure their interview approach, or the questions that they ask, obtain as much information as possible during the interview.

Building a psychological portrait

An individual's psychological profile includes many different factors, all of which influence how they think, interpret situations around them, and most importantly, why they may commit a criminal offence. These factors include:

▶ age
▶ gender
▶ personality
▶ behavioural habits, such as obsessive traits
▶ behavioural consistency; how they typically occupy their time, or which route they take to work.
▶ intellect
▶ health.

Knowledge of these psychological factors can help with predictions about future offences, as well as helping to identify individuals that may match some of these factors.

Discussion

Reflect on your own psychological characteristics. If someone were to profile you as a person (not as an offender) what would be written about you?

Ask a friend to write a profile about you, as well as writing your own. Compare them and see how accurate the profile written by your friend is.

Building a social portrait

While a psychological portrait looks at factors internal to the individual, social portraits look at the environment that the individual has been exposed to and considers the previous experiences they may have had. These factors include:

▶ religious beliefs
▶ ethnicity
▶ social class
▶ marital status
▶ occupation
▶ residential area
▶ substance abuse history
▶ potential criminal history.

Clues as to the above social factors may be gained through the time of day the offences occur, whether there are a number of offences in a similar area, and the method of the offence.

Crime scene data collection

Psychologists do not specifically help to gather crime scene information, though they have a role in helping to understand the meaning behind some of the evidence that is gathered. Crime scene investigators will gather much of the physical evidence such as fingerprints. Other information may also be gathered using police databases, which helps to look at patterns of offences that may have occurred, and through talking to the victim or witnesses. The type of information gathered includes the:

▶ type of victim; their age, gender, race
▶ type of offence committed; the victim may be injured and able to talk about what happened, as well as reviewing the immediate environment in which it occurred
▶ location; in the victim's own home, public or isolated place, and so on
▶ time of offence; day, evening, night
▶ frequency of similar crimes in the area; historical as well as recent offences may be considered
▶ physical evidence at the crime scene; crime weapon, blood spatter, footprints.

A multi-factor approach, including the use of physical evidence, databases and psychological profiling can help in understanding the importance of different parts of the crime scene, ensuring that information is not overlooked. This then helps the police find the offender.

Limitations of offender profiling

Offender profiling has been used for many years within some investigations, and has shown some success in a number of cases. As with all methods of investigation, there are a number of limitations that need to be considered, to appreciate the use of offender profiling fully.

Case study

John Duffy - Railway Rapist Between 1975 and 1986 there were 24 sexual assaults and two rapes committed in and around London, near railway stations. All offences were against young women.

David Canter developed a psychological profile based on key information known about the offences, including the offender trying to talk to the victims before and during the assault and that they were all approached near train stations. The profile was considered to be particularly accurate. Following Mr Duffy's conviction (13 years later) a male accomplice was given a life sentence for his involvement in the offences. There had been ongoing suspicions that he had an accomplice committing the offences with him, though there was no specific evidence at the time.

The profile shown in Table 4.3 highlights the accuracy, and therefore the strengths, of an offender profiling approach to crime. Cases such as that of John Duffy demonstrate that profiling can indeed be helpful to catch an offender.

▶ **Table 4.3:** Comparing the 'Railway Rapist' offender profile with John Duffy

Profile information	John Duffy
From London	Lived in Kilburn, London
Age 20-30	28-years-old when arrested
Married with no children	Married with no children
Marriage problems	Separated
Small man	5 feet 4 inches tall
Carpentry skills	Trained carpenter
Martial arts interest	Member of martial arts club
Linked to the railways and British Rail	Ex-British Rail employee

Problems and issues

Appropriateness

Offender profiling is usually reserved for the most serious of cases. These often relate to offences including murder. Holmes & Holmes (1996) studied the value of offender profiling in assisting the police in violent cases. They argued that the use of profiling *must* be applied only to a specific number of cases in order for the profile to be valid, and therefore helpful.

The only offences they believe offender profiling can be applied to are:
▶ sadistic torture
▶ evisceration (removing internal organs)
▶ cutting a body after death
▶ rape
▶ motiveless fire starting
▶ satanic and ritualistic crime.

Empirical investigation

The FBI top-down approach can be considered too subjective to be accurate as, in each case, the profiler has to interpret a lot of data, which someone else might look at differently. The original FBI profiling was based on convicted criminals who had committed murders. However, profiling is often applied to other crimes, and not just murder. This means that it can be argued that there are minimal types of crimes that this form of profiling is suitable for.

One way to learn if a technique is effective is to undertake research to assess its effectiveness. Many of the literature reviews that have studied offender profiling suggest that the popularity of offender profiling is less as a result of research showing that it works, but more because profiling has been heavily exposed by the media.

For example, there are many films that have looked at fictional profilers that make the role seem glamorous. When profiling has been used successfully in a real crime, the media has reported on it widely, leading to (arguably) a mismatch between what has been reported and what offender profiling can actually achieve. More research is needed in order to be confident about the effectiveness of offender profiling.

▶ The media can be accused of glamorising the role of profilers

Reductionist

Top-down profiling can be considered **reductionist** as classifying offenders in only two categories – organised and disorganised – is too simple a categorisation to reflect all the different types of offenders. Offenders may show both features within one crime so they cannot be classified as simply one category. This approach fails to consider the complexity of the offence and the offender committing them.

It is possible that an offender becomes more organised as they become more experienced in their offending, (for example, they wear gloves when committing a burglary to avoid leaving fingerprints) or become clearer on what they want to achieve by committing the offences (they burgle a house with the explicit means to steal a particular item, for example, car keys). As a result, to classify someone as either organised or disorganised overlooks the potential for the offending behaviour to change.

Police analysis bias

Many of the predictions made within profiles are vague and difficult to prove even if the offender is eventually caught. This means that large parts of a profile are considered **unverifiable**. There is the potential for investigating police officers to creatively interpret profiles because the information within them is vague. This can lead to the police being guided more by the profile that has been created than by the evidence gathered and other measurable information.

It is particularly complex when the profile provides information that is so vague that the profile can be interpreted in different ways. As there is no formal training consistently offered to the police about how to interpret profiles, this increases the potential for there to be a bias in how the profile is interpreted.

Normally, the police consider the profile to be accurate, and so they don't question it. This is because the police will have their own assumptions about offenders and why and when they will commit crimes. A vague profile increases the likelihood that the investigators' own assumptions can be confirmed within the profile. This can lead to the acceptance of an inaccurate profile, which therefore will have limited help in catching the offender.

There is also the tendency to believe the accuracy of the profile without challenging it, as they consider the offender profiler to be knowledgeable, and therefore accurate. The tendency to accept vague or general personality descriptions as being specific is known as the Barnum effect. An example of the Barnum effect is demonstrated in the work of Kocsis & Hayes (2003).

> **Key term**
>
> **Unverifiable** – not possible to prove the accuracy or truth of a hypothesis.

> **Research**
>
> Research the study completed by Kocsis and Hayes (2003) and discuss the outcomes. What does this study tell you about how profiles can be interpreted?

Ethics

Offender profiling has not always had the success of cases such as John Duffy. There have been other attempts to use profiling as a means of supporting the police where the outcome has been less successful, and indeed raised questions about the application of offender profiling.

The death of Rachel Nickell in 1992, and how the investigation was influenced by its profiler, psychologist Paul Britton, raised ethical questions about the use of profiling.

Paul Britton was approached to try and help the police gather evidence against a suspect for the murder of Rachel Nickell. They attempted to gain evidence by having an undercover policewoman form a relationship with the suspect, in an attempt to have him reveal fantasies that could have led to murder. There was a reduced level of objectivity in gathering the evidence relating to his possible involvement, with topics of conversation intentionally introduced. This raised ethical issues about the possibility of the suspect being manipulated by the investigators.

This approach was severely criticised during the original trial of the case, as it made the evidence obtained through this approach unreliable and so not usable in court. This case led to wider criticism of the credibility of profiling as a scientific, and therefore reliable, approach.

Hint

Extend

Close the book and summarise the three learning aims. Which do you feel most confident with? Review those you are less confident with.

How many explanations of criminal behaviour are there?

What may be some of the ways to punish an offender, and do they work?

What advice would you give to someone who wanted to be a profiler about the different approaches to profiling?

Assessment activity 4.3

Select a well-known crime that has been reported in the media. Obtaining as much information as you can about the offence, start to think about who might have committed it.

Working in small groups, one half of the group will use a top-down approach to develop a profile. The other half of the group will use a bottom-up approach.

Both halves of the group will present their psychological profile to each other, providing information about why you have made decisions about which characteristics within the offence you think are important.

You will need to be able to justify why you chose the approach you did in your profile, so an evaluative knowledge of the chosen approach is needed.

Plan
- Where might I find more information that would help me with my profile?
- How does the group share out the tasks so that everyone is involved?

Do
- I can apply my chosen profiling approach to the crime identified.
- I can recognise when I have enough information to answer the question.

Review
- I can justify my decisions within the task.
- I can understand the decision making for the other group, and therefore how I would use that approach in the future.

Further reading and resources

Bartol, C. & Bartol, A. (2012) *Criminal and behavioural profiling*, London, England: SAGE

Hollin, C. (1992) *Criminal behaviour: A psychological approach to explanation and prevention*, London, England: Routledge

Websites

Legislation: https://www. legislation.gov.uk
Information about punishment options for offenders

THINK ▶▶FUTURE

Safia Jones

Assistant psychologist

I have been working with people who have committed crimes for two years now and have had the opportunity to deliver a number of different treatment techniques designed to try to prevent people from committing similar offences again. This has included helping people to understand the consequences of their behaviour, helping them to address their drug use and giving them skills to better manage their anger.

It is important when deciding what treatment a person may need that I think about the reasons *why* they committed the offence. This helps to look at what skills people may need to learn to prevent this in the future, or what they need to change about their thinking that influences their decision to commit a crime. Once I have this information about a person, I am more likely to be able to offer treatment that is relevant to their offending.

Some of the treatment options work for some people, though others seem to keep committing offences. Sometimes they commit a different type of offence, sometimes it is because their personal circumstances changed and sometimes it may be because the treatment wasn't enough, or wasn't the right treatment.

Sometimes my job can be difficult, especially if I am listening to people talk about particularly violent crimes. My supervisor provides me guidance and support when it is needed. My job is not to judge people for what they have done, and to focus on giving them skills that they didn't have before.

Focusing on your skills

No place for judgement

It is important to be able to work with offenders without judging them. You can make sure that you remain supportive and professional by:

- always having information about their offences from a reliable source
- considering why they may have offended
- being clear of your role and the limits within it

Getting experience

Experience in professionally supporting others can be gained in a number of ways.

- Consider any voluntary work that gives you an opportunity to interact with individuals in a supportive, responsible way, such as in care homes, etc.
- Think about skills you have that help you to manage difficult situations. Developing resilience skills will make it easier to listen to difficult information.

Getting ready for assessment

Elijah is working towards a BTEC National in Applied Psychology. He was given an assignment with the following title 'Which explanation of criminal behaviour is the most reliable?' for Learning aim A.

He had to write a report that explained the different explanations of criminal behaviour and evaluate them to draw a conclusion. The report had to:

▶ include information on the biological, social and individual differences explanations of crime
▶ discuss the research which supports each of these explanations.

Elijah shared his experience below.

How I got started

First I collected all my notes on this topic and put them into a folder. I decided to divide my work into the three different explanations so I had all of the information together in the same place. I decided to use the three different explanations as headings within my report. I thought this would make it easier to guide the reader to the different areas. This also helped me to make sure that I had enough information about each of the three explanations.

I made sure that I had information about not only the different explanations of crime, but also research that had been undertaken that either supported or went against each of these explanations.

How I brought it all together

I decided to use a variety of fonts, colours and pictures to make the work look interesting. To start, I wrote a short introduction to the article. For each explanation of crime I:

▶ created a table explaining specific explanation (for example, genes) and provided a brief summary of each explanation
▶ referenced at least one research study for each explanation
▶ assessed the limitations and strengths of each explanation to support my argument about which explanation I considered most helpful.

Where possible I used specific examples of crimes to further demonstrate my understanding of each of the explanations.

What I learned from the experience

It was helpful for me to be really organised when writing my report. At first I did not have a clear structure and this made it difficult for me to reassure myself that I had answered the question. Next time I will start to use headings from the start when writing my report. It will certainly save me a lot of time!

There are quite a lot of research studies for some explanations and I needed to focus on a smaller number of research studies in my evaluation, rather than talking about them all. This helped to focus my argument as well as meaning that I could write more detail about each one, rather than a small amount of information on a large number of studies.

Think about it

▶ Have you written a plan with timings so you can complete your assignment by the agreed submission date?
▶ Do you have notes on each research study of crime that will help you when evaluating the effectiveness of the explanation?
▶ Is your information written in your own words and referenced clearly where you have used quotations or information from a book, journal or website?

Promoting Children's Psychological Development

5

Getting to know your unit

Understanding how to promote children's healthy psychological development is fundamental to many areas of applied psychology. The child is an active participant in their own learning and your role in supporting them is crucial to their later healthy development. In this unit you will learn about how children's psychological development is theorised and viewed, and how it forms the basis of approaches to preventing, diagnosing and treating developmental-related issues.

How you will be assessed

This unit will be assessed by a series of internally assessed tasks set by your tutor. Throughout the unit you will find assessment activities that will help you work towards your assessment. Completing these activities will not mean that you have achieved a particular grade, but you will have carried out useful research or preparation that will be relevant when it comes to your final assignment.

In order for you to achieve the tasks in your assignment, it is important to check that you have met all of the Pass grading criteria. You can do this as you work your way through the assignment.

If you are hoping to gain a Merit or Distinction, you should also make sure that you present the information in your assignment in the style that is required by the relevant assessment criterion. For example, Merit criteria require you to analyse and discuss, and Distinction criteria require you to assess and evaluate.

The assignment set by your tutor will consist of a number of tasks designed to meet the criteria in the table. This is likely to consist of a written assignment but may also include activities such as:

▶ developing a report that explores the ideas of childhood and theories of development illustrating their contribution in understanding and promoting health growth, development and mental wellbeing

▶ developing a report that links theory to case studies of psychological developmental issues that demonstrate the ways that healthy development could be promoted.

Assessment criteria

This table shows what you must do in order to achieve a **Pass**, **Merit** or **Distinction** grade, and where you can find activities to help you.

Pass	Merit	Distinction

Learning aim **A** Understand perspectives of childhood and theories of child development

Pass	Merit	Distinction
A.P1 Explain historical and current societal approaches to the nature of childhood. **Assessment activity 5.1** **A.P2** Explain how current psychological theories can inform professionals in promoting growth, development and mental wellbeing in children. **Assessment activity 5.1**	**A.M1** Analyse the contribution of societal approaches to childhood and the psychological theories of child development to the promotion of healthy growth, development and mental wellbeing in children. **Assessment activity 5.1**	**A.D1** Evaluate the impact of societal approaches to childhood and the psychological theories of child development in promoting healthy growth, development and mental wellbeing in children. **Assessment activity 5.1**

Learning aim **B** Examine factors affecting a child's healthy development and the role of professionals involved in supporting children, parents and carers

Pass	Merit	Distinction
B.P3 Explain factors affecting healthy development in children. **Assessment activity 5.2** **B.P4** Explain the roles of professionals in supporting children and their parents or carers. **Assessment activity 5.2**	**B.M2** Assess the importance of contributory factors, and the role of professional support, in the healthy development of children. **Assessment activity 5.2**	**B.D2** Evaluate the impact of contributory factors on the development of children and the impact of professionals in providing support to children, their parents or carers. **Assessment activity 5.2**

Learning aim **C** Investigate the use of theories of psychological development to explain and inform prevention of later dysfunctional psychopathy

Pass	Merit	Distinction
C.P5 Explain problems of psychological development in children. **Assessment activity 5.3** **C.P6** Explain professional approaches to treating dysfunctional psychopathy in children. **Assessment activity 5.3**	**C.M3** Analyse approaches taken by professionals in the treatment of dysfunctional psychopathy in children. **Assessment activity 5.3**	**C.D3** Evaluate the use of theories of child development in approaches taken by professionals in the treatment of dysfunctional psychopathy in children. **Assessment activity 5.3**

Getting started

Promoting children's development can support health and mental wellbeing. Write down a list of all the ways that you can think of to promote children's positive growth and development. When you have completed this unit, see if you can add some more ways to your list.

A Understand perspectives of childhood and theories of child development

The nature of childhood

The concept of childhood and child development has changed over time and has had a significant influence on parenting and child care practices throughout history. Views on childhood have been heavily influenced by society's laws, through their beliefs, assumptions and attitudes. It is important to understand these influences and the impact they have had on how professionals support children's healthy psychological development. A phrase often used is that childhood is 'socially constructed'. This means that the ideas of childhood are shaped by the way people think, believe and act, and what we see as 'normal' in society.

Historical perspectives

There have been a number of theorists over the years who have concentrated on the period of childhood.

▸ John Locke (1632–1704) was an English philosopher who believed children were born as 'blank slates' (tabula rasa). He felt the child's mind was malleable and that the parent's role was to mould the child through the teaching of virtue, wisdom and learning.

▸ Jean-Jacques Rousseau (1712–78) believed in the inherent goodness of children. He formulated a romantic attitude towards children in his famous 1762 novel *Emile, or On Education* and viewed children as only becoming corrupted through their experiences of the world.

▸ Philippe Ariès (1914–84) proposed that in the Middle Ages childhood did not exist. He believed that, in this time period, children were seen as no different to adults and that it was only from the thirteenth century onwards that notions of childhood appeared, with distinct phases from childhood to adulthood. He believed that these phases were socially constructed.

Cultural perspectives

Cultural differences in the way childhood is regarded are common. Some practices may appear unacceptable or unusual compared to the standards of your own culture. For example, in Norway children are often left to nap in very cold temperatures, something that they have done for many generations but this may seem cruel to British parents. In some cultures, such as on the Polynesian Islands, it is normal for toddlers and pre-school children to care for their younger siblings and even younger children from their parent's wider social circle.

Beliefs and cultural systems

A widely debated issue is whether children are influenced by their biological makeup (nature) or whether their behaviours, personality and beliefs are influenced through their environment (nurture). For example, a common view in many cultures and societies is that a child needs to be taught to be an adult, and that this process takes around 18 years. Cultures and societies that hold this view believe that a child needs a long period of time where they are protected, nurtured and socialised to prepare them for 'adult' society. However, other cultures believe that a child is ready to take on the role of an adult at a much younger age.

Broadly speaking many cultures and societies believe there are four distinct phases of life: childhood, adolescence, adulthood and old age. These phases of life provide a clear distinction between childhood and adulthood. For this reason, childhood is often viewed as a 'golden age'; an age of innocence and a period of life where the child requires protecting from the realities of adult life. This idea, however, is not common in all cultures. For example, Firth (1970) found that children from the Western Pacific were within their rights to dismiss orders from parents. He held the view that parents should earn the child's respect.

Religion

There is little evidence that shows an influence of religious beliefs on parenting, but religion does influence approaches to parenting and children's resulting behaviours. A parent's religious identity may influence the way the child thinks and behaves. Religious practices also determine the child's progression from childhood to adulthood through diverse ceremonial practices such as the **Bar Mitzvah.**

> **Key term**
>
> **Bar Mitzvah** – a Jewish practice where boys, when they reach 13 years old, become accountable for their actions and have a coming-of-age ceremony. Girls become a Bat Mitzvah at the age of 12.

Law

The ways that children are perceived and treated are also enshrined or determined by legal systems. In the UK, for example, a child is not legally an adult until they reach the age of 18. They can be married with the consent of their parents at 16 years old but cannot vote or drink alcohol until they reach the age of 18.

> **Research**
>
> In the 1800s there were many reforms on child labour and education, through the introduction of new legislation. With a partner, search for the types of laws and reforms that were introduced in the 1800s. What was the reason for these reforms? Can you identify the ways in which society at the time influenced these reforms?

Norms

Any person in a society is expected to behave appropriately so that everyone gets along – these are called the **norms** of society. People are expected to work together and socialise together in a way that is acceptable to everyone else. Norms dictate the way that society should operate and they act as an efficient way to achieve social welfare and solve collective problems. This is also reflected in the way that individual families operate within their own mini-cultures, which will be explored later in this unit. It is important to understand that the norms that have been defined in any one culture influence the way that adults raise their children. For example, in Japan children are seen to be the centre of a family and there are strong bonds between all family members. In a Kibbutz (a community in Israel), children would be raised communally by all the adults in the group.

> **Key term**
>
> **Norms** – the patterns or normative aspects of development or expectations in a society that are collectively devised and followed by a group.

Child-rearing practices

Child-rearing practices (or parenting) is a term used to describe the way that parents raise their children and support their physical, emotional, social and intellectual development from infancy to adulthood. In modern society this responsibility is often shared by parents, schools and regulating authorities. They are all responsible for ensuring children grow and thrive in positive environments.

There are a number of different parenting styles. Figure 5.1 shows how these parenting styles relate to each other. The following are different parenting styles.

- **Authoritarian**: the 'children should be seen and not heard' style. Rules are set by parents and children's feelings or needs may not be taken into account. A typical response to a question might be 'because I said so' with no explanation or discussion, and punishments may be used. Children of authoritarian parents tend to conform to rules and are obedient to authority figures but there is evidence to suggest that this style of parenting may have an effect on a child's later functioning in terms of self-esteem issues and aggressive or hostile behaviours.
- **Permissive**: a more relaxed style in its approach to rules and consequences. These may be set but not enforced by the parents, as they feel the child learns best when left with little parental involvement. Parents who follow this style can be very forgiving and may have a tendency to allow the child to 'win' any discussions if the child persists (begs). For a child of a permissive parent long-term effects are hard to determine, but children may be prone to self-esteem issues and depression. In adolescence they may be prone to substance use, school misconduct and lack of motivation in academic achievements. Behavioural problems may be due to being unable to accept authority and rules.
- **Authoritative**: parents using this style tend to invest effort into creating and maintaining a positive relationship with their children. Explanations to rules are provided, and when enforcing these, parents explain the consequences of breaking them to the child. The child's feelings and thoughts are taken into consideration. Parents use positive discipline strategies, such as rewards and praise, and they invest time in preventing negative behaviours before they occur. Children raised with authoritative parents tend to be happy and successful and are more likely to grow up to be responsible, confident adults. Some studies have shown that children raised with at least one authoritative parent report higher wellbeing and life satisfaction.
- **Uninvolved**: parents who have little to do with their child. They do not spend time with the child and may not know where the child is at times. Children receive little guidance and often are subject to few or no rules. Parents may be neglectful and lack knowledge of child development or they may be overwhelmed by other issues. Children of uninvolved parents suffer with poor self-esteem and poor school performance. They may have behavioural issues and there may also be longer term effects on mental health.

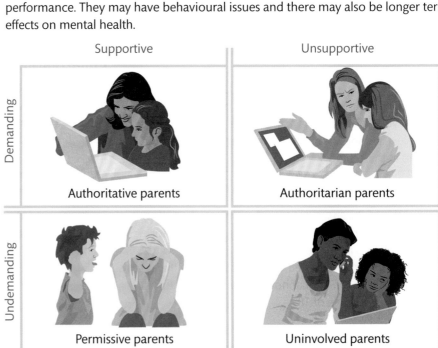

▶ **Figure 5.1:** The different parenting styles, and their relation to each other

Ⅱ PAUSE POINT
There are a number of theories about the way behaviour is formed. Consider these in relation to parenting styles. What do those studies tell you about parenting and a child's behaviour formation?

> Hint
You learned about behavioural theories in Unit 1. Look back at the approaches proposed by Skinner and Watson on conditioning and Bandura's social learning approach.

> Extend
Discuss what these theories could tell you about the long-term impact of parenting styles.

Modern-day views of childhood

The view Ariès held was that childhood is a socially constructed concept, a view many modern-day social scientists agree with.

Social construction of childhood

Social anthropologists have found that different cultures across the world have different views on how a society should behave, what they believe in and and what the social norms of their society look like.

Within a society or culture, beliefs, behaviours, and other norms exist that are common to all the members of that group or culture. Families also create their own systems of beliefs, behaviours and rules; and then live by those rules. Over the centuries, the concept of childhood has evolved, and legislation has played a significant role in changing the perception of children and childhood. For example, the Children's Acts of 1989 and 2004 define parental responsibility; they identify that organisations working with children have a duty to help safeguard and promote the welfare of children. The Early Years Foundation Stage curriculum (EYFS) defines the way in which children should be taught in early years and primary school settings.

> **Key term**
>
> **Social anthropologist** – someone who researches how people live in different societies.

In the modern day, children are viewed as:
▸ physically and psychologically immature compared to adults
▸ dependent on adults for a range of biological and emotional needs
▸ needing significant periods of time to develop mature socialisation skills
▸ being incapable of running their own lives or being held responsible for their actions.

Discussed earlier were the phases of life, including childhood, adolescence and adulthood. Experiences and perceptions of adolescence are not the same for all cultures. Although biologically, children move through to puberty and adolescence following very similar patterns, culturally this passage can be viewed very differently. The World Health Organization (WHO) defines an adolescent as any person between the ages of 10 and 19.

There are several agreed characteristics of adolescence, some of which include:
▸ biological growth and development, for example changes in the body and the onset of puberty
▸ undefined status, for example feeling like neither an adult nor a child
▸ increased decision making, for example a sense of responsibility grows as does judgement
▸ increased pressures, for example examinations (in some societies), social constraints and expectations
▸ search for the self, for example self-identity, worth, confidence and self-esteem.

Adolescence is viewed differently in other cultures and is sometimes defined as a 'rite of passage' often closely connected to the biological milestones of life, for example birth, maturity and reproduction. The **rites of passage** in Table 5.1 demonstrate how some cultures acknowledge adolescence differently.

> **Key term**
>
> **Rites of passage** – ceremonial events in cultures marking the passage from one social or age-related status to another.

▶ Can you think of any other rites of passage adolescents undergo?

Discussion

In a group, make a list of key terms that define 'adolescence'. Discuss the different definitions of adolescence and compare them to the way adolescence is defined in other cultures. Make a note of key similarities and differences, and how these definitions may be influenced.

▶ **Table 5.1:** Examples of rites of passage in different cultures

Ceremony	
Jewish: Bar or Bat Mitzvah	• Bar Mitzvah occurs when a boy turns 13 years old • The boy moves into manhood by reading the Torah • Bat Mitzvah is held when a girl turns 12 years old • The girl also reads the Torah at the Temple on the Sabbath
Amish and Mennonite: Rumspringa	• Means 'running around' in some Amish and Mennonite communities • Usually begins at 14–16 years old • Ends when a child chooses to be baptised within the community or leaves • Children spend a period of unsupervised weekends away from their family and are encouraged to do whatever pleases them. It is thought that the experience of the outside world will support them returning to the community
The Sateré-Mawé (indigenous people of Brazil)	• Known as the 'Bullet-Ant Initiation' • Boys as young as 12 years old mark their coming of age by searching the jungle for bullet ants which are then sedated and put into special gloves; the boys then wear the gloves for ten minutes • Once this ritual has been endured 20 times, the boy has earned the right to call himself a man
Malaysia: Khatam Al Koran	• Girls review the Koran in order to recite the final chapter before friends and family • Aged 11, this marks their growth to maturity at their local mosque
Maasai: Tanzania and Kenya	• There are several rites of passage for the Maasai • Boys aged between 10–20 years old are initiated as the new 'warrior class' • Boys undertake a circumcision ceremony: they sing, dance, drink alcohol, cows' blood and milk, and are then circumcised; this signifies their official transfer to manhood • They then spend ten years living in a dedicated area, known as a warrior's camp

In the 1950s, American psychiatrist Murray Bowen developed the Family Systems Theory. This viewed families as a whole, taking into account the way they collectively behave and the boundaries they set, and how these defined their personalities, emotions and behaviours.

These boundaries can either be open or closed, though never completely one or the other. All parts of a family are interrelated, and families have internal boundaries that define how their members relate to each other. For example, these could be rules that parents set for acceptable behaviours around the dinner table, acceptable language, and how conflict is dealt with. The boundaries that families set will be influenced by the outside environment such as laws of acceptable behaviour, sanctions and education. Family systems can be open or closed.

▶ **Open systems**: these have vague boundaries and allow elements of the external environment to influence the family system.
▶ **Closed systems:** these are exclusive and do not allow the external environment to influence the family system.

No system can be totally open or closed, however. To be totally closed would mean the family does not conform to the law, or norms of the wider society, such as attending schools. Figure 5.2 shows how family systems must interrelate with the outside world.

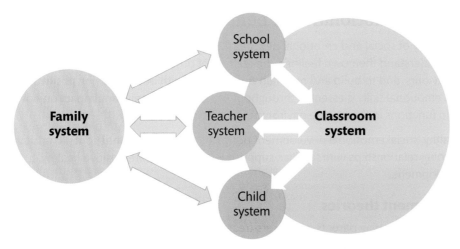

▶ **Figure 5.2:** How family systems interrelate with other systems of society

Rationale for view

The original social construction of childhood occurred at a specific time in history and so was related to the beliefs, values and norms of society at that time. Views on society and the norms within it have changed over the years. This in part can be attributed to the development of economic markets directed at children, as well as the recognition of the need to protect children.

In the 1800s in Britain, formal education became available to everyone, regardless of how wealthy they were. A range of legislation reformed the way that children were educated and, in 1880, brought in compulsory education to all up until the age of 10. Industrialisation, with a shift from agriculture to factory production, needed an educated workforce and so compulsory schooling to the young was introduced. These reforms changed perceptions of children and childhood as they moved children from factories to schools.

Children's rights

In 1992 (in the UK), the United Nations Convention on the Right of the Child (UNCRC) was introduced as a piece of legislation that gave children specific rights. It included a right to provisions (food, shelter and education), protection (against exploitation or abuse), and a right of participation with decisions made on their behalf. This law had far-reaching effects and changed the way that society viewed and treated children.

In many ways legislation has served to define what a child is, through reform and through the introduction of the Education Act (2006). Other forms of legislation include those listed below.

▶ The Human Rights Act (1998) is a set of basic human rights, including freedom of expression, right to work, education, equality and freedom from slavery, torture and degrading treatment.
▶ The Children's Act (1989, 2004) defines the ways that local authorities, courts and parents ensure children are safeguarded, and dictates how their welfare must be paramount when making any decisions as to their upbringing and care.
▶ The Sexual Offences Act (2003) sets out the law in the UK for the age of consent.

▶ Are there any other studies that involve animals imprinting?

Social, emotional and behavioural development

The study of social and emotional development explores the child's ability to identify and understand their own feelings, the feelings of others, controlling feelings and behaviours, and to build and maintain relationships with others. Having positive social and emotional skills is essential throughout life and has a significant impact on how a child functions in their home environments, schools and society.

Healthy, social emotional development occurs in an **interpersonal** context; positive ongoing relationships with familiar, supportive adults promote positive healthy development.

Attachment theories

From birth, the way parents and carers treat children has a significant impact on their learning and development. The study of attachment theories is useful to understand the effect of parenting styles and child-rearing practices on children's development and possible outcomes in later life. There are multiple attachment theories that attempt to explain how emotional bonds are formed between individuals and they describe how these bonds begin to emerge in early childhood.

John Bowlby first proposed his attachment theory in 1969. His student, Mary Ainsworth, developed this theory further. Attachment theory drew on ideas from **ethology, cybernetics, information processing**, developmental psychology and **psychoanalytics**. Bowlby was influenced by the work of Konrad Lorenz and Harry Harlow.

Konrad Lorenz (1952)

Konrad Lorenz proposed that organisms (humans and animals) have a biological tendency to form attachments with a single being. He explored the way that, during the first 15 hours after hatching, a period of time known as the 'critical period', goslings followed the first moving thing they saw. This process is known as called imprinting. In the absence of the mother goose, Lorenz was the first thing these goslings saw and so he became the attachment figure that the goslings followed. Lorenz found that this need to form an attachment was adaptive and an essential element towards survival. These ideas led Bowlby to consider the importance of a child's relationship with their mother and the importance of a strong social and emotional bond.

As the goslings imprinted very early in their lives, it suggests that there is a critical period and that attachment has a biological basis. Lorenz's study provided an insight into the importance of forming early bonds with children during a specific, critical period. Lorenz's studies have been replicated many times and so reliability was high. However, as it would be unethical to study humans in this way, his studies cannot be generalised to humans. Such studies do give insights, however, into the way that even from an early age, children may have an innate predisposition to copy the actions and behaviours of their parents or caregivers. Further studies have shown the impact on an infant when certain aspects of care are altered or removed.

Harry Harlow (1958)

Harry Harlow investigated **maternal deprivation** in rhesus monkeys, by placing new-born monkeys in a cage with two artificial wire monkeys that imitated a caregiver role. One of the wire monkeys provided food while the other did not but was wrapped in cloth, to simulate comfort. He found that the majority of the baby monkeys would spend most of their time with the cloth monkey, only going to the other model for food. He also found that, if scared, they would go to the cloth monkey for security. Harlow also found several common behavioural traits in the caged monkeys as opposed to those growing up in their natural environment, including that they:

- were more likely to be incredibly timid
- failed to socially interact with other monkeys
- were more likely to be bullied
- made inadequate mothers.

Harlow's findings provide an insight into how damaging maternal deprivation can be. Although this type of study could not be considered on human participants, Harlow's study helps with an understanding about the effects of maternal deprivation on children's positive mental growth and development. This study demonstrates the importance of positive emotional care and ensuring that children's needs are catered for beyond their physical needs; the understanding of this helps to support those working with children and families. Harlow's studies have significant implications for childcare practices, especially the importance of early experiences on long-term development.

Harlow's work has been criticised as being cruel (unethical) and limited in scope as it can only provide a small understanding as to the effects of deprivation in certain conditions. It is difficult to determine whether the results of this study could be applied to humans, as some of the monkeys were brought up in isolation. However, Harlow's study does provide a valuable insight into the development of attachment behaviours, and it also influenced the work of John Bowlby.

John Bowlby

Bowlby was influenced by the evolutionary perspective that children come into the world biologically pre-programmed to form attachments with others; his work was also influenced by the work of Lorenz and imprinting. He believed that the safety and security provided by a caregiver was adaptive and increased an infant's chances of survival.

Bowlby initially developed his ideas on attachment through research conducted on child delinquents and institutionalised children. His observations identified the negative effects that maternal deprivation could have on the infant if the mother was not available or non-responsive to the infant for long periods of time (around the first two years of life). He also found that the impact of maternal deprivation had long-term implications for a child's later life, including depression, aggression and other forms of psychopathy. He followed up these studies and, again influenced by Harlow's studies, concluded that rather than the classic approaches to attachment – which proposed that the goal of attachment was the satisfaction of needs (food) – he believed attachment was an intrinsic need that was formed from an emotional bond with a mother. He also believed that this extends beyond the need for these basic needs.

Bowlby had observed the anxiety of children when separated from their mothers and, even when fed by other caregivers, this anxiety did not reduce. Based on his observations, he theorised that infants have a universal need to seek close proximity with their caregiver when threatened or under stress, and he introduced the idea of **separation anxiety**. Bowlby thought that this need to form attachments with primary carers developed from an evolutionary process; that having this close bond would increase an infant's chance of survival. As a result of an attachment forming, a child who remained close to the caregiver would receive comfort and protection in return. Due to this attachment, the caregiver is able to provide appropriate responses to an infant's needs, allowing the infant to form a sense of security with the caregiver and providing them the ability to explore the world around them (Figure 5.3).

Bowlby proposed four characteristics of attachment which are shown below.

1 **Proximity maintenance:** this is the need for the child to be near the person they are attached to.
2 **Safe haven:** this is the child's ability to return to an attachment figure for comfort and security when faced with fear.
3 **Secure base:** the attachment figure is a figure of security for the child, allowing them to use the attachment figure as a base to explore their surrounding environment.
4 **Separation anxiety distress:** when the attachment figure is unavailable the child experiences anxiety.

> **Key term**
>
> **Separation anxiety** – fear of being away from an attachment figure, for example parents or caregivers.

Bowlby thought that children would only form one primary attachment (their mother). However, he later revised his theory to indicate that a child could form multiple attachments. He also suggested that there is a sensitive period for developing an attachment: between birth and five years of age. If an attachment is not formed within this sensitive period, a child might suffer negative developmental consequences, such as lower intelligence and behaviour problems.

Bowlby identified three main stages of attachment.

1 **From six weeks to around eight months:** an infant starts to develop trust and dependency upon primary caregivers (the mother).

2 **From around eight months to around two years old:** more defined or 'clear cut' attachments are formed between the infant and the mother. An infant may experience anxiety when the mother leaves.

3 **From around 18 months onwards:** more defined attachments are formed, separation anxiety declines and the infant can now understand that when a mother leaves she will return and a sense of security is defined.

Key term

Internal working model (IWM) – an approach that describes the mental representations a child forms of a relationship they have with their primary caregivers that then becomes internalised.

The attachments that infants form can have an impact on feelings of security and satisfaction in relationships with primary caregivers and other relationships throughout a child's life. A key concept of Bowlby's attachment theory was that of **internal working models (IWM)** which are the mental representation a child develops of themselves and their caregivers. A child develops a way of relating based upon what they observe and experience from their own parents or caregivers. It provides a template for the child to interact with their environment. This means that a child can approach new situations with a basis of knowledge formed from what they have experienced of how they can deal with possible threats. The IWM has three elements: the model of the self, the other (for example the mother), and the relationship between these two. These IWMs contain information about the availability and dependability of the mother and how forms of emotional discomfort may be met. So, the infant who experiences a mother who provides security and is responsive to their needs, creates a positive IWM. If, however, the infant experiences an insecure relationship with their mother (or primary caregiver), they may develop a negative IWM. These IWMs continue to be developed and refined throughout childhood and are important in shaping attitudes in adult relationships. Children who have positive IWMs will often have more positive adult relationships.

Morrison et al. (1997) found an association between attachment and adult relationships. College students completed a questionnaire relating to their current/most recent intimate relationships. They were also asked to complete an attachment inventory that assessed their attachment style. More securely-attached respondents described interdependence in their relationships, while those more insecurely-attached respondents (avoidant/ambivalent) reported more instances of hostility in intimate relationships.

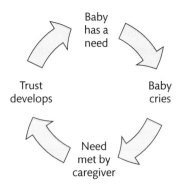

Baby has a need

Baby cries

Need met by caregiver

Trust develops

▶ **Figure 5.3:** Attachment theory

Discussion

Consider infants forming attachments. How do you think the attachment style of a child develops? Could a child's attachment be influenced by their caregiver's parenting style? Now consider them later in life, how do you think the attachment style of children influences the way they relate to their own children?

Mary Ainsworth

Mary Ainsworth expanded Bowlby's findings through studies that identified different forms, or types, of attachment that children formed with their primary caregivers. Ainsworth & Wittig (1969) developed an assessment technique called the Strange Situation Classification (SSC) whereby they observed the behaviours of children and their attachments to their mothers. The procedure used was as follows:

1 The mother interacts with her child in a room.

2 A stranger joins them.

3 After a short while the mother leaves the room.

4 The mother then returns and the stranger leaves.

5 The mother then leaves again and the child is then alone.

6 The stranger then returns.

7 Finally, the mother returns to the room and the stranger leaves.

Ainsworth observed the behaviour of the child when it was together with the parent, when they were separated and the child's behaviour on reuniting with the mother. Ainsworth initially identified three attachment styles, as described below.

1 Secure: the mother (or caregiver) meets the needs of the child who shows distress when the mother leaves and tends to avoid strangers when alone. The child is quick to soothe when the mother returns. The child uses the mother as a safe base to explore their environment and is often seen to check that the mother is there.

2 Insecure ambivalent/resistant: the child shows great distress when the mother leaves and avoids strangers, sometimes showing fear. When the mother re-enters the room, the child approaches her but shows resistance, for example pushing her away. The resistant child tends to cry more and explore less.

3 Insecure/avoidant: the child does not show distress when the mother leaves; they play normally when a stranger is present, and show little interest when the mother returns. The avoidant child is easily comforted by either the mother or the stranger.

A fourth attachment style was later identified by Main & Solomon (1986). They identified a disorganised-disoriented attachment style, which relates to children that have no predicable patterns of attachment behaviours. This attachment style is typically expressed through the child's odd behaviour. For example, a child may run up to their mother but immediately pull away, first seeking comfort and then when the parent is close, feeling fear and pulling away. This type of behaviour may be a result of a fearful relationship with the parents.

Attachment theories provide a good framework for understanding child development and especially for those working with children. They help professionals assess and treat children to achieve secure attachment styles. These theories have been used as a basis for providing secure environments for infants and toddlers in school settings where they use a key person approach. Key individuals and teachers in these settings form bonds with children to develop the child's sense of security. Attachment theory has been used to provide a basis of family therapy for children and adolescents in attachment-focused treatments for foster and adoptive families.

Attachment types in childhood have been mapped onto attachment types in adulthood. For example, a securely-attached adult would be more likely to have positive and close relationships with others without feeling the need to be near them physically. The anxious resistant adult may have formed insecure bonds and may display behaviours such as jealousy or being excessively upset by small issues.

Ainsworth's study provided **empirical evidence** to Bowlby's attachment theory. However, it can be argued that attachment theory places too much emphasis on the role of the mother figure, and not enough attention to how a father figure can influence attachment type. A child's temperament and how they behave could also be another factor in how a parent responds to them. For example, a child with very specific needs may need a carer who is extremely patient in order for a secure attachment to form. As discussed earlier, there needs to be consideration on the influences around the child as they grow older. Although internal working models are formed of primary caregivers, the environment and other relationships impact on the child's way of relating as the child grows and develops.

> **Key term**
>
> **Empirical evidence** – evidence that is gained through observation and experimentation.

You should also consider Ainsworth's studies in light of the parenting styles that may be associated with each of the attachment types involved. IWMs developed as a child influence the way adults behave towards others and their own children. Research has indicated that patterns established in childhood can have an impact on later relationships. Hazan & Shaver (1987) explored the beliefs about types of relationships in adulthood and found securely-attached adults tended to fall in love often, while those with avoidant attachment styles felt love was a rare and temporary state.

Case study

Charlotte is a 14-month-old baby and is being dropped off at day-care for the first time by her mother. Charlotte's mother spends a lot of time with Charlotte when she has free time and is always there to comfort her with cuddles and provide food when she is upset or hungry. Charlotte's mum knows what she needs when she is distressed and always gives her a warm and loving environment.

Thomas is 12 months old and he is also being dropped off for his first day at day-care. His parents are extremely busy with work and their personal lives and cannot spend much time with him. He is sometimes left crying for several hours a day and his parents do not have a very good idea of what needs he has.

1 What attachment style do you think Charlotte would have?

2 How do you think Charlotte would react after her mother leaves her at day-care?

3 What attachment style do you think Thomas would have?

4 How do you think Thomas would react after his parents leave him at day-care?

Key term

Ecological models – a view that the environment contains natural factors (biological, physical, chemical) that affect human life.

Ecological models

Ecological models suggest how a child's interaction with their environment can influence how they grow and develop.

Urie Bronfenbrenner proposed a model that explains the way children react to, and are influenced by, their environment and the way this affects or influences their social and emotional development. Bronfenbrenner proposed that a child moves through different environments throughout their lifespan and at every stage aspects of their environment may influence your behaviour to varying degrees, as demonstrated in Figure 5.4. These systems include the following:

▶ **Microsystem:** this refers to the direct environment around an infant such as their family, friends and neighbours.

▶ **Mesosystem:** this involves the relationships between the microsystem, such as a child's relationship with their school or classmates.

▶ **Exosystem:** this contains elements of the microsystem; effects on a child may be indirect. For example, if a mother has a new baby and experiences post-natal depression, this will have an indirect effect on the child.

▶ **Macrosystem:** this is the overall or all-encompassing level which includes all cultural beliefs, norms and rules of society.

▶ **Chronosystem**: this level involves the environmental events and transitions that occur throughout the child's life events. For example, a change in the family's structure, the death of a grandparent or changes in a parent's employment.

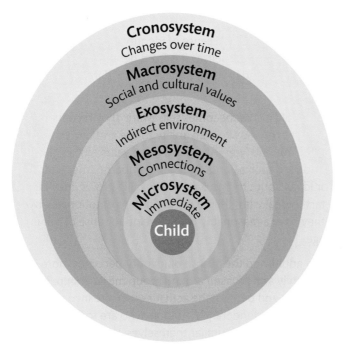

▶ **Figure 5.4:** Bronfenbrenner ecological model of child development

Bronfenbrenner's ideas have had a considerable impact on many areas in psychology, particularly on family systems therapy treatments. By understanding the influences of the family unit and the external environment on the child, this theory can help in the diagnosis and treatment of specific disorders. Each system plays a role in shaping and developing individuals. For example, a child who experiences a close secure family environment at home (microsystem/mesosystem) is more likely to be **prosocial** at school and form many positive relationships, find success in education and in other pursuits (exosystem). The child who grows in an environment with little or no structure with few, if any, bonds may not be so prosocial and will likely display more negative behaviours, which could lead to later mental-health issues.

▶ When comparing this model to theories of attachment and attachment types, you can see the important role the parent or carer has in supporting positive growth and development of children, and how they can influence a child's development at various stages of their life.

▶ Bronfenbrenner's theories have been shown to provide a holistic view of the influences on the growing child's internal and external environments. However, they have been criticised for their breadth of focus and that individual elements are often generalised; nor do they take account of individual differences across cultures.

Key term

Prosocial – behaviour that is positive and helpful, leading to social acceptance and friendship.

Social identity theories

To understand how children form a sense of identity it is necessary to understand how they first develop a sense of self, as it is from here that they start to compare themselves with others and adapt their behaviours to fit in with what they perceive as 'ideal'.

By around two years old a child becomes self-aware; they recognise themselves in photographs or the mirror and show an ability to use and understand self-referential language, such as 'I', 'me' and 'you'. At around three years old, a child displays more self-conscious emotions such as pride, guilt and embarrassment and has developed a self-concept or ideas about themselves. As the child grows, they rapidly become aware of (and start to deal with) their own and other's emotions. Between five and eight years old they have a reasonably fully-developed sense of self in the world and a positive self-image.

As a child grows to adulthood their sense of identity becomes more influenced by those outside the family and is based around group membership. Think about the way that children may dress and behave, the activities they are involved in such as sports, music or fashion. There is a tendency for people who are together in a social group or share similar interests to become similar themselves. What has been described here is social identity theory.

This idea was originally developed by Henri Tajfel and John Turner in 1979. In summary, they proposed that there were three mental processes involved in how individuals evaluated others and that these took place in a specific order, as shown in Figure 5.5.

▶ **Social categorisation:** individuals are assigned to a category that gives information about that person, for example a pop star, teacher or lifeguard.
▶ **Social identification:** an individual adopts the identity of the group they have been categorised as belonging to. For example, if you categorise yourself as a pop star you may act the way you think a pop star might act. Your self-esteem will also carry traits of the pop-star image. You are, in effect, part of an in-group and all things associated outside this pop-star image (say another alternative pop star) would be classified as the out-group.
▶ **Social comparison theory:** this was initially proposed by Leon Festinger (1954) and is based on the belief that individuals are driven to compare themselves to others on many different levels and these comparisons are influential in shaping an individual's identity and their place in the world with others. Tajfel and Turner viewed social comparison as a way of viewing identity as superior to the others it is derived from; the product of the in-group (their attitudes and beliefs) as compared with out-groups (who may have opposing beliefs and attitudes).

It is easy to understand how social identity theory, and the basis on which individuals form social relationships and identify with certain groups, can lead to prejudice and discrimination.

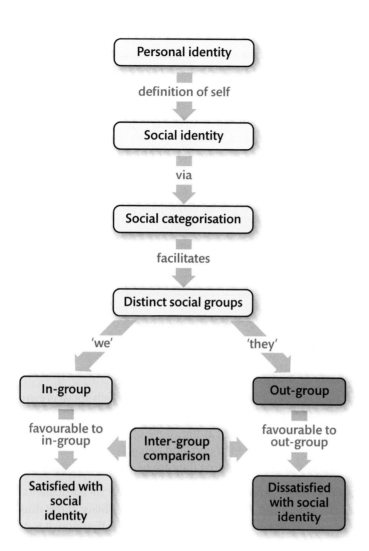

▶ **Figure 5.5:** Social identity theory

Tajfel and Turner's ideas demonstrate that social identity defines an individual's sense of who they are based on in their group membership. Having a sense of belonging to a group is important for self-esteem and confidence. Social identity theory proposes that group members will seek to find negative aspects of other groups to improve their own self-image. This forms the basis of prejudiced views between groups, for example the creation of friendship groups where individuals form friendships on the basis of popularity and interests. Understanding the ways that individuals form their social identity can support programmes of intervention for socially isolated individuals or help to understand issues of aggression.

Social identity theories have been criticised as they focused more on individuals and the way they form identity based on ideals, rather than on groups of individuals. As such it has been questioned whether these studies reflect individuals' true reactions in real life. Some studies have indicated that those who experience an increase in self-esteem as a result of positive in-group behaviours, is too short lived to have long term effects on personal identity. Therefore the effect of self-esteem should not be central to social identity theory. Further studies have indicated competitive individuals demonstrated greater in-group favouritism over cooperative individuals (Platow et al. 1990).

Link

Look back at Unit 1, page 18 to remind yourself about the concept of conformity and the key studies of Haney et al and Asch. Read Asch's study on page 20 as a reminder of the procedure.

Sherif's Robbers' Cave – Realistic Conflict Theory (1954, 58, 61) Sherif stated that conflict between groups happens when two or more groups are in competition. His experiment involved two groups of boys, aged around 12 years old. The boys did not know each other and were assigned to one of two groups. They were separated and had no knowledge of the other groups and were taken each day to a Scout camp. They were encouraged to bond in their groups and form attachments. After a number of sessions, the researchers introduced conflict situations (competitive sports) and brought the teams together. They also devised situations where one group appeared to be favoured over the other. This resulted in verbal and then physical aggression, and the researchers had to separate the children. Results demonstrated that conflict between groups can trigger prejudice and discriminatory behaviour that had not previously been observed.

1 Discuss the ways that the experiment helps understanding of issues of aggression in society.

2 How can this study help the understanding of issues of conformity and social categorisation?

Solomon Asch (1951) studied ideas of conformity and how a person conforms when there is either an ambiguous or obvious answer to a dilemma. He devised an experiment to investigate whether participants would conform to the obviously wrong judgement of a majority.

This study can support understanding of the extent to which social pressure from a majority group can affect how a person conforms to different situations. It helps with understanding how children conform as they develop, for example in gender roles and in their self-identify. It also helps to understand behavioural development and how children may conform to the groups that they are being raised within.

Criticisms have been raised about the sample in the study: all participants were male students of a similar age. This reduces the generalisability of the study. Some have criticised Asch's work as being culturally specific and therefore it is difficult to assess how individuals would conform in different cultures. For example, in Japan where obedience and respect are paramount, individuals may not question authority especially if those asserting the authority are older or male. Other criticisms focus on the time relevance of the study, for example, later studies that attempted to replicate Asch's findings, found that fewer students conformed. This demonstrates the importance of applying studies with caution and taking into consideration the cultural beliefs, norms and attitudes of individuals as well as the context, time and place.

Stanley Milgram (1963) conducted a study into obedience to authority. Similar to Haney's studies, he explored the way that individuals conform to authority and the lengths they go to in obeying instructions. In this study participants were assigned to pairs and then given the role of teacher or learner. The learner was actually a **confederate,** who was taken to a room and electrodes attached to his arms. The teacher was placed in a separate room in front of an electric-shock generator, with varying levels of voltage.

Learners were given a list of paired words to recall (a paired associate task) and the teacher was told to give an electric shock each time a mistake was made, increasing the intensity with every incorrect response. The learner (the confederate) answered using pre-recorded responses; a mix of correct and incorrect answers. The researcher was present in the room with the teacher, prompting the teacher to continue with the shock treatment. The study found that 65 per cent of participants continued to apply what they believed to be high levels of shocks (up to 450 volts). From this, Milgram concluded that people are likely to follow orders which are given by an authority figure.

Link

Look back at Unit 1 at Haney et al (1973) and the study of prisoners and guards in a simulated prison. This study looked at how social roles effect behaviour.

Key term

Confederate – or 'stooge'. Individuals who are part of an experiment and act exactly how the researcher instructs them. Other participants are led to believe that the confederate is a participant like them, but they are asked to behave/speak in a particular way that the researcher instructs them.

Again, this can help understanding of child development by considering how children react to authority figures. However, Milgram's studies were conducted in controlled environments and did not reflect real-life situations. Again, the sample was all male and was not representative of the population as his sample were self-selected. There were also ethical implications involved in this study as participants were deceived. Although this study demonstrates the possible effect that authority figures can have, replicating this type of study would be unethical due to the risks of psychological harm. However, similarities can be drawn from this study to real-life situations, such as teachers and learners, an army officer commanding soldiers, and so on.

> ⏸ **PAUSE POINT** You have reviewed ideas on social identity theory and conformity. Discuss your understanding of these studies and how you can apply them to child development.
>
> **Hint** Draw comparisons and links to other units you have studied in this qualification.
>
> **Extend** Think about how studies such as those explored could be used by professionals in different settings, such as schools or social-care facilities, to support children's friendship and behaviour development.

Behavioural theories

Behaviourists believe that all behaviours are learned through interaction with the environment. These ideas use an observational approach and are concerned with stimuli-response behaviours. This approach began in 1913 with the work of John Watson who set out a number of principles behind behaviour and discussed the role that environmental factors play in influencing behaviour. He based his ideas on the ideas of classical conditioning, in particular studies Pavlov conducted on dogs to learn more about the way that they associated an unconditioned (or neutral) stimulus to a particular response. Pavlov made his discovery from observing the way that dogs salivated on presentation of meat powder. However, he saw, over time, that the dogs were salivating before a meat powder was presented and identified that when paired with a certain stimulus it triggered a similar response. He then presented the meat powder at the same time as ringing a bell. He did this a number of times and then used the bell alone (neutral stimulus) and found that the bell had the ability to trigger the salivation.

> **Link**
>
> Look back at Unit 1 to remind yourself of the studies which are further discussed in this section.

Watson and Rayner (1920) conducted a study where they investigated whether classical conditioning could be applied to humans. They used a test subject, 'Little Albert', to demonstrate that phobic behaviours could be developed in children. This study demonstrates the importance of conditioning in child development, and the impact that this can have on a child's healthy development. There have been critiques of this work due to the use of a human subject and the distress it caused the child.

The 'Little Albert' study was a stimulus-response study. A number of studies that explored the stimuli-response ideas are listed below. They will help you understand the way that behaviourists believe behaviours can be controlled. They also form the basis of many child-rearing practices.

Burrhus Frederic Skinner's work was based on Thorndike's (1898) studies that proposed that a behaviour with favourable consequences is likely to be repeated, whereas if the behaviour is followed by unfavourable consequences it will not be repeated. His studies were known as reinforcement studies, and his most well-known study was 'Skinner's box'. This study was based on the idea of operant conditioning and demonstrated positive and negative reinforcement behaviours. While in a box, rats could hit a lever to have food dispensed, which they quickly learned to do (positive reinforcement). Skinner then demonstrated negative reinforcement with the rats being given electric shocks, until they hit the lever to stop them. Again, they quickly learned to do this.

Skinner's box study suggested that behaviours are learned rather than being innately present. However, these studies applied to animals and so may not be generalisable to humans. It would be **unethical** to carry out a similar experiment on humans. However, these theories have been used in practice to demonstrate ways to motivate positive behaviours. Reward systems are used in schools to encourage a repeat of certain behaviours and are also used in psychology to provide interventions to treat aggression and other learned behaviours.

Similarly, Albert Bandura's study showed that behaviour can be learned by children imitating people around them. In Bandura's study, results showed that children exposed to the aggressive model made more aggressive responses than those in the non-aggressive or control groups.

Lawrence Kohlberg (1984) explored moral development as a facet of behaviour. He presented a moral dilemma that posed a problem and then asked children of different ages a series of questions. He wanted to find out how moral reasoning changed as children got older. This was a **longitudinal** study and Kohlberg identified different levels, or stages, of moral development, which are outlined below. One of the key criticisms of Kohlberg's study was that the scenario used was hypothetical not real, and difficult to apply to a real-life situation. Also, again, the sample was all male. Studies have shown that there are distinct differences in the morality of men and women. Some studies have found that men focus more on principles of justice, while females focus on fairness and caring (Gilligan 1982). The subject of culture has also raised questions on Kohlberg's theory as interpretations of 'justice' and 'fairness' may have different connotations in different cultures.

The stages of moral development Kohlberg identified are as follows.
▶ **Level 1: Pre-conventional morality** – at around nine years old most children do not have a moral code. A child at this level would tend to behave well in order to not be punished. They also start to develop an understanding that different individuals have differing viewpoints.
▶ **Level 2: Conventional morality** – adolescents' (and adults') moral standards are internalised and reasoning is based on the norms of the group the individual exists in. During this stage, individuals display positive behaviours to seek approval from others and they become aware of, and follow, wider rules of society.
▶ **Level 3: Post-conventional morality** – an awareness that while rules and laws exist there are times when they may work against them in the interest of particular goals or situations. At this stage individuals have generally developed their own set of moral guidelines and are prepared to adhere to them at the risk of disapproval or punishment.

Heinz's wife was dying from a particular type of cancer. Doctors said that a new drug might save her. The drug had been discovered by a local chemist, and Heinz tried desperately to buy some, but the chemist was charging ten times the money it cost to make the drug. This was much more than Heinz could afford.

Heinz could only raise half the money, even after help from family and friends. He explained to the chemist that his wife was dying and asked if he could have the drug cheaper or pay the rest of the money later.

The chemist refused, saying that he had discovered the drug and was going to make money from it. The husband was desperate to save his wife, so later that night he broke into the chemist's premises and stole the drug.

1   Should Heinz have stolen the drug?

2   Would it change anything if Heinz did not love his wife?

3   What if the person dying was a stranger? Would it make any difference?

4   Should the police arrest the chemist for murder if the woman died?

Peer status

▶ How do you think your peers affect your behaviour?

As a child grows and they identify more with their peers at school they are often subject to judgement from these peers based upon the way they look or behave. The study of **sociometric** status explores the ideas around children who are rejected or favoured based on certain personal attributes. The following illustrate some of the attributes that define acceptance or rejection of peers when forming relationships with each other.

Key term

Sociometric – a quantitative method used for measuring the underlying social relationships between people.

- **Popularity and acceptance:** A child may be accepted or well liked based upon positive features and attributes such as physical appearance, body size or even someone's name. Generally, these children will be sociable and get on well with others. However, in some instances, children who display aggressive behaviours can still be accepted, for example the class bully. Other children may aspire to be part of a group with the bully, to ensure that they are protected.
- **Neglected**: They are not disliked by all, but they generally do not have a close social bond (a 'best friend'). They are generally passive and socially withdrawn.

- **Rejected**: This child may be subject to dislike by their peers and are not looked at as a friend. They also may suffer from depression and display aggressive behaviour.
- **Controversial**: Often disliked by all they can still form close social bonds and have a 'best friend'; this contradiction can cause confusion for the child as they are unsure where they fit in.

Kathryn Wentzel and Steven Asher (1995) conducted a study exploring the academic lives of neglected, rejected, popular and controversial children. 423 sixth- and seventh-grade children (11–13 years old) were selected to examine the academically relevant characteristics of different sociometric status groups. They found that neglected children tended to have positive academic profiles and teachers reported them as having higher levels of motivation when compared to average-status children. They were also more prosocial and compliant, being better liked by teachers.

Wentzel and colleagues conducted further studies in 1995, 1997 and 2003 on peer status and children's adjustments into school life. They found that compared to children with an average status (popular), controversial children attained lower grades and rejected children rated less prosocial and more irresponsible. Studies suggesting that children who are more popular achieve better grades are not conclusive. Other studies have shown that motivated (average-rated) students are more visible to teachers and so may receive more attention than controversial children. This may be because the popularity status of controversial children may be based on their identity as a 'class clown' (Skinner & Pitzer 2012); an identity that is likely to be viewed negatively by a teacher. In general, the more popular the child, the more likely they are to achieve and receive positive attention from their teachers, which will have a positive effect on their confidence and self-esteem.

Cognition, language and communication development

Development in children

Cognition is the way that children develop thought process, understand their environments, solve problems and develop language and communication skills. This brief definition provides a starting point for introducing some of the key theories that will help you understand how children build their knowledge and understanding. Cognitive development refers to the change in a child's mental abilities throughout their lifespan. Learning is not an easy process, but it is one of the most important abilities humans possess. It relies upon memory; the recording, organising and retrieval of information.

This section will explore contributions made by Piaget, Vygotsky, Chomsky and others to the way that children develop cognitive abilities, language and communication. You will learn how their research has led to an understanding of how children develop their skills through the following.
- **Thought processes**: the role of memory, construction of ideas and abstract thought and reasoning. (Theorist: Piaget.)
- **Understanding of environments**: to be able to learn, children need to be aware of their environments and how to interact with other individuals through socialisation and communication. (Theorist: Piaget.)
- **Problem solving**: this is a term used to describe the way that children reason and work out problems for example, completing a puzzle. (Theorist: Vygotsky.)
- **Language and communication**: the ability to interact with others and to communicate feelings, beliefs and understandings. (Theorists: Chomsky, Bruner, Skinner.)

Key principles and critiques of theories

Jean Piaget

Piaget was probably one the most influential figures who researched children's cognitive development. This research centred around the way a child learns about their world through the exploration of their environment. Piaget's cognitive developmental theory is a **constructivist theory**; he viewed children as active participants in their own learning. He believed that children sought out the knowledge to build their own understanding. He identified different stages of development that followed a structure from simple to complex, concrete to abstract. For example:

Simple to complex: a baby is fed with a bottle (a drinking vessel), they then grow and explore their environment and they find a beaker and associate that with a drinking vessel. They can drink from this so they then associate the beaker with a glass, mug and other drinking vessels.

Concrete to abstract: a child sees a large, hairy dog. They feel the dog and they get to understand the behaviours of the dog. They form a **mental representation** of the dog – that is they memorise that dogs have four legs and fur, and that they lick and bark. They then see another dog that is much smaller with very little hair, but the dog also has four legs and fur, and licks and barks. The child links this with the representation they hold for the hairy dog. The child is, in essence, building a dictionary in their mind about dogs. This example illustrates the idea of a **concept**.

When the child recognises the concept of the dog, their **schematic** knowledge is related to the concept of 'dog'. This means that they have ideas of a dog having four legs and fur that licks and barks. The child then finds out that the dog has sharp teeth and claws that can cause pain, so the concept of 'dog' then makes connections with another concept of 'pain'. So, a schema (or schemas) is how a child makes sense of experiences and how they develop their understanding to make wider associations with other concepts (i.e. linking the concept of dog and pain).

Piaget proposed that intellectual or cognitive growth is a process of adaptation. This means that, in certain situations, a child will try to understand a new concept by adapting, or trying to link existing schemas, with those they already know. If the child cannot find existing schemas to adapt, they will form new representations of what the object may be, and through categorising this object or forming new schemas, they move to a stage of equilibrium, where the child categorises the schema in a new store (Figure 5.6).

> **Key terms**
>
> **Constructivist theory** – a view that states that individuals gain knowledge from their experiences in their environments.
>
> **Mental representation** – the way that images or concepts are depicted internally.
>
> **Concept** – ideas, objects, people, experiences which/ who share the same properties.
>
> **Schemas** – repeatable patterns or organised ways of making sense of an experience or building blocks of knowledge.

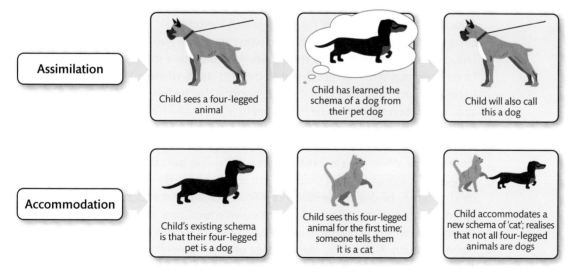

▶ **Figure 5.6:** The process of assimilation and accommodation

Piaget also proposed a staged development theory where children move through four different stages. These are the:

- sensorimotor stage, from birth to two years old
- pre-operational stage, from two to seven years old
- concrete operational stage, from seven to 11 years old
- formal operational stage, aged 11 upwards (adolescence to adulthood).

Each of these stages is categorised by the child's developing understanding of the world and are depicted in Table 5.2.

▶ **Table 5.2:** Piaget's stages of development.

Stage	Age	What the child develops and masters
Sensorimotor	Birth to 2 years	**Object permanence** – knowledge that an object still exists even if it is hidden. Children can form mental representations (a schema) of something.
Pre-operational	2–7 years	Children are capable of **symbolic thought.** They are able to form mental pictures of objects, people or events. Thinking is **egocentric**. Children have difficulty understanding or taking the viewpoint of others.
Concrete operational	7–11 years	This marks the beginning of **operational thought**. Children are able to use logic to their thoughts, for example they understand and can apply rules. Children can work things out internally (thinking). They can **conserve number, weight and mass.**
Formal operational	11 and over	Children develop the ability to think about abstract concepts and test **hypotheses.** For example, they may be able to work out complex problems or calculations.

Piaget's studies have been used extensively in practical situations. Most commonly his normative stages of development have been used to inform educational curriculums. These stages have been developed and incorporated into early years and primary curriculums, including the Early Years Foundation Stage (EYFS). The normative stages are also significant as they can support professionals in identifying where normative development milestones are delayed or affected and so allow them to treat people appropriately.

Criticism has been levelled at Piaget's research methods. He mainly observed his own children and a small sample of children who came from well-educated backgrounds, reducing generalisability of his studies. Some studies have shown that environmental factors may play a role in movement to the next stage, whereas Piaget observed it to be automatic. A further criticism of his work is that he misjudged the age children acquired certain abilities, as he happened to observe children master them at an earlier age. Although Piaget's work has informed the basis of educational curriculums, and treatments used by therapists and psychologists, its application remains controversial. While it is clear that children do tend to pass through the stages Piaget suggests, the age or stage of development at which they do so varies from child to child. This may be due to the influence of parental attachments and so the ways that parents relate to their children. A parent's own educational attainment could influence the speed in which a child develops certain skills, for example problem solving or communication. A child may reach a stage of development at an earlier age than a child whose parents have less a secure attachment with their child and do not engage in its education.

Research

Piaget constructed a study linked to the pre-operational stage of development. At this stage children are egocentric, meaning they cannot see things from another person's perspective. He constructed a task for children called the 'Three Mountains Task'.

Martin Hughes (1975) conducted a further study which critiqued the 'Three Mountains Task'.

Research and evaluate their findings. Discuss your views as to children's ability to decentre and see things from another person's perspective. Consider how this can be applied in practical situations.

Lev Vygotsky

Vygotsky believed that a child's development was dependent upon the support it received from others. Despite dying at a young age, meaning his work was left incomplete, Vygotsky's theories provided a significantly different approach to Piaget's four-stage model of development. Vygotsky placed more emphasis on the social factors that contribute towards cognitive development. He proposed that it is the social interactions that a child has with others that are important for development. Piaget, for example, proposed that language was dependent on thought (i.e. thought comes before language) whereas Vygotsky proposed that thought and language are initially separate systems that combine at around three years old and result in verbal thought (inner speech).

Adults are an important figure in promoting children's cognitive development and Vygotsky proposed that adults support a child's learning to the next level of development. He proposed a model known as the Zone of Proximal Development (ZPD) (Figure 5.7). Vygotsky's model demonstrates the difference between what a child can achieve alone and what they can achieve with guidance and support from an adult. For example, a child cannot construct a toy alone with building blocks but with the help of their parent is able to construct several toys.

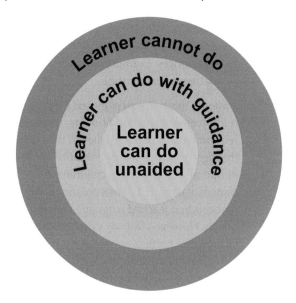

▶ **Figure 5.7:** Vygotsky's Zone of Proximal Development

Vygotsky believed that language develops from social interactions. It is the main way adults transfer information to children. Thought and language are separate until around three years old where they merge, and speech and thought become interdependent, which means that the child's thinking becomes verbal. Although Vygotsky proposed the significance of a child working with others to gain knowledge and move through the Zone of Proximal Development, it was Wood, Bruner & Ross (1976) who gave a name to the role of the adult in this situation, through what they called **scaffolding**.

> **Key term**
>
> **Scaffolding** – the way that an adult or someone more capable than a child supports a child's learning. They provide enough assistance to give the child motivation to complete a task on their own.

A child who cannot complete an activity alone is supported by a 'more able other' who would support the child and then slowly withdraw their support until the child can achieve a task independently. The term scaffolding has been adapted many times and you may hear other phrases that refer to this such as guided participation, collaborative learning, or sustained shared thinking.

Vygotsky introduced the term internalisation which describes the ways that children internalise information about their world. Children copy adults' behaviours and ask further questions until they can internalise the information, to guide their own behaviour, for example, a child could be given a jigsaw. Alone they may have difficulty completing the puzzle, but they can complete it with the support of someone who describes where pieces should go or demonstrates this. After repeated attempts and praise, the child can complete the jigsaw successfully on their own. Vygotsky's ideas have been compared with those of Piaget. Where Piaget stated that cognition was driven by a child's innate tendency to adapt to new experiences, Vygotsky focused on the importance of social interaction and emphasised the importance of instruction and guidance. Piaget, however, believed children learned through a process of self-discovery.

Language and communication acquisition

Naom Chomsky

Chomsky proposed that language is not learned, as Piaget and Vygotsky proposed, but is instead something that a child is born with. The means that he believed that language was **innate**. Chomsky believed that babies are born with a language acquisition device. He argued that the task of acquiring the correct tools to then process numerous types of language would be impossible for a child. Instead, Chomsky suggested a theory of universal grammar. This means that all humans are born with the knowledge of the rules of grammar. They are pre-programmed or innate. Chomsky, therefore, assumed that a child would only need to learn words (in their own language) and the grammatical rules would automatically be applied when they speak.

Jerome Bruner

Bruner also believed that language and thought were linked and that the way to support a child's cognitive development is through teaching children to use symbols. He also believed in the importance of adults in asking questions, which he believed would guide children's thinking. Bruner felt that learning was an active process and that children build new knowledge based on their current and past experiences. He identified three **modes of representation.**

> **Key terms**
>
> **Innate** – a term used in psychology to explain where something is natural; something an individual is born with.
>
> **Modes of representation** – how information or knowledge is stored and encoded in memory.

- **Enactive:** 0–1 years old – the child represents events through motor response, action-based information and storing in memory. Example: a child develops muscle memory to perform motor tasks such as shaking a rattle.
- **Iconic:** 1–6 years old – mental images are stored in memory. Example: a child sees a dog and so stores a mental image of the 'dog'.
- **Symbolic:** 7 years old onwards – the final stage is where information is stored in the form of a code or symbol or language, i.e. the use of words and symbols to describe experiences. Example: an understanding of the use of mathematical symbols.

Earlier in this unit you explored behaviourist ideas of reinforcement and conditioning. In line with his ideas on reinforcement, Skinner believed that language is acquired through the principles of conditioning. Through the process of operant conditioning, children would receive rewards for using language in a correct manner. Skinner also believed that children learned language through the imitation of others. However, Skinner's theories are problematic when faced with practical applications. They do not explain how, if a child learns through imitation, they still make grammatical errors. Chomsky was a critic of Skinner's ideas and did not believe that children could learn language in the way Skinner described. He believed that a child has an innate ability for language acquisition, for example meaning that they would innately understand the rules of grammar.

Role of adults

Many of the theorists in the section have emphasised the importance of adults in supporting and promoting **optimal** learning and development opportunities. Adults can do this in many ways.

▶ They can identify what a child likes and can use this knowledge to develop learning activities to promote different areas of development. For example, a child who is seen playing pirates could be introduced to books which explore different types of boat.

▶ From conducting observations adults can identify and implement strategies to support children to develop areas where they are not reaching milestones. For example, a child may not be using language appropriately and so, through a system of reward and reinforcement, adults can support language development.

Assessment activity 5.1

5A.P2 5A.P2 5A.M1 5A.D1

You are working in a primary school setting in a class of children aged four to five years old. There are 20 children in the class, with a higher number of boys. Six of the children come from different cultural backgrounds and two children have special needs relating to language and communication. One of these children appears very shy and nervous to join in with activities and is always found close to the class teacher.

Produce a report that considers how societal concepts of childhood can be used to understand the ways that children are treated and perceived in a school environment. Consider any influences that may come from the family, from teachers and from classmates.

Consider the ways that children at this age may be influenced by their friends and how they form relationships. Also include any thoughts on attachments and how children behave in an acceptable way.

Finally consider theories of cognitive, language and communication development. In your report, explain how this knowledge can support you when working with children. You will need to provide an evaluation of the impact these approaches and theories have on how you will work with children.

Plan

- What is the task? What am I being asked to do?
- How confident do I feel in my own abilities to complete this task? Are there any areas I think I may struggle with?

Do

- I know what it is I'm doing and what I want to achieve.
- I can identify when I've gone wrong and adjust my thinking/approach to get myself back on course.

Review

- I can explain what the task was and how I approached the task.
- I can explain how I would approach the hard elements differently next time (i.e. what I would do differently).
- I can evaluate the ways that cultural and societal beliefs have influenced approaches to understanding children's psychological development.

B Examine factors affecting a child's healthy development and the role of professionals involved in supporting children, parents and carers

Supporting children's optimal development

Provision of high-quality care for children has a significant impact on their learning and development. Those who support children's development play a pivotal role in ensuring children in schools, hospitals and childcare centres receive the best possible care to encourage their positive mental health and wellbeing. This section will explore the role of some of these professionals and look at some of the other factors that can affect how a child learns and develops.

Abraham Maslow developed a motivational theory that comprises five levels within a pyramid. It was initially proposed as a life-course model but was adapted by child developmentalists to demonstrate the needs of a child. Figure 5.8 illustrates the way a child progresses through each of the stages, from the bottom level of psychological needs to the top level of finding independence or self-actualisation. The model illustrates the needs of children at each level to ensure positive mental growth and acts as a guide for those supporting children's positive growth and development.

Figure 5.8: Maslow's Hierarchy of Needs adapted for child development

Factors impacting on children's development, learning and mental health

Consider all the things that influence the way that you dress, think and behave. Where do you think these influences affecting your personality and behaviour have come from? Have you ever reflected on these and consciously made a choice to change your behaviour? Influences come from many different sources, from your friends, family and also include those imposed upon you by society to encourage you to conform to society's norms. Children's development can be affected by factors before birth as well as throughout their life.

Personal and biological factors

Several factors can affect a child's development while they are still in the womb.

Prenatal factors

▶ **Maternal health:** some diseases can attack the placenta (HIV) and reduce nutrients passed to the fetus. Other diseases that affect the fetus include chicken pox, syphilis, flu and rubella.

▶ **Diet and lifestyle:** babies in the womb are directly affected by the diet and lifestyle of the mother. It is important that the mother maintains a healthy diet and lifestyle (such as exercise and avoiding some of the other factors below) throughout her pregnancy. A lack of or excess of certain vitamins can either help prevent neural tube defects (vitamin B) or lower the incidence of congenital abnormalities.

▶ What other ways can a pregnant woman ensure she maintains a healthy lifestyle?

▶ **Addiction and substance abuse:** As with diet, anything that the mother does to her body has a direct effect on the baby. If the mother abuses substances, and even becomes addicted to them, there are often poor consequences for the baby. Recreational drugs may cause congenital abnormalities, low birth weight or premature birth. Smoking nicotine constricts blood vessels reducing the blood flow and nutrients to the placenta, which results in a risk to birth weight, miscarriage or premature birth or still birth. Alcohol results in smaller babies with smaller brains, and some babies display fetal alcohol syndrome. This syndrome can affect different areas of development, including causing developmental delay, learning difficulties and impaired growth.

▶ **Heredity and genetic disorders:** When defective genes (or mutants) occur they cause disorders that can affect prenatal growth. Some of the most common diseases are cystic fibrosis, where the gene can be passed down through many generations without any of the carriers showing signs of the disease. Sickle cell anaemia haemophilia and Down's Syndrome are other examples of disorders that are caused by genetic defects. Developmental abnormalities during embryonic states can also affect a baby's growth although the reason for this is unclear. Some examples include spina bifida and cleft lip or palette.

Link

Look back at Unit 1 to remind yourself about a human's genetic make up.

▶ **Nature–nurture:** The development of the fetus in the womb is impacted by both nature and the environment it is developing within, nurture. For example, if the parent is exposed to certain chemicals from the environment, this can have an effect on fetal development. Then, from birth, a child grows and learns through this interplay between biology programmed already to develop and perform certain abilities, and the environment which provides the stimulation. For example, to demonstrate the way that nature and nurture work together the example of early brain development is useful to consider; in the first three years of life the brain establishes and strengthens connections with other neurons. A child's experiences of the physical environment provide stimulation that spark activity and boost neuronal development.

Biological and health factors

Some of the biological factors at the prenatal stage are present throughout a child's development. Other biological factors can occur throughout a child's development.

▶ **Disabilities and long-term medical conditions:** Short- and long-term illnesses and medical conditions, including disabilities, can affect the way that a child develops and learns. If a child spends long periods of time in hospital, they can fall behind on school work and therefore their intellectual development may become delayed. They may be unable to play and interact with their peers; this can affect their social and emotional development. Children with disabilities may develop low self-esteem due to this, which in turn can affect later healthy mental functioning.

▶ **Short/long-term illness:** Depression and anxiety are examples of illnesses that can impact on prenatal growth. For example, some studies have shown that the mother's emotional state during pregnancy can have an effect on the baby's brain. Prenatal stress has also been linked to neurological and physical problems. A person with a chronic, long-term illness may experience high levels of stress and anxiety and this can be transmitted to the fetus.

▶ **Learning difficulties:** Having learning difficulties can affect the mother's choices. For example, they may lack understanding of ways to ensure appropriate prenatal care or make healthy choices in relation to their lifestyle or nutrition. A child with learning difficulties may require more assistance, or special schooling and may not be able to live independently in adulthood.

Personal, social and emotional factors

In this next section you will explore the role of personal, social and emotional factors in influencing children's healthy development. As these are very much linked to the environment and not biology, you will notice some close links to environmental and societal factors.

▶ **Attachment and friendship orientations:** The forms of attachment that individuals develop with others change over time and as a child grows to be more prosocial, they move from general attachments that provide their basic and essential needs, towards establishing strong relationships and friendships. When children create attachments in the first few years of their lives, they develop internal working models (IWM) of their primary attachments. These IWM's form the basis of – and guide – a child's future behaviours. The child will adapt these IWM's as they develop relationships with extended family and then friendships. An example of an IWM is where a mother has formed a secure bond with their child and responds to the child's needs immediately. The child therefore constructs an IWM where they see themselves as capable of calling for attention when they need it and therefore worthy of receiving that attention.

▶ **Security:** A child needs a secure base from which to explore their environment, normally from a primary caregiver that they feel sure will attend to their needs if they become distressed. If a secure attachment is missing, growth and development may be affected as the child may become wary of strangers, they may not engage in social and educational activities, and may become withdrawn and isolated.

▶ **Abuse:** The effect of abuse on children's overall development can be significant. A child who is emotionally or psychologically abused may become withdrawn and experience difficulties communicating effectively with others. They may have difficulty in developing friendships, which will affect their language development. Sexual or physical abuse can result in immediate and long-term psychological disorders, such as depression or self-harm.

▶ **Bullying:** This can affect the physical and emotional health and development of a child. Bullying can have a short- and long-term impact and can lead to self-harm and social and emotional problems. Bullying can affect a child's ability to make friendships and there is a risk of later mental health problems. A child who is bullied may also experience physical conditions such as headaches, sleep problems and anxiety.

▶ **Transitions:** A child's development can be affected when they experience significant life events (transitions). Some examples are shown in Table 5.3.

▶ **Table 5.3:** Transitions a child may experience

Transition	Scenario	Possible effects
Moving house/location	Joe aged 4 years and his family have recently moved to a new location that is very different from his last home, which was in the middle of a big city. He has moved to a rural location where there are no near neighbours.	**Social and emotional development:** Joe has left close friendships behind. He may struggle to develop new friendships. His may experience low self-esteem and reduced confidence.
Moving to a new school	Muhammed aged 5 years has recently moved house and has had start a new school midway through term time.	**Cognitive development:** Muhammed is experiencing a new area of the curriculum that he was not covering at his old school. He is behind his peers in his learning. This can affect his confidence and self esteem in developing social relationships as well as affecting his ability to achieve expected curriculum outcomes.
Divorce and separation	Clare is aged 3 years and her parents have recently divorced. Her mother has moved to a new location and so she has little face-to-face contact with Clare.	**Social and emotional development:** Clare may experience anxiety and depression as she misses her mother. She may become withdrawn and isolated, and may lose confidence.
Separations	Sam is five years old. His father is an officer in the army and is going on a work-related course abroad for six months. Sam's mother remains at home to look after Sam and his three-month-old sister, Jess.	**Social and emotional development and cognitive development:** Sam may experience anxiety and a loss of self-esteem while his father is away. He may feel left out as his mother has to care for Jess. He may take on certain roles in the home to support his mother and potentially may miss out on friendships at school.

Family systems factors

Factors operating within and around family systems can also have a significant impact on a child's growth and development. Earlier you saw the way that Bronfenbrenner's model demonstrated how a child may be influenced by their immediate environments.

▶ **Work, leisure and home life:** A parent's work can have a significant impact on a child's development; consider the parenting types discussed earlier in this unit. For example, a parent who works long hours may be more tired and irritable and have little time to interact with their child. This may affect a child's social and personal development. Cognitive development can be affected by a parent's unwillingness or lack of time to read to their child or help with homework, for example.

- Older children may be left to care for younger siblings, affecting their ability to socialise with peer groups.
- Leisure activities influence a child's development.
- There has been research on the effects of computer games and TV on children's social development. Some evidence suggests that these technologies can impact on a child's social and communication skills.

▶ **Society:** Earlier in this unit you explored the way that the wider society influences a child's development, through social norms. Law is one example of a societal influence as it places responsibility on parents to ensure their child receives an education and behaves in a socially acceptable way.

▶ **Parenting styles:** Parenting styles can affect a child's mental health. For example, a child's emotional confidence and self-esteem may be negatively affected by the authoritarian parent who upholds a strict regime with little negotiation and high order. A child may become involved in deviant behaviours and miss schooling where the parents are permissive or uninvolved.

▶ **Attachments with family and friends:** You have explored the impact of attachments and friendships and how they can influence a child's development. It is useful to

> **Link**
>
> Look back at page 248 to remind yourself about Bronfenbrenner's ecological model of child development.

consider here the effects of family systems. Each of the family members dynamically interact with, and influence, each other's behaviours. For example, a parent who restricts a child's social activity when they have behaved inappropriately, may in turn be affected by the child's subsequent behaviours. This then affects the way the parent reacts to that child or other members of the family. Repeated disagreements between family members impact upon the way each member reacts and behaves.

▶ **Education and income:** Some research has demonstrated that educated parents have more resources (both financial and physical) available with which to support and meet their child's needs. Resources are not necessarily financial resources, but physical or **social capital** resources. This is the time and effort a parent puts into supporting a child in their school work which could include helping them with homework, volunteering at schools or engaging with their children's teachers to develop strategies to support children's learning. Some research has argued that the better educated the parent, the more able they are to invest in their child's educational success.

Environmental and societal factors

As well as personal and biological factors, the environment and society that children experience can affect their development, learning and mental health.

Environmental factors

Housing, and the location of housing, can have an impact on a child growing up. If a child's home is located near to amenities including schools, clubs and play activities, this can have a significant impact. A child who grows up in a deprived neighbourhood in a rural location with few amenities may not be able to develop strong bonds with others; their learning may be affected as the location of amenities such as playgrounds and libraries may be inaccessible.

The quality of housing can also affect a child's development, learning and mental health. If a child, for example, has to share a room or lives in a small home with no dedicated space to study then they may not have the space required to complete school work. This can have an obvious effect on

their educational attainment. They might also suffer poor mental health from not having any space to themselves.

> **Reflect**
>
> Reflect on your own childhood. Can you identify with any of the factors? How have they affected the way you have developed?

Social and political factors

Another environmental factor you need to consider is the effect of policies, services and strategies, for example the systems that govern health services. The Mental Health Act 2007 provides information regarding the rights of people with mental-health disorders and how they must be treated. This also includes a code of practice that describes the forms and procedures for supporting individuals with these disorders. The Act describes the forms of support that individuals should expect from professionals. However, constraints on services impact on the ability of an individual to gain support, and these constraints can be linked to where an individual lives.

Wealth, which can be linked to social class, is another factor that affects development; social class has often been attributed to better mental health and wellbeing in children. However, this is not universal or necessarily true. James Coleman spoke of the concept of social capital, discussed earlier. Coleman believed that where parents did not make this investment in their child's education, it would have a negative impact on their child's educational outcomes. Coleman's description of social capital provides an explanation of the importance of a child developing rich bonds with their parents, peers and teachers, and illustrates Vygotsky's concept of the importance of others in contributing to a child's learning.

Cultural factors

Earlier you explored social identity theory and the way in which in-group and out-group attitudes, beliefs and behaviours can develop through individual and group relationships as children grow. This includes the local community that children grow up within. A close, local community can impact on a child's development as they may create additional attachments and feel secure in their environment. Another form of community may be the religious community that a child is raised within for example a Muslim, Catholic or Protestant community. These groups can often provide family support as well as a safe space for children to explore their environment.

Attitudes on gender can also influence a child's development.

There are cultural differences in the perception of men and women. For example, in Japan traditional gender roles of men being the main income provider and women staying at home with the family, tend to be more prevalent than in Western societies. Beliefs like this are subject to change. For example, the rise of feminism since the 1960s has caused a change in the family structure in many Western households, with some traditionally female tasks now taken on by the males in the household as well.

Theory into practice

Pick a culture that interests you. Consider that culture's rules, their values, customs and practices. Consider also the role of gender, race and local community within that culture.

How do you think each of these can influence the way that a child develops or the possible impact on future mental health?

Link

Look back at learning aim A on page 243 for information on the impact of beliefs, values and society norms on a child's development.

Professionals involved in supporting children's development

In this section you will briefly explore the role of those who work with children in supporting their growth development and healthy mental wellbeing. Observations are key to all professionals working with children. Through these, they are able to identify where a child may be deviating from milestones. They can either treat or refer children for specialist treatment. There are a number of professionals in different areas that support children: Tables 5.4 and 5.5 identify these.

▶ **Table 5.4:** Professionals' roles and responsibilities in education

Profession	Responsibilities
Teacher	• Creates supportive learning environments for children, role models, teaching knowledge to children • Can be one of the first to identify areas of developmental delay
Support worker	• Supports the needs of children with specific needs through helping them with their daily needs, supporting education • Can assist with personal care needs and general mobility • Can support professionals in administering therapies
Nursery or pre-school professional	• Similar role to the teacher but much of knowledge taught is through play-based activities • May be able to identify developmental delay much earlier
Teaching assistant	• Supports the teacher in delivering learning • Often supports smaller groups of children who may be experiencing difficulties • They do not identify and treat developmental problems but work with professionals to support children
Health visitor	• Works with school nurses to protect and ensure children are safe • Supports school programmes to promote health, for example healthy eating, exercise
School nurse	• Provides preventative and screening services, health education, immunisation against diseases, etc.
Special Needs Coordinator (SENCO)	• Responsible for finding and providing support for children with specific learning difficulties or needs

> **Table 5.5:** Professionals in health, social and other professionals

Profession	Role
Clinical psychologist	• Conducts observations and interviews • Identifies and treats mental, emotional behavioural problems
Educational psychologist	• Conducts observations and interviews • Sets tasks with children to identify difficulties they may experience with learning • Makes assessments based on children's reactions to tasks set • Does not adopt the same procedures to identify psychological problems but can prescribe medication and refer patients to specialised provision and services
General practitioner of medicine (GPs)	• Normally treats common medical conditions and makes referrals to hospitals and other specialist medical services
Health worker	• Promotes good mental health in the community • Supports and signposts individuals to services • Identifies and designs plans for specific treatments • May specialise in some therapies, for example cognitive behavioural therapy (CBT)
Social worker	• Could work with children in foster care, or residential placements • Works alongside other professionals to ensure child receives the right care, education and health services
Police	• Psychology-related roles within the police force can include safety and enforcement • May perform assessments and support individuals with post-traumatic events
Child and adolescent psychiatrist (CAP)	• Works with children and young people (up to 18 years old) treating a wide range of mental health conditions, for example anxiety, stress, substance misuse, eating disorders, autism, etc.
Midwife	• Provides support through pregnancy, labour and childbirth • May provide parenting classes and support the physical, psychological and emotional needs of mothers
Counsellor	• Deals with children who are depressed, who may have suffered abuse and other emotional and mental problems • Provides a supportive environment where a child may open up to the counsellor in a number of ways such as through art, role play or just by talking

Other support services

In addition to the professionals above, there are a number of other services that provide support to children and families. Other than the professionals named above there are a number of other services that are there to help children and their families. These include charities such as Barnardo's. Set up by John Barnardo in the late 1800s, he believed that children were best supported in small family style groups and adopted a 'cottage style' model in his children's homes. The modern-day Barnardo's has taken on a more holistic approach of supporting families, providing support for disabled children, young people and safeguarding.

Mencap was first conceived by Judy Fryd in the mid-1900s who formed the National Association of Parents of Backward Children (later becoming Mencap). Campaigns initiated by Mencap have resulted in people with learning disabilities being included in the Further and Higher Education Act 1992. Today Mencap provides services including 24-hour care, enabling people to join local leisure activities; providing advice and information on employment; and providing education and support for various psychological, emotional and social needs.

Self-help groups are community groups where people can attend and gain support from those in similar situations, and sometimes professional help from organisers or guests. An example could include a group for autistic children and their caregivers.

Research

Mencap conducted a longitudinal study called the Brooklands Experiment. Research online to find out more about the outcomes of this study and what impact it had on the provision of support and services for those with learning disabilities.

Assessment activity 5.2

5B.P3 5B.P4 5B.M2 5B.D2

Research a different culture to your own and look at how this culture impacts on child development. You should consider the society's rules, values, customs and practices. You should also think about the role of gender, race and local community, and how these contributory factors can impact on the ability and way professionals support children. Consider how this culture influences the way a child develops and any possible impact on future mental health.

Write a report that compares the culture you have chosen to research with that of the UK. What are the key differences in this culture in how it influences and raises children?

Consider factors such as poverty, wealth, social status, parental and family factors, and where the child might live.

Consider how these influences could affect a child in this culture. What is the potential to their future mental health outcomes?

Select a biological and environmental factor that can impact on a child's development and evaluate the role of the professional in supporting a child.

Plan

- What is the task? What am I being asked to do?
- How confident do I feel in my own abilities to complete this task? Are there any areas I think I may struggle with?

Do

- I know what it is I'm doing and what I want to achieve.
- I can identify when I've gone wrong and adjust my thinking/approach to get myself back on course.
- I can evaluate different factors and the way they impact on the way professionals support children's development.

Review

- I can explain what the task was and how I approached the task.
- I can explain how I would approach the hard elements differently next time (i.e. what I would do differently)

Key terms

Dysfunction – an abnormality or disruption in the way some aspects of the human condition function. In the case of applied psychology this could be a disturbance in cognitive, emotional and/or social functioning.

Deprivation – in psychology, this is the loss of an attachment figure; where an individual does not receive the basic necessities required for a healthy life.

Social and economic deprivation – where an individual does not receive the social and economic requirements for healthy cognitive, social and emotional development. This could include a lack of financial support, or social exclusion due to discrimination.

Privation – where a child has never received the care, love, security of a primary caregiver and has not formed any specific attachments.

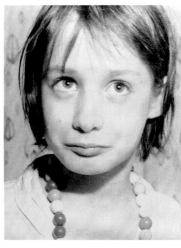

▶ The case of Genie Wiley provided a lot of information for researchers about the critical period for language development

C Investigate the use of theories of psychological development to explain and inform prevention of later dysfunctional psychopathy

Instances of deprivation and abuse

To be able to understand how professionals can support children's positive health and wellbeing, it is useful to consider situations where no support and/or neglect has been identified and where this has had a significantly negative impact on children's mental wellbeing. Exploring areas of **dysfunction** is important to demonstrate the likely outcomes if children are not supported. **Deprivation** is a term used to describe a situation where an individual does not have the conditions that are considered essential for a normal healthy life. This, generally is an attachment to a primary caregiver, but also includes food, shelter, warmth, love and security (which can be defined as **social and economic deprivation**). Some of the cases covered in this section will focus on situations where children have been unable to form specific attachments with primary caregivers; this has been defined by Michael Rutter (1981) as **privation**. To summarise: deprivation can be defined as the loss of something, whereas privation indicates that the child never had that 'something' to lose in the first place.

Deprivation

You will explore three studies on deprivation: Genie; the Czech Twins; and Hodges and Tizard (1989).

Genie

Genie (real name Susan Wiley) was born in April 1957 in Arcadia, California, USA. She was found by social services at 13 years old having been kept in extreme isolation. She wore nappies and her speech was like that of a baby, she weighed less than 59 pounds and walked strangely, holding her hands like a rabbit. She had been beaten by her father if she made any noise and could speak no more than 20 words/phrases. At the time scientists had identified that as a child develops, they learn specific things during specific periods, called critical periods and that language was one of these specific things. They believed Genie had missed this period and so had missed her chance to develop language. However, as Genie grew and developed, she engaged enthusiastically with her environment and learned words, though not the rules of grammar or sentence construction. It was felt that the left side of the brain responsible for language had diminished. As she was not exposed to words and language during the critical period, that part of her brain failed to mature and started to disconnect. Starved of stimulation, Genie's brain had not developed the capacity for full language acquisition.

The Czech Twins

Jarmila Koluchova (1976) studied a pair of twins who were brought up in an institution for a year and then by an aunt for six months. The first 18 months of their lives were comparatively normal and it is assumed that they were experiencing a normal upbringing and would have formed some attachments. After their father remarried and they returned home, their stepmother abused the children over the next five years by locking them in a room and beating them. When they were found at seven years old, they both had developed bone disease and were small for their age. Their developmental ages were estimated at around three years old as they could not talk or recognise pictures and were afraid of people. After time spent in a number of schools, the twins were adopted by a woman who provided them special care and by the age of 11, the twins had caught up in terms of development and their speech was normal for their age. In a follow-up study, Koluchova found that both were married with children, in stable, happy relationships. This study demonstrates that as the children had experienced early attachments during the critical period, the effects of subsequent abuse could be reversed, and they were able to lead healthy adult lives.

Hodges and Tizard (1989)

Jill Hodges and Barbara Tizard conducted a study to explore the effects of privation on later attachments in children who had an institutional upbringing to understand whether the effects of early deprivation could be reversed or modified and whether there is a **critical/sensitive period** for the development of behaviours. This was a longitudinal study with a sample of 65 children who had been in residential care from a few months old to around four years old. Although the children received good quality care, they were not encouraged to form attachments. The children were observed for four years when some of the children were either adopted or returned to their family and observations continued in these environments. Hodges and Tizard found that the children who returned to their natural homes showed weaker attachment and behavioural problems than those children spending time in institutions who demonstrated more attention seeking behaviours and social relationship problems.

> **Key term**
>
> **Critical/sensitive period** – a period (up to two and a half years old) where a child needs to form an attachment with a caregiver.

Feral children

Studies of feral children have also served to provide valuable evidence of the importance of learning and nurturing during critical periods and the effects on long-term development, learning and mental health.

Victor of Aveyron

Victor was found when he was aged around 12 years old, after growing up in isolation from human communities. Victor not only had no experience of language but also had not learned socially acceptable behaviours. He did not respond to sounds, not even loud noises. He would only respond to those sounds that he was familiar with from living in nature, such as cracking nuts. He had no speech, only guttural noises and had no social skills; he did not care to be around others and was happy by himself. He was adopted by Jean-Marc Gaspard Itard, a medical student, and

Victor lived with him in his house. Under Itard's care, Victor was able to learn several phrases and adopt some limited social skills. This case occurred in the 1700s and at this time there was no understanding of the concept of critical periods. However, Itard introduced behavioural modification techniques that supported Victor's language development.

Oxana Malaya

Born in 1983 in Novaya Blagoveshchenka, Ukraine, Oxana was neglected by her alcoholic parents and when she was three years old she was left outside one night. She retreated to a kennel, alongside dogs, for warmth and learned animal behaviours to survive. After six years of eating raw meat, barking and walking on all fours she was found by police and taken into care. Before she was abandoned, she had acquired some language and so was able to relearn this, and at 22 years old she was assessed as having the mental capacity of a six-year-old child. This study highlights that the critical period of language acquisition, up to five years old, has some relevance as Oxana's 're-acquisition' demonstrates.

Romanian orphans

In the 1980s and 1990s children were discovered in overcrowded orphanages in Romania. The care they were receiving was poor, and children were only provided with their basic needs (food, clothing and warmth), with many never receiving any love or emotional care. Michael Rutter's study (2007) followed a group of children adopted by British families, with the youngest adopted at under six months old. This was a longitudinal study and children were assessed at the ages of four, six and 11. Rutter and his colleagues found that children who were adopted younger than six months old developed normally, while those who were older formed attachments indiscriminately (with any adult rather than one) and experienced difficultly in forming friendships. This study demonstrated that if attachments are provided before a child was six months old the effects of deprivation can be overcome; after this time the effects appear to be more permanent.

Evaluation and application

Studies of deprivation and privation have provided professionals with valuable tools to identify atypical development patterns in children. Longitudinal studies have helped them to identify effective treatments and therapies to overcome the effects of early deprivation and recover cognitive, social, emotional and language skills that have been lost during their periods of isolation and abandonment. These studies demonstrate the oversimplification of Bowlby's theory of a critical period as they demonstrate how children can recover from early-attachment deprivation to lead healthy, normal lives, given the right circumstances and environment.

Effects of family and society systems

Family and societal systems have been discussed earlier in this unit and you have learned how the family can influence the family system through its own interactions as well as being influenced by society. The family sets their own rules for social behaviours and are influenced by society's legal and social norms of behaving. However, when a family system is disrupted or becomes dysfunctional, problems can arise within the family unit and often the children suffer consequences as a result of a lack of parental care and nurturing. All professionals working with children and adults with parental responsibilities have a duty to safeguard children, and the effects on a child who suffers forms of abuse can be severe and last well into adulthood, or abuse can tragically lead to a child's death.

Child protection is part of safeguarding. Safeguarding is a wider approach where professionals actively promote the safety and welfare of children, while child protection means keeping children safe from harm who are being abused or are in danger of being abused.

Victoria Climbié

The case of Victoria Climbié caused a significant review of child protection arrangements in the UK. It illustrates the importance of the role of professionals in identifying issues in the home. Victoria left her home in the Ivory Coast to live in the care of her aunt, who lived with her partner. She suffered abuse at the hands of her aunt's partner, which led to torture and her death. Victoria was admitted to hospital on several occasions and authorities missed these opportunities to identify that she was being abused. After her death, this oversight resulted in social workers being dismissed for gross misconduct. An in-depth review on this case led by Lord Laming put forward some 58 recommendations based on evidence to improve child

protection in the UK. The review provided a strategic approach for child protection priorities to ensure that all professionals working with children are able to maintain a vigilant and robust approach towards ensuring the safety and welfare of all children.

Liam Fee

In a similar case, child protection officers were found guilty of enabling the murder of two-and-a-half-year-old Liam Fee. He died at the hands of his mother and partner, who had subjected him to continued physical abuse. Rachel and Nyomi Fee were convicted of murder and abuse, of not only Liam but also abuse of other children. A case review confirmed that while Liam's death could not have been predicted, as the mother and her partner were 'manipulative' and controlling, there were missed opportunities across services to raise concerns. Even though a number of people had raised concerns about Liam, including staff in his nursery and his childminder, the case went undetected due to a catalogue of missed opportunities and failures on the part of other support services.

Evaluation and application

While these types of cases are rare, they illustrate the important role that those working with children must undertake to support children's normative development proactively and to identify when there are issues that impact on that child's healthy development. Professionals working with children and young people should be trained to recognise signs and symptoms of abuse in order that they can act promptly to prevent tragic incidents, such as the cases of Victoria Climbié and Liam Fee. These cases both impacted on legislation in the UK to help children's safeguarding.

Forms of trauma

Earlier you explored the social and emotional factors that can affect a child's normative development. You explored the different forms of transitions that children may experience that could have a significant impact on their later healthy mental functioning. Factors that influence child development can come from the environment the child grows up within and the people around the child. The most influential figures in the first few years of a child's life are the parents; their parenting styles can impact significantly on normative development. You also looked at other factors that could impact both negatively and positively on a child's development, such as the following.

▶ **Bullying**: Children can be bullied by peers but also bullying can be by parents if they adopt authoritarian parenting styles. A bullied child may become withdrawn, lose confidence and may be unable to make meaningful friendships, which will have a significant negative impact on their overall development.

▶ **Divorce**: Children whose parents separate and divorce may experience emotional difficulties as they come to terms with their parent's separation. Very often separations can be acrimonious (angry and bitter), and parents fight over financial and physical resources. This can also affect the way children are treated and the parenting style may change as a result of the divorce. A parent may become more permissive; buying presents to gain a child's favour or they may become overprotective, for example restricting the child's visits to the absent parent.

▶ **Death**: The death of a family member can cause anxiety and stress to children as they see their own parents or other close caregivers coming to terms with the death of a loved one. The death of a parent or other carer can cause significant trauma to a child as they lose a primary attachment, as well as the child having to deal with a change in their family situation. Parenting styles may change as a result, as the living parent may have to assume the deceased partner's position in the family. This can cause significant stress to a child and lead to anxiety and self-esteem issues.

▶ **Physical/sexual abuse:** The studies you have explored illustrate the potential impact that abusive behaviour can have on a child's development and potential to achieve healthy outcomes. Often the parents are the instigator of this abuse, but if children become withdrawn or antisocial due to the impact of abuse, parents may change their parenting style in order to try and deal with the trauma their child has suffered.

Discussion

There are several forms of abuse that professionals need to be aware of when they are involved in the safeguarding of children. Research the roles and responsibilities of professionals in identifying and reporting possible incidents of abuse. Discuss how having this knowledge will help professionals in supporting children's welfare. The NSPCC and Childline websites may be useful for this activity, and can be found at the end of this unit.

▶ **Natural disasters:** These are events such as floods, earthquakes, hurricanes and tsunamis. Natural disasters can have devastating effects on families and communities. As well as causing death and injury to family members, children may find their family displaced from their home location sometimes losing their siblings, friends and parents. For example, floods and landslides in Sri Lanka in 2017 left 213 dead and 415,000 affected, with 30 per cent of those being children.

Research

Research one of the natural disasters listed below.
- **Mexico:** Puebla earthquake (2017) – 225 lives lost, millions affected.
- **Colombia:** landslide (2017) – 300 lives lost, 200 injured.
- **Sierra Leone:** mudslides (2017) – 600 lives lost, 6000 affected.
- **Bangladesh and Nepal:** flooding and landslides (2017) – 600 lives lost 41 million affected.

1 Can you identify the type of response, and who initiated the response to these disasters?

2 What forms of support would have been given to children in these situations to support their social and emotional needs?

3 How do you think such disasters can affect long-term mental health?

4 How do you think professionals could support children who have experienced this type of trauma?

Post-Traumatic Stress Disorder (PTSD) is an anxiety disorder that is caused by frightening or distressing events, including war. Those suffering with PTSD can often relive traumatic events through nightmares and flashbacks. For a child, the risk of them developing PTSD depends on a number of factors including:

▶ how close the child is to the trauma

▶ how severe the trauma is to the child

- how long the trauma lasts for
- whether the trauma occurs more than once
- how well the child can cope with the trauma (how resilient they are)
- what support (resources and people) the child receives after the trauma.

A traumatic event for a child might be:
- an incident of abuse (physical, sexual, emotional, neglect)
- violence
- animal attacks
- serious accidents.

Parents of children with PTSD need to provide a secure reassuring base for children to be able to talk about their experiences. Parents themselves may also be suffering from PTSD, particularly in instances where the trauma was from the experience of war. Children may react in different ways and this can be challenging for a parent also suffering from PTSD as their own parenting style may be affected. Behaviours children may display include acting disruptively, depression, aggression, disengagement and, in adolescents, substance abuse. For a child who has experienced life in a war zone these symptoms may be more extreme and include isolation, severe anxiety and fear for their own life.

Parents may also suffer from PTSD when their children do not, for example parents who were in the armed forces returning from active duty. PTSD can affect the ways that parents' function in family systems. A parent may appear self-consumed and unable to interact or contribute to their family. The other parent may take on the dual role of mother and father and take over daily household responsibilities. Children are significantly affected by role changes because parenting styles are often dramatically affected through increased responsibilities in the household. This impacts on their own social relationships and education and may also have a detrimental impact on their own mental wellbeing as they struggle to come to terms with the difficulties within the family unit. Attachments may be severely affected and children may develop behavioural and personality difficulties as a result.

Effects on young carers

There are various situations in which children take on the roles of adults. These include when children have to take responsibility for the care of either their parents or younger siblings. Such cases also demonstrate the importance of the role of professionals and of intervention.

Sometimes a parent may be so overwhelmed by their anxiety that the child may take on the role of that parent in order to support them. The examples provided earlier in this section on PTSD provide a good example of this type of situation. This is a form of **boundary dissolution**, where the child takes on a parent's role and the distinct roles that you would expect each to play become blurred.

Society is seeing more young children taking on the role of their parents in household duties when their parents are unable to care for their own needs due to long-term illness or disabilities that restrict their ability to lead normal lives. Children become the primary source of care for some parents. However, this can have a significant impact on the child's own development, which is a concern for developmentalists as they see these children missing critical parts of their development.

Young carer's lives may be dominated by adult-type roles, such as cleaning and caring for others. They may miss after-school events, or even school itself, to ensure that they are in the home for as much time as possible. The implications of this is that they effectively

Key term

Boundary dissolution – where the lines between the role of parent/carer and child become blurred.

miss out on the social aspects of their own life, their friends and their own interests, as they are taking on adult roles and responsibilities. Young carers may have a limited childhood or adolescence phase, progressing to adulthood before the majority of their peers in Western society. This can have significant impact on their ability to socialise and interact with others, as well as impacting on their educational outcomes, due to potentially missing time from school, not having space or time to complete homework, or just having other more critical concerns than their education.

Role reversal is another element of boundary dissolution. Role reversal describes the process in which parents turn to their children for emotional support. It can be an exploitative relationship where parents' expectations exceed a child's capacities and where a child's developmental needs are ignored. This does not mean the parent is unsupportive, but the emotional needs of the parent are seen to be greater. Research has shown that children experiencing role reversal are often unable to meet developmental norms and experience difficulty in regulating their own behaviour and emotions.

▶ What impact do you think being a young carer would have on friendships?

Prenatal effects

During prenatal stages and through the first few years of a child's life, the brain and body develop at a rapid pace and it is during this time that a child's exposure to influences in the environment have a significant effect on them. A child needs stimulation to learn and develop. They need to be immersed in language at an early age, during the critical period, in order to acquire the skills necessary to socialise and engage with others. Addiction and substance abuse by the mother during pregnancy has been found to be particularly harmful to the baby and can lead to psychiatric problems, delayed development and reduced emotional control problems (AHD). Recreational drugs have been linked to mood, attention and hyperactivity during adolescence, as well as being a potential cause of autism. Here are a few more examples.

▶ **Certain toxins:** Prenatal chemical exposure can have lasting detrimental effects on children's development and can cause diseases. Some chemicals such as mercury found in fish can influence IQ. Lead found in houses (pre-1978) can lead to behavioural disorders. Pesticides found in some foods can have an effect on

> **Link**
>
> Look back at page 263 in which you explored the prenatal factors that can affect a child in later life and how some of these can have serious mental-health implications.

cognitive functioning. Solvents can cause fetal loss (miscarriage) and have been linked to disrupted brain exposure and behavioural and attention difficulties.

▶ **Exposure to intimate partner violence (IPV):** Although difficult to find reliable data, IPV is thought to lead to premature birth and low-birth weight, which are associated with increases in attention, behavioural and psychological disorders in children.

▶ **Influence of mental stress:** Mothers experiencing mental-health issues such as depression, prenatal or postnatal stress and anxiety may not engage with their young babies and may sometimes reject them. This has a significant impact on a child's ability to form bonds and socialise as well as impacting on language development.

▶ **Poor diet:** This can affect healthy growth and development of children. A healthy diet also helps to prevent illnesses such as heart disease and diabetes. Lack of folic acid intake in pregnancy has been linked to birth defects of the baby's brain and spina bifida. Hunger as a result of low household income and other resources for food may result in undernutrition, which not only affects the physical but also the psychological health of children.

▶ **Addiction:** According to the NSPCC most parents/carers who drink alcohol or use drugs do so in moderation, so as not to pose a risk of harm to their own children. The risk of harm to children with parents who do misuse alcohol and drugs is higher, due to the mental and physical health problems associated with substance abuse. The impact on children can be substantial. Substance abuse during pregnancy puts the fetus at risk, but after birth and whilst the child grows, the child of a parent who has an addiction is more at risk of:
  - abuse from a parent
  - poor educational attainment
  - social problems
  - taking substances themselves
  - turning to offending behaviours.

Environmental effects

The environment a child is raised in can have a significant impact on their healthy development. The professional's role is to identify ways to support and provide interventions for those suffering adverse effects of their environment. The following points provide examples of how professionals can support individuals who experience these different situations.

There are over four million children in poverty in the UK and lone parent families are twice as likely to be in poverty as couples with children. The Child Poverty Act 2010 places responsibility on local authorities to tackle child poverty in their areas. Each authority is required to set out plans to reduce and mitigate the effects of child poverty.

Intelligence/parental education levels – It has been widely debated as to whether children's development can be influenced by intelligence (IQ) and parental education levels; research has offered valid arguments for each side. It could be assumed that children living in poverty may not receive the same support and care of parents with higher incomes and more stable environments. There has been some argument that the better educated a parent, the more likely the child is to achieve success based on the parent's academic achievements. This assumption is based on weak evidence, however. The concept of social capital could have more of an impact here, rather than purely a measure of parental intelligence.

Earlier you discussed the impact on lifestyle and income on children's healthy development within their family systems, including looking at Bronfenbrenner's ecological model. Professionals use models such as these to inform their own practice

Link

Look back at page 266 which discusses social capital.

and to help them understand the factors that are operating in the background that can affect a child's development. These models help professionals in educational settings to interpret children's behaviours, highlight concerns, and seek specific interventions to support children from **multi-agency professionals**.

Income, for example, can have dramatic effects on children's healthy development; the effects of poverty can result in poor living conditions and lack of nutrition. Income also affects lifestyle factors such as leisure pursuits and availability of amenities.

Deviance from norms of society – Norms of society are the unwritten rules of behaviour that are considered acceptable in a culture or society. They create the basis of expected behaviours between individuals and groups such as respect and cooperation and can also form the basis for laws, customs and practices that define the limits of acceptable and unacceptable behaviours. Where an individual deviate from the norms this means they act in a way that society does not approve. For example, a child who plays truant from school repeatedly.

Case study

Tochi is ten years old. He has recently moved to the UK from Northern India with his mother, father and his younger sibling, Satpriya. He has recently joined the local primary school. His mother speaks little English and Tochi struggles with his reading. His mother buys the reading books the school is using and learns to read them herself so she can help Tochi with his education.

Tochi's mother has 'invested' social capital to help Tochi succeed at school. Therefore, it is not necessarily the intelligence or education of a parent that is the most crucial factor, but rather the time and resources parents invest in their children's overall wellbeing.

1 Discuss this example and how other types of support can be provided to children to enable their healthy development.

2 Discuss the impact of poverty, intelligence and family systems on children's later psychological wellbeing.

3 Can you think of examples in your own upbringing where you can identify forms of social capital invested by parents or friends in helping you achieve.

Genetics and heredity

You have explored biological explanations of factors influencing children's development and compared these with environmental factors. Professionals use evidence and studies from various areas to determine how best to treat certain conditions and put in place preventative measures to mitigate against longer term ill mental health.

Twin studies have been successful in exploring effects of certain environmental factors on a child's later mental health. They have been used to investigate the effects of nature (biology or genes) and nurture (environment or upbringing) on behaviours of children. Research using twin studies are used as it is possible to make inferences between two types of twins: monozygotic (MZ) and dizygotic (DZ). Comparing the **concordance** of behaviours between MZs compared to DZs you can understand whether a given behaviour is likely to result from nature or nurture.

As MZ twins share all their genes (100 per cent identical) and DZ twins only half, studying the differences in their behaviours reveals a lot about the influences of nature (genetics). For example, the role of nature is demonstrated in a study that found MZ and DZ twins displayed similar personalities despite being separated at birth, adopted and brought up in different family environments (nurture).

Professionals have also used adoption studies to illustrate the impact of the environment on a child's development and demonstrated the influence of nature (biology) and nurture (environment). It is important to consider, however, that professionals should adopt a more holistic approach to diagnosing and treating individuals and that environment alone cannot always account for primary causes.

Case study

A well-documented example of twin studies is the Genain quadruplets. These were identical (MZ) quadruplets who were born in 1930. Both their mother's and father's family had a history of mental illness and the children also developed schizophrenia. This study illustrates the likelihood of a 'schizophrenic gene' impacting on the quadruplet's mental health. Gottesman & Shields (1966) used twin studies to provide further evidence to establish a genetic component to schizophrenia.

Brendgen et al. (2005) used questionnaires as a method to establish whether there was a connection between social aggression (taunting) and physical aggression. This study compared identical (MZ) and non-identical (DZ) twins. This study looked for the **concordance** between sets of MZ twins, compared to DZ twins. They found there was a link between physical aggression and genes, but a weaker link between social aggression and genes. The study concluded that physical aggression was linked to nature while social aggression was linked to nurture.

1 How can the above studies support professionals in diagnosing and treating conditions?

2 Discuss your thoughts on the influence of biology and the environment on determining development.

Application of theories to working practice

Influence of known cases for professionals

The value of understanding the factors surrounding cases of different forms of deprivation and abuse is important as it provides professionals insight into the possible impact on a child's future development. This allows them to put in place support strategies and treatments to tackle issues early on in life before they have opportunity to affect later psychological health.

Drawing together knowledge of children's psychological development and reviewing known cases of dysfunction have had a profound effect on both policy and practice, influencing the way that professionals work with children in their roles. This section will explore some of the theories discussed earlier in this unit to illustrate the links that professionals draw on to inform their understanding and decisions when applying intervention strategies to promote healthy development.

How theories can inform the way professionals interpret known cases of dysfunctional development

Knowledge of theories help support professionals in diagnosing and treating causes and effects of possible dysfunctional or **atypical** development. Cognitive theory is one of the theories that professionals use.

This understanding of possible negative outcomes on children's psychological development can help professionals put in place preventative measures and strategies to be able to identify and treat symptoms and causes earlier. For example, Piaget's staged approach towards cognitive development has been used to support professionals, particularly educationalists, as a diagnostic tool in identifying possible atypical development in children. Both Piaget's and Vygotsky's theories are used by educationalists in curriculum practice and elements of both theories have been incorporated in curriculum frameworks in the UK (the Early Years Foundation Stage (EYFS)). Professionals have used these curriculum frameworks as a guide to track children's progress and identify when development deviates from the norm. For example, Piaget's stages of cognitive development are used to monitor children's developmental progress through school and can be used as a tool to identify developmental delay. Vygotsky and Bruner's approach towards ZPD and scaffolding is used to support teachers in developing activities that guide or scaffold children's learning to help them become independent learners.

An understanding of the effects of factors on the unborn child help health workers and midwives in educating pregnant mothers of the dangers of drinking, smoking, substance abuse and exposure to certain toxins. These preventative measures ensure children's positive prenatal growth.

Knowledge of the causes and effects on children on a parent suffering from PTSD support psychologists and other multi-agency professionals in compiling strategies and support for children and families. These strategies include: counselling for parents and children, and extra educational support for children.

Studies of feral children have helped professionals gain insight into how normative development of areas, such as language and communication, are affected by deprivation.

▶ The case of Genie, kept in extreme isolation during the critical period for language acquisition, provided professionals insight into how language develops. The fact that Genie was later able to develop some language provides insight for professionals into how children can and will learn language at different stages of development.

▶ The case of Oxana Malaya, who developed animal behaviours after being forced to live with a pack of dogs, also provides insight into language acquisition for professionals. As Oxana was able to 're-acquire' some language, this has implications for how language is developed and retained. Her behaviour with the dogs, by mimicking their 'language' was also important information for professionals.

All these cases link back to the importance of early attachments and critical periods, not only for attachments with key individuals but also for learning language. It also demonstrates and helps to distinguish between whether the acquisition of language is an innate capacity or something that is learned through imitating others.

The insights gained from these cases are valuable for teachers and educationalists and inform their day-to-day practice delivering curriculum activities that support language and communication and encouraging language and communication in social situations. Speech therapists use this knowledge to support children whose speech is delayed or children who may have experienced forms of deprivation who choose not to speak.

Key term

Atypical – a term used where a child does not follow the normal course of development or milestones.

The effect of attachments, attachment styles and parenting within family systems can have a profound effect on children's developmental outcomes.

A mother with **postpartum depression** may not be able to form essential bonds with their baby which could extend over long periods.

A single parent with low education, in poverty, or with addiction may not provide adequate care and support for a child.

In both of the situations above, the parent may experience difficulty creating bonds with their child. The child may form insecure or disorganised attachments, experience delayed language and cognitive development and behavioural problems as well as other mental health conditions including depression.

Cases such as Liam Fee and Victoria Climbié provide professionals with the understanding of the effects of maltreatment on children, where parents fail to form positive supportive attachments with their children. Professionals including health workers, social workers, psychologists and the police work together using a multi-agency approach, observing, diagnosing and treating symptoms and causes. From this they are able to put in place interventions.

Table 5.6 provides further examples of where theories and case studies link together illustrating how professionals use this information to develop ideas on diagnosing and treating children.

▶ **Table 5.6:** The influence of cases on professionals' understanding of child development

Theory	Theorist	Condition	Case studies	How this influences professionals' approaches (what has been learned and applied)
Language and communication	Chomsky Bruner Vygotsky Skinner	Lack of speech	Genie	There are many theories that can be used to understand Genie's where extreme isolation had a profound effect on her ability to learn language. Vygotsky emphasised the importance of social interactions in developing language and communication skills. Skinner believed that children learn language from their environment and through positive reinforcement provided by their parent when they vocalise which encourages the child to speak more Professionals use this knowledge to understand causes for cases and apply these in different situations, for example a speech therapist may use understanding to develop therapies for a child whose speech is delayed. Professionals applying theory/case studies to practice: Teachers, SENCOs, speech therapists, psychologists.
Psychopathological development	Bowlby Ainsworth	Attachment problems	Czech twins	This case is useful to help professionals understand the importance of the formation of bonds with parents/carers during the 'critical period' and demonstrates that as the children lived their first 18 months in a supportive environment, the effects of the abuse they received could be reversed as they grew to lead healthy adult lives Professionals applying theory/case studies to practice: Nursery practitioners, health workers, GPs, behaviour therapists, psychiatrists.

Psychical and psychological development	Lord Laming	Abuse	Victoria Climbié Liam Fee	This case and the subsequent report by Lord Laming support professionals in developing a multi professional workforce that provides services to children and families to support healthy physical and psychological development. The report highlighted the importance of professionals working together to be able to more readily respond to concerns over the safety of children.
				Legislation (the Children's Act 2004) was created as a result of the report placing a duty on all professionals or authorities working with children and young people to cooperate and work together with other agencies to promote children's wellbeing. Professionals in schools, hospitals, social care services and others use this legislation to guide best practice to ensure this type of tragic event does not reoccur.
				Professionals applying theory/case studies to practice: Teachers, SENCOs, social workers, Drs, psychologists
Social development	Bowlby Ainsworth	Attachment problems	Romanian orphans	In this case children in orphanages received poor quality care and were not able to form attachments. The case illustrated the importance for forming attachments within the first six months of life.
				Findings of this study help professionals develop strategies to encourage secure bonds with caregivers and develop positive friendship orientations.
				Professionals applying theory/case studies to practice: Teachers, SENCOs, foster and social care services, behaviour therapists
Twin Studies	Brendgen et al	Schizophrenia	MZ and DZ twins	Brendgen et al's study is just one example of how valuable the study of twins can be in helping professionals understand whether behaviours and personalities are genetic (nurture) or the environment (nature). In this study a link was found between physical aggression and genes (nature) and a weaker link between social aggression to genes (nurture). This knowledge helps professionals to develop strategies for intervention, support for children, especially in foster care situations.
				Professionals applying theory/case studies to practice. Psychiatrists, psychologists, behaviour therapists

Theory into practice

Look back at the case of Victor of Aveyron. The table provides an example of Genie and language and communication. Which other theory or theories could be linked to this case study? How would professionals use this knowledge when diagnosing and treating children.

Table 5.7 identifies some of the professionals involved in promoting children's healthy development, their role in supporting children's psychological development and some of the theories they may draw from to support them in diagnosing and treating psychological conditions.

Job role	What they do	Areas of focus
Educational psychologist	Often qualified teachers, they advise on children and young people's educational needs. They assess learning and emotional needs and support therapeutic and behaviour management programmes.	Cognition, social and emotional development, supporting children in reaching normative milestones
Psychotherapist	They work with individuals who have mental difficulties such as depression, phobias, stress, anxiety, physical and psychological problems. It is often known as a 'talk therapy' as this is an important part of treatment. They help individuals cope with feelings and change their behaviours.	Mental health
Psychoanalyst	Founded on the work of Sigmund Freud, they work with people who suffer from a range of emotional problems, similar to those of the psychotherapist. They explore the unconscious factors that affect behaviour.	Mental health
Speech therapist	They work in hospitals and the community with children and adults. They support speech, language and swallowing difficulties by developing programmes for developing speech and communication skills.	Language and communication
Health visitors	They are qualified and registered nurses or midwives. They work in education and health care and support health education. They also support the health and wellbeing of families. They can assess the health needs of individuals, families and wider communities and provide advice and support on good health and ways to prevent illness. They may also work with 'at risk' people (homeless, addicts, travellers) or deprived children.	Physical and mental health and wellbeing
School nurse	They provide preventative and screening services for children in schools. They assess health needs and provide education and advice, immunisation, and deal with safeguarding. They can also support children with healthy eating as well as identifying areas of concern in cognitive and physical health.	Physical and mental health and wellbeing
General practitioner (GP)	They provide general health care and physical examinations for conditions and injuries. They refer patients to specialist consultants and surgeons for more specialised conditions.	Physical and mental health and wellbeing
Midwives	Midwives provide support and advice to mothers throughout pregnancy, at childbirth and after birth.	Physical and mental health and wellbeing of mothers during pregnancy and in first few months of life

---

Theory into practice

Look at one of the professional roles above or find another that interests you. Explain their role and the type of work they do. What theories or case studies do you feel would be useful for them to understand when supporting children in their role?

Multidisciplinary workforce

Earlier in the unit you identified a number of professionals involved in diagnosing and treating children's atypical development. In the UK, The Children Act 2004 saw the introduction of an integrated approach to working with children's services and its aim was to make joint working between agencies easier, to ensure the protection of children. An integrated approach enables professionals to:

▶ support improvements in professionals' relationships with children and families
▶ quickly respond to situations
▶ provide focused expertise in specific areas, for example child psychologists and speech therapists
▶ share information in order to find the most effective support

---

- ensure the needs of the child are central to all decisions
- define roles and professional boundaries
- understand the role of other agencies
- ensure a joined-up approach to meeting children's individual needs
- support school planning and review of curriculum practice
- ensure enhanced and improved outcomes for children and young people
- improve understanding and raise awareness of issues and professional practice
- promote trust and facilitates joint planning.

There are many roles within a multidisciplinary workforce, and Table 5.8 outlines some of these.

▶ **Table 5.8:** Components of a multidisciplinary workforce

Educationalists: childcare workers, teachers, SENCOs, teaching assistants	Through monitoring children's developmental activities, they are able to identify when developmental norms are not being achieved and where there may be causes for concern, for example safeguarding. They report concerns to social services or police, or other services such as speech therapists, psychologists or GPs.
Police	Involvement occurs where there is a suspected issue such as abuse of a child by parents or others. They investigate allegations or concerns and take protective measures such as removing vulnerable children from their home or other abusive situations. They work with the other agencies and advise on matters of law and policy.
Social services: social workers, social support staff	They have a statutory obligation to safeguard and promote the welfare of vulnerable children and adults. Social workers work with educationalists, professionals (such as psychologists) and families to provide support and guidance. They monitor the level of care provided for children and can be responsible for placing children into care and supporting them with foster carers or adoption services.

It is useful to consider some of the challenges a multidisciplinary workforce may experience, as these may affect their ability to meet children's individual needs.

- **Time:** With a rising number of children and young people experiencing educational and psychological difficulties, many services are becoming overwhelmed and are unable to give the right kind of support for prolonged periods. An example of this is the increased use of online counselling, due to the lack of available time to always provide face-to-face support.
- **Lack of clarity:** There may be instances where communications are misinterpreted or overlooked, and this may have a significant impact on a child's diagnosis or treatment.
- **Use of language:** Different professionals use different terminology. Some use acronyms or technical language and it is important to ensure that the terminology used is clear to members of other agencies.
- **Crossing boundaries:** Some may assume knowledge in one area and give advice which cannot be relied upon, which again can have serious consequences on diagnosis or ongoing treatment.

Nathan and Jayden are three-year-old twins. They have recently moved to a new area and have joined a new pre-school setting.

The boys had a turbulent first three years of life as their mother and father were alcoholics. Their father was prone to violent outbursts that sometimes involved hitting his wife and shouting at the children. They separated when the twins were a year old and their mother took them to live with their grandparents, who live in a rural village where there are few neighbours making it difficult for the boys to socialise with other children. Both parents spent time in rehabilitation, but the father has since disappeared. Their mother has formed a strong relationship with another man who has supported her and the children over this period and they now have a stable relationship in their new home.

Practitioners have conducted observations of the children in their first week of pre-school and identified that they are not meeting developmental norms in the following areas.

Cognitive ability: They appear around eight months behind their peers. They have difficulty understanding the difference between past and future and do not use their imagination.

Language: They have difficulty talking in sentences and only have a limited vocabulary.

Social skills: They lack confidence and often play alone with each other. They become distressed if they are apart.

Consider the impact on the children where they might have observed aggressive behaviour between their parents and how this might affect their mental health and development.

Consider the role of the professionals in school and other professionals who might be involved in supporting and promoting the boys' mental health and wellbeing.

Produce a report that evaluates the theories that could be used to understand Nathan's and Jayden's current developmental progress and the possible ways these theories could be used to support professionals in identifying approaches to promote their development.

You should consider the possible long-term psychological impact on the boys' mental health caused by their past experiences and explain how theories can help understand how to apply different strategies and support.

Plan
- What is the task? What am I being asked to do?
- How confident do I feel in my own abilities to complete this task? Are there any areas I think I may struggle with?

Do
- I know what it is I'm doing and what I want to achieve.
- I can identify when I've gone wrong and adjust my thinking/approach to get myself back on course.

Review
- I can explain what the task was and how I approached the task.
- I can explain how I would approach the hard elements differently next time (i.e. what I would do differently)
- I can evaluate the different ways professionals use theories to help them treat aspects of dysfunctional psychopathy in children.

Further reading and resources

Herbert, M. (2003) *Typical and Atypical Development: From Conception to Adolescence* Oxon: BPS Blackwell

Smith, P.K., Cowie, H., Blades, M. (2015) *Understanding Children's Development (Basic Psychology)* (6th ed.), West Sussex: J Wiley

Thompson, M., Hooper, C., Laver-Bradbury, C., Gale, C. (2012) *Child and Adolescent Mental Health Theory and Practice* (2nd ed.), FL: Taylor & Francis

NSPCC: https://www.nspcc.org.uk/

Childline: https://www.childline.org.uk/

UK Government: https://www.nidirect.gov.uk/

THINK ▶FUTURE

Richard Ng

Foster care worker

I have been working in a foster care agency for a few years. Foster carers have a tough job, supporting children who have often had some pretty horrific experiences with their biological parents. It is very hard not to get emotionally involved with cases, but you have to try to do the best you can to make the children's lives better if even for a short while.

When I completed a psychology course, I particularly enjoyed the nature-nurture debate. I remember having great discussions about whether you learn behaviours, or whether they are innate. After I left school I went to work with the local council in their children's services department. I then completed a degree in social work which meant I could work in different settings.

My job is really interesting as I get lots of opportunities to meet people. I meet clients and assess their needs, often in their own homes. I communicate with other organisations to make sure that provision is in place and I work with the families to make their homes ready for children coming to them. Of course, there are some aspects which are not so great like the case conferences which can be quite upsetting. But it means that all the teams are working together to do the best for the children in our care. Just knowing that I make a positive difference to children's lives is reward enough for me.

I am keen to progress in my career and have taken a Masters degree in Psychology and I intend to then take a PhD in Clinical Psychology. This will help me work in more senior roles but I am particularly interested in researching foster care and the children who need those services.

Focusing on your skills

Promoting children's psychological development

- Understanding the way that children develop and learn is fundamental. Having the knowledge and skills to be able to identify patterns of growth and development is core to being able to apply these skills in practical situations.

- Before applying theory to practice, make sure you have a clear idea of the fundamental principles provided in this unit.

- Always keep an open mind and question everything. Never apply an assumption to one thing just because a theory says so.

Introduction to Psychopathology

6

Getting to know your unit

Mental disorders can have significant impact on the life of the individual with the condition, and those around them. Psychopathology considers the nature and cause of mental disorder. This knowledge helps to inform how such conditions are treated. The aim is to promote recovery for the individual wherever possible.

How you will be assessed

This unit will be assessed by a series of internally assessed tasks set by your tutor. Throughout this unit you will find assessment activities that will help you work towards your assessment. Completing these activities will not mean that you have achieved a particular grade, but you will have carried out useful research or preparation that will be relevant when it comes to your final assignment.

In order for you to achieve the tasks in your assignment, it is important to check that you have met all of the Pass grading criteria. You can do this as you work your way through the assignment.

If you are hoping to gain a Merit or Distinction, you should also make sure that you present the information in your assignment in the style that is required by the relevant assessment criterion. For example, Merit criteria require you to analyse and discuss, and Distinction criteria require you to assess and evaluate.

The assignment set by your tutor will consist of a number of tasks designed to meet the criteria in the table. This is likely to consist of a written assignment but may also include activities such as:

▸ developing a poster to reflect the different causal factors of mental disorder
▸ watching documentaries that reflect the personal experiences of those with specific mental conditions
▸ drawing a flowchart to reflect the route an individual may take in getting treatment for a specific disorder.

Assessment criteria

This table shows what you must do in order to achieve a **Pass**, **Merit** or **Distinction** grade, and where you can find activities to help you.

Pass	Merit	Distinction
Learning aim **A** Understand modern and historical concepts of psychopathology in society		
A.P1 Explain ways in which psychopathology is defined. **Assessment activity 6.1**	**A.M1** Analyse the historical development of the concept of psychopathology. **Assessment activity 6.1**	**A.D1** Evaluate how the concept of psychopathology has been viewed historically. **Assessment activity 6.1**
A.P2 Explain how perceptions of psychopathology have developed over time. **Assessment activity 6.1**		
Learning aim **B** Examine causes, types and characteristics of mental disorders		
B.P3 Discuss different causal factors that may lead to mental disorders in individuals. **Assessment activity 6.2**	**B.M2** Assess causal factors that contribute to one mental disorder in relation to its associated characteristics. **Assessment activity 6.2**	**B.D2** Evaluate the impact of causal factors that contribute to one mental disorder in relation to its associated characteristics. **Assessment activity 6.2**
Learning aim **C** Explore professional approaches to the treatment of mental disorders		
C.P5 Explain appropriate treatments for one form of mental disorder. **Assessment activity 6.3**	**C.M3** Analyse the ways in which professionals can contribute to the treatment of individuals with one form of mental disorder. **Assessment activity 6.3**	**C.D3** Evaluate the importance of the role of professionals and treatments for one mental disorder. **Assessment activity 6.3**
C.P6 Discuss the role of professionals involved in diagnosing and treating one mental disorder. **Assessment activity 6.3**		

A Understand modern and historical concepts of psychopathology in society

Mental illness has always been present. The language used to describe **psychopathology** and the treatment of it, however, has changed significantly over time. There have been formal changes in how it is diagnosed, as well as changes in understanding why people develop psychopathology.

Defining psychopathology

The aim of creating definitions is to help in understanding a topic, in this case psychopathology. In having clearly defined symptoms relating to different mental disorders, there is a common language for everyone to use when discussing mental disorders.

Mental health and wellbeing

Mental health is considered to be on a spectrum, ranging from being psychologically healthy, to being psychologically unhealthy and experiencing psychological ill health or disorders.

Mental health is considered to be a state of wellbeing in which every individual can achieve their potential in life, can cope with the normal stresses of life, can work productively and fruitfully, and is able to make a contribution to the community (World Health Organization, 2014). For those with mental-health conditions, wellbeing can be achieved by promoting recovery from the condition as much as possible and helping the individual to remain focused on what they are able to achieve, despite the presence of any mental-health issues.

Behaviour that can be psychologically unhealthy can be described as abnormal behaviour, which is behaviour that is not displayed by the majority of the population. Psychopathology aims to understand and treat this abnormal behaviour, which may include hearing voices when there is no one in the room or being unable to control anxiety when faced with something you are scared of.

From the concept of mental 'health' comes the premise that anything beyond what is healthy is considered **pathological** or diseased in some way, which therefore needs to be fixed and made healthy again. To try and avoid experiencing ill health, focus needs to be on positive health promotion.

Historically, behaviour that has been considered 'out of the norm' has been pathologised as an indication of poor mental health. Using a medical approach, mental illnesses are described using the terms 'signs' and 'symptoms'.

▸ **Symptoms:** These are only visible to the individual, for example pain or visual disturbances.
▸ **Signs:** These are indicators of a problem which can be observed by others, for example **hypomania** or rapid breathing.

Individuals who experience symptoms of a mental disorder may be referred to as 'patients'.

Statistical definitions

Statistics help to determine if the presence of particular psychological symptoms is so significantly different from the general population (the 'norm') that it can be considered a psychopathology. The statistical norm is the mean (average) or modal (most frequent) example of a particular behaviour.

Deviation from norms

Many people display traits of anxiety. For one person to be diagnosed with an anxiety disorder, they would need to show significantly greater anxiety than the rest of the population. The benchmark of statistical norms helps to see how different a person may be in their presentation of signs than those around them.

Norms are often used in this way to explain psychopathology, that is those with high levels of anxiety who would benefit from anxiety management techniques. However, you also need to consider those at the other end of the anxiety spectrum (those with very low anxiety). This part of the population may have no need to have any anxiety management intervention, yet they also deviate from the norm.

Norms are used in many areas of psychopathology. When considering the presence of low intelligence, a factor within learning disabilities, the intelligence of the individual is compared to the norms of others of the same age.

Figure 6.1 identifies the normal distribution of intelligence. Those with 'average' intelligence are within the middle two sections (in orange). Those who have intelligence lower than the average (norm value) are to the left of this, and those with higher intelligence are to the right. Most people fall within the 'average' range.

Figure 6.1 shows a **normal distribution**.

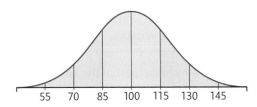

▸ **Figure 6.1:** Normal distribution of intelligence

In the figure above, the highest peak of the curve reflects level of intelligence that is most common in the general population (IQ=85-115). IQ scores on ether side of this peak reflect other levels of intelligence that are less common. The very edges of the distribution data (very low and very high intelligence) occur most infrequently.

Social and political norms

Extremes of what is statistically normal only reflects the frequency at which a behaviour happens. The labelling of what is then considered psychopathological can be affected by additional influences. Social and political norms can influence what is clinically psychopathological. Behaviour that is substantially at odds with what is considered acceptable within society is often considered to be in some way abnormal.

This may differ from what is statistically abnormal.

What is acceptable, and therefore what is abnormal, is usually specific to cultures, and specific to particular times in history. The politics of a country at the time also influences norms. In the UK, up until 1967, being a male homosexual was illegal. This resulted in homosexuals being criminalised; they were often sent to prison as a result. It also resulted in homosexuals being forced to undertake behaviour therapy to try and 'cure' them of what was considered an illness. This involved being given drug treatment, electric shocks to the head (known as electroconvulsive therapy – ECT) and aversion therapy.

Research

There have been many changes in norms over the years, both political and social, in relation to gender. Using the internet, explore some of the areas in which norms have changed for both men and women. As a starting point you may want to explore some of the gender-specific norms relating to the role of women within the family, and how they have changed over the years. Other topic areas to consider could include:

- women voting
- stereotypical toys for boys and girls
- males showing emotions, and so on.

Approaches to defining psychopathology

A number of explanations for psychopathology have been proposed over the years. When trying to understand why a person may develop, for example, schizophrenia, it may be the case that one explanation on its own is not sufficient to explain the presentation of that particular disorder. There are two main approaches used to explain psychopathology: biological (genes and neurotransmitters), and psychological (psychodynamic, behaviour and cognitions).

Biological models

The biological approach argues that there are a number of influences on mental disorder.

Link

Look back at Unit 1 for more information on the biological approach.

Genetics: Exploring psychopathology within families and within sets of twins can help to understand the likelihood that a family member may also develop a psychological disorder. This likelihood is known as the **concordance rate** which suggest that the disorder is, at least in part, genetic.

Key term

Concordance rate – the likelihood that a family member will develop the same psychological disorder as another member of their family (who shares the same genes).

Link

Look back at Units 1 and 5 to remind yourself about twin studies (which are a common theme in the study of psychology). Also look back at Unit 4 in which you read about the diathesis–stress model and its key principles.

The diathesis–stress model can be used to explain how some individuals will have an inherited, predisposed vulnerability to developing a psychological disorder if exposed to certain stressors within the environment. This is particularly relevant to conditions relating to psychosis, such as schizophrenia.

Neuroscience: This is another way that biology can be used to explain mental disorders. It focuses on brain structure and function with consideration of the influence of hormones on the brain.

Damage to the frontal lobes (the section of the brain involved with problem solving and planning) have been shown to contribute to many disorders including attention disorders, lack of motivation, poor planning and a reduction in emotional range. Any malfunctioning in this area may also contribute to aggression and impulsive behaviour.

Link

Look back at Unit 4 which covered the role of the amygdala in detail.

The amygdala (part of the limbic system) helps to process emotions. This area of the brain plays a key role in the development and control of phobias and anxieties. It has been found that people with phobias display a greater level of brain activity within the amygdala when they are exposed to their phobia. A smaller amygdala has been associated with a greater fear of spiders (Fisler et al. 2013). This suggests that a smaller amygdala may lead to vulnerabilities for phobias.

The chemicals in the brain that help the messages to be sent through the body (neurotransmitters) have been linked with a number of mental disorders, partially to psychosis and mood disorders. Table 6.1 shows some neurotransmitters and the mental disorders they have been linked to.

Table 6.1: Neurotransmitters and their related mental disorders

Neurotransmitter	Mental disorder
Low levels of serotonin	Depression and anxiety
High levels of dopamine	Psychosis and Attention Deficit Hyperactivity Disorder (ADHD)
Low levels of norepinephrine	Attention Deficit Hyperactivity Disorder (ADHD)
Low levels of gamma-aminobutyric acid (GABA)	Drug or alcohol addictions

Biological models fail to fully consider the influence of thoughts and experiences on the individual and the role such experiences may have on certain conditions.

Psychological models

These models propose that disruption or dysfunction in psychological processes (such as how a person thinks or interprets situations) can lead to the development of mental disorders. It considers symptoms of distress as often being a normal response to a difficult experience, though the development of a disorder can result from prolonged responses or faulty thinking that can both cause and then continue the feelings of distress.

Psychodynamic model: This is the unconscious feelings from early trauma that contribute to later **hysteria**. The mind attempts to protect against later distress by repressing memories that would cause upset. This means that the individual does not recall the traumatic incident, which arguably prevents the development of psychopathology. Repression is considered a **defence mechanism.**

When there is conflict between the three elements of a person's personality (id, ego and superego), the individual is vulnerable to experiencing stressors. The use of defence mechanisms once again help to prevent the development of anxiety.

Behavioural model: Psychopathology is based on learned reactions to life experiences. Dysfunctional behaviour, including psychosis or low mood is learned over time.

Those with obsessive compulsive disorder (OCD), for example, experience a brief reduction in distress when they engage in their compulsive behaviours. This then reinforces that this behaviour helps to reduce the distress (albeit for a brief period of time). This would be a form of operant learning.

The association between a traumatic event and a phobic object can result in the development of wider phobias, for example being bitten by one dog leads to a generalisation and so a fear of all dogs. This would be an example of classical conditioning as applied to psychopathology.

Cognitive model: A mental disorder is a result of 'faulty' or irrational thinking. When presented with a stimulus, it is *how* the stimulus is interpreted or viewed that results in distress, for example thinking that a spider will jump up at you, leading to a fear of the spider. Similarly, in cases of depression a person may have developed the belief that they are worthless, which leads to the development of depressive symptoms.

It is argued that these faulty thoughts not only contribute to the development of the symptoms, but also maintain the symptoms. The cognitive approach to understanding psychopathology has significantly influenced the treatment of such conditions.

A final explanation is a humanist approach. If individuals can develop psychological distress, this can be resolved through developing insight and a sense of meaning in life. The distress is the result of limited awareness, and an absence of important values.

Key terms

Hysteria- excessive or uncontrollable emotions that seem out of context for the situation. Emotions may include fear or panic.

Defence mechanism – process by which an individual unconsciously uses psychological strategies to protect themselves from anxiety. Examples may include: repressing a memory, finding a rational explanation for something you have done wrong, or denying the existence of the anxiety.

Link

Look back at Unit 1 for information about behavioural theories and their key principles.

Link

Go to page 323 for information about cognitive therapies.

Classification systems

There are two main classification systems that are used to diagnose the presence of a mental disorder. Classification systems serve as a tool for reporting and grouping conditions or factors that influence health. Their emphasis is not solely on mental health but cover a broader topic of diseases and health-related conditions.

The International Classification of Diseases (ICD) was first published in 1948 by the World Health Organization (WHO). In 1952 the American Psychiatric Association (APA) produced the first edition of the Diagnostic and Statistical Manual (DSM). Within both systems, conditions are grouped together based on common presenting symptoms, for example anxiety. These classification systems are used to diagnose various medical conditions, including mental disorders.

They provide diagnostic criteria that describe the essential features of a condition, the threshold that is considered 'beyond normal' for that condition as well as features that help to differentiate one condition from another.

Over the years there have been a number of changes made to each of these classification systems. ICD is currently on its tenth edition. The recently released ICD-11 will come into effect from 2022. The DSM was updated in 2013 and is currently on version DSM-5. Changes to classification systems reflect both growing scientific knowledge and changes to social and political norms.

Both classifications group mental health conditions into distinct areas for example schizophrenia and delusional disorders, personality disorders, and so on. There is a degree of overlap in the type of conditions covered, though there may be subtle differences in the criteria required for diagnosing a condition.

Both classification systems are trying to develop general categories within which individual behaviour and symptoms can be explained. A challenge with this approach is that there can be differences across individuals' presentation of a disorder, often due to there being a number of features for each condition. Classifications need to consider all presentations of the condition. There can also be overlap across disorders meaning that the clinician needs to consider which disorder the individual's symptoms most closely link with.

There are a number of other limitations associated with a classification system approach.

▶ **Interpretation of the definitions:** Clinicians will have to consider which classification, and therefore which diagnosis, most closely fits the symptoms. This may mean the clinician has to interpret the meaning of the conditions to consider which is most appropriate. This can lead to different diagnoses of the same symptoms from different clinicians.

▶ **Effect of labelling:** Some disorders carry a degree of **stigma** and attaching a diagnosis to someone can cause them to be viewed unsympathetically by others.

▶ **Treatment implications:** Some treatments are inappropriate for some conditions. If someone has been wrongly diagnosed and then given an inappropriate treatment, this could be potentially harmful.

▶ **Access to support:** Some support services are only available for individuals who have specific diagnoses, even though they could be useful for those with other diagnoses.

PAUSE POINT

Stigma in mental health can occur for many reasons and can come from many sources.

> Hint

Review newspaper articles to see how mental disorder has been documented in the media. What are the key labels associated with mental illness, whether in general or regarding specific conditions?

> Extend

How accurate are the labels you have identified in the media?

Design a five-minute presentation in a small group that presents ideas that may help challenge some of the stigmas you have read about. Present this to your peers.

Origins of psychopathology

Throughout history, individuals who don't necessarily follow society's norms, including being unpredictable or potentially harmful, have been labelled by others in society as 'mad' or by other such terms. The explanations for this behaviour have changed over history, as medical and scientific knowledge develops.

Early perceptions

Mental disorders can result in rapid changes in a person's personality or behaviour, or a loss of skills or engagement in activities they used to enjoy. History has seen a number of changes in what were considered to be the causes of such behaviour.

Ancient beliefs dating back to ancient Greece were heavily influenced by religion and a belief in the Greek gods. In this culture it was considered that symptoms of mental illness were the result of having wronged the gods in some way. Individuals would look to the gods to try and cure the individual. For example, they may have prayed to Asclepius, the healing god and god of medicine, in the hope of a cure.

The rod of the ancient god Asclepius is used within medical symbols in the modern world, reflecting an on-going affiliation to the history of medicine. For example, the symbol of the World Health Organization (an organisation concerned with international health) includes the rod of Asclepius in its logo.

▶ The Rod of Asclepius has been associated with healthcare practices since Ancient Greek times

Significant changes in the person's behaviour, which may occur with limited warning or build up has contributed to early beliefs that an individual was in some way 'possessed'.

In **demonology** (a view held among ancient civilisations) such possession was considered to be by 'bad spirits'. They believed that the only way to treat the presence of the bad spirits was to cleanse the individual of the spirits through specific rituals, often involving torture, in an attempt to force the spirit out of the individual's physical body. This process of getting rid of bad spirits was known as an **exorcism**.

The idea of demonology remained present within Western societies through explanations of witchcraft and possession used within the eighteenth century to explain mental illness. The idea that psychopathology is the result of an individual being possessed by a spirit is still used as an explanation of certain mental disorders, such as psychosis, in some African cultures today. Neuner et al. (2012) found a high level of reported sprit possession among Ugandan boys and young men who had been abducted and forced to work as child soldiers.

> **Key terms**
>
> **Demonology** – the study of demons and other unnatural harmful beings.
>
> **Exorcism** – the attempted removal of a supposed evil spirit from a place or person.

▶ What impact could a 'diagnosis' of spirit possession of these children have on the families left behind?

Key term

Naturalism – the belief that mental disorder is a result of natural causes.

Even when individuals have been known to have a medically diagnosed mental disorder, exorcism may still be attempted in these cultures. Tajima-Pozo et al. (2011) suggested that possession is still considered an explanation of mental illness.

Naturalism (or objectivism) maintains that concepts of health and mental disorders are mainly driven by objective natural categories of biological function and dysfunction. Biological functioning may interact with social values and norms but exists independently of them. Any malfunctioning of the individual would be considered a 'disease'. Early beliefs would therefore label an individual as diseased if they presented any symptoms that were not the social norm or atypical for most people.

Attitudes towards mental illness vary among individuals, families, ethnicities, cultures, and countries. Cultural and religious teachings often influence beliefs about the origins and nature of mental illness, and shape attitudes towards the mentally ill. What is considered psychologically healthy in one culture may be very different to the views of another. Hearing voices, a symptom of psychosis, is viewed differently by cultures. Some are very accepting and others less so.

While some Native American tribes do not stigmatise any mental illnesses, others stigmatise only some mental illnesses, and other tribes stigmatise all mental illnesses. In Asia, where many cultures value conformity to the norm, mental illnesses are often stigmatised and seen as a source of shame. Some of this shame is influenced by what the culture perceives to be the reason for the mental disorder.

WonPat-Borja Yang, Link & Phelan (2012) wanted to explore how people's beliefs about mental illness may change if the mental illness has a genetic basis.

Participants were given scenarios about a person displaying symptoms of either schizophrenia or clinical depression. The ethnicity and gender of the character being described in the scenario was matched to the participant. Many participants considered mental disorder to be a result of genetics, and therefore believed mental illness was hereditary.

They found that Chinese-American participants were more likely to want to know if there was mental illness in the family when choosing a partner and requested genetic testing prior to getting married, more than European–Americans.

They also found that there was a reduction in stigma among Chinese-American participants if they believed mental illness was genetic. In European–Americans, the belief of a genetic basis for mental illness increased stigma.

When considering the views of the participant about marriage or having children with someone with a genetic mental disorder, European–Americans were more reluctant to marry or have children with someone with a mental disorder than Americans of Chinese descent. This suggested that Chinese-Americans were more accepting of mental disorder.

1 What does this study tell you about cultural variations in stigmatisation of mental illness?

2 Can you think of any reasons why these differences might exist?

3 How do you think these cultural variations might affect clinicians' diagnoses of mental disorders?

In Ghana, it is an accepted belief that spirits may speak to individuals. As such, hearing voices in this culture is viewed in a very positive way, by the individual experiencing the voices and those around them. Alternatively, Americans who have the same symptoms are more inclined to view them in a very negative way. In many Western cultures, the cultural perception of hearing voices is seen as a symptom of a mental disorder. Such different perceptions can lead to differences in the way (or even whether) the sufferer seeks help. Diagnostic classifications (discussed later in this unit) aim to be 'culture neutral' to reduce any discrepancy in diagnoses across the world.

In the early twentieth century, Sigmund Freud described religion and its rituals as a form of 'collective neuroses'. He identified similarities between religious rituals and obsessional rituals characterised within some mental disorders. He argued that guilt is created when religious rituals are not carried out, and this guilt is reduced when they are, so a self-perpetuating 'ritualaholic' cycle is set up. Religion has, however, been proved to enhance psychological wellbeing for many individuals, with prayer being considered a helpful means of addressing stress in the short term.

Despite the early views of Freud, there is no indication that high levels of guilt lead to anxiety and depression, and measures of religiosity do not predict clinical obsessions, such as that found within obsessive–compulsive disorder (Lewis 1998).

Classifications

Early classifications of mental disorder focused on the consideration of mania (over-activity) and melancholia (under-activity). Admissions to asylums in the 1800s often identified these diagnoses as the reason for the patient being admitted to the asylum. There were clearly defined definitions of these classifications and there are indications that they differed in meaning throughout the country.

Classifications were later redefined, and the two terms more closely started to resemble the type of clinical diagnoses that are recognisable today.

▶ **Mania:** This is classified as a manic episode such as that associated with bipolar affective disorder.

▶ **Melancholia:** This is depression, or a depressive episode, which may occur within other conditions, such as bipolar disorder.

It is thought that the two conditions are cyclical, meaning that melancholia follows mania and vice versa. As such, the two conditions are associated with each other. The transition from one to another can be a subtle change or a more intense shift in mental state.

Medical model

The development of medical understanding has led to the consideration that mental illness is a result of a medical problem, or a disease within the body. This approach, known as the medical model, marks a more scientific move to explaining mental disorder. There are a number of physical illnesses that can have a negative effect on the psychology or mental health of an individual, therefore demonstrating a relationship between physical and mental health.

Syphilis, for example, is a sexually transmitted infection that has physical symptoms including a rash, ulcers, high temperatures and joint pains. If left untreated, the bacterial infection can spread to the brain, at which stage the syphilis becomes known as neurosyphilis. This leads to problems with the nerve function in the body, paralysis and dementia. These are all symptoms of the brain disease **general paresis**.

General paresis is a type of neurosyphilis. Symptoms may emerge more than ten years after being infected with syphilis if the syphilis has been left untreated. Other symptoms, besides dementia-type symptoms such as memory difficulties, include:

▶ delusions, hallucinations
▶ language problems, such as saying or writing words incorrectly
▶ difficulty in problem solving, making decisions
▶ mood changes.

The condition can be treated with antibiotics, but it is not always possible to reverse any damage caused to the brain as a result of the original syphilis infection.

The relationship between the physical syphilis infection and the general paresis that can emerge suggests there might be other mental disorders that have a biological or medical explanation. This idea became known as the **somatogenic hypothesis**.

> **Key terms**
>
> **General paresis** – a problem with mental function due to damage to the brain from untreated syphilis. It is a type of neurosyphilis.
>
> **Somatogenic hypothesis** – the belief that your mental state, and more specifically mental disorder are signs and symptoms of how well the body is functioning. Mental disorder is a result of physical or biological impairments in the body.

The medical model led to the emergence of medical specialists that focused on mental illness and how to treat it. These doctors became known as psychiatrists, working in the field of psychiatry. Psychiatry is now a well-established medical profession. The aim is to treat the symptoms of mental disorder using medication that impacts on the biological functioning of the body.

The medical model offers treatment options for mental disorders, on the basis that there is a medical issue that needs to be treated and so this model treats mental disorders as they would any other disease. However, the model has a number of flaws in its approach.

1 It ignores the role of learning within psychopathology

The medical model ignores the fact that mental disorders may be influenced by the environment or through people's learning experiences within such environments. Observing others is a recognised way in which other behaviours are learned, and this can also apply to mental health symptoms.

2 It assumes the body of the patient is dysfunctional, rather than their experiences

The medical model does not consider the influence of thoughts on a person's behaviour. They may have learned to interpret situations in a particular way, for example learning to be paranoid and suspicious as a result of, perhaps, traumatic experiences. The individual is therefore simply experiencing a normal reaction to an abnormal situation.

3 It is reductionist

It only considers one explanation for mental disorder. This explanation is somewhat simplistic in that it overlooks the complexities of a human being (their thoughts, interpretations, emotions, and so on) and tries to find a single explanation for the distress or symptoms they present.

> **Key term**
>
> **Reductionist** – attempting to explain a complex situation by breaking it down into its most simple forms.

4 It assumes psychopathology is a 'problem'

The medical model assumes that something in the body is not working properly and must therefore be fixed. It ignores the idea that symptoms may be an extreme version of a normal state that is experienced by everyone. For example, everyone gets fed up at some point and may change their mind about meeting up with a friend, as they just 'aren't in the mood'. Some people may have an extreme reaction which affects their ability to interact with others and so they withdraw from any form of activity. This behaviour may gain a diagnosis of depression if it occurs frequently enough that it becomes a problem in the person's everyday life. This suggests that mental health is on a dimension (functional to less functional), rather than being a separate issue.

Considering psychopathology a 'problematic' behaviour can result in additional distress to an individual experiencing symptoms of a particular condition. The potential for them to be labelled (by themselves or others) as someone with a problem, or someone who is imperfect in some way, can affect the person's recovery and the quality of support they receive from society.

Asylum and community care models

Asylums

Psychiatric services aim to resolve the symptoms of those experiencing mental disorders. The first psychiatric service in the UK opened in 1247 in a monastic priory (The Priory of St Mary of Bethlehem) in London. In 1330 it became known as Bethlem Hospital. It treated both physical illness and insanity. This and other such hospitals were known as **asylums**.

The hospital regime was a mixture of punishment and religious devotion. The shock of corporal (physical) punishment was believed to cure some conditions, while isolation was thought to help a person 'come to their senses'.

In 1676, the first specially commissioned hospital for the insane was built, and this became the new site for Bethlem Hospital. The Victorian era saw government reform, including provision for better care and treatment of those with lunacy (Lunacy Act 1890). Individuals now had to be certified insane before admission to an asylum. Asylums became a 'last resort' for those with mental disorders.

Bethlem Hospital continued to accept voluntary patients, who were not certified insane. This led to the vast majority of patients being self-certified as requiring inpatient support. Medical officers in asylums labelled patients as either curable or incurable. A rise in the number of 'incurable' patients led to significant increases in the number of people within asylums. Other asylums started to adopt the Bethlem's voluntary admission procedure.

> **Key term**
>
> **Asylum** – a hospital that treated both physical illness and insanity.

▶ Bethlem Royal Hospital

The Mental Treatment Act 1930 triggered the start of an outpatient approach to the treatment of mental disorder, with patients only voluntarily admitted if the clinical need was too great to treat in the community. Further laws and the introduction of the National Health Service has contributed to the growth in community psychiatric services (and the eventual closure of many asylums).

Phillipe Pinel introduced humane treatment during his time in charge of a French asylum. He removed the use of physical restraints and encouraged exercise in the open air. He believed mental disorders could be caused by stress or injury. Not only did he want to encourage a positive relationship between doctor and patient, he also introduced the process of keeping detailed patient records to help with treatment.

From Pinel's work emerged an approach known as moral treatment. The focus of this approach, developed by the Quaker movement in the UK, was to develop understanding, hope and moral responsibility as a way of reducing symptoms of mental disorder. This approach placed emphasis on:

▶ humanity
▶ polite conversation
▶ self-discipline
▶ simple rewards and punishments
▶ occupational therapy.

Critics of this approach argue it does little to cure the mental disorder the patient is experiencing. Instead it provides a framework within which to interact with patients.

Increasing numbers of patients in hospitals led to a reduction in the quality of care being offered within a hospital setting. Attempts to change the routine clinical environment from that of restraint and an unrewarding environment to a more nurturing environment led to the development of therapeutic communities.

Theory into practice

Imagine you were a member of staff working in an asylum that focused on moral treatment.

Discuss in a group what activities and interactions you would want to make available to a patient with depression.

You may want to consider specific rewards and punishments that would be appropriate for the individual.

Milieu therapy is an early form of a therapeutic community; a clinical setting that is focused on psychological principles, designed to improve wellbeing, and based on psychotherapy techniques. Many of its values are shared with those of the moral treatment approach, including:

▶ productivity
▶ independence
▶ responsibility
▶ feelings of self-respect.

Milieu therapy creates a relationship of mutual respect between patients and staff, and encourages activities, either recreational or vocational. This led to a reduction in the length of admission with patients being less likely to relapse if they had undertaken this therapeutic approach (Paul & Lentz 1977).

An additional development within hospital environments was that of token economy programmes. Patients were given 'tokens' for engaging in certain behaviours within the hospital, such as social activities or washing their hair. These tokens could then be exchanged for rewards such as chocolate. This led to a greater degree of positive activity within such settings. However, token economy programmes can have ethical issues relating to patients having restricted access to niceties such as treats. It is also difficult for a patient to continue such behaviour outside of the hospital if the same rewards are no longer present. As a result, there is a greater chance of relapse on discharge from hospital.

Case study

In 1960, a female patient was admitted as an informal patient to the Devon County Mental hospital. Her general practitioner (GP) had referred her to the hospital as he said that she was confused and was refusing to eat or drink anything. He also said she kept taking her clothes off. Her records showed that she had never before needed any psychiatric treatment. She had been living in care but had started to deteriorate over the past few weeks; it was assumed that her deteriorating health was due to her advanced age.

In hospital, a doctor diagnosed 'senile psychosis' although his notes do also stress that there were no signs of senile dementia. However, on review of her notes, it seems she was only seen by a doctor twice.

Nurses notes say that the patient on admission was pleasant and easy to look after – she was clean and ate well. This was in stark conflict to the GP's description of the patient. Her medical notes only listed two barbiturates as her regular medication.

Ten days after her admission, the hospital doctor made notes about her discharge arrangements, where she was to go into the care of her daughter and should continue with her medication. On discharge, the patient seemed relieved and refused any after care. Her discharge letter said she was not showing any mental or physical symptoms other than those due to her age. Her only care recommendations were to have lots of company, light nursing care and some gentle sedation.

1 After reading the case study above, reflect on the treatment she received in the hospital. Did being in hospital help her in any way?

2 What would be the possible treatment options for an elderly lady in a similar situation in the twenty-first century? Discuss your ideas in a group.

Community care

From the 1910's general hospitals started to provide outpatient mental-health treatment, as they had for many years with physical illnesses. There has also been an increase in other community-based services for people with mental illnesses, such as supported housing, day services and the availability of community mental-health nurses. This approach has become known as community care.

Christopher Clunis was a paranoid schizophrenic who went on to murder Jonathan Zito in 1992 at a tube station in London. An enquiry suggested that there was a failure in the coordination of his community care, as there was no single contact person overseeing his involvement with community services to ensure that he received all the support he required. Fortunately this is a rare situation, though a serious one if it occurs.

To avoid a similar occurrence, community care is now coordinated via a Care Programme Approach. This approach ensures that key issues of clinical need are not overlooked by the various agencies typically involved in an individual's care. If an individual moves geographical areas, the person coordinating the care (Care Coordinator) will speak to the equivalent person in the new area. This aims to prevent patients being overlooked within the system, while encouraging the patient to remain as independent as possible.

Link

Look back at Unit 4, page 223, to remind yourself about token economy programmes, as applied in prison settings.

Think about how the inpatient care of those with mental disorder has changed over the years. Look at the YouTube series 'Bedlam Mental Health Inpatient UK Documentary 2013'.

    Hint   Modern psychiatric hospitals are very different to the original asylums. What are some of the key changes that have occurred within this time?

    Extend   Did the programme confirm or deny your expectations of an inpatient setting? How does this differ from that described within the original Bethlem hospital and other asylums?

Assessment activity 6.2

6A.P1 6A.M1 6A.D1 6A.P2

A mental health nurse is asked to give a presentation to the student nurses to help them understand the role of mental-health nursing in the modern NHS.

The nurse is keen for them to understand the differences that have taken place over time, in particular the change in views on psychopathology.

Develop a timeline to reflect the various significant changes in history regarding your understanding of mental disorder.

Within this you should include consideration of how mental disorder is currently, and was previously, defined and how models of mental disorder have progressed with advances in medical understanding.

Plan

- What is the task? What am I being asked to do?
- How confident do I feel in my ability to perform this task?
- What areas might I struggle with?

Do

- I know what I am doing and my aims.
- I know where I have gone wrong and have adjusted my approach to get myself back on task.

Review

- I can explain the task and how I approached it.
- I can explain how I might do it differently next time.

Examine causes, types and characteristics of mental disorders

Understanding the reasons why mental disorders develop helps in thinking about suitable treatment options for patients. This understanding can also provide guidance on how to prevent the development of some conditions. Using a clear diagnostic system provides an insight into the characteristics of each condition and an understanding of what clinical input might be appropriate.

Causal factors associated with mental disorders

Over time there have been numerous factors identified as possible **causal factors** for different mental health conditions. For many conditions there is more than one possible causal factor.

Prenatal factors

When a baby is in the womb, prior to birth, it receives nutrients solely from the mother. The blood exchange between the mother and the baby means that the fetus (unborn child) is vulnerable to any negative influences. If the mother's diet and lifestyle is not conducive to a healthy pregnancy, then this will affect the baby. This can have an effect on the development of the fetus, including brain development.

Factors than can affect the fetus include:
- alcohol use
- substance use
- smoking
- poor diet
- maternal stress.

If the mother has any form of addiction, such as taking illegal drugs or extensive alcohol use, or is taking any prescribed medication that has addictive properties, it is possible for the child to be born with an addiction itself. As a result the baby will be required to withdraw from the substance in the days following birth. Babies born with addiction are at risk for long-term health problems, ranging from birth defects to mental or emotional problems in adulthood. A child born to a mother addicted to alcohol has the potential to have fetal alcohol syndrome. Symptoms can include learning difficulties, mood disorder and coordination problems which last throughout the life of the child.

Some disorders are thought to be hereditary, in that they are passed down via genes through generations. Conditions such as autism, attention deficit hyperactivity disorder (ADHD), bipolar disorder, major depression and schizophrenia appear to be inherited more frequently than other conditions, suggesting some hereditary links.

Schizophrenia, in particular, is a condition that appears vulnerable to maternal stressors, including mothers experiencing bereavements while pregnant. There is a correlation between maternal depression during pregnancy and the baby developing depression in later life. Prenatal maternal anxiety contributes to anxiety and greater stress responses in the child from adolescence.

Some conditions are influenced by the environment the mother is exposed to and others appear to have a genetic basis. This offers alternative viewpoints of the nature–nurture debate.

> **Key term**
>
> **Causal factor** – a factor that is believed to lead to the development of a mental disorder.

> **Link**
>
> Look back at Unit 5, page 263 for more information on the effect of prenatal factors on child development.

- Nature argues that behaviour, including mental disorder, is inherited.
- Nurture argues that behaviour is influenced by external factors after conception, for example the product of exposure, experience and learning on an individual.

Biology and health factors

An individual's physical health can contribute to psychological health concerns. Some individuals appear to have a greater vulnerability to developing mental health issues due to the presence of other, pre-existing conditions. Much of the emphasis has been on the development of depression, and to a smaller degree, anxiety.

Long-term medical conditions are those which can be managed, but often not cured. The long-term nature of the condition often requires significant adaptations to the individual's lifestyle and activity levels. Individuals with conditions such as diabetes or cardiovascular disease commonly experience mental-health problems such as depression and anxiety, or dementia in the case of older people. They are two to three times more likely to experience mental-health issues, such as depression, than people without these conditions. For those with chronic obstructive pulmonary disease (COPD), the prevalence of a panic disorder is 10 times that of the general population (Livermore et al. 2010).

As a result of these **comorbid** problems, a person's long-term condition and the quality of life they experience can both deteriorate.

> **Key term**
>
> **Comorbid** – when an individual has more than one condition, such as anxiety and diabetes.

Mental-health conditions can contribute to physical health problems, as well as physical health problems contributing to mental-health worries. For example, stress suppresses the body's immune system, reduces resistance to disease and might increase the risk of coronary heart disease (Stewart-Brown 1998). This introduces a degree of uncertainty as to the causal relationship between physical and mental health. Some physical impairments may be the result of side effects from medications such as anti-psychotics (for example tremors).

Physical disabilities, such as multiple sclerosis, are correlated (statistically linked) with high levels of depression, and higher rates of suicide (Sadovnick et al. 1996). Disabilities caused by accidents or trauma can lead to the development of specific mental disorders such as **Post-Traumatic Stress Disorder (PTSD)**.

> **Discussion**
>
> Choose one physical condition, for example multiple sclerosis, diabetes, etc. and use the internet to explore some of the symptoms of the condition you have chosen. Think about the challenges someone with this condition may face.
>
> In a group, reflect on the effect of this condition on mental health and discuss why you think a person with the condition you chose may be more susceptible to mental-health disorders.

> **Key term**
>
> **Post-Traumatic Stress Disorder (PTSD)** – an anxiety disorder caused by stressful, fearful or life-changing events. It is characterised by specific nightmares relating to the stressor, flashbacks, emotional numbing and a heightened awareness (hyper-vigilance) to potential threats.

> **Link**
>
> Look back at Unit 5, page 273, for more information on how PTSD can affect development and learning.

Given the significant adjustment usually required to come to terms with events of this type that have led to, for example a loss of limbs, wheelchair use, and so on, physical disabilities can contribute to the development of depression. There is a high prevalence of mental-health conditions among war veterans who have suffered serious physical injury in combat. This is often a comorbidity of conditions such as PTSD and depression.

Illnesses that lead to pain, either in the short or long term, have a relationship with depression. They may also lead to individuals overusing medication or seeking other substances in an attempt at pain management. This then leads to further issues with addiction. Chronic pain can also lead to a form of somatisation disorder (a psychological condition where the individual presents with various vague physical ailments). A challenge to medical professionals is that pain is also a symptom of somatisation disorder. There is a diagnostic confusion as to whether pain is a symptom of a physical illness or is indicative of an underlying psychological concern.

Individuals with learning difficulties may take longer to learn new skills and require additional support with complicated information and unfamiliar tasks. They are more prone to developing mental illness than those without learning disabilities. The reason for this is unclear. Biological approaches argue that the individual may be biologically more vulnerable to developing mental illness. Other explanations suggest that social and environmental experiences affect people with learning difficulties. It is possible they may be subjected to heightened stressors, and a difficulty in establishing relationships may lead to increased isolation. This can lead to anxiety and low mood.

Family systems factor

The learning approach suggests that individuals are influenced by their experiences. A chaotic home life and poor parenting can lead to neuroses that are characterised by anxiety.

Attachment theory states that interactions with inconsistent, unreliable, or insensitive attachment figures (i.e. parents) interfere with the development of a secure, stable mental foundation. This reduces resilience in coping with stressful life events, making distress and anxiety at times of crisis more likely. This means that people with insecure attachments may be more vulnerable to mental disorders, and insecure attachments may contribute to the development of personality disorders.

Lots of conflict between a parent and a child can contribute to childhood anxiety, depression, aggression and low self-esteem. Positive parenting approaches, such as parental support (for example educational activities) can result in a reduced presence of childhood depression (Smowkowski et al. 2004). This suggests parental support may help to protect the child from developing mood disorders in their adolescence.

The parenting style an individual is exposed to within their developmental years correlates with future adolescent mental health. An authoritative parenting style is one that has high expectations of the child yet is also highly responsive to the needs of the child. It encourages the child to have a degree of independence, with support available when needed. The parent nurtures the skills and emotional needs of the child, with sensitivity. This parenting style has fewer negative psychological outcomes for the child than for other parenting styles.

Other parenting styles include:

▶ **authoritarian:** high expectations; low level of responsivity to the needs of the child; high levels of restriction on the child
▶ **permissive**: few demands made on the child; high level of responsivity to the needs of the child; minimal use of punishment
▶ **uninvolved:** few demands made on the child; low level of responsivity to the needs of the child; lack of involvement with the child.

> **Link**
>
> Look back at Unit 5, page 239, for more information on child-rearing practices.

Abuse, or other distressing environmental exposure, whether it is in the family home or another caregiver situation can have a significant impact on the attachment an individual has with those around them, thereby exposing the same vulnerabilities to further distress.

Experiencing of, or witnessing abuse, can specifically result in PTSD, in much the same way as war veterans develop it following combat situations. There is also a relationship between abuse and other anxiety disorders, such as OCD. It is hypothesised that this can be in part due to an abuse survivor trying to gain control in, or following, an abusive situation in which control may have been taken away from them. The need for control in an often uncontrollable situation results in them expressing heightened levels of control over themselves, such as an excessive need to be tidy or restricting food intake, etc.

Stressful life events are associated with mood disorders in adults. The same can be found in adolescents, with a degree of similarity of stressor. All sources of personal stress relate to depression symptoms. Significant life events include:

▶ exams or academic pressures
▶ romantic breakups
▶ family disruption, including parental separation, new parental relationships, etc.
▶ change in accommodation or employment.

In addition to the above increasing depressive symptoms, they also correlate with increased alcohol use, smoking and, for some, illegal drug use.

> **Theory into practice**
>
> It is likely that you will have academic assessments soon, for this and other courses you may be studying. The link between stressful life events such as exams, and the increase of issues with mood, such as feeling low or anxious is well documented. Management of these stressors can be undertaken individually, through learning and using skills.
>
> Working on your own, complete the following task.
>
> 1 Write a list of activities that you like to do that helps you to feel better when anxious, low in mood or stressed, such as going for a walk, having a cup of tea, etc.
>
> 2 Identify what conditions you may learn in most effectively, for example a quiet environment, textbooks to hand, etc.
>
> 3 Make a plan about what you may need to do to protect your mental health and manage any possible symptoms of stress in the build-up to your exams.

▶ Even happy events can cause stress in the short term

Positive transitions, including starting a new job, buying a house or getting married can contribute to heightened stress, even if only in the short term. If these symptoms are not effectively managed, this can contribute to longer-term anxiety disorders.

Environmental factors

The environment in which a person is raised can contribute to levels of psychosocial stress. Greater exposure to such stress generates heightened emotions in the individual, which can lean them towards specific conditions. For example, an individual who regularly experiences fear due to the environment, may go on to develop anxiety symptoms.

Housing pressures, including cost of accommodation, and the potential for poor living conditions, have been found to be present among high numbers of people with sleep problems, anxiety and stress.

Areas of high **population density** are found to correlate with higher mental distress, specifically in those people who may already have limited social support (Lepore & Evans 1991). Living in very busy, compact environments can increase the likelihood that an individual will withdraw from the community, which in itself can contribute to mental-health issues such as depression. High levels of psychosis can often be found among highly populated settings.

Individuals facing housing pressures may live in high-density populations (such as inner cities) or in areas of lower socioeconomic status. As a result, they have less available money to help them to move out of the current environment.

It is not fully clear if the housing pressures are the sole cause of subsequent mental distress or act as contributing factors that increase the likelihood of mental disorders developing. Individuals with housing concerns are at increased risk of having employment difficulties, and potentially a low income, which can also negatively affect psychological wellbeing.

Such locations are often those with limited access to recreational amenities, such as leisure centres, or those that may help to increase the positive wellbeing of the residents, such as community centres. There may be limited funding available to try and resolve the absence of such facilities.

Social and political factors

As previously mentioned, socioeconomic status influences many domains of an individual's life such as employment options, income, education access, accommodation style and locations. For those of lower socioeconomic status, and therefore of lower social class, this means that there are numerous variables which they must contend with that are associated with mental-health concerns. They are therefore more likely to develop mental-health conditions at some stage of their lives than someone of a higher social class.

The provision and availability of mental-health services are often dependent on geographical location, with concerns about a '**postcode lottery**' existing for mental health support.

The current government recognises the need for increased mental-health support, which is outlined within the NHS England's 'Five Year Forward View' policy document. Within this, there is a recognition that various social factors (as well as health factors) increase vulnerability to mental conditions. Policies have been created and government funding given for the development of community services aimed to address common mental-health issues (anxiety and depression) via psychological means. This approach has led to an explosion of Improving Access to Psychological Therapies (IAPT) services throughout England.

The challenge faced by mental-health services in the current economic climate is that there is only a limited amount of money which healthcare providers are given. With this money they need to provide a range of services, but there may be insufficient funding. As a result, healthcare services often have the difficult challenge of deciding which service will receive money, and money given may not be as much as is needed to run the best possible service. This places enormous pressure on the services and has the potential for some important services being unavailable to those who need it.

Research

Using the internet, find a copy of the NHS England's 'Five Year Forward View' document. Spend some time reading the content, specifically information relating to mental health.

1 What positive influence will these proposals have on those with mental-health conditions?

2 What are the benefits of considering a long-term plan for those with mental-health issues?

Studies have found that the lower the socioeconomic status (SES) of an individual, the higher the likelihood for mental illness. SES is often associated with the amount of education a person has received, and their annual income. Greater educational exposure increases the potential for an individual to earn more money, and therefore has the potential to improve their SES.

The National Comorbidity Study in the US looked at the mental-health status of over 8000 US citizens aged 15–54 years old . Yu & Williams (1999) used data gathered by this study to look at the relationship between mental health and education and income levels. They used this information to estimate the likelihood of psychiatric disorders. Using an **odds ratio**, they investigated the likelihood of disorders such as clinical depression, mania, panic disorder, social phobia and psychosis.

The study found that the likelihood of disorders decreases as the number of years in education increases. It also found that the likelihood of disorders decreases as the individual's income increases. The results of this study suggest that more years spent in education appears to reduce the likelihood of mental disorders developing. Those with fewer than 12 years of education, for example, were found to be 2.82 times more likely than the general population to develop an anxiety disorder.

Similarly, it shows that low-income individuals are more likely to experience mental disorders; for example, the study found substance abuse disorder to be 1.92 times more frequent in this lower earning group. There is an increased likelihood (over three times more likely than the general population) for the low-earning or low-education groups to experience more than three mental disorders.

It has been suggested that the education and income status may not influence mental disorder, as suggested in this study. Instead, it is argued that the presence of a mental disorder may lead to difficulties in gaining high-income jobs, and lead to low educational achievement. The presence of the mental disorder therefore can result in a person moving into a lower SES group because of their mental disorder, not the SES group causing the mental disorder.

Key term

Odds Ratio – using statistics, it represents the odds (likelihood) that an outcome will occur, given an exposure, that is, the likelihood someone from a low SES will develop a mental-health condition.

Cultural factors

The effect of society on the individual can result in the individual either feeling as if they are a valued member of society or that they are at odds with the belief system of the culture in which they live. This culture can be the wider attitudes of their country or the specific attitudes of a local community. Discrimination due to a person's mental ill health can come from society at large, as well as from within a person's own community. The negative beliefs (or stigmas) attached to someone with a mental disorder can prevent those with mental-health conditions from seeking support.

If the individual presents with views or behaviours that differ from their culture it can lead to a sense of isolation. This in turn can develop into a reluctance to interact with others for fear of recrimination or judgement, or a social phobia. Some groups within a community may perceive themselves to be more different from others and can be considered more vulnerable to the negative effects of self-perception or bias.

Cultural and religious teachings often influence beliefs about the origins and nature of mental illness, and shape attitudes towards the mentally ill. Abdullah & Brown (2011) highlight the wide range of cultural beliefs surrounding mental health. For instance, while some Native American tribes do not stigmatise mental illness, others stigmatise only some mental illnesses, and other tribes stigmatise all mental illnesses. In Asia, where many cultures value conformity to society's norms and place value on emotional self-control, mental illnesses are often seen as a source of shame.

As discussed earlier in this unit, cultural beliefs can influence whether an individual's out-of-the-norm behaviour is considered the result of a demonic possession or a mental illness, for example. What a culture believes to be the basis for the mental illness can also contribute to the seeking of help for the disorder, and whether there is the potential for the family as a whole to be viewed negatively as a result of mental illness.

The Vietnamese, who believe in Karma, consider mental illness as a form of punishment for the sufferers who may have sinned in their previous life. According to Buddhist belief, a person's suffering may be a result of their previous misdeeds, or those of their family. Family members of individuals with mental illnesses may therefore feel reluctant to disclose or even admit that their relatives have a mental illness. Even family members who have a greater understanding of mental illness may feel reluctant to seek help. This can leave the family isolated, avoiding contact with friends, relatives and medical professionals.

Family plays a fundamental role in determining whether Arabic clients will utilise mental-health services. Traditionally, in Arab culture, an individual's behaviour is an indication of the degree to which the entire family upholds social values, norms and expectations. Social reputation is of significant value in Arabic culture and enormous efforts are made to avoid any shame that may negatively influence the family reputation. Families can act as a protective shield against stress but can also be a source of stress if an individual deviates from their collective values.

▶ Society's norms have a strong impact on how mental disorders are viewed, even within a family

Case study

Becker et al. (2002) looked at the effect of TV being introduced onto the island of Fiji on adolescents living on the island. Specifically, they were focused on investigating attitudes and behaviours of adolescent girls towards food after TV was introduced.

Prior to this, women who were larger in build were seen culturally to be stronger, with girls therefore tending to be larger.

Procedure: In 1995, within a few weeks of TV being introduced to Fiji, 63 girls aged between 16 and 18, were given a questionnaire that assessed their eating attitudes. They were also physically weighed. They were then interviewed so they could explain their comments from the questionnaire. Three years later the same data was collected from a group of 65 girls (aged 15-18) from the same island.

Findings: There was no difference in the weight of the two groups. The 1998 group displayed significantly higher attitudes that supported dieting and self-induced vomiting than the 1995 sample. There had been no reported self-induced vomiting to control weight in 1995, though by 1998, 11.3 per cent of the sample had used this method. Those living in a house with a TV set were three times more likely to give responses in the questionnaire that suggested they had distorted views about eating. The physical weight of the individual did not influence if they would engage in self-induced vomiting. Instead it appeared that perceptions about their weight were a critical factor. 83 per cent of the 1998 sample believed that the TV had influenced their views on their body weight.

Conclusion: The introduction of TV to Fiji demonstrated a negative effect on disordered eating attitudes and behaviour on a community that had been previously absent of eating disorders.

1   What does this study tell you about the impact of causal factors on mental disorders?

2   What impact, if any, do you think this study may have had on the people of Fiji?

While TV is potentially one of many social factors contributing to the attitudes and behaviours noted within the Fiji study, the nature of the introduction to TV provides a unique opportunity to assess its influence.

The two groups within this study contained different girls, and it is therefore possible, that the difference in results is due to pre-existing beliefs rather than the effect of the TV itself.

Expectations are placed on individuals as a result of their gender. These are known as societal **norms**. Men have culturally been expected to be strong in character, serving in the role as a protector for women and children. Societal expectations have often been critical of men who display their emotions, with this being interpreted as a sign of weakness.

There are significant differences between men and women in relation to mental health, and particularly accessing treatment for mental-health concerns. This suggests that there are possible cultural barriers, relating to how individuals expect men to behave, or the expectations men have on themselves as a result, that contributes to the differing statistics between genders.

- Three out of four suicides are by men, with suicide being the biggest cause of male death under the age of 35.
- They are three times more likely to become alcohol dependent.
- Only 36 per cent of the referrals to community psychological services known as IAPT are for men.

Men tend to wait longer before seeking medical help for mental-health conditions than they would for physical health concerns, and in comparison to women. There is therefore the potential for men to be under diagnosed within mental-health statistics, therefore delaying the treatment they may benefit from.

Key term

Norms – social expectations that guide behaviour.

High levels of distress among the transgender population contributes to significantly higher levels of anxiety and depression in this population than is found in the general population. This primarily arises in response to the discrimination (actual or perceived), stigma, lack of acceptance, and hostility they may face within the community they live.

Individuals from minority ethnic groups are over-represented in a number of areas relating to mental health (Mental Health Foundation 2018). They are:

▶ more likely to be diagnosed with mental-health problems
▶ more likely to be diagnosed and admitted to hospital
▶ more likely to experience a poor outcome from treatment
▶ more likely to disengage from mainstream mental-health services, leading to social exclusion and a deterioration in their mental health.

There may be reluctance among minority groups to engage in mainstream mental-health services, and as such there are concerns that mental health within this population is under-reported.

There are two distinct forms of discrimination that can be experienced by minority ethnic people with mental health difficulties: racial discrimination and discrimination because of mental ill health. This adds additional barriers for them to overcome, which further serves to isolate them.

❚❚ PAUSE POINT
There are many different causes of mental disorder. Different causes may contribute to the development of different mental disorders.

Hint
Recall as many causal factors associated with mental disorders as you can, thinking of biological, social and environmental factors.

Extend
Review newspaper and media articles relating to mental health. Which of the causal factors identified are more commonly represented within the media?

Types and characteristics of mental disorders

There are many different types of mental disorders, and within these there is a lot of variation in the level of mental distress people suffer and the severity of their conditions. Disorders related to people hurting themselves and personality disorders are sometimes grouped into the wider umbrella term of 'mental disorder'.

Personality disorders

Personality reflects the way that a person thinks and interprets the world around them. Personality is the individual differences between people about how they feel and behave. A personality disorder is related to personality traits that may be over-rigid or extreme. A formal diagnosis of a personality disorder may be given if the following applies to the person.

▶ It presents with difficulties in several areas of functioning, for example affectivity, arousal, impulse control, ways of perceiving and thinking, and style of relating to others.
▶ The abnormal behaviour pattern is enduring of long standing, and not limited to, episodes of mental illness.
▶ It causes difficulties in a broad range of personal and social situations.
▶ It appeared during childhood or adolescence and continues into adulthood.
▶ The disorder leads to considerable personal distress.
▶ There is a presence of significant problems in occupational and social performance.

Using the ICD-10 classification system, there are nine different personality disorders. These include: paranoid, emotionally unstable (including impulsive type) and anxious avoidant types.

Paranoid personality disorder

The following features are characteristic of this disorder.
- Being sensitive to setbacks and a tendency to bear grudges.
- Viewing interactions from others as having suspicious motives.
- Suspecting infidelity in relationships without evidence.
- Found in between 1 and 4 per cent of the general population (Lee, 2017), and more common in men.

Emotionally unstable personality disorder (EUPD)

This disorder shows a tendency to act impulsively without considering the consequences; the person's emotions are often unstable. The ability to plan ahead may be minimal, and outbursts of intense anger may often lead to violence or extreme behaviour. There are two types of EUPD: both share elements of impulsiveness and lack of self-control.

1 EUPD (Impulsive type):
- Emotional instability and lack of impulse control.
- Outbursts of violence or threatening behaviour are common, often when criticised by others.

2 EUPD (Borderline type):
- Emotional instability is present.
- Person's own self-image, aims, and internal preferences are often unclear or disturbed.
- Often chronic feelings of emptiness.
- Tendency to have intense and unstable relationships that lead to repeated emotional crises and a fear of abandonment.
- Suicidal threats or self-harm behaviours.
- Found in one per cent of the general population, and three times more likely in women than men.

Anxious (avoidant) personality disorder

The following features are characteristic of this disorder.
- Constant and unavoidable feelings of tension and apprehension.
- Person believes they are socially unskilled, unappealing or inferior to others; they have a strong fixation on being criticised or rejected in social situations; they are unwilling to become involved with people unless certain of being liked.
- Restricts lifestyle because of the need to have physical security; avoidance of social or occupational activities that involve significant contact with others because of fear of criticism, disapproval, or rejection.
- Less than one per cent of the general population have this personality disorder.

Self-injury and suicide

Self-injury, often described as self-harm, happens when someone hurts themselves deliberately. It does not include when a person is hurt in an accident, for example someone cutting themselves with a knife while trying to cut a loaf of bread. Self-injury can involve many different methods, including cutting, burning, swallowing things or head banging. It can also include reckless behaviour such as binge drinking or drug use.

Self-harm usually happens when the person is in a state of high emotion or distress.

Some people plan it in advance; for others, it may happen on the spur of the moment. Some people self-harm only once or twice, but others do it regularly and can find it hard to stop.

The UK has some of the highest rates of self-harm among European countries. It is estimated that one in every 250 people self-harm, though it is possible that there are more who do so but do not tell anyone about it. There is a higher likelihood of self-harm among those with emotionally unstable personality disorders (borderline type).

There is often a cycle that occurs when an individual self-harms. The distress experienced is reduced by the self-harm, but there is temporary respite as a result of the self-harm. Feelings of regret for engaging in self-harm only serves to increase the overall sense of the distress. This cycle is demonstrated in Figure 6.2.

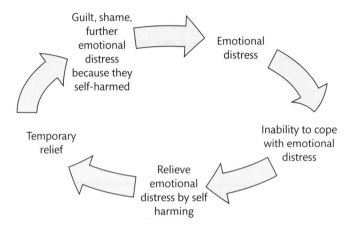

▶ **Figure 6.2:** Diagram of the self-harm cycle

People who engage in self-harming behaviour are not more likely to end their life by suicide. Suicide is not a mental illness in itself. Instead it is a serious consequence of a number of treatable mental disorders, including depression, some personality disorders and schizophrenia.

It can be difficult to identify when a person may be considering suicide, as they may not talk about their plans to other people. Some characteristics however may be warning signs that a person may be thinking about ending their life. There may be many other indications of suicidal thoughts that are specific to that person. Thoughts of suicide may follow a recent trauma or life crisis or may be a result of a build-up of distress. Characteristics may include:

▶ excessive sadness or moodiness
▶ sense of extreme hopelessness
▶ giving away possessions
▶ saying that they want to die (or similar).

If you are worried about a person, it is important to get them help immediately. Crisis services can help at critical times. These may include if the person is having frequent thoughts about wanting to die or hurting themselves or is starting to act in a way that is increasingly concerning. It is possible that if the person is supported to resolve their concerns (i.e. the reason why they want to die), this may help to reduce their suicidal thinking. This can take a long period of time to achieve.

Schizophrenia and psychotic disorders

Schizophrenia is a severe form of psychosis. A **psychotic disorder** is one where the individual will lose sense of reality as well as reduced insight into their own behaviour and thinking. This reduces their awareness of both their immediate situation and their own mental state. There are a number of different types of psychotic disorders, with different characteristics, and they range in severity.

Approximately one per cent of the population has schizophrenia, with a further two-three per cent experiencing milder forms of the disorder. Given the range of severity within this condition, schizophrenia is on a spectrum, with a greater severity of symptoms experienced by some individuals. Within this spectrum of symptoms, it may be that some individuals display some symptoms but do not display them sufficiently to be given a full diagnosis of schizophrenia. These individuals may later go on and develop a greater severity of symptoms.

Men tend to develop schizophrenia earlier than women. Symptoms for men start to emerge between the ages of 16 and 25, and between 25 to 30 in women. It is rare to have a child under the age of 10 to be diagnosed, or for an adult over the age of 40 to start showing symptoms for the first time.

There is a strong genetic link with schizophrenia, as it tends to run in families. Symptoms of schizophrenia are classified into 'positive' and 'negative' symptoms, as shown in Table 6.2.

▶ **Positive**: Symptoms not seen among the general population; an addition to the individual's typical behaviour.
▶ **Negative**: Disruption to normal emotions or behaviours; a removal of the existing behaviour.

▶ **Table 6.2:** Examples of schizophrenic symptoms

Positive symptoms	Negative symptoms
• Hallucinations (i.e. in hearing or smell) • Delusions • Agitated body movements • Thought disorders (unusual ways of thinking)	• Flat 'affect' (reduced expression of emotions) • Difficulty sustaining activities • Limited feelings of pleasure • Reduced movement or speech (catatonia)
There is a third category of symptoms: Cognitive symptoms • Memory problems • Disorganised thoughts • Problems with focusing or sustained attention	

There are a number of different types of schizophrenia, all with different symptoms:
▶ **paranoid:** beliefs of being persecuted, hearing threatening voices
▶ **hebephrenic:** flattened mood or inappropriate mood, disjointed speech or behaviour
▶ **catatonic:** becoming mute or unreactive to environment, bizarre postures, rigid posture.
▶ **undifferentiated:** often used when there are insufficient symptoms to categorise the condition as a more specific type of schizophrenia or showing symptoms for more than one of the schizophrenic subtypes.

The main treatment for schizophrenia is the use of **antipsychotics**, with psychological therapies helping to support the individual to cope with symptoms of psychosis. It is possible for the symptoms to resolve over time. When this occurs, it is known as being in **remission**.

Key term

Psychotic disorder – a mental disorder that causes abnormal thinking or experiences. People may hear voices that are not possible heard by others or see things that others cannot. They may have unusual beliefs about themselves or others, i.e. that they are the Queen of England.

Key terms

Antipsychotics – medication taken to reduce the symptoms of the psychosis.

Remission – when symptoms of a mental disorder (or other condition) are no longer present in an individual, i.e. they are experiencing a period of time when they do not have any hallucinations.

Schizophrenia is considered the main psychotic disorder. Individuals can, however, present with psychosis in the absence of having schizophrenia. **Substance-induced psychosis** relates to a psychotic episode that is the result of abuse of stimulant drugs (such as amphetamine) or other drugs, a negative reaction to prescription drugs, or excess use of alcohol. Substance-induced psychosis often presents the same way as schizophrenia, i.e. hallucinations and delusions. One of the many dangers of substance abuse is that substance-induced psychosis can occur some time after using the substance (even a number of years later).

Individuals may experience symptoms of psychosis within other mental disorders, though would not be diagnosed with an additional psychotic disorder if this occurred. For example, individuals experiencing the mania associated with bipolar disorder may experience delusional thinking, hallucinations or may not be thinking in a logical way. The reason for the psychosis would be as a result of their bipolar disorder.

Key term

Substance-induced psychosis – symptoms of psychosis that are the result of substance abuse.

Phobias and anxiety disorders

Anxiety is a common emotion experienced by many people. For most this is an emotion that helps to identify potentially dangerous situations and allows you to be prepared to manage such situations. For some people these experiences happen all too frequently or to a greater extent than is possible to manage. Long-term symptoms of anxiety may be considered an anxiety disorder.

Anxiety disorders may be the result of a traumatic event or loss, such as bereavement. They can also be caused by a stress response due to a person's inability to manage the pressures placed on them. The causes of many anxiety disorders are often unique to the individual. There are some indications of a genetic basis to the development of anxiety disorders.

Anxiety disorders can have very different triggers resulting in a number of different diagnostic anxiety disorders such as:
- generalised anxiety disorder (GAD)
- phobias
- obsessive compulsive disorders (OCD).

There is however a degree of overlap between these three types of anxiety disorders.

Generalised anxiety disorder (GAD) reflects a chronic state of anxiety that does not have a specific trigger. Anxieties can relate to impending worries, health concerns and other pressures of daily living. For many with GAD there may be no clear pattern in the causes of the anxiety, and it represents a more general concern about being able to relax. Anxiety may increase in severity across time, with the impact on the individual's ability to manage the symptoms of anxiety varying as a result.

Other anxieties can come in the form of social anxiety, a worry of being in social settings, or when there is a high likelihood of having to talk to someone else. Social anxiety may also be considered a social phobia. Some individuals can have specific fears relating to health conditions, often resulting in time spent researching physical characteristics for fear of them being related to an illness, known as a health anxiety.

Phobias are an extreme form of anxiety triggered by fears relating to specific situations or objects. These fears can be present even if the feared object does not present any direct danger. Phobias may include:
- **agoraphobia:** a fear of being in situations or places where escape may be difficult or where help may not be present if it was needed
- **arachnophobia:** a fear of spiders
- **claustrophobia:** a fear of being enclosed in a small space
- **globophobia:** fear of balloons.

▶ What other phobias can you find out about?

Obsessive compulsive disorder (OCD) is an anxiety-based disorder. It differs from other disorders due to the presence of obsessions and compulsions in the individual's thoughts and behaviours. These can lead to a high level of distress when experiencing these. OCD tends to emerge gradually and can often be triggered by a stressful event.

▶ **Obsessions:** These are unwanted thoughts or urges which the person keeps experiencing and is unable to control.

▶ **Compulsions:** These are repetitive behaviours that the person feels they must keep doing to try and reduce the unpleasant thoughts that result from their obsession.

Common OCD-type behaviours include having to check doors and locks to the home multiple times, for fear of being burgled. Alternatively, someone may wash their hands multiple times a day, and excessively when doing so, for fear of contamination by germs. Individuals who hoard lots of objects within the home may do so because they are worried that one day they will need it or would miss the item too much, even if the item is something like old newspapers.

Many people may double-check their front door is locked or hesitate before they throw something away. That doesn't automatically mean that they have this disorder. OCD is the result of such behaviour occurring over time and being associated with high levels of anxiety associated with these behaviours. Those with OCD have high levels of distress if they are unable to carry out their ritual compulsion, and it has a significant effect on their daily routines. Some individuals in extreme cases may stop leaving the house at all as the anxiety caused by checking locks and doors becomes too distressing. Treatment aims to help them to manage both the obsessive thoughts and overcome the compulsive behaviours.

Case study

Siobhan lived alone. While at work one day, an intruder burgled her house having broken the lock on the patio door. The house was ransacked; Siobhan came home to find clothes pulled out of drawers and furniture knocked over. Nothing of sentimental value was taken but she had to replace the electrical items that were stolen.

In the following weeks, Siobhan started to worry when at work that she had left the patio door unlocked, and that she was going to be burgled again. This caused her much anxiety. She started to make sure she always locked the patio door behind her when she used that door. Quickly she found she was reluctant to use that door at all, in case she left it open.

She found herself starting to check the front door was locked multiple times when leaving the house for work, in case someone broke in that way. However, soon she was spending increasing time rattling the front door handle to make sure it was locked, which started to make her late for work. When at work she had difficulty concentrating, worried she had not locked the door and would therefore be burgled.

Over some months she started to call in sick at work as she couldn't cope with spending the day worrying about the door locks. Siobhan started to miss out on outings with friends as she would have to leave the house. Over time, friends became reluctant to go to Siobhan's house each time they wanted to see her, and they started to visit less often.

Siobhan started to become isolated, worried to leave the house because it meant she would have to lock the front door. She knew the process of locking the door could take a long time with her continued checking of the door, and she knew she wouldn't be able to relax. She spent more and more time on her own, in her house, with the doors locked.

1 Siobhan's initial worry was that she would be burgled again. What appears to be her concern at the end of the case study?

2 What may be some of the obsessions she is having?

3 Identify the compulsions she is experiencing.

Mood disorders

Depression is a condition covered under the wider classification of mood disorders. It can affect the emotions, thoughts, motivation and behaviours of the person with depression. The severity of symptoms can range from mild, brief episodes of low mood to more severe and long-lasting depression.

▶ **Emotions:** People have feelings of sadness and hopelessness. There may also be anxiety.

▶ **Motivation:** There is a lack of interest in hobbies. People may not want to do any activities, often including even basic self-care.

▶ **Behaviours:** People can be tearful, have slowness of speech or movement, be physically inactive, or experience poor sleep.

▶ **Thoughts:** People have a negative view of themselves and their future. They may be pessimistic, have reduced problem solving, have thoughts that make them feel they would be better off dead. Among those with very severe depression there may be psychotic thoughts.

There are different types of depression.

Clinical depression may often be referred to as major depression or unipolar depression. It is a mood disorder that occurs without the presence of mania.

It can affect anyone of any age. Given the severity of the symptoms, it is likely that there will be noticeable problems with the person's relationships with others, school or work and their engagement in social activities.

This type of depression can occur for a single episode or can be a pattern of reoccurring depressive episodes. The characteristics noted above are present, though there may be some variation between individuals as to which characteristics are present. Symptoms usually need to have been present for at least two weeks, except in cases of unusually severe depression, in order to be diagnosed with depression.

Depression differs to grief, which often occurs following the death of a loved one. For those experiencing grief there are still moments of respite from the sadness, and there remains a degree of being able to look towards the future. Depression, on the other hand, is a more constant state of sadness.

Bipolar disorder is a mood disorder that has alternating episodes of depression and mania. The time period between changes in mood can be very fast (known as 'rapid cycling') or may occur more gradually (see Figure 6.3).

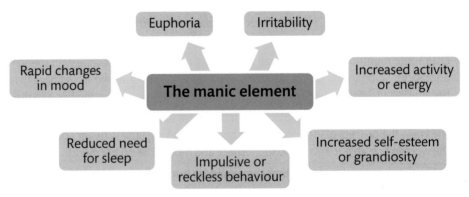

▶ **Figure 6.3:** The key features of the manic element of bipolar disorder

The depressive symptoms of bipolar disorder are the same as for unipolar depression described above.

There are three subtypes of bipolar disorder, outlined below.

▶ **Bipolar Type I**: Manic episodes are pronounced, as are depressive episodes. Both manic and depressive symptoms have an impact on functioning.

▶ **Bipolar Type II:** The mania experienced is lower in severity than for Type I (known as hypomania). Depression has a significant impact on functioning.

▶ **Cyclothymic disorder:** Hypomania is present, as are depressive symptoms, but not to the extent that it meets the severity of being labelled as 'depression'.

Bipolar disorder can be a very debilitating mental disorder, with a significant impact on the person's ability to function. There can be high rates of relapse, which can often be due to individuals being non-compliant with medication. At times when the person's mood improves and they feel less depressed, they are at an increased risk of choosing to discontinue medication as they feel 'better'. When manic, their insight into the need to take medication is significantly reduced.

Figure 6.4 shows the variation in mood range, from depression to mania for those with depression, and Bipolar Type I and Bipolar Type II, in comparison to the usual mood fluctuations of someone without a mood disorder.

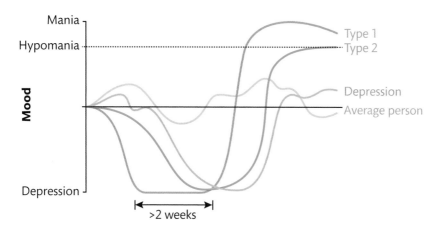

▶ **Figure 6.4:** The range in mood for various mood disorders, versus someone without a mood disorder

Other mood disorders can include Seasonal Affective Disorder (SAD), whereby the individual experiences unipolar depression in the winter, with improved mood in the summer. SAD is most common in countries like the UK where there are large changes in the weather and daylight hours in the different seasons. It can also worsen symptoms of existing depression that people experience throughout the year. It is not fully considered to be a separate condition on its own, but can be argued that it is an extended, heightened mood cycle. Individuals who have mood disorders, such as bipolar disorder or depression, are more likely to display symptoms of SAD than those who do not have bipolar or depression.

SAD can be more common in Scandinavian countries which experience long periods of darkness in winter months. Despite this, contrary to beliefs, there is no indication that the suicide rates of Scandinavian countries such as Sweden, Norway and Denmark are significantly higher than other countries with greater sunlight. Many people who experience seasonal mood changes do not experience such significant variety in their mood compared to summer months to lead to a diagnosis of SAD. Such individuals may be described as having the 'winter blues' which is a mild variation in their mood in winter months. Individuals with the winter blues may feel slightly less happy in winter, but would not be considered to be depressed (and therefore do not have SAD).

There is an increased likelihood of a person with any type of mood disorder to engage in self-harm behaviour, particularly at times of low mood. Suicide rates among those known to have depression are higher than those without mood disorders. This identifies the need for appropriate treatment of the mood disorders in order to prevent such behaviour.

Addiction

You will have covered how addictions develop in Unit 3. Specifically, you will have looked in detail at the topics of smoking, gambling and alcohol use. This section focuses on the characteristics of these, and some other, forms of addictions.

> **Link**
>
> Look back at Unit 3 for more information about different types of addiction while working through this section.

Eating disorders

These are a group of behaviours characterised by unusual eating habits. These may include restrictive or excessive food intake that can have a negative effect on physical or mental health. Eating disorders are typically more common in females, though the numbers of males being diagnosed with this condition is increasing.

Types of this disorder include those listed below.

▶ **Anorexia nervosa**: a pathological fear of gaining weight, and weight loss that is induced by the individual. An individual may engage in excessive exercise in order to lose further weight. Use of diuretics and appetite suppressants may be evident. There may be intrusive thoughts about their own appearance and weight.

▶ **Bulimia nervosa:** repeated bouts of overeating and an excessive preoccupation with the control of body weight followed by vomiting or use of laxatives. This disorder shares many psychological features with anorexia nervosa, including an over-concern with body shape and weight. Repeated vomiting is likely to result in physical complications. There may be a history of anorexia nervosa.

▶ **Binge-eating disorder** can be considered a form of atypical bulimia. There may be episodes of binge eating, in the absence of purging or fasting as with bulimia nervosa.

Substance abuse

This may refer to the taking of a number of different substances, including alcohol, drugs and nicotine (smoking). All of these, and many others, can affect how a person's mind works, sometimes not always for the better. With continued use an addiction can develop, meaning that it is difficult for the individual to stop using the substance. People may misuse substances that are legal (alcohol, caffeine, nicotine) or those that are illegal (such as cannabis, 'spice' and cocaine).

For behaviour to be considered substance abuse, the individual needs to be aware of the potential negative consequences of taking it while choosing to take it anyway.

Substance dependency refers to the psychological, physical and behavioural symptoms an individual will experience; dependency occurs after repeated exposure to the substances. It will include a strong desire to take the drug, difficulties in controlling its use, persisting in its use despite harmful consequences, a higher priority given to drug use than to other activities and obligations, increased tolerance, and sometimes a physical withdrawal state.

The dependence syndrome may be present for a specific substance (for example tobacco or alcohol), for a class of substances (for example opioid drugs, such as heroin), or for a wider range of different substances.

Individuals may experience the 'withdrawal state' when they stop taking the substance. This is a time-limited set of physical and psychological symptoms which occur as a direct result of the substance withdrawing from the body. These symptoms can include convulsions or delirium.

When individuals choose to stop smoking, they may initially experience:

▶ cravings for a cigarette
▶ feeling irritable and restless
▶ have trouble thinking clearly.

These negative effects can make an individual reluctant to try and stop smoking. After all, the feeling of smoking may be more reinforcing than the feeling of trying to stop smoking. The negative experiences when trying to stop smoking contributes to the high levels of people who do not succeed in stopping for any prolonged amount of time. Individuals in this situation could be described as physically dependent on the nicotine within the cigarettes. As the cigarettes may help to relax them when stressed, the person may also be psychologically dependent, believing that they cannot manage stressors without cigarettes. This creates an additional barrier to overcoming the addiction.

A psychotic disorder can develop either immediately or after many years of substance abuse. This is more common in relation to drug or alcohol abuse, rather than for those who have smoked cigarettes for many years. It is, however, becoming more evident for those who chose to smoke drugs other than nicotine in their cigarettes. This would be known as substance-related psychosis. A psychotic disorder mirrors many of the symptoms for schizophrenia, including hallucinations and paranoid delusions. These will need to be treated by clinicians in the same way as for schizophrenia and other psychosis.

Gambling

Pathological gambling, sometimes known as compulsive gambling, consists of frequent, repeated episodes of gambling that dominate the individual's life. This can often lead to difficulties in engaging in social activities, work, family life and can cause financial concerns. An individual with a gambling addiction will have a thought process which focuses overwhelmingly on gambling, it may be specific to one form of gambling, such as slot machines, though can also generalise to any form of gambling, such as making a bet on whether it will snow at Christmas.

Gambling that is seen as significantly problematic can be classified as a mental disorder known as pathological gambling (using ICD10) if it meets the criteria listed below.

▶ Repeated (two or more) episodes of gambling over a period of at least one year.
▶ Episodes do not have a profitable outcome for the person but are continued, despite personal distress and interference with daily living.
▶ The person describes an intense urge to gamble which is difficult to control, and reports that he or she is unable to stop gambling by an effort of will.
▶ The person is preoccupied with thoughts or mental images of the act of gambling or the circumstances surrounding the act.

▶ What other types of gambling can you think of?

Other mental health conditions may also result in the individual taking part in gambling, such as someone suffering from bipolar disorder gambling during a manic period, when risk taking is high. The gambling behaviour may therefore be considered a symptom of their bipolar disorder rather than the individual also being diagnosed with pathological gambling. For many other people pathological gambling is not related to any other known mental-health condition, and their only mental-health concern is the severity of their gambling behaviour.

⏸ PAUSE POINT

Think about your behaviour or habits that you have that you believe that you *must* do. What would it feel like if you were unable to do this behaviour, or if it was harmful to you?

Hint

Addiction can be present among many people. It may not always be knowingly harmful. What harm can be caused by addictions

Extend

How would you know if the behaviour you chose was becoming an 'addiction'? What might you think, say or do that would suggest this?

Assessment activity 6.2

`6B.P3` `6B.M2` `6B.D2`

Doctors at a local surgery are wanting to increase the amount of health promotion literature in the practice.

They are keen to ensure that the literature they have is as accessible to as many people as possible, while also sharing an important health promotion message.

Design an information leaflet that could be given to visitors to the doctors' surgery that highlights the factors known to lead to mental disorder.

Choose one mental disorder and design a poster that the GPs could use within the practice.

Include information about signs and symptoms and any advice that would be helpful to share.

When designing the poster, consider that people may only view the poster quickly; it is important to catch their attention for this short amount of time.

It may be helpful to look at existing health promotion information in order to get further ideas.

Plan
- What is the task? What am I being asked to do?
- How confident do I feel in my ability to perform this task?
- What areas might I struggle with?

Do
- I know what I am doing and my aims.
- I know where I have gone wrong and have adjusted my approach to get myself back on task.

Review
- I can explain the task and how I approached it.
- I can explain how I might do it differently next time.

C # Explore professional approaches to the treatment of mental disorders

Approaches to the treatment of mental disorders

Treatment options for mental disorders differ depending on the nature and severity of the disorder. Patient choice is considered wherever possible when considering treatment. Medication may be considered appropriate for some, whereas a more psychological approach is often favoured by many individuals and for many conditions.

Psychodynamic approaches

Psychodynamic therapy aims to identify unconscious issues that are contributing to an individual's current distress. It is influenced by Sigmund Freud's psychodynamic theory and psychoanalysis. In identifying and then rectifying the unconscious issues, this therapy aims to reduce symptoms of, for example, anxiety and depression which can be considered symptoms of the repressed issues.

▶ The structure of the treatment sessions is less structured than other therapies, and is based on **free association**. This is a process where, during the session, the individual talks about anything that is on their mind. Through this process individuals may provide indications of unconscious worries that are leading to their current symptoms.

▶ Individuals are encouraged to discuss their dreams, as another way of gaining insight into the unconscious. Interpretation of dreams is known as **dream analysis**. It aims to distinguish between the manifest content (the literal content of the dream) and the latent content (the underlying meaning of the dream).

▶ Within the therapeutic setting, a therapeutic relationship emerges between the individual receiving the treatment and the therapist. **Transference** can occur within this dynamic. This is where the individual may unconsciously direct feelings towards the therapist that they are feeling towards others. This can lead to the individual treating the therapist as if they were the other person the individual is thinking about. Often this reflects a relationship they may have had with someone in their childhood, such as a parent or sibling. This process helps the therapist to better understand some of the unconscious issues driving their current concerns.

> **Key terms**
>
> **Free association** – a therapist asks an individual to share anything that comes into their mind, including words, images, and so on.
>
> **Dream analysis** – the process of finding meaning in the dreams an individual has when they are asleep.
>
> **Transference** – the feelings an individual has for a person that are directed towards the therapist.

> **Theory into practice**
>
> Keep a diary for one week of the dreams you have, if you can remember them. Record as much detail as possible. Research some of the general suggestions within dream analysis and look at the suggested meaning for the content of the dreams you experienced.
>
> 1 Reflect on the suggested meaning of your dream. Does it seem to have some relevance to you?
>
> 2 How would it feel discussing your dreams and having them analysed by a therapist?

Psychotherapy can be a long-term treatment option, and this extended timeframe can result in individuals choosing not to continue with intervention. This can impact on success rates if treatment is not completed. Having therapy can also be distressing to the individual. To identify unconscious worries, individuals must process the emotions that may arise as a result.

Psychotherapy is based on the therapist **subjectively** interpreting the information the individual is providing. As it is subjective, there is the possibility that the therapist may misinterpret the information. For example, when working with an individual with an eating disorder, the psychotherapist may interpret events reported by the individual as being more significant, and therefore more related to the eating disorder than the individual would. Similarly, dream analysis is a particularly subjective element of psychotherapy, when the therapist's understanding of the dream significantly influences what meaning they communicate to the individual.

> **Key term**
>
> **Subjective** – interpretation of a situation or information based on your own feelings and beliefs (rather than based on fact).

Behaviour therapy

Using principles of classical and operant conditioning, behaviour therapy tries to develop new associations between a stimulus and the individual. It is influenced by the learning approach as this approach assumes that all behaviour is acquired through learning. Behaviour therapy is particularly effective when applied to phobias or other anxiety conditions.

> **Link**
>
> Look back at Unit 1, page 253, to remind yourself of the key principles of classical and operant conditioning.

Classical conditioning therapies

Treatments based on classical conditioning principles support the idea that, through conditioning, such behaviours can be changed, and new associations formed. Conditioning works by forming associations between stimuli, resulting in specific behaviour on later exposure to the same stimulus. The process of changing associations between a stimulus and a phobic response is known as extinction (such as being up a ladder and having a fear of falling, changing to being up a ladder and having a feeling of calm).

Extinction can be achieved through several different exposure therapies, in which a new association is developed through a structured introduction to a feared stimulus. Exposure therapies include those listed below.

1 **Flooding:** An individual is exposed to the source of their phobia with no prior build up or any means of escape from the situation. Exposure may be actual or imagined exposure. The individual is taught relaxation techniques to be used at the point of exposure. They are unable to avoid the phobia and, as a result, anxiety reduces.

Flooding has been found to be as effective as other exposure therapies (Ougrin 2011) for simple phobias, though less effective for phobias such as agoraphobia. While this approach may provide good value for money in that it requires only one session, it can be highly traumatic for the individual. This increases the likelihood that the individual will not complete the treatment, even if it is only for a short period of time.

2 **Counter conditioning:** This aims to replace a response to a stimulus with a new response. It aims to deter people from the original response. For example, for someone with a smoking addiction, it aims to remove feelings of positivity associated with smoking, and replace them with one that will reduce the likelihood of further smoking.

Counter conditioning approaches include:

▶ **Aversion therapy:** The individual learns to experience an 'aversive' or negative feeling when near a stimulus. It is commonly used for treatment of addictions, such as smoking, alcohol use, and so on.

Certain medications are available for an individual to take if they want to stop smoking. If they then have a cigarette, it induces a feeling of nausea which serves to put the person off wanting another cigarette. Any positive feelings they used to have from smoking are therefore replaced with negative experiences. Over time the individual will learn to associate a cigarette with feeling sick and will no longer want one.

An individual needs to be aware of the implications of using the substance while taking the medication, as it is not a pleasant experience to feel nauseous. As the feelings of nausea are induced only while the person is taking the medication, there is a possibility that the individual may return to using the substance if they stop taking the medication, based on them remembering the previous positive association they had with the substance.

▶ **Systematic desensitisation**: This approach is used to reduce anxiety or phobic responses to specific triggers. It has limited use in the absence of a trigger, as the individual needs to be exposed to the source of their anxiety. Whereas flooding is an extreme exposure to a feared object, systematic desensitisation is more gradual in nature. It is therefore more ethical as it causes less distress to the individual, despite being a longer treatment option.

It follows the following process.
1 The individual learns relaxation techniques.
2 They develop an anxiety hierarchy (a list of anxiety-provoking situations, from least to most feared).
3 They are introduced to the lowest-rated object, and with support from the therapist, apply the taught relaxation skills while being exposed to the object.

4 Once they can show they can remain calm when exposed to the object, the individual can move to the next object on the hierarchy.

5 The individual is supported by the therapist as they progress through the hierarchy until they reach the most feared object.

The process results in a gradual desensitisation, in which a new pairing between the feared object and a feeling of relaxation is developed. The individual will then associate the feared object with relaxation when exposed in the future.

Systematic desensitisation works on the basis of reciprocal inhibition. This is the idea that it is not possible to experience two emotional states at the same time. An individual is not able to be relaxed and anxious at the same time. Therefore, with repeated practice, relaxation becomes the dominant emotion when exposed to the phobic object.

This process results in heightened anxiety on initial exposure, hence the need for a good level of competence in using relaxation skills prior to any exposure taking place. This means it should always be completed by a qualified therapist, in order to be able to appropriately resolve any anxiety. As progression through the hierarchy is dependent on the individual's progress, it places the individual in control of the rate at which the therapy progresses.

Operant conditioning therapies

These therapies are often referred to as behaviour modification (or behaviour analysis), using the idea that mental illness is learned and can therefore be unlearned, leading to different, more 'psychologically healthy' behaviours.

It focuses on the consequences of a behaviour as a way of understanding what reinforces that behaviour, and therefore making it more likely that it will happen again. Behaviour analysis (also known as a 'functional analysis'), undertaken by a therapist, will try to understand the 'function' of a behaviour, that is why the individual may continue to display the behaviour. This is done by observing the consequences for the individual of displaying the problem behaviour.

Once the function is understood, such as why a person restricts their food or why someone may self-harm, the treatment will aim to disrupt the reinforcement that this behaviour provides, or to support the development of the same reinforcement by displaying a new behaviour.

For example, a person may find that their stress levels temporarily reduce when they self-harm. This leads them to continue to self-harm when stressed in the future. The treatment to manage the individual's association between self-harm and feeling less stressed would be to replace the self-harm behaviour with another behaviour that also helps them to feel less stressed. Next time the individual feels stressed, they may be encouraged to have a cup of tea or try a relaxation exercise, for example. If this behaviour is used each time the person feels stressed, the relationship between self-harm and feeling less stressed is reduced, and the individual will be reinforced to try relaxation each time they are stressed.

Response shaping encourages new behaviours to occur. The therapist will reinforce behaviours that currently take place that are similar to the desired behaviours. Reinforcement is given only for behaviours that get progressively closer to the desired behaviour.

For example, an individual with depression may have a reduced interest in any form of activity. Showing an interest in an activity, even if they do not want to do it, may be reinforced. This reinforcement is progressively adapted, for example the person says they want to *watch* an activity. Further reinforcement will then take place as the motivation to undertake an activity increases, hopefully finishing in an increased level of participation in an activity.

The process of operant conditioning does not need to be overseen by a therapist. Instead it provides the individual with the ability to control their own behaviour. The self-directed use of the principles of operant conditioning is known as behavioural self-control. It has been successfully applied to a number of psychopathologies, including addiction, obsessions and behaviour problems.

Cognitive therapy

There is a degree of overlap between cognitive therapy and behaviour therapy, as cognitive therapy explores the thinking behind an individual's actions, while also working to change behaviour as well. Working on the premise that faulty thinking leads to mental disorders, cognitive therapies aim to reduce or remove the presence of such faulty thoughts and replace them with more rational thinking.

Cognitive therapy aims to break the vicious cycle between thoughts and behaviours that can maintain the symptoms of a mental disorder. Looking at Figure 6.5, it is possible to see the cycle of OCD, for example. Cognitive therapy will seek to provide assistance at a number of stages, which may include:

▶ **Stage 1:** Skills to challenge the obsessive thought, i.e. to replace it with a less obsessive thought, or use a distraction technique.

▶ **Stage 2:** Emotional management to reduce symptoms of anxiety.

▶ **Stage 3:** Self talk to try and reduce likelihood they will undertake the compulsive behaviour.

▶ **Stage 4:** Reflection on the long-term value of addressing the OCD.

An individual will be provided with the skills to manage all stages of the cycle, allowing them to break it at any stage, even if they engage in some part of the cycle.

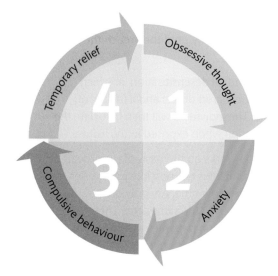

Types of cognitive therapy include those listed below.

▸ **Rational emotive behaviour therapy (REBT):** This aims to change how an individual interprets their experiences, rather than changing the experience itself. Through challenging irrational beliefs and emotions and replacing them with more functional ones, it allows the person to overcome the difficulty they have in interpreting their experiences positively.

▸ **Cognitive behaviour therapy (CBT):** This is similar to REBT in that it aims to overcome irrationality, but this has an emphasis on changing thoughts. It helps to manage the negative thoughts associated with many conditions including anxiety, depression and psychosis.

▸ **Mindfulness-based cognitive therapy (MBCT):** This therapy was originally designed as a form of relapse prevention for depression and a way of helping to reduce distress following trauma. It contains influences from the practice of meditation. A central element of the therapy involves the individual becoming increasingly aware of their current emotional and cognitive state as a form of distraction from a low mood.

▸ **Acceptance and commitment therapy (ACT):** This is a form of mindfulness-based therapy. This therapy is based on the idea of accepting situations that cannot be changed or accepting strong emotions in order to be able to move away from those feelings. It also requires the individual to use cognitive skills to further reduce or defuse the heightened emotions by learning to change their thinking from that of high emotions to calm thoughts.

Family systems therapy

This treatment works on the theory that it is necessary to understand the family unit of a person in order to understand the individual themselves. Family therapy is a form of psychotherapy, where individuals within the family work together to understand how their actions affect the whole family. It aims to get families working together to address concerns. It can be used with mental-health concerns to understand the basis for some of the individual's symptoms, as well as developing solutions to address any concerns there may be in order to support the individual's recovery.

For it to work, family members need to agree to engage in the process, and there is an emphasis on honesty throughout in order for it to be effective.

Drug treatments

Medication approaches can work in isolation for a condition, or in conjunction with psychological techniques. They may be used if psychological techniques have limited success, or as a means of controlling symptoms, allowing for psychological interventions to have greater impact. Different medications serve different purposes, as they work on the body in various ways.

Antidepressants aim to treat symptoms of low mood and clinical depression. They can also be prescribed for those with generalised anxiety disorder or obsessive-compulsive disorder. The idea is that they help to balance hormones and neurotransmitters so that when these biological factors are balanced, it helps to keep an individual's mood more regulated. The most common type of antidepressants are selective serotonin reuptake inhibitors (SSRIs), which are favoured as they have a limited number of side effects.

Other antidepressants include:
- tricyclic antidepressants, an older form of SSRIs, that are now less used due to the relationship between medication use and suicidal thoughts
- serotonin and norepinephrine reuptake inhibitors (SNRIs) that block the reabsorption (reuptake) of the neurotransmitters serotonin and norepinephrine in the brain
- monoamine oxidase inhibitors (MAOIs) that maintain levels of the neurotransmitters norepinephrine, serotonin and dopamine in the brain.

Anxiolytics inhibit feelings of anxiety and may have some sedative effects. They can lead to addiction if overused and are therefore often prescribed only for short-term use. Benzodiazepines are a particular form of anxiolytics with highly addictive properties. They boost the effect of the neurotransmitter gamma-aminobutyric acid (GABA), which usually has a calming effect in the human brain.

Antipsychotics are typically prescribed for schizophrenia or bipolar disorder, or for severe anxiety and depression. They help to reduce the activity of the dopamine system, where over-activation can lead to hallucinations. Antipsychotics may be taken daily as a tablet or liquid medication, or via an injection (known as a depot) every 2–4 weeks. They are not addictive, but the body gets used to having them, so any reduction should be done gradually.

Additional therapies

Counselling is a talking therapy that focuses on discussion of an individual's thoughts and feelings about a situation. It is often used to deal with heightened emotions and mental-health conditions There are many different approaches a counsellor may take with the individual, much of which is chosen to suit the issues being presented and the individual's preferences.

Many interventions are responding positively to the technological era. CBT and other therapies are now being offered via the internet in the form of computerised CBT (**cCBT**) or other online self-help therapies to help to address conditions such as anxieties and depression. Clinicians can engage in individualised therapy sessions via online chat forums, email and through telephone-based interventions.

> **Link**
>
> Look back at Unit 1, page 39, for more information on neurotransmitters which play an important role in how antidepressants work.

> **Key term**
>
> **cCBT** – CBT therapy undertaken via an online forum or email exchange rather than face-to-face as with CBT.

Mental health professionals

There is a wide range of professionals working within mental-health settings. They all have very specific roles, with the same goal of supporting individuals in their recovery from their mental-health symptoms.

Diagnosing and treating disorders

When you feel unwell for any reason, your first contact with medical professionals is through your General Practitioner (GP). This includes any concerns relating to mental health. They can guide individuals in a number of ways to assist them with their mental-health concerns. They may prescribe physical activity or other forms of recreation as a starting point for low mood or anxiety. They may also make a referral to community psychological IAPT services that undertake short-term CBT.

In trying these approaches first, the GP tries to avoid medication, only using this when considered clinically necessary. If using medication for anxiety and low mood the aim is always that it will only be a short-term treatment approach, as long-term medication use can cause additional physical complications.

If the mental-health concern is for more complex conditions that require on-going specialist treatment and monitoring, the GP is likely to refer the individual to a psychiatrist.

Diagnosis of complex mental-health conditions is most frequently undertaken by a psychiatrist. A psychiatrist is a medical doctor who specialises in the diagnosis and treatment of mental illness such as schizophrenia or bipolar disorder. They can start patients on special medications to help treat their symptoms and continue to review their mental state while they are on such treatment, with help from the patient's GP.

Psychiatrists will refer to the relevant diagnostic classification tool to help them to make the diagnosis based on the patient's history and current symptoms.

Psychologists often work alongside psychiatrists and GPs to help with the treatment of mental disorders. Using some of the techniques discussed previously, they will aim to support the patient to manage their symptoms effectively. Some psychologists are involved with the diagnosis of some mental disorders if they have had specialist training. The information a psychologist obtains from working with the patients can also help with the psychiatrist's diagnosis of the patient. A psychologist does not prescribe medication.

Occasionally other professionals may be involved in diagnosis and treatment of mental illnesses. This may include neurologists who may play a role if the reason why the person has the disorder is due to a fault in their brain, such as due to a tumour. They will be involved in the treatment of any such tumour while the mental disorder is dealt with by mental-health specialists.

Mental-health workers

Within any mental-health team are a number of staff working alongside the psychiatrist and psychologist. There will be a number of nurses who have trained as Registered Mental-Health Nurses (RMNs). They will work directly with the patient to support them through a mental-health crisis and will often have therapy skills to be able to provide specific treatment relating to symptom management.

Many nurses have additional qualifications that allow them to prescribe some of the mental-health medications a patient may need. If a patient needs medication given to them by injection, it is usually the RMNs who will give them this medicine.

The support given by a mental-health workers usually provided within a community setting, with the individual living in their own homes. They may attend a local GP surgery to see the mental-health team, or more often attend specialist mental-health centres (known as 'hubs') where many different mental-health professionals may be based. It is only at times of serious difficulty when an individual may receive mental-health support in a hospital or other in-patient service.

An individual can be considered vulnerable at times of acute mental distress. Social workers play a key role in addressing some of these vulnerabilities. They offer support for issues that are indirectly related to their mental health, such as accommodation, access to their children, and so on. Social workers are also very experienced at working with the family of the patient (with the patient's consent) to maximise the patient's recovery.

A case manager will coordinate the different professions for a particular patient and ensure that the treatment plan is achievable. Each patient will have a case manager assigned to them. They will often be the contact person for a patient on their case load.

Additional professionals may contribute to mental-health teams when needed to help with specific issues as they arise. These include:

- **paediatricians** who provide medical consultation specifically for children
- **occupational therapists** who help with the

development of meaningful activities or development of skills related to everyday tasks such as cooking

▶ **counsellors** who offer talking-based therapy to help resolve problems.

communication difficulties. They teach practical skills to encourage a child to be able to maximise their communication abilities. Communication difficulties can reduce access to educational opportunities and can result in student distress.

Case study

Declan is 19 years old. He has grown up in care and has started to feel suicidal. When he was 18 years old he attempted suicide because he felt so low. Following his suicide attempt he spent a brief period of time in an acute hospital ward where he saw a psychiatrist who diagnosed him with depression, and prescribed him with anti-depressants. Mental-health nurses helped him to understand what depression was, and how this explained how he had felt for so long. A psychologist helped him to develop skills to manage himself when his mood was low, and to try and avoid a future suicide attempt.

Since he was discharged from hospital, he has continued to work with the community mental-health team and sees a mental-health nurse every two weeks to discuss how he is feeling. A social worker has been helping him to sort out his housing, which was a source of his worries. He is looking forward to having somewhere secure to live and possibly starting college in the near future. He sees the psychiatrist every three months to check his medication is still helping him. He knows he can also visit his GP should he start to get worried about his mood.

1 List all the different professionals that have been involved in looking after Declan and his mental health.

2 What have been the responsibilities of each of the professionals involved?

Professionals in educational organisations

Schools and other education settings have a responsibility to support the mental wellbeing of their students. Children can experience a range of mental-health concerns. Schools serve a critical role in early identification of mental-health difficulties. Staff often include those listed below.

▶ **Health visitor:** A registered nurse working with parents of children from age 0–5 years. Their aim is to safeguard and protect children, recognising signs of abuse or neglect and making appropriate referrals to address such issues as they arise. They work with parents to educate them on promoting the positive mental health of the child, and the parent.

▶ **School nurse:** They provide a link between community services, i.e. the GP practice and the school, working with children from age 5–19 years. They continue the health-education role started by health visitors and undertake health assessments, including mental-health assessments as needed. They will provide advice to the school on student wellbeing.

▶ **Special educational needs coordinator (SENCO):** A qualified teacher coordinating the provision of education for children with special educational needs or disabilities in schools. They coordinate with the parents of children to maximise the engagement and learning of the student.

▶ **Speech therapist:** They assess and treat children (and adults) with specific language, speech and

Support groups

There are many charitable or government organised initiatives that focus on addressing the symptoms of mental health disorders or raising awareness to the general population about such disorders. In improving the knowledge people have about specific conditions, it is hoped that people will be less judgemental of those who are experiencing the disorders.

These groups are of benefit to individuals with a mental-health disorder, parents, relatives or friends of those with a condition, and to clinicians for providing further guidance on how to support someone with a specific disorder.

Mind

This charity aims to provide access and support to as many people as possible with mental-health conditions. They also campaign to raise awareness, improve services and promote understanding among the wider population about mental disorders. This has included influencing governments by communicating how to improve existing services and support consideration of new mental-health initiatives.

It operates telephone contact services for individuals in distress, emergency services needing personal help, and they provide legal information and advice on mental-health related law.

Young Minds

As its name suggests, this charity focuses on the provision of mental-health support for children and young people. They aim to increase the resilience of children, so they are more able to deal with difficulties they may experience in life. It provides advice to both children and their parents.

In sharing information about how children and young people feel distress from common experiences, such as bullying and grief, it potentially reduces the worry that how the individual is feeling is 'not normal'. It provides skills and information to help to protect an individual from starting to feel distressed.

Rethink

Rethink provides national help and support for individuals with mental disorders, and their caregivers. They run commissioned mental-health services, including sheltered housing, recovery houses and at-home community support. This helps to increase the access of support that people can receive. The charity campaigns for an improvement of the lives of those with mental illness, which is achieved in part by encouraging the government to prioritise mental-health needs.

Alongside Mind, Rethink leads the 'Time to Change' programme, England's most ambitious programme to end the stigma and discrimination experienced by people with mental-health problems. This campaign has been running since 2007. The campaign has led to a significant positive change in the way mental health is viewed in England.

❚❚ PAUSE POINT There are many different organisations available to help individuals with mental-health disorders, either general support or specific to one condition.

Hint What sort of information is made available by the charities named above (and others)?

Extend Undertake some independent research looking at the information that is made available on their websites.

Have a conversation with peers about your views on approaching these charities if needed.

Assessment activity 6.3

6C.P5 6C.M3 6C.D3 6C.P6

The local community mental-health team has a vacancy for one more staff member. There is some debate about what type of profession they should advertise the new role as. There is already a psychiatrist, psychologist and a mental-health nurse within the team.

Within a group setting, discuss the roles of each profession that will be needed within a mental-health team including what type of work each professional could do and the benefit this will have to the team. Identify the profession that you consider to be most needed within the community team.

Develop a job description for the job advert, considering what work the job role will involve, and what skills and qualities the person will need to undertake this job.

You will need to have a clear argument as to why you have chosen this profession above other possible roles.

Plan
- What is the task? What am I being asked to do?
- How confident do I feel in my ability to perform this task?
- What areas might I struggle with?

Do
- I know what I am doing and my aims.
- I know where I have gone wrong and have adjusted my approach to get myself back on task.

Review
- I can explain the task and how I approached it.
- I can explain how I might do it differently next time.

Further reading and resources

Davey, G. (2014) *Psychopathology; Research, assessment and treatment in clinical psychology* London: John Wiley & Sons.

ICD-10 diagnostic criteria: https://icd.who.int/browse10/2016/en

YouTube: Bedlam Mental Health Inpatient UK Documentary 2013

THINK ▶FUTURE

Azra Demir

Mental-health support worker

Working with patients with mental-health issues has been the most challenging and rewarding job I have ever done. Before I started this job, I didn't fully appreciate the level of distress they can experience when they are having a reduction in their mental health. Some patients need lots of support from us as staff at that time.

The doctors I work with help to sort medication out, and the psychologists will often work with a patient to manage their symptoms. My role is different. I'm there to support them at any time of the day, to help them when they are distressed and involve them in positive activities to try and keep them well.

It's nice when you see someone settled in their mental health, especially when they often arrived at the hospital acting very differently. I enjoy doing activities with them. I just enjoy seeing them being able to concentrate on an activity that makes them feel good about themselves. That goes a long way to helping someone recover from a mental illness.

Focusing on your skills

Know the history

It is important to understand the mental-health history of the individual as well as the history of psychopathology in general. You will be able to support an individual with a mental disorder more effectively if you are clear about their specific circumstances. Key questions could include:

- How long have they had the symptoms they currently report?

- Have they had these, or similar symptoms, previously?

- Do they have any diagnosed mental disorders?

- What support do they currently have from others?

- What previous treatment have they tried, and what was the outcome?

- What do they want to happen in their treatment?

- Are there any suicide/self-harm concerns?

- What are their immediate needs?

Getting experience

Many mental health organisations will allow volunteers to work with them. This may be in person undertaking fundraising or supporting an individual. There are agencies who provide telephone support such as the Samaritans.

- Think about which mental health organisations share the same aims and values as you do.

- See if there is any voluntary work that you can do for them. Even fundraising for a charity can help expand knowledge of specific mental disorders.

Getting ready for assessment

Amelie is working towards a BTEC National in Applied Psychology.

She was given an assignment with the following title 'What is the most effective treatment approach for depression?' for Learning aim C.

She had to write a report that explained the different treatment options for depression and evaluate which was the most effective: The report had to:

▸ include information about at least three different treatment approaches of depression, i.e. psychodynamic, behaviour, drug, cognitive
▸ discuss the effectiveness of each of these treatment methods and how they applied to depression.

Amelie shared her experience below.

How I got started

First, I collected all my notes on treatments of mental disorders. These notes were already separated into the different groups of treatment, i.e. psychodynamic, cognitive, etc. I separated all the information out that related to depression and kept information about the other conditions safely in a folder for future use.

I decided to structure the report using headings of the different approaches. This was to make sure that I covered all treatment options relevant to this disorder.

I reviewed the evaluations I had for each approach so that I made sure I answered all parts of the question I needed to answer in the report. This included looking on the internet for up-to-date evaluations of treatment approaches.

How I brought it all together

I made sure I had a large amount of time that I could spend on the report in one go to help me to focus on the report.

For each treatment approach, I:
▸ created a bullet point list of what the treatment for depression involved
▸ referenced at least one research study for each approach
▸ assessed the limitations and strengths of each treatment to support my argument.

What I learned from the experience

The report felt overwhelming at first, as there are so many treatment options that could be used for depression. There is quite a bit of overlap between some of the treatment approaches and I needed to have a clear understanding of each of them to make sure I did not confuse my discussion of them in the report. Once I understood the overlap it did not feel so overwhelming.

By taking each treatment approach in turn, I was able to remain focused on each method. This gave me a natural structure to the report. If future reports do not have the same type of structure, I will spend time developing a structure that fits the report.

Many of the evaluations about therapies helpfully make clear which condition they are referring to, so I was able to rule out evidence that was not related to depression. I found that there are many websites that have up-to-date research about the effectiveness of different treatments that will be helpful for similar reports in the future.

Think about it

When planning the assignment it is worth considering the following:
▸ What am I being asked to do? Make sure you fully understand the question you have been asked to answer.
▸ What do I know about this topic? It may help to summarise key points of your knowledge
▸ How will I show my knowledge? Designing a plan for the content you tend to include can help to structure your answers.

Applied Sport Psychology 7

Getting to know your unit

A growing area of psychology is its application to sports performance. To benefit from training sessions and to succeed in competitions, sportspeople must achieve an appropriate mindset. Understanding psychological techniques can help them achieve this mindset by providing interventions to manage their thoughts and emotions, and to support their performance needs.

How you will be assessed

This unit will be assessed by a series of internally assessed tasks set by your tutor. Throughout this unit you will find assessment activities that will help you work towards your assessment. Completing these activities will not mean that you have achieved a particular grade, but you will have carried out useful research or preparation that will be relevant when it comes to your final assignment.

In order for you to achieve the tasks in your assignment, it is important to check that you have met all of the Pass grading criteria. You can do this as you work your way through the assignment.

If you are hoping to gain a Merit or Distinction, you should also make sure that you present the information in your assignment in the style that is required by the relevant assessment criterion. For example, Merit criteria require you to analyse and discuss, and Distinction criteria require you to assess and evaluate.

The assignment set by your tutor will consist of a number of tasks designed to meet the criteria in the table. This is likely to consist of a written assignment but may also include activities such as the following.
- A report on key psychological theories and their application within sports environments.
- Designing psychological intervention programmes that could benefit a sportsperson's performance.

Assessment criteria

This table shows what you must do in order to achieve a **Pass**, **Merit** or **Distinction** grade, and where you can find activities to help you.

Pass	Merit	Distinction

Learning aim **A** Understand key psychological theories underpinning performance in sport

Pass	Merit	Distinction
A.P1 Explain key principles of theories of motivation and self-confidence in sport. Assessment activity 7.1	**A.M1** Discuss the extent to which psychological theories can account for changes in motivation, self-confidence and arousal levels of sportspeople. Assessment activity 7.1	**A.D1** Evaluate how far psychological theories can account for changes in motivation, self-confidence and arousal levels in sportspeople. Assessment activity 7.1
A.P2 Explain key principles of arousal and anxiety in sport. Assessment activity 7.1		

Learning aim **B** Investigate how psychological theories can be applied to sporting situations

Pass	Merit	Distinction
B.P3 Explain how motivation and self-confidence factors impact on sports performance. Assessment activity 7.1	**B.M2** Discuss how motivation, self-confidence, arousal and anxiety levels impact on sports performance. Assessment activity 7.1	**B.D2** Evaluate the impact on sports performance of the relationship between motivation, self-confidence and arousal levels. Assessment activity 7.1
B.P4 Explain how arousal and anxiety levels impact on sports performance. Assessment activity 7.1		

Learning aim **C** Recommend psychological interventions to meet sports performance needs.

Pass	Merit	Distinction
C.P5 Produce an outline programme of recommended psychological interventions to address the performance needs of a selected sportsperson. Assessment activity 7.2	**C.M3** Produce a programme of recommended psychological interventions for a selected sportsperson, analysing their suitability in addressing performance needs. Assessment activity 7.2	**C.D3** Produce a detailed programme of recommended psychological interventions for a selected sportsperson, evaluating their suitability in addressing performance needs. Assessment activity 7.2
C.P6 Explain the suitability of the programme to benefit a selected sportsperson. Assessment activity 7.2		

Getting started

Think about the very best sportspeople in the world. You are probably thinking about people like Serena Williams, Usain Bolt, Cristiano Ronaldo or Lucy Bronze. Which psychological qualities have helped these sportspeople reach their outstanding performance levels and how do you think these qualities have helped?

 A

Understand key psychological theories underpinning performance in sport

Key terms

Motivation – the direction and intensity of one's effort.

Self-confidence – the belief that you can successfully perform a desired behaviour.

Arousal – a state of alertness and anticipation that prepares the body for action. It involves both psychological and physiological activation.

Anxiety – a negative emotional state associated with feelings of nervousness, apprehension or worry.

When you think about how well an athlete has performed in sport, often the explanations for performance or success are linked to factors related to **motivation**, **self-confidence**, **arousal** or **anxiety** levels. Throughout this section you will learn about theories associated with these important parts of sport psychology, as well as the strengths and limitations of these theories.

Theories of motivation in sport

There are many different theories that help you understand motivation in sport. Each have different elements of motivation and their impact on sports performance. First, though, it important to know the definition of motivation.

Definition of motivation

Think about how you feel and behave when you are motivated. How does your body feel? What do you think about? How does your performance level change? All these things will help you to understand why the most widely accepted definition of motivation is possibly 'the direction and intensity of one's effort' (Sage, 1977). The direction of your effort means the thing that you are working towards (for example training goals) and the intensity of your effort refers to how hard you will work to achieve something.

Need achievement theory

Need achievement theory was created my McClelland (1961) and later built upon by Atkinson (1974). They suggested that the way people behave in sports environments is best explained by understanding the interaction between different personal factors (for example motive to achieve success, or motive to avoid failure), and situational factors (for example how likely you are to be successful or the value that you place on success). This theory is made up of five parts: personality factors, situational factors, resultant tendencies, emotional reactions, and achievement behaviour (Figure 7.1).

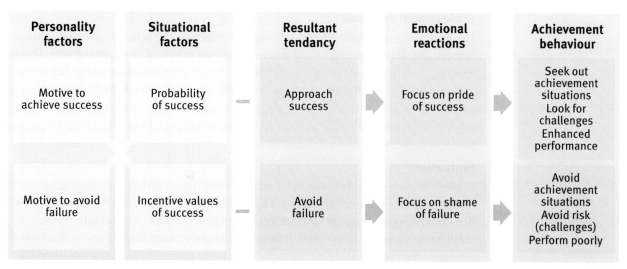

▸ **Figure 7.1:** Need achievement theory

Personality factors

Every sportsperson has two achievement motives. These are the **motive to achieve success** and the **motive to avoid failure**. The balance of these two motives will impact on a sportsperson's behaviour in sports environments. Athletes with high motive to achieve success are more likely to be comfortable evaluating their own sports performance and are unlikely to let themselves get worried about failing. Conversely, those who have a high motive to avoid failure are less comfortable evaluating their performance and are more likely to worry about failure.

Situational factors

The sporting situation that an athlete experiences also plays a role in their sporting behaviours. The need achievement theory suggests that **probability of success** and **incentive value of success** are two important situational factors that influence behaviour. The probability of success is linked to the difficulty of a task: your own skill or ability and that of your opponents. For example, you are less likely to win a 100-metre sprint race against Tori Bowie than you are against an athlete of a lesser level than yourself. However, competing against such a high-level athlete might alter your perceptions of success and you might place more value on just being able to compete against them than that of a lesser-level athlete. In other words, the act of being able to compete against an athlete of that ability would be enough for you, rather than any expectation of winning.

Resultant tendencies

The resultant tendency relates to a sportsperson's behaviour as a result of the personality and situational factors involved (for example the probability of success and the incentive value of success). It is the degree to which a sportsperson will approach success or avoid failure. This theory best predicts an athlete's behaviour when they have a 50–50 chance of success (for example competing against somebody who is equally as good as them). In these circumstances, athletes who are high achievers are more likely to seek out this type of challenge and enjoy taking part in sporting activities that are neither too difficult, nor too easy.

Emotional reactions

The emotional reaction is the amount of pride or shame that a sportsperson experiences during a sporting event. Typically, high achievers will focus on the pride of success whereas low achievers will focus on the shame of failure.

Key terms

Motive to achieve success – a sportsperson's capacity to take pride in their sporting accomplishments.

Motive to avoid failure – a sportsperson's capacity to feel or experience shame as a result of failure.

Probability of success – how likely it is that you will experience success (for example winning) in sport.

Incentive value of success – how much value you place on the success you experience in sport.

Achievement behaviour

The final component of the need achievement theory is the achievement behaviour component. This is the product of interaction of the previous four components. This is what the sportsperson will do under different sporting circumstances. High achievers are likely to look for challenging situations; they will be comfortable and perform better in situations where they are being evaluated. Low achievers, conversely, will tend to avoid challenging situations, opting more for tasks in which they are guaranteed to win or lose.

Evaluation

One of the main benefits of the need achievement theory is that it allows you to understand how different athletes will behave under different performance scenarios (for example against people who are equally as good as them, much better than them, or much worse than them). It helps you to understand how people will act who are either high or low in their motivation to achieve success or in their motivation to avoid failure, particularly in 50–50 situations. However, it does not work as well as a predictor of performance when athletes have moderate motives to achieve success or to avoid failure.

Achievement goal theory

Achievement Goal Theory (AGT) (Duda & Hall, 2001) suggests that three factors – achievement goals, perceived ability and achievement behaviours – interact to produce an athlete's levels of motivation (see Figure 7.2). This theory suggests that if you want to understand an athlete's motivation, you must understand what success means to them.

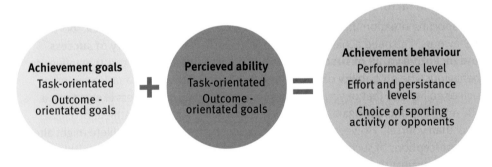

▶ **Figure 7.2:** Thinking about your own sport, how can the AGT explain your own levels of motivation?

Task orientation

Task orientation focuses on the athlete comparing their own performance to their previous performance; it emphasises personal improvement. This can help motivation as the athlete is more in control of whether they achieve the goal or not. A task-orientated approach is often recommended for athletes as it allows them to control how they achieve their goals. It can also enhance an athlete's performance and can help them maintain effort levels and wellbeing.

Outcome or ego orientation

Outcome or ego orientation involves comparing performance with that of others; it has an emphasis on beating opponents and winning prizes. Outcome-orientated athletes, when facing much higher-level opponents, are more likely to reduce their effort levels, will often make excuses for losing and can feel bad about themselves when they lose.

Sportspeople can be both task- and outcome-orientated at the same time; they might want to win an event at the same time as achieving a personal-best performance. It is widely accepted, however, that most sportspeople will be higher in one orientation than the other.

Evaluation

A major strength of the AGT is that it helps you understand the ways that different goal orientations can impact on performance and wellbeing. This can help psychologists to understand how to motivate athletes in the best way possible.

Self-determination theory

This is a **meta theory** created by Deci & Ryan (2000). This theory has helped sport psychologists understand different sport experiences, including sports injury rehabilitation, sport dropout rates and psychological wellbeing in coaches and athletes.

> **Key term**
>
> **Meta theory** – a theory that is made up of several smaller theories to provide an understanding of a topic.

Individual needs for autonomy, relatedness and competence

The most popular of the sub-theories is the Basic psychological needs theory (BPNT), which argues that you have three basic needs which must be satisfied in order for you to be motivated. These are:

▶ **competence:** your perception that you can successfully complete a task to the required/desired quality

▶ **autonomy:** your perception that you have choice or control over events happening in your life

▶ **relatedness:** your perception of connectedness or belonging to others.

If these three psychological needs are met, people are more likely to be motivated towards a particular activity. This means they may try hard, keep going when things go wrong, and appreciate the experience of growth from taking part in sport and exercise.

> **Reflect**
>
> Think about a time when you either felt you were not very good at a sporting activity, that you constantly felt you were being told what to do with no choice in activities, or times when you felt isolated from the rest of a group. Did you want to carry on with your activity?

Intrinsic motivation

Intrinsic motivation refers to someone participating in an activity without an external reward and/or without the primary motivation being the achievement of an external reward. This is motivation that is internal ('comes from within'). 'Fun' is the most common form of intrinsic motivation, but aside from this there are three key elements that can affect it. These are:

▶ **accomplishments:** when athletes wish to increase their level of skill to get a sense of accomplishment

▶ **stimulation:** seeking an 'adrenaline rush' or some form of excitement

▶ **knowledge:** being curious about performance; wanting to know more about it and to develop new techniques or skills that benefit performance.

Extrinsic motivation

Extrinsic motivation is motivation that comes from an external source. Within the self-determination theory, there are four different levels of extrinsic motivation, as detailed below.

▶ **External regulation:** This is the least **autonomous** form of motivation and a sportsperson will undertake behaviours because of an external demand (for example a coach telling an athlete they must do it); a possible tangible reward (for example a trophy); or an intangible reward (for example praise).

▶ **Introjected regulation:** This is where a sportsperson takes the behaviours on board but doesn't fully accept them as their own. It might be that they try to do something to receive approval from other people.

▶ **Identified regulation:** This is a more autonomous form of behaviour where undertaking the behaviour has personal value to the sportsperson.

▶ **Integrated regulation:** This is the most autonomous form of extrinsic motivation where goals are viewed as being part of the sportsperson's 'self'; they will strive to achieve them for external reasons, such as a trophy or praise.

> **Key terms**
>
> **Intrinsic motivation** – motivation that comes from within.
>
> **Extrinsic motivation** – motivation that comes from an external source.
>
> **Autonomous** – being independent and feeling able to make your own decisions.

▶ What do you find motivates you to complete a sporting activity?

⏸ PAUSE POINT   Can you understand how to contrast and link intrinsic and extrinsic motivation?

Hint   Close this book and produce a table that provides examples of intrinsic and extrinsic motivation.

Extend   How do you think that intrinsic and extrinsic motivation can interact to influence sports performance, both positively and negatively?

Amotivation

Amotivation is absence of motivation. It can be caused by a lack of perceived competence or autonomy, a negative self-perception, or the athlete not valuing the activity they are going to take part in.

Evaluation

A key strength of the SDT is that it has been able to explain motivation across a range of different contexts. It can help to design ways of working with athletes that enable them to be more motivated, more productive and feel better about themselves as a result.

> **Research**
>
> Visit the self-determination theory (SDT) website (www.selfdeterminationtheory.org) and look at some of the research that has used this theory. What problems or questions has it been used to answer?

⏸ PAUSE POINT   Can you explain the different theories of motivation?

Hint   Close the book and draw a table that summarises the key parts of each theory.

Extend   Add two extra columns to your original table and complete this with the strengths and limitations of different theories.

Theories of self-confidence in sport

Self-confidence is a psychological state empowered by the belief athletes have in their ability to perform and achieve specific outcomes. An individual's level of self-confidence can be influenced by their experiences in training and games, so it is important to know how to enhance the opportunities for people to build their confidence during sport sessions. Sport psychologists often work with coaches, managers and athletes during their training sessions or games, to support confidence development. Think of confidence as an impenetrable brick wall – your job is to help athletes build their wall, brick by brick. Understanding theories of self-confidence in sport helps you to know how you can help athletes improve their self-confidence.

Reflect

Think about a time when a coach has told you that you needed to be more confident. How did you behave during that event and how would you change your behaviour in future to show your increased confidence?

Definition of self-confidence

Self-confidence is the belief that you can successfully perform a **desired behaviour** (Weinberg & Gould, 2015). 'Desired behaviour' can be any sporting activity, such as hitting a bulls-eye in darts or scoring a penalty in football. The key part about sport confidence is that you believe you will be successful.

Key term

Desired behaviour – the behaviour that a sportsperson is aiming to achieve.

Discussion

Name an athlete who you think performs in a confident way. What is it about this athlete's behaviour in sport, that makes you think they are confident?

Vealey's Multidimensional Model of Sport Confidence (1986, 2001)

Vealey et al. devised the Multidimensional Model of Sport Confidence. This is a model that helps to understand the different factors that influence confidence within sport. It has four main components: factors influencing sport confidence; sources of sport confidence; constructs of sport confidence; and consequences of sport confidence.

Factors influencing sport confidence

Factors linked to personality, demographics (data about population groups) and organisational structure will influence levels of sport confidence. Personality factors (such as the athlete's level of optimism) will increase or decrease their confidence. Those with a more positive outlook (that is, those who are more optimistic) tend to be more confident. Evidence suggests that demographic characteristics such as gender can also influence confidence levels, but there are many conflicting findings surrounding this. Finally, the organisational structure such as the coach's behaviour, level of competition that the athlete is competing in and the **motivational climate** can all affect levels of self-confidence too.

Key term

Motivational climate – the environment that is created by coaches, parents and team mates that can help motivate athletes during training and competition.

Sources of sport confidence

There are a number of sources of sport confidence. Male athletes may report outperforming their competitors as a source of confidence, while female athletes report self-development and improvement (for example improving their own sports performance) as a source of confidence. Previously experiencing success can help increase levels of self-confidence for future events as the athlete will have a greater belief that they can repeat previous results. Believing they are more talented than opponents can also build confidence, partly because this contributes to feelings of having a competitive advantage over an opponent. Vealey, Hayashi, Garner-Holan, and Giacobbi (1998) outlined nine sources of sport confidence.

1 **Mastery:** developing and improving skills.
2 **Demonstration of ability:** showing ability by winning and outperforming opponents.
3 **Physical and mental preparation:** staying focused on goals and being prepared to give your all.
4 **Physical self-presentation:** feeling good about yourself (for example physical appearance, body weight).
5 **Social support:** getting support from peers, family and coaches.
6 **Coaches' leadership:** feeling that you can trust the coaches' decisions and having a belief in their ability.
7 **Vicarious experiences:** seeing others do well.
8 **Environmental comfort:** feeling comfortable in the environment where you will perform.
9 **Situational favourableness:** feeling that everything is going well and that you are getting the bit of luck that you need to succeed.

Constructs of sport confidence

The term 'constructs' means all the things that make up sport confidence. In the model Vealey et al. proposed, these include:

▶ decision-making skills (for example being able to decide which pass to play and when)
▶ physical skills (for example running, jumping, tackling)
▶ anticipatory skills (for example understanding the ways different opponents may play and being able to predict what they might do)
▶ the capacity to learn and develop (for example being able to acquire new sport skills).

Consequences of sport confidence

The consequences of sport confidence are linked to 'ABCs' – Affect, Behaviour and Cognition. If the athlete has higher levels of confidence, these factors are more likely to have a more positive effect (or emotion), they are likely to try harder (behaviours) and they are likely to pay closer attention to their sport to keep improving (cognitions).

Evaluation

Limitations in early versions of this model were that it did not accurately predict performance and that it did not fully consider each of the different factors that contribute to making up self-confidence. The more recent version of the theory is much better at predicting the relationship between self-confidence and sports performance. The theory now has helped to provide lots of different factors that coaches and sport psychologists can consider when trying to enhance confidence and performance in athletes.

Bandura's self-efficacy theory

Self-efficacy is an athlete's belief in their ability to complete a set task successfully. A prominent psychologist, Albert Bandura produced the self-efficacy theory (1977, 1986, 1997). This theory details how self-efficacy and, as a result, self-confidence and sporting performance can be developed. It is important to understand the principles of building self-confidence into your everyday sport sessions. The self-efficacy theory tells you that performance accomplishments, vicarious experiences, verbal persuasion and emotional arousal will create efficacy expectations, which will increase the chances of heightened athletic performance (see Figure 7.3).

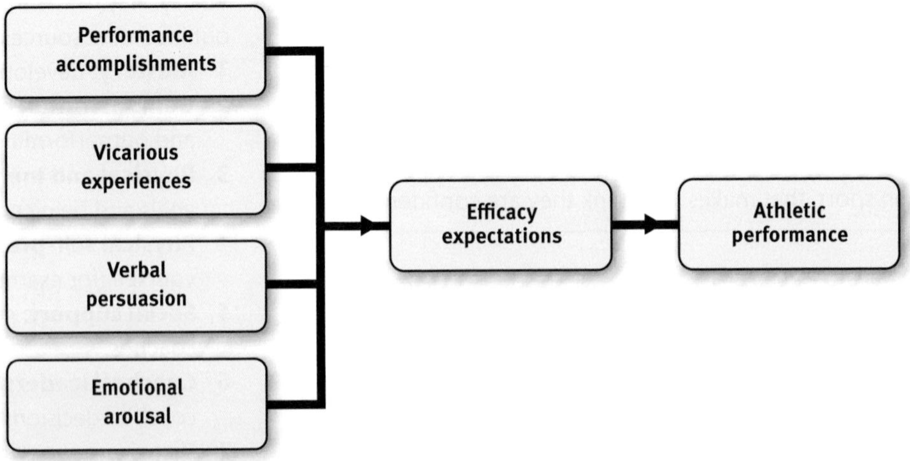

Key term

Self-efficacy – a belief in your ability to succeed in specific situations or accomplish a task. It reflects confidence in the ability to exert control over your own motivation, behaviour and social environment.

Link

Look back at Unit 3 for more information on self-efficacy.

▶ **Figure 7.3:** How can you apply Bandura's self-efficacy theory to your favourite sport?

Performance accomplishments

Think about when you recently performed well in your sport. How did you feel afterwards? You probably enjoyed it and could not wait to play again. Recent performance accomplishments are the strongest source of self-confidence. It is therefore important, particularly with children and young people or those returning to sport after a lengthy absence, to structure practices to allow for achievement of challenges and for athletes to receive feedback on these accomplishments.

A key consideration for coaches and sport leaders is to give specific examples of accomplishments and to praise or reinforce the effort that it has taken to reach the accomplishment. For example, if a young basketball player successfully performs their first three-point jump shot, do not just praise the outcome of the event (that is scoring the three points), make sure you also praise the effort they have put in (for example the time they have spent practising).

Vicarious experiences

The second strongest source of self-confidence is vicarious experience – this occurs when an athlete sees somebody who is similar to them (for example the same age or similar performance level) perform a skill successfully. This can enhance their self-belief in being able to do the same. It can have a modelling effect that is enhanced if the athlete observed is somebody significant to them, such as a close friend or a talented team mate.

To enhance the modelling effect, some coaches also use video footage of elite athletes performing a task. This can often give athletes something to aspire to, without creating any negative social comparisons between team mates. This is important as recent research in football has shown that negative social comparisons between team mates can reduce a player's chances of reaching an elite level in football, due to the effects it can have on their confidence (Gledhill & Harwood, 2015).

Verbal persuasion

This is a useful way to enhance self-confidence and occurs when somebody who is important to the player (for example a coach or team captain) tells the player they believe in them and that they can perform well. This is a similar idea to positive motivational self-talk but it comes from an external source, persuading the athlete that they are good enough. For coaches, it is important to model this behaviour for two main reasons.

▶ Have you been part of a sports team that has helped you to succeed?

▶ As a coach, you are likely to be the most influential person in a young athlete's sporting life, closely followed by their team mates and parents, so the message from you is likely to have the most impact.

▶ If, as a coach, you model the behaviour of verbal persuasion, you are more likely to have the athletes you work with model that behaviour too. This means that they are more likely to use positive self-talk with their team mates. This will help create a climate of confidence-building in your athletes and is more likely to create social support networks within the team. These networks are hugely important during setbacks, such as slumps in performance or serious injury, as athletes will feel more empowered and able to cope with these situations, and have a greater sense of team cohesion (unity).

Emotional arousal

This is the least impactful factor affecting self-efficacy. If an athlete is sad or upset prior to a competition, this may lower their confidence in their ability to succeed. It can have a negative effect on sports performance.

Efficacy expectations

These are an athlete's beliefs and expectations about their ability to perform tasks. How persistent they are in practising an activity or behaviour can play a role in how successful they are.

Athletic performance

The athletic performance is the resultant performance, influenced by each of the different factors. Typically, if self-efficacy is high, performance will increase.

Evaluation

Research has consistently supported the idea that the self-efficacy theory and its different elements have a significant impact on sports performance. These relationships are seen in both team and individual sports and with different types of athletes.

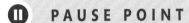

PAUSE POINT   How does the self-efficacy theory explain performance?

> Hint   Describe each of the sections of the self-efficacy theory.

> Extend   Provide a sport-based example of the self-efficacy theory.

Key terms

Anxiety – a negative emotional state associated with feelings of nervousness, apprehension or worry. For example, if an athlete is concerned about an event, they may experience anxiety in the weeks leading up to it.

Continuum – a continuous, gradual sequence from one extreme to another but along which there are no clearly marked distinctions.

Theories of arousal and anxiety in sports performance

Psychological definitions of arousal and anxiety

Arousal is a state of alertness and anticipation that prepares the body for action. It involves both physiological activation (increased heart rate, sweating rate or respiratory rate) and psychological activity (increased attention). Arousal can be seen as a **continuum**, with deep sleep at one extreme and excitement at the other. For example, an athlete may experience arousal throughout an event – before, during and after – at different points on the continuum.

Drive theory – linear relationship between arousal and performance

Hull (1943) proposed the drive theory, which views the arousal–performance relationship as linear. This means that as arousal increases, so does performance. The more 'learned' a skill is, the more likely it is that a high level of arousal will result in a better performance (see Figure 7.4). If the skill is not well learned, performance will deteriorate as arousal increases.

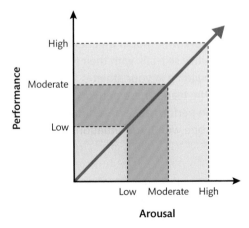

▶ **Figure 7.4:** According to the drive theory, what is the arousal–performance relationship?

This theory can help to explain why beginners find it difficult to perform under pressure. However, there is little research to support this theory as there is evidence to suggest that athletic performance is benefited by arousal only up to a point. As arousal increases, athletes may revert to using previously learned skills as they are well learned, but they may not be correct – for example, reverting to poor form in a volleyball match as arousal increases throughout the match. This does not equate to a clear, linear relationship between arousal and performance.

Inverted-U hypothesis – curvilinear relationship between arousal and performance

Yerkes & Dodson (1908) created the inverted-U hypothesis due to the limitations of the drive theory. It states that at optimal arousal levels (usually a moderate level of arousal), performance levels will be at their highest. When arousal is too low or too high, performance levels will be lower (see Figure 7.5). It argues that performance levels will be lower because the athlete is neither physiologically nor psychologically ready (for example, heart rate and concentration levels may be too low or too high).

The final key argument from this theory is that the performance decreases after the optimal level of arousal gradually. For example, the quality of a tennis player's serve might gradually worsen the further they get away from their optimal point of arousal.

The inverted-U hypothesis is more widely accepted than the drive theory because most athletes and coaches can report personal experiences of under-arousal (boredom), over-arousal (excitement to the point of lack of concentration), and optimum arousal (focusing on nothing but sports performance). However, there are questions over the type of curve demonstrated.

▸ Is the optimal arousal always a single point or do some athletes experience optimal arousal for a longer period of time?

▸ Is the decrease in performance always a steady decline or can it be more dramatic?

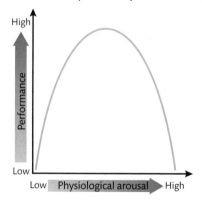

▸ **Figure 7.5:** According to the inverted-U theory, what is the arousal–performance relationship?

Catastrophe theory

Created by Hardy (1990, 1996), the catastrophe theory expands on the inverted-U theory by suggesting that performance is affected by arousal in an inverted-U fashion only when the individual has low levels of **cognitive anxiety**. If an athlete is experiencing higher levels of cognitive anxiety, and arousal levels increase up to the athlete's threshold, the player experiences a dramatic (or catastrophic) drop in performance levels (see Figure 7.6). This is a sudden decrement in performance, rather than a gradual decline. The key difference between catastrophe theory and the inverted-U theory is that the drop in performance does not have to be a gradual decline when arousal levels become too high.

Key term

Cognitive anxiety – the thought processes that occur when a person is anxious, such as concern or worry.

The catastrophe theory does not argue that cognitive anxiety is completely negative. The theory suggests that the athlete will perform at a higher level if they have a degree of cognitive anxiety because their attention and concentration levels increase. It is only when levels of cognitive anxiety are combined with extremely elevated levels of arousal that performance levels decrease dramatically. However, this theory is still questioned by some over claims that everybody's optimal arousal is the same single, moderate point.

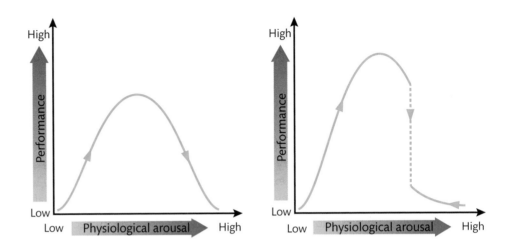

▶ **Figure 7.6:** According to the catastrophe theory, what is the arousal–performance relationship?

Theory into practice

Discuss the different theories that try to explain the arousal–performance relationship with your peers and come up with sporting examples that explain each of the theories. Which do you think best explains the arousal–performance relationship, and why?

Multidimensional anxiety theory

The multidimensional anxiety theory (Martens et al. 1990) suggests somatic and cognitive anxiety can affect performance in different ways and that their levels will change in the build-up to an event. Generally, cognitive anxiety is thought to decrease performance, while somatic anxiety is thought to enhance performance (to a certain point).

However, there are exceptions. For example, where **somatic anxiety** is low in the build-up to an event, having slightly elevated levels of cognitive anxiety can enhance performance. This slight increase can arouse and direct an athlete's attention towards ensuring they have a good performance. However, if the cognitive anxiety becomes too great, performance will be reduced.

State and trait components

Anxiety is a negative emotional state associated with feelings of nervousness, apprehension or worry.

▶ **Trait anxiety** is an aspect of the personality and part of an individual's pattern of behaviour. Someone with a high level of trait anxiety is likely to become worried in a variety of situations, even non-threatening situations. Athletes with high levels of trait anxiety are usually more state-anxious in highly pressured, highly competitive situations where there is a great deal of evaluation.

Key term

Somatic anxiety – the physical symptoms of anxiety, such as stomach pains and an increased heart rate.

▸ **State anxiety** is a temporary, ever-changing mood state that is an emotional response to any situation considered threatening. For example, at the start of an Olympic 400-metre event, the runner may have higher levels of state anxiety that drop once the event begins. State anxiety levels may increase again when coming up to the final bend and be at their highest level when coming towards the finish line when they are neck-and-neck with their strongest rival.

Cognitive, somatic and behavioural components

Anxiety also has cognitive, somatic and behavioural components as discussed below.

▸ **Cognitive anxiety** refers to the negative thoughts, nervousness or worry experienced by some in certain situations, such as prior to a large sporting event. Symptoms of cognitive anxiety include concentration problems, fear and bad decision making.

▸ **Somatic anxiety** relates to physiological changes (such as increases in heart rate, sweating and increased body heat) in certain situation, such as when you are participating in a large sporting event, and the awareness and perception of these changes. For example, an athlete could be concerned because they sense an increased heart rate if they have gone into a game less prepared than usual. This increase in heart rate is necessary for performance but is seen as negative by the athlete.

▸ **Behavioural anxiety** refers to how nerves affect behaviours. Signs and symptoms of this type of anxiety include 'playing safe' (not taking acceptable risks such as a risky pass), changes in posture, fidgeting, rapid speech and avoiding eye contact.

Reversal theory of anxiety

Kerr (1985, 1997) produced the reversal theory. This theory suggests that it is the perception of arousal that can influence performance. For example, if an athlete perceives the symptoms of arousal as positive, they are more likely to enhance performance or perceive their performance as more positive. Conversely, if arousal symptoms are viewed as negative, the athlete is likely to perform worse, or perceive their level of performance to be worse. This explains why some sport psychologists highlight the role of some of the signs and symptoms of arousal (for example increased heart rate, increased breathing rate, increased temperature) in successful performance, turning arousal from an unpleasant worry into a pleasant excitement.

Investigate how psychological theories can be applied to sporting situations

Motivation theories in sporting environments

As you learned previously, there are many different theories that can help you understand motivation in sporting environments. This section will develop these theories and show you how they can be applied to specific aspects of sporting events.

Need achievement theory

Athletes with a high need to achieve (NACH) and high need to avoid failure (NAF): choosing competitions and opponents

Athletes can be grouped into two categories: those who need to achieve (NACH) and those who need to avoid failure (NAF). NACH athletes tend to strive for success; they keep trying when things go wrong, and feel a sense of pride in accomplishments. There is less focus on comparing skill, ability or performance against other athletes, with a greater emphasis on realistic and challenging personal goals.

High-achiever NACH athletes typically set themselves challenging goals, prefer competition against worthy opponents and perform well when being evaluated. NAF athletes tend to avoid these scenarios. For example, an athlete with low achievement motivation will prefer playing against a weaker opponent where success is virtually guaranteed, or against an opponent who is so good that they are guaranteed to fail.

Everyone has aspects of both NACH and NAF, but the balance of the two determines a person's achievement motivation.

Impact of levels of achievement motivation on task persistence and mastery

Arguably, the need achievement theory is best at predicting an athlete's behaviour during situations where there is a 50–50 chance of success or failure. In these situations, athletes who are high achievers are likely to approach challenges, seek out opportunities to improve, persist with tasks that they are set, and seek to master new skills.

Conversely, low achievers are likely to avoid such 50–50 situations, where there is an equal chance of success or failure. An example of a 50–50 situation is one where they may be competing against an athlete who is just as good as them. They are more likely to approach situations only where a task is very easy and so there is no chance of failure (for example playing against an athlete who is much worse than them). Equally, they are more likely to approach impossible-looking situations where there is no chance of success, as they would not feel any shame, worry or disappointment about losing in that situation.

Effect of being evaluated on performance of high and low achievers

Athletes with high achievement motivation tend to like being in situations where they will be evaluated, partly because that evaluation provides them with an opportunity to receive feedback that can help them to improve further. They are less concerned about any negative consequences of being evaluated and are more likely to approach situations where they are being evaluated. The opposite is the case for people with low levels of achievement motivation.

Achievement goal theory

Value of task orientation on work ethic, persistence and optimal performance

There is some debate over whether outcome- or task-orientated goals are better for motivation. Traditionally, task-orientated goals have been shown to:

▸ increase levels of work ethic, effort and persistence
▸ reduce levels of disappointment or frustration
▸ reduce fear of failure.

The main argument to support these points is that the athlete is more in control of goal achievement when adopting task-orientated goals. By being more in control of goal achievement (for example by having a goal which relates to self-improvement as opposed to beating an opponent), athletes are more likely to want to improve so will try harder and continue when things get difficult. Athletes are also less likely to get frustrated. Consider a time you have tried to outperform somebody who is significantly better than you: it can be frustrating because – no matter how hard you try – you always struggle to win. By making self-comparisons related to self-improvement, you are much less likely to experience this frustration as the only person you are competing against is yourself. Equally, by comparing yourself to yourself and setting goals that are linked to controllable factors, you are much less likely to fear failing.

Drawbacks of a sportsperson adopting an outcome or ego orientation

Outcome-orientated goals have been shown to result in lower levels of perceived competence, effort and persistence, as well as athletes tending to blame failure on things that are beyond their control. This could be a result of the athlete feeling less in control over the goal. For example, if you are constantly competing against people who are much better than you and all you value is beating your opponents, you are more likely to become frustrated and your self-confidence will diminish. This is because you know that you are always probably going to lose in spite of your best efforts.

The debate over the benefits and limitations of task versus ego orientation centres on the simplicity of the arguments. For example, if a sportsperson places a great deal of meaning on an event's outcome then they may be more likely to persist in trying to achieve, even if they are at first unsuccessful. Equally, an athlete constantly using task-orientated goals who is unsuccessful in improving may see their motivation to improve decrease.

Discussion

Some situations result in people demonstrating both task orientation and outcome orientation. How do you think this can happen? Think about it in a sporting context.

Theory into practice

Ashleigh is a competitive bodybuilder. She trains hard because she wants to see her personal physique improve. Her major competition is against herself and she sets challenging goals related to self-improvement. However, in competitions Ashleigh always focuses on beating her opponents. She will often look to see which bodybuilders are competing in upcoming events and can get concerned even before the competition if she sees that there are people competing that she has previously lost to. If she does not win, she usually has a lull in her training regime and tells herself that she is not good enough.

How do Ashleigh's goals, and her reaction to them, change according to her situation?

Self-determination theory

Participation in sport meets individual needs for autonomy, relatedness and competence

Sport participation can help people:

▸ experience a sense of control over their own experiences (autonomy satisfaction)
▸ connect and interact with other people (relatedness satisfaction)
▸ feel as though they are good at something and able to achieve a desired outcome (competence satisfaction).

Collectively, when these needs are satisfied, a sportsperson is likely to experience greater psychological wellbeing and achieve higher levels of performance.

Importance of self-determined behaviour and its impact on persistence, ability to cope with stress and produce peak performance

Athletes who demonstrate self-determined behaviour are:

▸ less likely to drop out of sport
▸ more likely to experience higher levels of psychological wellbeing
▸ likely to experience improved performance
▸ more likely to respond to stressful situations more positively and, in so doing, more likely to produce peak performances.

Impact of extrinsic rewards on intrinsic motivation

For extrinsic motivation to be effective, rewards must be effective. If a reward is given frequently, it will be of less value to the athlete, removing its impact on performance. Equally, if an athlete places too much emphasis on the reward and it is subsequently removed, it is possible their intrinsic motivation levels will decrease. A coach needs to have an in-depth knowledge of their athletes to maximise the effectiveness of extrinsic rewards.

Discussion

How can extrinsic motivation positively and negatively influence intrinsic motivation? Consider this in the context of a sporting activity of your choice.

Self-confidence theories in sporting environments

Vealey's multidimensional model of sport confidence

Impact of different levels of sport confidence on sports performance

Self-confidence can arouse positive emotions, help concentration, increase effort and influence game strategy. For example, a player with a high level of self-confidence may want to take responsibility for set pieces in football (influencing game strategy) because they feel they have paid attention to positions and behaviours of team mates (concentration), which they feel increase the chances of success.

Optimal levels of self-confidence can help increase and maintain an enhanced level of performance. If an athlete has lower levels of confidence, or is over-confident, there is a strong chance performance can decrease, affecting overall psychological wellbeing and increasing injury risk. If an athlete lacks confidence or is over-confident, they may begin to miss relevant information because they are paying less attention.

Research

Research the term 'over-confidence'. Find as many sources and consequences of over-confidence as you can. For each one that you find, provide an example of how it may negatively affect sports performance or an athlete's wellbeing.

Consequences of sport confidence on sports performance

Within Vealey's Multidimensional Model of Sport Confidence, the 'ABC Triangle' was produced to show the consequences of sport confidence and explain the relationship between affect, behaviour and cognition. An optimal (usually high) level of sport confidence will positively affect emotions, more adaptive achievement behaviours (for example trying harder when things are difficult), and better use of cognitive resources (for example attentional skills/concentration). Collectively, these changes are likely to increase sports performance. Athletes who feel better about themselves (and can pay attention to a variety of different factors) are likely to perform better in their chosen sport.

Bandura's self-efficacy theory

Manipulating sources of self-efficacy

There are six main sources of self-efficacy that a coach can manipulate in order to influence a sportsperson's expectations of success.

1 **Performance accomplishments:** they can manipulate opportunities for success, in order to increase the sportsperson's perceptions of performance accomplishments. This could be achieved in different ways, including altering playing area size, providing feedback on progress and altering rules to provide a greater opportunity for athletes of different ability levels.
2 **Vicarious experiences:** Seeing team mates or opponents complete different skills can help a sportsperson believe that they also can complete that activity successfully. They can achieve this through modelling behaviours and skills.
3 **Verbal persuasion:** They can receive persuasion from an external source (for example another coach or a physiotherapist), to persuade them that it is possible to complete an activity successfully. This could be a coach telling a hockey player that they are excellent at taking penalties, that they don't need to worry that they have missed some in the last game and that they just need to keep calm and try again in order to be successful.
4 **Imaginal experiences:** They can use imagery techniques to create successful experiences in their mind. This gives them the opportunity to imagine that they are good at a certain behaviour or skill, which can then increase their belief in their ability to complete a task successfully.

Link

Go to page 357 for more information on imagery techniques.

1 **Physiological states:** Changes in physiological states (for example heart rate and breathing rate) can either increase or decrease an athlete's belief in their ability to complete a task. Altering their perception of the meaning of these physiological changes (for example that the changes are beneficial for performance as opposed to being something that indicates they are not well prepared) can also influence self-efficacy levels.

2 **Emotional states:** Helping an athlete to have positive emotional responses to (or preparation for) an activity (for example helping them to feel more energised or more at peace) can lead to improved expectations of success. This can be achieved through completing different psychological skills-training activities, such as self-talk, imagery or breathing activities.

Collectively, these six points can all impact on an athlete's efficacy expectations. In turn, these efficacy expectations can impact on the sportsperson's performance.

Influence of expectations of success on sports performance

The term 'expectations of success' relates to an athlete's beliefs and expectations about their ability to perform tasks and achieve desired outcomes (for example to win the game or event). Research, such as that carried out by Samson & Solomon (2011) shows that having positive performance expectations can enhance performance levels. This can be as a result of increased confidence or increased effort and persistence. Typically, this will be the case unless an athlete becomes complacent.

> **Discussion**
>
> In pairs, discuss how a sportsperson could reduce their opponent's expectations of success using the theories discussed.

Arousal and anxiety theories in sporting environments

Drive theory: relationship of increases in arousal to performance

There are very few applications of this theory within sports environments. As the theory suggests that performance will increase alongside arousal levels, with no specific end point, there is very little support for the application of this theory.

Inverted-U hypothesis

As with the drive theory, there is little evidence to support the inverted-U hypothesis and potential applications

within sports environments. While there are many athletes, coaches and sport psychologists who can relate to the concept of athletes who are under- and over-aroused not performing as well as they should, and athletes who are optimally aroused performing consistently well, there is little support for the universal shape of the curve. There is also little support for the idea that every athlete's optimal point of arousal is the mid-point of the curve, suggesting that a more individualised understanding of optimal arousal is needed.

Catastrophe theory

Choking due to the impact of high cognitive anxiety

Performance **decrements** that occur in high-pressure situations are sometimes referred to as 'choking'. An example of this might be when a golfer misses an easy putt that is required to win the Open Championship. However, choking also includes the process that leads up to the decreased performance. It is an extreme form of nervousness and it is largely based on the subjective importance of the event (i.e. what the event means to the individual athlete). Choking can be more apparent in the presence of parents, peers or large audiences.

> **Key term**
>
> **Decrement** – a reduction in something.

Characteristics of a sportsperson experiencing choking

The characteristics of a sportsperson choking are that they will perform to a sub-standard level (i.e. worse than normal) when they are in high-pressure situations. There is debate about whether this can be any type of decrease in performance, or whether the decrease needs to be very sudden and very severe. Typically, athletes who are experiencing choking will suffer symptoms such as muscle tension, an inability to think properly or concentrate, and even an inability to move correctly. These things all contribute to decreased performance.

Impact of high arousal levels of attentional focus, muscle tension and aggressive behaviour

During heightened states of arousal, the attentional field, which focuses attention and concentration, becomes narrowed. This means that the more aroused you become, the lower the number of relevant cues you can concentrate on. For example, in a game of basketball, at optimal states of arousal, the point guard will be able to focus on the opposing player in possession of the ball as well as their own and the other players' positions on the court. But during heightened states of arousal they may only be able to focus on the opposition player and may disregard other important cues.

Just as a heightened state of arousal can narrow the player's attention, it can also broaden it to the point where performance is decreased. In this scenario, the point guard player would be concentrating on irrelevant information like crowd noise as well as the relevant game cues.

Case study

Jemima is a 16-year-old gymnast. She has very high-performance standards and always compares herself to other gymnasts. Jemima's coach constantly tells her that if she is ever going to make it as an Olympic gymnast with any chance of winning a medal, then she needs to get used to putting the 'extra work' in and that she needs to start performing better than her competitors.

Jemima's parents are friends with her coach and regularly talk with her coach about Jemima's performance levels. After one of the most recent reviews, Jemima's parents have reminded her about the amount of money that they have spent helping her get to the level she has achieved. They have also reminded her about the number of hours that they have spent taking her to and from competitions and training, and have started talking more about the number of sacrifices that they have made in their own personal life, in order to support her in her gymnastic development.

It is the morning of a representative squad selection event, where Jemima needs to perform well in order to make the team. In the car on the way to the event, Jemima's parents remind her of these conversations and that they are expecting big things of her. Jemima's coach told her father that a gymnast who regularly beats Jemima is competing today as well, so they should make sure Jemima is 'ready to compete'. In the car on the way to the event, Jemima's father constantly reminds her of the expectations that are on her and that she must win. He also tells Jemima that she 'can't let them down now, not when she is so close'.

At the event, Jemima really struggles with what is usually her strongest event: the floor routine. She can't concentrate on the routine she is supposed to be completing, her muscles feel tight and she can't relax into her movement patterns. Before every part of her routine, Jemima looks into the crowd and sees her father looking very nervous and her mum with her head in her hands. Jemima prepares to attempt the major tumbling element of her routine and trips as she starts her run up, falls over and immediately starts crying, before leaving the floor.

1 Do you think that Jemima choked during this situation? Justify your answer using specific details from the case study.

2 What factors do you think played a role in Jemima's performance?

3 Which arousal–performance theory do you think is best to explain this case?

⏸ PAUSE POINT What are the theories of about the arousal–performance relationship?

> Hint Close the book and produce a timeline with descriptions of the different theories around the arousal–performance relationship.

> Extend Highlight how the limitations of earlier theories contributed to developments of later theories.

Multidimensional anxiety theory

State and trait components

Earlier in the unit, you learned about the differences between state and trait components. Think now about two darts players, each with equal levels of skill. They need to hit a double-16 to be able to win the World Darts Championship for the first time in their career. The player who is low-trait anxious (i.e. more relaxed and laid back) is more likely to view this situation as less threatening (i.e. have less state anxiety) and will probably be more successful in their performance. Conversely, the player who is high-trait anxious (i.e. more worried or with more of a tendency to view situations as negative and threatening) may perceive the situation as being more threatening and worry more about it (i.e. experience more state anxiety). This may mean they are less likely to be successful when trying to hit the double-16. Experienced athletes who are high-trait anxious may be able to cope more effectively with changes in state anxiety due to different skills developed during their career. They may also be able to use their experience to reduce how negatively they view challenging or evaluative situations.

▶ How do you deal with anxiety before a sporting event?

Increases in cognitive anxiety negatively affect performance

Think about times that you have been extremely worried or had lots of negative thoughts that you struggled to control. These are examples of increased cognitive anxiety. During sports performance, this can distract your attention from the task at hand, lead to you doubting your ability as a sportsperson and can reduce the level of effort or persistence that you put into an event. All these factors can have a negative impact on performance in the long term.

Increases in somatic anxiety positively influence performance

There are some suggestions that an awareness of changes in a sportsperson's physiological state can improve performance. Working over a period of time with athletes will help understand that these physiological changes are beneficial for performance, as opposed to being negative for performance. For example, an athlete might perceive a sudden change in body temperature and heart rate early in a game as a sign that they are unfit, when these are simply ways that the body prepares them for competitive sport. According to the Multidimensional Anxiety Theory, the relationship between somatic anxiety and performance is an inverted-U.

Inverse relationship between cognitive anxiety and self-confidence

As well as having a negative impact on sports performance, high levels of cognitive anxiety are also associated with lower levels of self-confidence.

Reversal theory

Characteristics of a sportsperson who interprets anxiety as a positive emotion

High levels of arousal or anxiety being perceived as positive usually occur in athletes who are quite playful, spontaneous, and often enjoy being in the present.

Characteristics of a sportsperson who interprets anxiety as a negative emotion

High levels of arousal or anxiety being less pleasurable usually occur in athletes who are quite serious, are less comfortable being spontaneous and feel that they must plan things out in advance and often spend a lot of time thinking about the future.

There are three main factors that can determine whether anxiety or arousal will be perceived as positive or negative. These are explained below.

1 **Changes in the environment:** A golfer who has been playing well in good weather conditions may notice changes in their arousal and anxiety levels/symptoms if there is a sudden change in the weather. If they associate these arousal changes with the changes in weather, the changes may be perceived more negatively.

2 **Frustration:** If a tennis player becomes frustrated with a line-call and they notice their heart rate, body temperature and sweating rates change, they could view these changes as negative and start to perform at a lower level.

3 **Satiation:** If an athlete prefers a particular type of practice or tactic and is repeatedly asked to do something different, this could result in them reacting more negatively to any changes in arousal.

Assessment activity 7.1 | A.P1 | A.P2 | B.P3 | B.P4 | A.M1 | B.M2 | A.D1 | B.D2

You have applied for a work placement position with a regional sports organisation. As part of this, your role will be to observe and support the lead practitioner in producing coaching information that can help to support athlete development.

The specific aspects that the organisation is working on are the different factors that can influence their athletes' motivation, self-confidence, arousal and anxiety.

This is a highly competitive placement position, so involves a selection event. For this event, you have been asked to produce a series of coaching information leaflets (one each for motivation, self-confidence, anxiety and arousal) that explain the different theories.

Make sure that you use relevant sporting examples to illustrate each of the different theories. Consider both the strengths and limitations of how each element (motivation, self-confidence, anxiety and arousal) can influence sports performance, and think about the strengths and limitations of the theories.

Plan
- What is the task? What am I being asked to do?
- How confident do I feel in my own abilities to complete this task? Are there any areas I think I may struggle with?

Do
- I know what it is I'm doing and what I want to achieve.
- I can identify when I've gone wrong and adjust my thinking/approach to get myself back on course.

Review
- I can explain what the task was and how I approached the task.
- I can explain how I would approach the hard elements differently next time (i.e. what I would do differently).

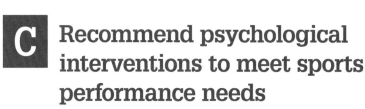

C Recommend psychological interventions to meet sports performance needs

Psychological interventions to influence motivation of sportspeople

Psychological interventions are used to enhance the motivation of sportspeople. Each method of enhancing motivation has various uses and what benefits one person won't benefit another. It is important to understand the strengths and limitations of different techniques, so that you know how to use them effectively. The main intervention techniques used to enhance motivation in sport are performance profiling and goal setting.

Performance profiling – uses and processes

Performance profiling is a way of understanding a sportsperson's views of their sporting qualities and can be used to help them to improve their performance by increasing their motivation. Profiling helps in understanding the sportsperson's perspective and will increase their motivation to develop. It also encourages the sportsperson to reflect on their performance, helping them to reach an elite level and experience greater psychological wellbeing. The process of performance profiling in general follows several stages. These are:

▶ eliciting constructs
▶ assessment of constructs
▶ utilising the results of the assessment (for example to set appropriate goals that will help increase performance).

Eliciting constructs – ten psychological factors important for performance

The term '**eliciting constructs**' refers to identifying the qualities that athletes, coaches and sport psychologists view as being important for successful sports performance. Within this stage, a sport psychologist would introduce the idea by asking the athlete what psychological factors they think are important for top performance. When using performance profiling in a sports setting, the athlete could be asked to think of an elite performer and write down the athlete's qualities. This could also be completed together with a coach or a sport psychologist. To avoid any confusion, it is important that an agreed definition for the different constructs is included as part of the performance profile. It will also be helpful to discuss why the sportsperson thinks that these constructs are the most important for their sport. Psychological factors that are often included in this stage include confidence, concentration, commitment, motivation and many others. They will often be sport-specific.

Assessment of constructs

Depending on the purpose of the performance profiling, this assessment can be done either solely by the sportsperson or independently by both the sportsperson and the coach. Opinions are then gathered and differences assessed. The sportsperson would rate themselves from 0–10 for each construct. This is usually recorded on a circular grid, as shown in Figure 7.7, which shows examples of different psychological factors that could be included on a performance profile and their possible rating out of 10. It isn't uncommon that coaches and athletes may offer different ratings, as this is a subjective process.

Key terms

Psychological interventions – techniques used to try to enhance health, wellbeing and/or performance of athletes.

Performance profiling – a way of identifying strengths and areas for development in sports performance, that can be used to set goals and improve motivation.

Eliciting constructs – identifying the key psychological factors that are important for successful sports performance.

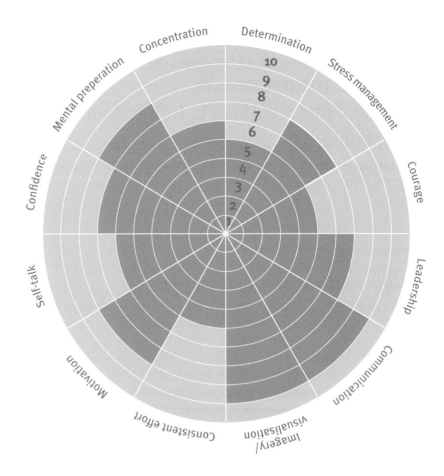

▶ **Figure 7.7:** Assessment of constructs rating

Utilising the results from an assessment

It is possible to use the results of performance profiling as the basis of goal setting with a sportsperson, to help them improve their overall sports performance. You might look to the areas that have scored the lowest and use this as the basis for improvement. Equally, you might also look at the psychological factors that you think are the most important and then seek to improve these, if there is obvious room for improvement. Whichever way you choose to use the results, it is important that the sportsperson is central to the decision-making process over areas for improvement and any associated goals. By being actively involved in this process, the sportsperson is likely to feel more autonomous in their goal setting, which will often increase their motivation.

Discussion

Why do you think that an athlete might be resistant to change and how do you think you could help them to become less resistant?

Areas resistant to change

Sometimes, a sportsperson might be reluctant to change a particular area of the performance profile. This might be because they don't think it is important to change, because they are not sure how they can improve it, or that they are uncomfortable with suggestions made about improving their performance. Regardless of the reason for their resistance, it is important to support athletes in reducing these levels of resistance.

Evaluation of performance profiling

Performance profiling is a proven, effective way of improving motivation and performance in a range of athletes. For it to be most effective, the athlete must be fully engaged with the process and be committed in considering which qualities are important for their sport and why. If an athlete is not prepared to do this, it is likely that the performance profiling will be less effective.

Goal setting

Timescale for goals

You should set goals in a coherent, progressive and linked manner. You should use a combination of short-term, medium-term and long-term goals. Having only a long-term goal has little effect on performance and motivation. Achieving short-term and medium-term goals are important as they can guide the athlete towards realistic long-term goals. Having the constant sense of achievement through reaching the short-term and medium-term goals enhances the athlete's motivation to continue.

You should avoid being too prescriptive with timescales for some goals and allow flexibility for them to be revised if the athlete is struggling to achieve them all. Table 7.1 shows an example of short-term, medium-term and long-term goals that might be used for an international rugby player who has ruptured their anterior cruciate ligament and had this surgically repaired.

▸ **Table 7.1:** Why do you think it is important to have a logical progression of goals?

Goal setting for an athlete who is recovering from anterior cruciate ligament reconstruction surgery	
Duration of goal	**Example**
Short-term	Progress to standing up with full weight bearing within 72 hours of surgery
Short-term	Have swelling eliminated and approximately up to 100° range of movement within two weeks post-surgery
Short-term to medium-term	Be able to perform a full squat, have unrestricted balance and control when walking and have approximately 130° of knee flexion within two weeks to three months post-surgery
Medium-term	Have full range of motion, full strength and straight-line running ability by three to five months post-surgery
Medium-term to long-term	Be able to perform change of direction running and return to restricted sport-specific drills within four to six months post-surgery
Long-term	Have a full return to competitive sport within six to twelve months post-surgery

Types of goals

As well as establishing goals for sportspeople to follow, you also need to determine the type of goal you are setting them.

Outcome, performance and process goals

▸ Outcome goals focus on the result of the event, like winning a match. These are often the least effective for motivation as goal achievement depends on the opposition as well as the athlete. For example, if you run a personal best in the 400 metres but finish last and the outcome goal was to win, this could negatively affect motivation. Too much time thinking about this type of goal just before or during competition can increase anxiety and decrease concentration, reducing motivation. However, this type of goal can improve short-term motivation (losing to somebody can spur you on to train harder so you beat them next time).

▸ Performance goals focus on your performance and comparing your current performance to previous performances, so are independent of other athletes and give you a greater sense of control over the goal. Having greater control over goal achievement is highly beneficial for motivating an athlete.

▸ Process goals are based on what the athlete must do to improve their performance. An example would be a basketball player wanting to improve their jump-shot accuracy by making sure they release the ball at the height of the jump. This type of goal is useful for improving motivation as it gives a specific element of performance to focus on, which facilitates learning and development.

It is important to incorporate all types of goal when completing goal setting with athletes rather than using just one type of goal. When used correctly, they will all complement each other and are more likely to enhance motivation. Often outcome, performance and process goals can be viewed on a continuum (see Figure 7.8).

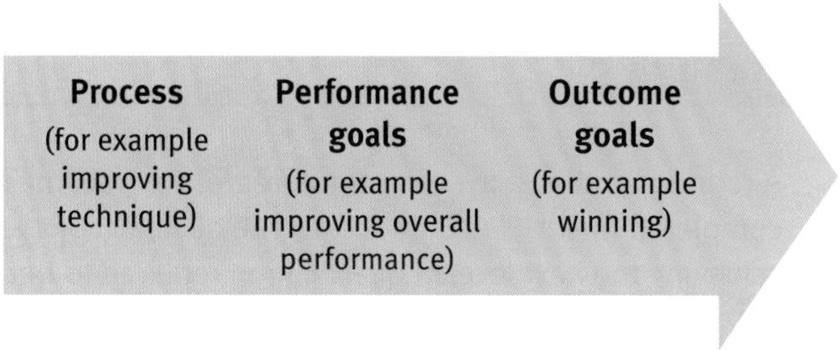

Process
(for example improving technique)

Performance goals
(for example improving overall performance)

Outcome goals
(for example winning)

▸ **Figure 7.8:** How do the different types of goal link together?

Mastery goals

Mastery goals (sometimes referred to as task or learning goals) focus on self-challenge and improvement, or at least not doing any worse than a previous performance. You do not make any comparisons between the athlete and other competitors – you focus only on setting goals that relate to the athlete surpassing their previous performance. Some sport psychologists argue these goals are best for enhancing motivation as they help an athlete strive for greater competence and because the athlete is more in control of whether these goals are achieved. There are two types of these goals: mastery-approach goals (MAp) and mastery-avoidance goals (MAv).

▶ MAp goals focus on performing a task well and outperforming previous personal achievements (for example setting new personal best times or learning a new skill). These goals tend to create the greatest levels of intrinsic motivation in athletes and can have positive effects on performance.

▶ MAv goals focus on not making mistakes or not letting your performance decrease from previous levels. These goals can have negative effects on an athlete's wellbeing but do not always decrease performance.

Competitive goals

Competitive goals focus on demonstrating superiority over another athlete, or not being out-performed. While some people think these goals are bad for motivation because whether they are achieved is not fully in control of the athlete, they can be good for motivation if the athlete setting the goals has a high perception of competence. There are two types of this goal: performance-approach goals (PAp) and performance-avoidance goals (PAv).

▶ PAp goals can have a beneficial effect on motivation, especially when an athlete feels more competent, and have been shown to enhance performance in competitive situations.

▶ PAv goals are widely recognised as the worst type of goal as they focus heavily on negative aspects of sport and can create higher levels of stress and anxiety and lower levels of motivation as a result.

SMARTS principle of goal setting

While setting goals, you should follow the SMARTS acronym. This stands for:

▶ Specific – the goal should say exactly what needs to be done
▶ Measurable – the goal should be quantifiable and evaluated on a regular basis
▶ Action-orientated – the sportsperson should have to do something to achieve the goal
▶ Realistic – goals should be challenging enough so that they are not too easy, but not so hard that they can't be achieved
▶ Time-orientated – goals should have a timeframe for completion
▶ Self-determined – the sportsperson should preferably set or at least have an input into setting the goals, so that they feel a greater degree of autonomy over the goals.

Link

Look back at Unit 2, page 114, for more information about SMART goals.

Discussion

When thinking about their impact on motivation, why are the 'action-orientated' and 'self-determined' aspects of the SMARTS principle important?

Case study

A retiring football player wants to progress to become a head coach of a premier-league football team. They completed their UEFA 'B' and 'A' license qualifications while playing. They have set themselves the target of achieving the next level of qualification required to become a head coach. The goal that they set is:

Complete the UEFA Pro-License Coaching qualification within four years of retiring from professional football.

1 Can you identify from this goal, how it is:
- specific
- measurable
- action-orientated
- realistic
- time-orientated?

2 Now, imagine you have just completed a 10k race and would like to run a marathon next. What would be an appropriate SMART goal that might help you achieve this goal?

Psychological interventions to influence self-confidence of sportspeople

Imagery – types and applications

Imagery is one of the most widely-used techniques within sport psychology. It can be used in training, before, during and after competitions, or away from the sporting environment altogether. Imagery involves creating or recreating images in your mind, rather than physically practising a sports skill or technique. It should involve as many senses as possible, as well as recreating emotions experienced through the activity you take part in. The most effective imagery uses **visual**, **auditory**, **tactile**, **olfactory** and **kinaesthetic** senses. Of these, visual and kinaesthetic imagery techniques are used most often.

There are two main perspectives of imagery. These are internal and external imagery. Internal imagery is imagery that happens from a first-person perspective, for example visualising the activity you are undertaking as though you were seeing it through your own eyes. External imagery is when you conduct the imagery as though you are watching yourself on a video. It is common that sportspeople will use both internal and external imagery but will often prefer one over the other. This enhances confidence by providing the athlete the opportunity to see themselves being successful within different sporting scenarios, which increases their belief in their ability.

| Key terms |

Visual – you concentrate on the different things that you can see during the movement.

Auditory – you concentrate on the different sounds that you associate with a sporting movement.

Tactile – you concentrate on the sense of touch during the sporting action.

Olfactory – you concentrate on the different smells that you associate with a sporting action.

Kinaesthetic – you concentrate on the feel of the movement.

| Theory into practice |

Shut your eyes and imagine you are standing and waiting to take a free throw in basketball. Imagine yourself standing on the free throw line looking forwards toward the basket. You bounce the ball a couple of times and then set yourself for the shot. You shoot, feeling your body move in the correct sequence, seeing your hand release the ball and feeling the body position at the point of release. You can see the ball travelling towards the basket then sinking into the basket.

| Theory into practice |

Shut your eyes and imagine you are about to take the basketball free throw again, only this time it is as if you are watching yourself on a video. You can see yourself bounce the ball a couple of times and then set yourself for the shot. This time you can see that you aren't quite square to the basket and your left foot is slightly further forward than your right foot. You can see that your shooting elbow is pointing straight towards the basket immediately prior to releasing the ball and that you have released the ball at the height of your shot.

There are five main functions of imagery: motivational specific, motivational general (mastery), motivational general (arousal), cognitive specific, and cognitive general.

- **Motivational specific imagery:** Imagine yourself in a highly motivating sport setting such as scoring the winning goal in a football match. This is an example of motivational specific imagery and is aimed at increasing motivation levels in athletes.
- **Motivational general (mastery) imagery:** Now imagine yourself in a situation where you must concentrate and think positively, such as at the start of a 100m sprint. This is an example of motivational general (mastery) imagery and is aimed at helping athletes to remain focused and have confidence in their ability.

- **Motivational general (arousal) imagery:** This time, imagine yourself breathing deeply just before you start a run to the vault in gymnastics and how you feel once you have taken the deep breath. This is an example of motivational general (arousal) imagery and is aimed at helping you to control arousal and anxiety levels.
- **Cognitive specific imagery:** Imagine yourself correctly executing a sports skill of your choice, such as putting a golf ball or potting a snooker ball. This is an example of cognitive specific imagery and is aimed at acquiring, practising and correcting sports skills.
- **Cognitive general imagery:** imagine yourself playing an active part in your team's overall tactics, for example providing an overlapping run for your winger in football so that you can get a cross into the box. This is an example of cognitive general imagery and is aimed at acquiring and practising team strategies or tactics.

Imagery can be used for a variety of purposes, including those listed below.
- **Reducing anxiety and stress:** Imagining emotions associated with relaxation (sometimes used alongside other techniques such as breathing exercises) can more effectively control anxiety, arousal and stress levels.
- **Influencing self-confidence:** Through imagery, the athlete will be able to experience feelings of success and will be able to come up with strategies as to how they can be successful in performance. As the athlete sees that they can complete the performance successfully (if only in their minds), their levels of self-confidence will increase.
- **Imagining goals:** Imagery can be used to create a mental experience of you achieving your set goals (for example the process of winning a medal or surpassing your personal best) which provides motivation to then achieve that goal.
- **Mental rehearsal and pre-performance routines:** Imagery can be used as part of all types of pre-performance routines as it helps the athlete to mentally rehearse the action before performing the activity physically.
- **Injury rehabilitation:** Imagery can be used to help develop or maintain skills during injury rehabilitation. It can help to increase an athlete's confidence in preparation for their return to sport, and there are even suggestions that it can have neuromuscular benefits that can be helpful in reducing the risk of re-injury.

Imagery is a type of skill and, as with any other type of skill, it requires practice in order to perfect it. One of the most common ways of introducing imagery with a sportsperson is using an **imagery script**.

When planning your imagery script, you should consider the 5Ws of imagery script planning (see Figure 7.9):
- **W**ho will use the script?
- **W**here will the script be used?
- **W**hen will the script be used?
- **W**hy is the script being used?
- **W**hat will be imagined?

Research

Research the term 'PETTLEP Imagery'. What does this mean and how does it help you understand how you can use imagery with sportspeople?

Key term

Imagery script – a script that is written either for or with the athlete, that details a scenario that the athlete can use to enhance their performance. It is one of the most common modes of delivering imagery training.

Imagery Script Checklist

Who

Gender ☐ Male ☐ Female   **Age** _____

Competative level _____

Sport characteristics _____
_____

Imagery experience

Imagery use
⌐_____⌐
Never   All the time

Imagery ability
⌐_____⌐
Poor   Very good

☐ **1PP**   ☐ **3PP**   ☐ **Combination**

Other details to consider _____
_____

Where and when

Where _____

☐ Training   ☐ Competition   ☐ Away from training/competition

When

☐ Before   ☐ During   ☐ After

Other details to consider _____
_____

Why (e.g. learn /improve skills/strategies, increase confidence, control arousal/anxiety e.t.c)
_____
_____

What (content tailored to the Who, Where, When and Why)
_____
_____

Important sensory modalities

☐ **Visual**   ☐ **Kinesthetic**   ☐ **Auditory**   ☐ **Olfactory**   **Other** _____

Personalised details _____
_____

▶ **Figure 7.9:** How can you use this checklist to produce your imagery script?

Evaluation of imagery techniques

These techniques have proved to be successful for many sportspeople. The main limitation to their success is whether the athlete is prepared to take the time to learn to use them properly. The evidence surrounding imagery interventions to enhance confidence is extremely robust.

Self-talk – types and uses

Have you ever played in a match and said something to yourself like 'Come on!' or 'Focus! Keep your eye on the ball'? This is self-talk and is something most athletes do, sometimes without even doing it for any specific purpose. Self-talk is a psychological skill used to enhance learning, increase performance and to motivate athletes. The two main categories of self-talk are positive and negative self-talk (see Figure 7.10):

▶ **Positive self-talk (PST)** is often used for motivation, aiming to increase energy levels and produce a more positive attitude in athletes. It usually involves statements such as 'Keep going!' or 'I can do this!' rather than task-specific instructions. Sometimes athletes use **cue words** instead of phrases; some even write cue words on their hand or wrist, or even sew them into sports implements. Historically sport psychologists believed positive self-talk was beneficial for all sporting activities. However, more recent research (for example Tod, Hardy & Oliver (2011) has suggested that positive, motivational self-talk may not be as effective for sports requiring fine movements.

▶ **Negative self-talk (NST)** is historically believed to be a negative aspect of performance. It is a self-critical process which some sport psychologists have argued hinders an athlete from achieving goals and fosters self-doubt. Common self-talk statements include 'That was a stupid mistake to make' and 'I can't believe how bad I was'. However, more recently some researchers have argued negative self-talk does not always reduce performance and that it can actually be motivational for athletes, as it can draw their attention to areas they can improve and can make them want to improve further.

▶ **Figure 7.10:** The benefits of psychological skills training during injury rehabilitation

PAUSE POINT   Think of some situations when you might use self-talk.

> **Hint**   Write a description of each type of self-talk.

> **Extend**   Using sporting examples, discuss how you think that the different types of self-talk positively and negatively affect performance.

There are several uses for self-talk.

▶ **Self-confidence:** Self-talk can help to enhance self-confidence as it gives the athlete a sense of belief in what they are doing. PST can redirect the athlete's attention away from negative thoughts or things that have gone wrong, which then increases the athlete's level of confidence.

▶ **Arousal control:** Self-talk can be useful to regulate arousal as cue words or positive phrases can be used to redirect the athlete's attention away from negative aspects of performance that are the cause of higher levels of arousal.

▶ **Pre-performance routines:** Athletes can often use positive self-talk and another form of self-talk – **instructional self-talk** – as part of pre-performance routines. PST helps to motivate athletes towards the upcoming games, whereas instructional self-talk can be used to provide sport-specific instructions for the athlete to concentrate on during games.

Psychological interventions to influence arousal levels of sportspeople

Arousal in sport runs on a continuum from deep sleep to hyperactivity. Athletes may need help to influence their arousal levels to any point on this continuum in order to help them perform at their best. If athletes need to reduce their arousal levels, they would use relaxation techniques. However, if the athlete needed to increase their arousal levels, they would need to use energising techniques.

Relaxation techniques

Relaxation techniques are techniques that can be used to reduce arousal levels. These techniques include progressive muscular relaxation, mind-to-muscle techniques and breathing control.

Progressive muscular relaxation

An easy-to-use technique that helps to reduce muscle tension. It is a useful technique because it raises your awareness of levels of muscle tension and, through the relaxation phase, helps to distinguish between what is a state of tension and relaxation. The technique involves tensing and relaxing groups of muscles in turn over the whole body. The process involves tensing a muscle group for five seconds, releasing the tension for five seconds, taking a deep breath and repeating. It is called progressive muscular relaxation because an athlete progresses from one muscle group to the next until all muscles have been tensed and relaxed.

Mind-to-muscle techniques

Relaxation imagery is an example of a mind-to-muscle technique that is used to reduce levels of arousal, stress and anxiety. It is often used to help athletes who are struggling to manage performance pressures or with athletes who have long-term injuries. Relaxation imagery can be supported by either imagery scripts (such as the one shown below), images or videos. Knowing about different scenarios that can help relax athletes is important – a commonly used scenario is relaxing on a warm beach.

Imagine that you are on a hot beach. You can feel the warm sun beating down on you. You can see the golden white sands and can see where they meet the clear blue waters. You can see the blue sky that is clear, except for a few white fluffy clouds. You are now walking towards the water and you can feel the sand between your toes as you walk. You can hear the waves roll in as you get closer to the water's edge. The water starts to splash against you, and you can feel its cooling effect on your skin. You are now stepping into the water. As you walk in deeper you feel the cool sensation on your feet, your ankles and then on your legs. You dive into the water and enjoy the cooling sensation. Everything is peaceful here. You are completely at peace, calm, warm and relaxed.

Breathing control

This is a slow and deliberate inhalation–exhalation process. It is best used during breaks in play and is useful when athletes are getting anxious. A simple method is to work on a 1:2 ratio of breathing in to breathing out, with people most commonly taught to breathe in for four seconds and then breathe out for eight seconds. Physiological benefits include oxygen transport, carbon dioxide removal, reduced muscle fatigue and reduced chances of injuries such as cramp.

The psychological benefits are also important. One of the biggest problems with over-arousal is the reduced concentration levels that accompany it. For example, focusing on negative aspects, such as muscle tension, increased heart rate and (in some cases) nausea can be symptoms of over-arousal. Using breathing control techniques can be beneficial in reducing arousal in two ways.

▶ It reduces the physiological symptoms of arousal and anxiety.
▶ It focuses an athlete's attention away from the negative aspects, because they must concentrate on getting the breathing techniques correct.

The results of these benefits are increased concentration, confidence, control and wellbeing. The best time to use breathing control in a competitive situation is when there is a break in the play, because it gives an athlete the chance to be slow and deliberate in their breathing technique. This helps them regain their composure.

Safety tip

Before starting any breath control techniques with an athlete, you should find out if they have any respiratory conditions – such as asthma – that could affect their ability to breathe in deeply.

Discussion

Do you think there are any sports or athlete groups that would be resistant to these types of relaxation techniques?

Energising techniques

Energising techniques are different techniques that are used to increase an athlete's arousal levels.

Common energising techniques are outlined below.

▶ **Pep talk:** This is a short talk that is designed to instil enthusiasm in athletes and increase their determination to succeed. Pep talks are usually quite informal but will be passionate. In team situations, pep talks are usually delivered by a leader in the group (for example a coach or captain) but can be delivered by anybody in different situations.

▶ **Listening to music:** Think about when you have seen athletes like Michael Phelps walk to a swimming pool with his headphones on. Why do you think athletes listen to music at this time? Listening to music can narrow a performer's attention and divert it from tiredness. Exciting music can increase body temperature, heart rate and breathing rate, all of which can improve sports performance. Music is also helpful for avoiding negative thoughts.

▶ **Use of energising imagery:** This can be achieved using high-energy images of competition (for example a hard tackle in rugby), playing well (for example crossing the finish line first in a race) and high levels of effort (for example being able to lift a new weight in the gym).

▶ What do you do before a sporting event to relax?

Assessment activity 7.2
`C.P5` `C.P6` `C.M3` `C.D3`

Great news! You made it through the selection event and have been invited to interview for the placement position. You are one of only ten people who got shortlisted.

As part of your interview, you are required to deliver a presentation in whichever form you prefer (Microsoft Powerpoint, Prezi, poster etc.) on psychological interventions to meet sports performance needs.

You have been asked to select a well-known athlete and complete the following tasks.
- Give a background to the athlete and the demands of their sport.
- Produce a psychological intervention programme that links the benefits and limitations of techniques to the needs of the sport and the athlete.
- Considers the strengths and limitations of each of the intervention techniques, to show that you can make sound judgements about the different techniques.

Plan
- What is the task? What am I being asked to do?
- How confident do I feel in my own abilities to complete this task? Are there any areas I think I may struggle with?

Do
- I know what it is I'm doing and what I want to achieve.
- I can identify when I've gone wrong and adjust my thinking/approach to get myself back on course.

Review
- I can explain what the task was and how I approached the task.
- I can explain how I would approach the hard elements differently next time (i.e. what I would do differently).

Further reading and resources

Books

Bush, A., Brierley, J., Carr, S., Gledhill, A., Mackay, N., Manley, A., Morgan, H., Roberts, W. and Willsmer, N. (2012) *Foundations in Sports Coaching*, Harlow, Essex: Pearson Education.

Bush, A., Garrard, M., Gledhill, A., Mackay, N. and Sutton, L. (2012) *Foundations in Sports Science*, Harlow, Essex: Pearson Education.

Gledhill, A., Adams, M., et al. (2016) *BTEC Nationals Sport and Exercise Science Student Book,* Harlow, Essex: Pearson Education.

Harwood, C. and Anderson, R. (2015) *Coaching Psychological Skills in Youth Football*, Oakamoor: Bennion Kearny.

Karageorghis, C. and Terry, P. (2010) *Inside Sport Psychology*, Champaign, IL: Human Kinetics.

Kornspan, A. S. (2009) *Fundamentals of Sport and Exercise Psychology*, Champaign, IL: Human Kinetics.

Weinberg, R.S. and Gould, D. (2014) *Foundations of Sport and Exercise Psychology*, 6th edition, Champaign, IL: Human Kinetics.

Websites

http://believeperform.com – Believe Perform: Sport psychology website with a range of podcasts, infographics and other resources about a range of sport psychology topics.

https://www.psychologytoday.com/topics/sport-and-competition – *Psychology Today*: the sport and competition section of *Psychology Today*, which contains articles and blogs associated with different sport-related topics

www.selfdeterminationtheory.org – Self-determination Theory: A website devoted to self-determination theory that includes descriptions of each theory and discusses research underpinned by this theory.

Podcasts

https://soundcloud.com/bmjpodcasts/i-cant-return-to-play-when-fear-of-reinjury-dominates-after-acl-reconstruction-adam-gledhill – 'I can't return to play': A British Journal of Sports Medicine podcast that looks at a sports injury case study, using imagery and self-talk as a way of enhancing an injured athlete's sport and injury-related confidence.

THINK ▶FUTURE

Jamal Ejakita

Sport psychologist in professional rugby league

I've been working as a sport psychologist in professional rugby for four years. After I completed my BTEC Level 3 Applied Psychology course, I went to university and completed a BPS-approved degree in Psychology and then further postgraduate training in sport and exercise psychology, as I needed this to be able to use the title 'Psychologist'. This complemented my rugby coaching qualifications and my playing experience, so I'm happy that I have the subject knowledge as well as an understanding of the sport.

Having an understanding of the sport you work in is essential for effective work as a sport psychologist. So is the ability to develop and maintain effective working relationships with different individuals. In doing so, you are more likely to be able to get to know your athlete which is useful when designing psychological skills-training programmes. If you want to gain any experience, you should approach either the British Psychological Society or the British Association of Sport and Exercise Sciences, or sport psychologists within your locality, to see if there are opportunities for observational work placements.

Focusing on your skills

Designing psychological skills interventions

It is important that sport psychologists are able to design safe and effective psychological skills interventions for athletes. Below are some top tips.

1 Before completing any work with an athlete, make sure that you have their fully informed consent.

2 Make sure that you conduct an appropriate needs analysis, so that you can effectively plan around their specific needs.

3 Find out if the athlete has any previous experience of using psychological skills training techniques. If they have used different techniques previously, they may already have a preference for working in a particular way.

4 Make sure you can provide a clear rationale for including particular psychological skills-training techniques by linking the needs of the athlete with the proposed benefits of the different techniques you have chosen.

5 Review the athlete's progress at scheduled times – to monitor improvements amend the skills-training programme accordingly.

6 Always work within your limitations of practice. If you are unsure speak to another professional or refer your athlete to them.

Getting ready for assessment

Franco is working towards a BTEC National in Applied Psychology. He was given an assignment with the following title: 'Designing psychological skills-training programmes for a sportsperson' for Learning Aim C. He had to produce a psychological skills-training programme for a sportsperson in a sport of his choice and deliver this as a presentation with accompanying presentation notes. The presentation had to:

▶ discuss the different psychological skills that can be used with athletes in sport
▶ produce a psychological skills-training programme for an athlete and discuss how the programme would benefit the athlete.

How I got started

First, I decided on which athlete I wanted to base my report on. I chose my favourite sport because I knew this would motivate me to do the work and would help me to learn about something that might benefit my own sports performance.

I collated all my notes for this particular learning aim and separated them down into different sections that looked at the different psychological skills and how to design a psychological skills-training programme. After this, I produced a summary table of each of the different psychological skills and their different benefits and looked at how these might link to the athlete I had chosen.

Then I looked at the different ways that you can assess the strengths and areas for improvement of athletes, and how I could identify the demand of the different sports. Then, using the information I had learned about the different psychological skills, I looked at how I could organise the different skills that would benefit my athlete into a coherent psychological skills-training programme.

How I brought it all together

To start, I prepared a short introduction that outlined the purpose of the work that I was doing. After this, I discussed each of the psychological skills that can be used in sport. Within this, I discussed:

▶ an introduction to each of the different psychological skills
▶ a discussion of the proposed benefits of the psychological skills for different athletes.

After doing this, I planned out my psychological skills-training programme for my athlete, ensuring that I covered all the unit content. I made sure that I included the key benefits of the psychological skills-training programme for my athlete, as well as suggesting any alternatives in case my athlete wanted different psychological skills-training activities to do.

What I learned from the experience

There are lots of different psychological skills-training activities that can be used with athletes, so it is important to be able to link the proposed benefits of these activities to the needs of athletes. This made the assignment a little bit difficult at times because I was unsure which to select.

Next time, I would group my psychological skills-training activities under headings (for example psychological skills that can enhance relaxation), look at the key benefits and any difficulties athletes might have when learning these, and use all that information to select the best ones for my athlete.

I think I spent a bit too much time focusing on the structure and layout of my psychological skills-training programme and not enough time providing evidence to support the arguments that I was making, so I would look to rectify this if I was to do the same assignment again.

Think about it

▶ Have you planned out your assignment so that you know you will be able to complete it by the submission deadline?
▶ Do you have the recommended resources as well as your class notes to help you to provide evidence and references to support and develop the arguments that you plan to make?
▶ Is your assignment written in your own words?

Glossary

A

Adaptive advantage – in evolutionary terms, any characteristic of an organism that increases its chances of survival.

Acute stress – the immediate response to a traumatic or stressful situation which produces a strong emotional response.

ADHD – Attention deficit hyperactivity disorder.

Adrenal cortex – the area of the brain that surrounds (and is immediately adjacent to) the adrenal gland.

Adrenal gland – produces hormones to help the body function; can help control heart rate, blood pressure and stress reactions.

Adrenal medulla – inner part of the adrenal gland controlling hormones that initiate the fight-or-flight response.

Adrenaline – hormone that is released during stress that helps to prepare the body for action.

Affectionless psychopathy – an inability to show affection or concern for others. Those with affectionless psychopathy have little remorse or guilt for any bad behaviour.

Ambiguity/Ambiguous – situation where there is no clear and obvious way to act.

Amygdala – a set of neurons that forms part of the limbic system, responsible for emotions, including anger.

Analogy – a comparison between one thing and another for the purpose of explanation.

Androgyny – gender identity that has characteristics associated with being both masculine and feminine.

Antigens – any substance foreign to the body that produces a response such as creating antibodies to the foreign (harmful) invader.

Antipsychotics – medication taken to reduce the symptoms of the psychosis.

Anxiety – a negative emotional state associated with feelings of nervousness, apprehension or worry.

Application – the way the findings of a study are used in society.

Arousal – a state of alertness and anticipation that prepares the body for action. It involves both psychological and physiological activation.

Assumption – a decision about something based on minimal knowledge.

Asylum – a hospital that treated both physical illness and insanity.

Attention – selectively attending to some of the information in the environment.

Attitude – a predisposition towards an object or situation.

Atypical – A term used where a child does not follow the normal course of development or milestones.

Atypical gender identity – gender identity that does not reflect a person's biological sex.

Auditory – you concentrate on the different sounds that you associate with a sporting movement.

Automatic processing – a behaviour that, after repeating over and over, happens without giving it much thought.

Autonomic nervous system – part of the nervous system responsible for bodily functions such as breathing, heartbeat and the digestive process. is not in their best interests.

Autonomous – being independent and feeling able to make your own decisions.

Aversion therapy – therapy aimed to stop a particular behaviour using classical conditioning to associate the behaviour with negative feelings.

Aversive stimulus – an unpleasant event that when presented with a consequence that is negative will reduce the likelihood of the behaviour happening again.

B

Bandwagon effect – changing behaviour to be similar to that of an increasingly popular movement.

Bar Mitzvah – a Jewish practice where boys, when they reach 13 years old, become accountable for their actions and have a coming-of-age ceremony. Girls become a Bat Mitzvah at the age of 12.

Behavioural techniques – is a broad term that refers to different treatments for mental health disorders.

Benzodiazepines (BZ) – anti-anxiety drugs which increase the amount of GABA in the brain.

Beta-blockers – drugs that reduce activity in the sympathetic branch of the autonomic nervous system.

Binary – a forced choice to one or other position, for example masculine or feminine.

Biofeedback – a technique that involves feedback about a person's physical stress reaction to a situation and how this can be managed.

Biomedical – focuses on physical, medical and biological explanations, for example genetics.

Biopsychosocial – an integrated approach to health which involves biological, psychological and social areas.

Blanket consent – sometimes given to provide authority to conduct research activity without requiring additional approval.

Boundary dissolution – where the lines between the role of parent/carer and child become blurred.

C

Category – grouping of things that are similar.

Causal factor – a factor that is believed to lead to the development of a mental disorder.

Causal relationships – where one variable causes a change in another. (Cause and effect).

cCBT – CBT therapy undertaken via an online forum or email exchange rather than face-to-face as with CBT.

Central nervous system (CNS) – the brain and the spinal cord.

Central route – involves being persuaded by the arguments or the content of the message.

Chromosomes – structures containing genetic material.

Chronic stress – the emotional response to stress over a long period of time involving continuous arousal.

Clinician – a general term to describe the clinical professional working with the individual. This may be a psychiatrist, psychologist, nurse or other professional.

Code – or coding data means that you would arrange data into categories to help analyse the data. So you might identify a common phrase that participants use.

Cognitive – working through thoughts to process information.

Cognitive anxiety – the thought processes that occur when a person is anxious, such as concern or worry.

Cognitive behavioural therapy – a therapeutic technique which gets a person to change their thinking, resulting in changing the addiction behaviour.

Cognitive or distorted bias – a type of thinking that allows people to make quick decisions which are drawn on expectations based on past experiences; these can be biased and lead to false information.

Cognitive paralysis – involves over-thinking a situation resulting in paralysis so the situation cannot be dealt with.

Comorbid – when an individual has more than one condition, such as anxiety and diabetes.

Concept – ideas, objects, people, experiences which/who share the same properties.

Concordance – an agreement between two views or things. In twin studies, the presence of the same trait in both twins being examined.

Concordance rate – the likelihood that a family member will develop the same psychological disorder as another member of their family (who shares the same genes).

Confabulation – unconsciously mixing up of memories from different sources to create a different memory.

Conditioned response (CR) – a learned response to a specific stimulus.

Conditioned stimulus (CS) – an object or event that has acquired the power to cause a specific response through association.

Conditioning – a theory that the response to an object or event can be changed by learning.

Conditioning phase – the period during conditioning where the neutral stimulus is presented alongside the unconditioned stimulus in order to acquire its power.

Conditions – in an experiment, a condition is the way the tested variable is applied to the participants.

Confederate (or 'stooge') – people who are part of an experiment and act exactly how the researcher instructs them. Other participants are led to believe that the confederate is a participant like them, but they are asked to behave/speak in a particular way that the researcher instructs them.

Confirmation bias – the focus is directed towards information that is consistent with your opinions and/or knowledge.

Conformity – changing your mind or behaviour to that of the group.

Confounding variable (CV) – a variable that affects both the independent and dependent variables and causes the appearance of an association that may not necessarily be correct and could influence the results of a study.

Conservation of mass, volume and size – the ability to understand that something stays the same even though its appearance changes.

Constructive feedback – feedback that focuses on providing insights that someone can use to improve their work and/or behaviour.

Constructivist theory – a view that states that individuals gain knowledge from their experiences in their environments.

Continuum – a continuous sequence, where changes within the sequence are gradual.

Controls – in research, it is essential to hold as many **variables** constant as possible so as only the variable being tested changes between the conditions.

Correlation – a relationship or association between two variables that can be positive, negative or zero (no relationship).

Cortisol – hormone released from adrenal gland in response to stress signals from the brain.

Cost-benefit – an evaluative process that judges and compares the situation to determine if it is worth doing.

Covert sensitisation – a form of **aversion therapy** using words or images to change behaviour.

Critical/sensitive period – a period (up to two and a half years old) where a child needs to form an attachment with a caregiver.

Cue reactivity – external environmental cues can trigger initiation of an addictive behaviour.

Cue words – single words that are a form of self-talk and used to trigger a desired response by an athlete. Common cue words include 'believe', 'relax', 'focus' and 'strong'.

Culture – the ideas, customs and social behaviour of a particular society.

Cybernetics – science of communications and automatic control systems (machines and humans).

D

Daily hassles – minor events from everyday life such as misplacing your shoes or missing the train to work.

Data – information gathered during the course of research applied to a specific question.

Debriefing – a process when research is completed to provide an opportunity for the participant to discuss the procedure and findings with the researcher.

Decrement – a reduction in something.

Deductive reasoning (from general to specific) – starting with a conclusion and then presenting facts and examples.

Defence mechanism – process by which an individual unconsciously uses psychological strategies to protect themselves from anxiety.

Demand characteristics – participants change their behaviour to fit with the aims of the experiment.

Demographic variables – statistics about people that include information of gender, class, education, family size and age.

Demonology – the study of demons and other unnatural harmful beings.

Dependent variable (DV) – the variable the experimenter measures. This is the result of a study.

Deprivation – in psychology, this is the loss of an attachment figure; where an individual does not receive the basic necessities required for a healthy life.

Desensitisation (tolerance) – a treatment that reduces emotional responsiveness to a stimulus after repeated exposure to it.

Desired behaviour – the behaviour that a sportsperson is aiming to achieve.

Direct reinforcement – as in classical conditioning you experience reinforcement for what you do.

Dizygotic twins (DZ) – are non-identical. They may be either the same sex, or a boy and a girl. They will look slightly different. They share 50 per cent of their DNA.

Dopamine – neurotransmitter involved in many functions in the brain including reward.

Double-blind procedure – neither the participants nor the experimenters knows who is receiving a particular treatment.

Dream analysis – the process of finding meaning in the dreams an individual has when they are asleep.

Dysfunction – an abnormality or disruption in the way some aspects of the human condition function. In the case of applied psychology this could be a disturbance in cognitive, emotional and/or social functioning.

E

Early separation – when a child is separated from his or her mother when the child is young.

Ecological models – a view that the environment contains natural factors (biological, physical, chemical) that affect human life.

Ecological validity – how much the study's procedure and/or conclusions genuinely reflect real life events and behaviour.

Egocentric – inability to put themselves in the position or viewpoint of others. See Piaget's famous 'Three Mountains Task' and the 'Hughes Policeman Doll Study'.

Electroencephalograph (EEG) – machine that measures the electrical activity in the brain producing a visual pattern of brain activity.

Eliciting constructs – identifying the key psychological factors that are important for successful sports performance.

Emetic drugs – used in medicine to induce nausea or vomiting.

Emotional response analysis (ERA) – using data from brain scans to assess the emotional impact of something.

Empirical evidence – evidence that is gained through observation and experimentation.

Empirically tested – tested using information obtained through observation or experimentation.

Environment of evolutionary adaptation (EEA) – the conditions that existed during the period of evolutionary change.

Environmental fit – the degree to which the environment and individual match.

Ethics committee – a panel that looks at your research proposal and says whether it is safe and ethical. It will confirm whether you can start work on your project.

Ethology – the study of human behaviour and social organisation.

Evolution – the process of change through genetic mutations interacting with the environment over successive generations.

Exorcism – the attempted removal of a supposed evil spirit from a place or person.

Experimentation – a design where the researcher manipulates a particular variable and observes the effect of this manipulation on an outcome such as a participant's behaviour.

External motivation – wanting to do something because of the influence of someone or something else.

Extraneous variable (EV) – a variable that is not an independent variable but could affect the results (the DV) of the experiment.

Extrinsic motivation – motivation that comes from an external source.

Eye tracking – technique used to measure the duration and direction of gaze. This could involve the viewer wearing glasses or taking video of the eyes during exposure to the stimuli and analysing what they focused on.

F

Fear appeals – messages that are often used to influence attitudes and behaviour in terms of making people aware of the potential harm to them if they do not accept what the message is saying.

Femininity – psychological characteristics associated with being female.

Fight-or-flight – a physiological reaction that occurs when a person feels under attack or perceives a threat to their survival.

First-degree relative – a blood relative with whom you share at least 50 per cent of genes, for example parents and siblings.

Focus group – technique for gaining opinions about things. A group of people is assembled and they are then asked to discuss the topic being investigated. Their responses are analysed in order to draw conclusions.

Free association – a therapist asks an individual to share anything that comes into their mind, including words, images, and so on.

Functional magnetic resonance imager (fMRI) – large machine that detects changes in oxygen use across the brain showing areas currently being most used when doing a specific task.

Fundamental attribution error – the tendency to underestimate the effect of your own motives or behaviour in a situation but overestimate the motives or behaviour of others in the event.

G

GABA – a neurotransmitter which suppresses the activity of other neurotransmitters in the brain.

Gatekeeper – someone who acts as an intermediary between the participants and the researcher. They may also have power to grant or deny access to research participants.

Gender dysphoria – a condition where the person feels that their biological sex and their gender do not match.

Gender salience – salience means to make relevant, so gender salience is to make gender relevant, for example by reminding people of the stereotype it makes it more important.

Gender-fluid – taking the view that gender is not fixed throughout life but can change.

General paresis – a problem with mental function due to damage to the brain from untreated syphilis. It is a type of neurosyphilis.

Generalisability – how far we can apply our findings of our research to the target population we are interested in.

Generalisable – a term to describe the extent to which research findings can be applied to the rest of the population.

Generalisation – the tendency to respond in the same way to different but similar stimuli, for example liquids.

Genes – units of inheritance that provide the basic plan for physical makeup.

Genetic predisposition – the increased chance of developing a disease or pattern of behaviour based on our inherited genes.

Genome – all the hereditary information contained in the genes of an organism.

Genome lag – the idea that evolution works slowly, so genes that developed in the past are still present even though the environment is very different.

Genotype – genetic makeup of a person present from birth.

Geographical profiling – a process of evaluating the location of connected serial crimes, such as murder or burglary to decide the most likely area in which the offender will live.

H

Hardiness – a type of personality that shows resilience when faced with stress; hardy people are controlled and embrace a challenge.

Health continuum – a type of scale. At one end of the scale your health is very good and at the other it is very poor. Different factors, for example physical or psychological, will influence where you are on that scale in terms of your health.

Hemisphere – one of two sides of the brain which make up the whole.

Heuristic – a mental shortcut, like an algorithm in a computer.

Hippocampus – a small organ within the limbic system, responsible for the processing and storage of short-term memory.

Holistically – looking at a person's health in terms of both their mind and body.

Hormones – chemical molecules that are released into the blood stream that have an impact on organs of the body including the brain.

Hostile aggression – reactive, often angry aggression in response to a perceived threat. It has an emotional basis.

Hostile attribution bias – the tendency to think that the ordinary behaviour of other people is actually threatening towards you.

Hypertension is another name for high blood pressure which involves a state of high physiological arousal.

Hypomania – an emotional state that may include irritability or overexcitement. More severe types of irritability or overexcitement may be called mania.

Hypothesis – a prediction about what is (or could be) happening.

Hysteria- excessive or uncontrollable emotions that seem out of context for the situation. Emotions may include fear or panic.

I

Identify – becoming more like another person, taking some of their characteristics into yourself.

Imagery script – a script that is written either for or with the athlete, that details a scenario that the athlete can use to enhance their performance. It is one of the most common modes of delivering imagery training.

Imitate – to copy the behaviour of another person.

Imitation – copying the behaviour of others.

Implicit bias – unconscious and non-deliberate attribution of specific qualities to a member of a social group.

Incapacitation – aim of preventing future crimes by taking away the offender's ability to commit them (such as placing them in prison).

Incentive value of success – how much value you place on the success you experience in sport.

Independent variable (IV) – the variable the experimenter manipulates or changes. This is something the researcher thinks will have a direct effect on the dependent variable.

Inductive reasoning (from specific to general) – drawing conclusions from the facts and examples that you observe.

Information processing – a model used by cognitive psychologists to explain thinking processes and how they are similar to the way a computer works.

Informational social influence – changing your mind or behaviour to that of the group in order to do the right thing in a situation where you are uncertain.

Informed consent – consent provided by a participant to take part in a study. Participants have the full knowledge of the possible consequences of their involvement.

Innate – a term used in psychology to explain where something is natural; something an individual is born with.

Internal working model (IWM) – an approach that describes the mental representations a child forms of a relationship they have with their primary caregivers that then becomes internalised.

Interpersonal – skills used by a person to interact with others properly.

Initiation – refers to the beginning of the addiction.

Institutionalised – a developed dependency after a long period of time in an institution.

Instructional self-talk – a task-specific form of self-talk that involves the athlete giving instructions to themselves about different aspects of performance (for example technical or tactical elements).

Instrumental aggression – aggression that serves a purpose. It could be described as cold-blooded; it is rational in order to accomplish an aim.

Interpersonal coherence – the similarities between a crime or victim and the offender's behaviour within their every day lives.

Intrinsic motivation – motivation that comes from within.

Investigator effects – a participant's behaviour may be affected by the relationship with the researcher. A number of different factors could affect the participant's responses and behaviours including age, gender, ethnic group, appearance, expressions and communication styles.

K

Kinaesthetic – you concentrate on the feel of the movement.

L

Levelling – leaving out parts of original information resulting in shortening of the memory.

Life Change Unit (LCU) – refers to the number of points awarded on an item on the SRRS.

Life events – major changes in the circumstances of an individual such as death, moving to a new house, or getting married, which require the person to readjust in some way.

Likert scale – **quantitative** method of measuring attitudes by assigning numbers to levels of agreement.

Limbic system – a collection of structures in the mid-brain that is involved in processing memory and emotional information.

Lobes – sub-component of the hemispheres – four lobes in each one.

Localisation of function – area of the brain responsible for specific behaviour.

Locus of control – the extent to which people believe they have power over the events in their lives.

Longitudinal – a study taking place over a period of time, usually months or years.

Longitudinal research – research that tests the same people over a long period of time comparing their responses between time periods.

M

Maintenance – how the addiction keeps going.

Maladaptive behaviour – involves things that a person does that stops then from adjusting to healthy situations.

Manipulate – used where variables are changed on purpose. It can be termed as an independent variable.

Masculinity – psychological characteristics associated with being male.

Maternal deprivation – a lack of a mother or motherly figure in a child's life.

Memory – the process of encoding storing and recalling previously learned information.

Mental representation – the way that images or concepts are depicted internally.

Meta theory – a theory that is made up of several smaller theories to provide an understanding of a topic.

Meta-analysis – involves researchers using studies and results that already exist and drawing overall conclusions from their findings.

Model – a person you observe and may imitate.

Modes of representation – how information or knowledge is stored and encoded in memory.

Monozygotic (MZ) – twins who are identical. They are always the same sex – both boys or both girls who will look the same as each other. Their DNA is 100 per cent the same.

Motivation – drive to do something (behave in a certain way).

Motivational climate – the environment that is created by coaches, parents and team mates that can help motivate athletes during training and competition.

Motive to achieve success – a sportsperson's capacity to take pride in their sporting accomplishments.

Motive to avoid failure – a sportsperson's capacity to feel or experience shame as a result of failure.

Multi-agency professionals – a term used for those who work towards protecting and safeguarding children, young people and vulnerable adults (CYP/VA) in all areas of life.

N

Naturalism – the belief that mental disorder is a result of natural causes.

Nature – the relative contribution of our biological makeup on our behaviour (especially before birth).

Negative priming – stimulus that makes response to a prime slower.

Negative reinforcement – the avoidance of a negative consequence following certain behaviour.

Neural – relating to nerves which transmit information in the nervous system especially the brain.

Neurochemistry – the balance of chemicals in the brain.

Neuron – a specialised nerve cell that receives, processes and transmits information to other cells in the body.

Neuroendocrine stress response – a physical reaction to stress in the body that affects homeostasis involving the endocrine system.

Neurotransmitters – chemical molecules that are used in transmitting nerve signals across the nervous system.

Neutral stimulus (NS) – an object or event that initially has no power to cause behaviour.

Non-adherence – the extent to which patients do not follow the instructions they are given by medical professionals in following their recommended treatment programme.

Non-binary – view that there are multiple possible outcomes rather than the fixed two.

Noradrenaline – a hormone which activates the body into action when it is threatened, increasing arousal, for example.

Normal distribution – an arrangement of a set of data (i.e. intelligence scores) where most values collect in the middle of the range, with a symmetrical reduction on both sides of range.

Normative social influence – changing your mind or behaviour to that of the group in order to fit in with them and not stand out as different.

Norms – the patterns or normative aspects of development or expectations in a society that are collectively devised and followed by a group.

Nurture – the relative contribution of our environment on our behaviour.

O

Object permanence – knowledge that an object continues to exist when out of sight.

Objective – based on what is seen and reported factually, not influenced by opinions, feelings, or beliefs.

Odds ratio – using statistics, it represents the odds (likelihood) that an outcome will occur, given a exposure, that is, the likelihood someone from a low SES will develop a mental-health condition.

Offender profile – an investigation approach designed to identify likely suspects of a crime.

Office for National Statistics – government body that compiles statistics on the population and their behaviour. It is open to search on the internet.

Olfactory – you concentrate on the different smells that you associate with a sporting action.

Operational thought – is another term used for problem solving or hypothetical deductive reasoning proposed by Piaget. How a child's thinking becomes more sophisticated.

Optimal – meaning the best or most favourable option.

P

Parasympathetic nervous system – part of the involuntary nervous system, that slows the heart rate, increases intestinal and gland activity.

Participants – people recruited to take part in research.

Pathology – behaviour that is extreme or difficult to control.

Peer reviewed – work that has been examined by other experts in the field before it is published.

Perception – becoming cognitively aware through the processing of sensory information.

Performance profiling – a way of identifying strengths and areas for development in sports performance, that can be used to set goals and improve motivation.

Peripheral route – involves not being persuaded by the arguments or the content of the message, but could be based on who the speaker is in a debate, attractiveness of speaker, and so on.

Perspective – a specific way of seeing and explaining things.

Phenomenon – a term used to describe something that may exist or may happen but the cause cannot easily be explained.

Phenotype – the observable differences between people that develop as their genotype interacts with the environment.

Phobia – mental health disorder characterised by extreme irrational fear of an object or situation which affects daily life as the sufferer actively avoids the object.

Physiology – how human's and animal's bodies and plants function.

Pilot study – a small-scale study that researchers use to evaluate or test whether doing a bigger study into an area is feasible given the time, cost and other factors a researcher has available. It is also useful for assessing the approach and so potentially adapting it for the main study.

Pituitary gland – the main gland in the body which directs other glands to release hormones.

Plagiarism – the act of plagiarism is to steal or pass off ideas or words of another as your own. You can plagiarise work if you use someone else's work without their permission or present original ideas as a new idea.

Population density – lots of people living near each other, such as high-rise flats and large housing estates with houses close together.

Population validity – how much the characteristics of the participants reflect the characteristics in the general population.

Positive priming – stimulus that makes response to a prime faster.

Positive reinforcement – the production of a reward following certain behaviour.

Post-Traumatic Stress Disorder (PTSD) – an anxiety disorder caused by stressful, fearful or life-changing events. It is characterised by specific nightmares relating to the stressor, flashbacks, emotional numbing and a heightened awareness (hyper-vigilance) to potential threats.

Postcode lottery – a phrase developed to indicate how an individual's geographic location can affect the provision of support and services available to them.

Postpartum depression (postnatal depression) – a mother experiences intense emotion of sadness, hopelessness, anxiety. Often developed around 1 to 3 weeks after childbirth. Postpartum depression is thought to have a genetic cause.

Predisposition – a genetic characteristic you have inherited from your parents that makes you more likely to develop an illness.

Primary data – is a term to describe the data collected by a research which comes from first-hand sources e.g. surveys, interviews or experiments.

Primary reinforcer – reinforcement for a behaviour that meets a basic need, including sleep and food.

Priming/Prime – stimulus that subconsciously affects how you respond to something.

Privation – where a child has never received the care, love, security of a primary caregiver and has not formed any specific attachments.

Probability of success – how likely it is that you will experience success (for example winning) in sport.

Probation – the supervision of an offender in a community setting, either as an alternative to prison or those who have been released from prison. It is more typically known as community supervision.

Procreation – the act of sexual reproduction.

Prosocial – behaviour that is positive and helpful, leading to social acceptance and friendship.

Pseudonym – an alias or made-up name used to protect the identity of the participant.

Psychoanalytics – the study of personality. It was first proposed by Sigmund Freud in the late nineteenth century.

Psychological interventions – techniques used to try to enhance health, wellbeing and/or performance of athletes.

Psychopathology – the study of mental illness.

Psychosocial factors – information combining psychological and social influences.

Psychotic disorder – a mental disorder that causes abnormal thinking or experiences. People may hear voices that are not possible heard by others or see things that others cannot. They may have unusual beliefs about themselves or others, i.e. that they are the Queen of England.

Punitive – to inflict a punishment on an individual.

Punishment – negative consequence following certain behaviour.

Q

Quantitative – numerical data.

Questionnaire – self-report method where the participants give written answers to pre-determined questions.

R

Random allocation – putting participants from the sample into the conditions of the experiment using a random technique. This could be putting all names in a hat and drawing out one at a time until one group is populated, then doing the same for the next group if there are more than two conditions.

Rational non-adherence – involves the patient directly refusing to follow their recommended health treatment.

Rationalisation – unconsciously changing recall of a memory so it is more understandable to you.

Raw data – data that has not been analysed.

Recall – bring a memory back into one's mind; remember.

Recall bias – a systematic error that occurs when participants do not remember previous events and experiences accurately or leave out details.

Receptor – part of the nerve that receives and reads signals from other nerves, helping transfer information around the nervous system and brain.

Recidivism – the tendency for an offender to commit a further offence, or offences.

Recursive – repeating a process, for example you start with a question and you read something which changes your mind about the question. You then refine your question and search for new literature.

Reductionist – a theory that makes human behaviour too simple and therefore overlooks the complexities of humans.

Reflex – an innate (inborn) physical response to specific stimuli.

Regimen – is a prescribed course of medical treatment used to promote healthy behaviour that is suggested people to follow.

Rehabilitation – the belief that individuals who have committed criminal offences can be treated and can return to a crime-free lifestyle.

Reinforcer – outcome that strengthens a certain behavioural response.

Relapse – when the addict has resumed their addictive behaviour.

Remission – when symptoms of a mental disorder (or other condition) are no longer present in an individual, i.e. they are experiencing a period of time when they do not have any hallucinations.

Repeated reproduction – the same person repeatedly recalling information.

Replicable – a research study should produce the same results if repeated exactly. If a researcher follows all the procedures and uses the same methods as another study and their results were very different, this means that the original study was not very replicable, or it was not clear enough.

Replication – reproducing the behaviour of others.

Retention (Retain) – storing of information in the memory for future use.

Reward pathway – a specific limbic circuit within the brain that creates feelings of pleasure.

Rich data – informative or 'deep' data which provides a deep insight into an idea. Provides a good illustration or explanation of why a person feels the way they do rather than just giving a yes/no answer.

Rites of passage – ceremonial events in cultures marking the passage from one social or age-related status to another.

Role conflict – involves an individual being put in a position that requires them to behave in a way that they know is not in their best interests.

Role model – a person who is regarded as a suitable example for an observer, perhaps due to higher status and some shared similarities with the observer.

S

Sample – people selected to participate in a specific research study.

Sampling – a procedure for selecting a representative group from the population in a study.

Scaffolding – the way that an adult or someone more capable than a child supports a child's learning. They provide enough assistance to give the child motivation to complete a task on their own.

Schema – hypothetical cognitive framework that organises and stores information.

building blocks of knowledge.

Schemata – plural of schema.

Scientific – using the systematic approach associated with science to explain things.

Self-confidence – the belief that you can successfully perform a desired behaviour.

Self-efficacy – your belief in your ability to succeed in specific situations or accomplish a task. It reflects confidence in the ability to exert control over your own motivation, behaviour and social environment.

Self-efficacy – a belief in your ability to succeed in specific situations or accomplish a task. It reflects confidence in the ability to exert control over your own motivation, behaviour and social environment.

Self-harm behaviour – causing deliberate injury to oneself.

Self-inflicted death – a person dies as a result of a deliberate action they have done to themselves.

Self-medication model – when people use substances such as alcohol to compensate for underlying problems that have not been treated.

Self-reinforcement – individuals reward themselves when they achieve a certain outcome.

Self-report method – measurements such as questionnaires which are completed by participants themselves.

Semantic – the meaning of something.

Semi-structured methods – Are those such as interviews and focus groups that do not rely solely on a predetermined list of features to observe or questions to ask. They allow participants to expand from statements and questions.

Separation anxiety – fear of being away from an attachment figure, for example parents or caregivers.

Serial reproduction – a technique used in memory research where one person gives information to the next, who then gives it to another person, and so on. Similar to Chinese whispers.

Serotonin – neurotransmitter found in the brain and the body that is associated with mood. Note that some hormones are also neurotransmitters.

Sexual selection – evolutionary pressures operating to select a mate based on characteristics that would benefit the mating couple's offspring.

Sharpening – focusing on small details in the original memory so they become more important.

Siblings – brothers and sisters within a family.

Social and economic deprivation – where an individual does not receive the social and economic requirements for healthy cognitive, social and emotional development. This could include a lack of financial support, or social exclusion due to discrimination.

Social anthropologist – someone who researches how people live in different societies.

Social capital – a concept used to describe the different types of resources that people can provide. Resources could be wealth but can also mean the networks of friendships and families and what they can provide to a child such as their knowledge e.g. a father or mother may be good at maths and English so able to support their child with homework.

Social desirability bias – where participants are concerned about how they appear, so do not respond honestly. They may change their behaviour or responses to what they perceive as more favourable.

Social learning – learning that happens as a result of observing the behaviour of others.

Social proof – using information from other people to judge the quality of a person, product or event.

Social support – comes from friends, family, co-workers, or any other form of social network who can involve themselves in practical, emotional support and help boost self-esteem.

Socialised – the process of learning to behave in ways acceptable to society.

Societies – large groups of people living together with shared laws, values and traditions.

Socioeconomic – looks at how social and economic factors affect individuals.

Sociometric – a quantitative method used for measuring the underlying social relationships between people.

Somatic anxiety – the physical symptoms of anxiety, such as stomach pains and an increased heart rate.

Somatogenic hypothesis – the belief that your mental state, and more specifically mental disorder are signs and symptoms of how well the body is functioning. Mental disorder is a result of physical or biological impairments in the body.

SRY gene – gene responsible for initiation of male developmental process.

Status – perceived power of the person or group of people.

Stereotype – a common, but simplistic, view of a person or thing.

Stigma – a sense of disapproval directed to someone with a particular characteristic or engages in a specific behaviour, i.e. crime.

Stress – a state which occurs when the perceived demands of a situation exceed the perceived ability to cope.

Stress inoculation training – a form of cognitive behaviour therapy designed to maximise a person's ability to cope with stress. It involves teaching coping strategies to manage stress.

Stressor – An event or experience that causes stress to the individual.

Structured observations – where the researcher gathers data without direct involvement with the participants.

Subjective – interpretation of a situation or information based on your own feelings and beliefs (rather than based on fact).

Substance-induced psychosis – symptoms of psychosis that are the result of substance abuse.

Symbolic thought – where internal images are used to represent objects, people or events that are not present (imagination).

Sympathetic nervous system – part of the autonomic nervous system that influences the body to become aroused.

Synthesis – a combination of all the elements of the research project brought together to provide the reader with an overview of a document/ research project. A written discussion that draws on your research questions, findings and discussion that finishes with a statement as to the current situation and possible implications and future research areas.

Systematic desensitisation – a treatment for phobias in which the patient is exposed progressively to more anxiety-provoking behaviour. The behaviour is then paired with relaxation in order to cope with the anxiety caused by the phobia.

T

Tactile – you concentrate on the sense of touch during the sporting action.

Target population – the total number of people/ individuals from which a sample might be drawn.

Testosterone – male sex hormone.

Traits – characteristics.

Transgender – (also referred to as trans) moving from one gender identity to another.

Transference – the feelings an individual has for a person that are directed towards the therapist.

Type A Behaviour (TAB) – shows patterns of behaviour associated with hostility, competitiveness and impatience, which are aspects linked to stress-related illness.

Type B Behaviour (TBB) – relaxed, non-competitive style behaviour, which is generally non-aggressive.

Type C Behaviour (TCB) – behaviour characterised by patience, cooperation and a minimal negative emotional reaction.

Type D Behaviour (TDB) – behaviour in people who are prone to stress, anger and tension, and who generally have a pessimistic outlook.

Typical gender identity – gender identity that reflects a person's biological sex.

U

Unanimity – total agreement between members of the group.

Unconditioned response (UCR) – a naturally occurring reaction to a specific stimulus.

Unconditioned stimulus (UCS) – an object or event that naturally has the power to produce a reflex response.

Unethical – not following the proper rules of conduct and risking psychological or physical harm.

Unstructured observations – where the researcher records everything; there is no plan about what data to collect.

Unverifiable – not possible to prove the accuracy or truth of a hypothesis.

V

Variables – anything that can change.

Vicarious learning – learning through observing the consequences of others.

Vicarious reinforcement – seeing another person's actions being reinforced.

Visual – you concentrate on the different things that you can see during the movement.

W

Work-life balance – refers to ideal situations where workers have time for both work and family, for example.

X

X chromosome – a sex chromosome (in humans and other mammals) normally present in female cells, provided by the mother.

Y

Y chromosome – sex chromosome associated with masculine development provided by father's sperm which may contain either an X or a Y chromosome.

Index